1600+ Practice Questions for the GRE®

ONLINE + BOOK

This publication is designed to provide accurate information in regard to the subject matter covered as of its publication date, with the understanding that knowledge and best practice constantly evolve. The publisher is not engaged in rendering medical, legal, accounting, or other professional service. If medical or legal advice or other expert assistance is required, the services of a competent professional should be sought. This publication is not intended for use in clinical practice or the delivery of medical care. To the fullest extent of the law, neither the Publisher nor the Editors assume any liability for any injury and/or damage to persons or property arising out of or related to any use of the material contained in this book.

© 2016 by Kaplan, Inc.

Published by Kaplan Publishing, a division of Kaplan, Inc.
750 Third Avenue
New York, NY 10017

Printed in the United States of America

10 9 8 7 6 5 4 3 2 1

ISBN-13: 978-1-5062-0268-6

Kaplan Publishing print books are available at special quantity discounts to use for sales promotions, employee premiums, or educational purposes. For more information or to purchase books, please call the Simon & Schuster special sales department at 866-506-1949.

Table of Contents

Welcome

Congratulations on your decision to take the GRE, and thank you for choosing Grockit for your GRE preparation. With Grockit's online tools plus the practice in this book you get:

- 1,600+ practice questions with explanations for every answer
- video lessons with tips and strategies from top-rated Grockit experts
- Grockit's full suite of analytics, which allow you to understand the components of the GRE that you're struggling with and to review those questions until your weaknesses become your strengths
- Grockit's data on overall performance, plus insights to test timing, question difficulty, and concept frequency
- Grockit's advanced algorithm, which serves up practice targeted to your personal strike zone—questions that are not too hard and not too easy, but just right for you. The strike zone is where optimal learning takes place

To register for online access, go to: grockit.tv/gre1600

The material in this book is up-to-date at the time of publication. However, changes in the tests or test registration process may have occurred after this book was published. Be sure to carefully read the materials you receive when you register for the test.

For the most up-to-date information about the exam, helpful tips, and more, please visit us online at **grockit.tv/home**

Thanks for choosing Grockit, and best of luck with your studies.

Chapter 1

Introduction to the GRE

GRE: About the Test

THE PURPOSES OF THE GRE

The GRE, or Graduate Record Examination, is a computer-based exam designed to assess readiness for a wide variety of graduate programs. The ways in which graduate schools use GRE scores vary. Scores are often required as part of the application for entrance into a program, but they also can be used to award fellowships or financial aid. Each section of the GRE is designed to assess general skills necessary for graduate school. Some of these skills include the ability to read complex informational texts and understand high-level vocabulary words in the Verbal Reasoning section, the ability to respond to an issue in written form in the Analytical Writing section, and the ability to apply general mathematical concepts to a variety of problem types in the Quantitative Reasoning section. Graduate school admissions officers often view the GRE score as an important indicator of readiness for graduate-level studies. In addition, graduate school admissions officers are comparing hundreds or even thousands of applications, and having a quantitative factor, such as a GRE score, makes the job of comparing so many applicants much easier.

HOW THE GRE IS ORGANIZED

The GRE is administered on computer and is approximately four hours long, including breaks. The exam consists of six sections, with different amounts of time allotted for you to complete each section.

Basics of the GRE	
Exam Length	4 hours, including breaks
Scoring Scale	130–170 (1-point increments) for Verbal and Quantitative; 0–6 for Analytical Writing
Format	Multi-stage test (MST), a computer-based format that allows students to navigate forward and backward within each section of the test
Number of Test Sections	6 sections, including an experimental or research section
Breaks	One 10-minute break after your third section; 1-minute breaks between all other sections
Analytical Writing	One section with two 30-minute tasks: Analyze an Issue and Analyze an Argument
Verbal Reasoning	Two 30-minute sections with approximately 20 questions each
Quantitative Reasoning	Two 35-minute sections with approximately 20 questions each; onscreen calculator available

Your test may also include an unscored experimental section—an additional Verbal Reasoning or Quantitative Reasoning section. This experimental section is disguised to look like a real section—there is no way to identify it. On the day of the test, one of the subject areas may have three sections instead of two. Treat all sections as scored unless you are told otherwise.

Lastly, your test could contain a research section in place of the experimental section. This section is also unscored and will be indicated as such. If you have a research section on the test, it will be the last section. Pay careful attention to the directions at the beginning of the section.

SCORING

The Analytical Writing section is scored on a scale of 0–6 in half-point increments. The Verbal Reasoning and Quantitative Reasoning sections are scored within a range of 130–170 in one-point increments. Because there are so few possible scores—only 41—that you can get on the GRE, answering just one more question correctly could be enough to turn an average score into a great score. The following tables give a cross section of the percentile ranks that correspond with certain scaled scores on each section of the GRE. For the full percentile-to-score conversion tables, see **www.gre.org**.

Verbal Reasoning		Quantitative Reasoning		Analytical Writing	
Percentile Ranking	Scaled Score	Percentile Ranking	Scaled Score	Percentile Ranking	Scaled Score
99	169–170	98	170	99	6.0
95	165	95	168	98	5.5
87	161	86	163	93	5.0
78	158	78	160	80	4.5
63	154	64	156	56	4.0
50	151	52	153	38	3.5
36	148	37	149	15	3.0
22	144	21	145	7	2.5
10	140	10	141	2	2.0

CANCELLATION AND MULTIPLE SCORES

At the end of the test, you have the option to cancel your score. The trick is that you must decide whether you want to keep your scores before the computer shows them to you. If you cancel, your scores will be disregarded. (You also won't get to see them.) Canceling a score means that it won't count; however, you will not receive any refund for your test payment. If, due to illness or personal circumstances, you perform unusually poorly on that particular day, then it may be wise to cancel. But keep in mind that test takers historically underestimate their performance, especially immediately following the test. They tend to forget about all of the things that went right and focus on everything that went wrong. So unless your performance has been terribly marred by unforeseen circumstances, don't cancel your test.

The ScoreSelect® option lets you decide which test scores to send to schools. Your test fee entitles you to send scores to up to four graduate institutions on Test Day. With ScoreSelect®, you can send scores from your most recent test administration or from all administrations of the GRE taken in the last five years. After

Test Day, you can send selected scores for a fee when ordering Additional Score Reports. Scores for a test administration must be reported in their entirety.

You can take the GRE once every 21 days, up to five times within a rolling 12-month period. While you can take the GRE multiple times, it's best to test once and test confidently.

TEST REGISTRATION

The computer-based GRE General Test is offered year-round. To register for your GRE, visit **www.gre.org**. Registering earlier is strongly recommended because spaces often fill quickly.

HOW THE MULTI-STAGE TEST WORKS

A multi-stage test, or MST, is a computer-based test that you take at a special test center at a time you schedule. Below is a chart that highlights some of the key features of the GRE MST:

MST Features
The test adapts one section at a time, altering the difficulty level of your second Quantitative and Verbal sections based on your performance on the first.
You may answer questions in any order within a section and change your answers to previously answered questions within a section.
An onscreen calculator is provided for the Quantitative Reasoning sections.
Mark & Review buttons are available to help you keep track of questions you want to revisit.

Now that you have a sense of the overall format and structure of the GRE MST, let's look more closely at what the term "multi-stage test" means, how the MST adapts to your performance, and how these factors determine your score.

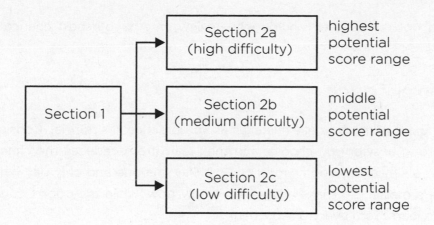

The chart above depicts a simplified version of how the MST adapts. Depending on your performance on the first Quantitative or Verbal section, you get channeled into a harder or easier second Quantitative or Verbal section. The difficulty of the second section determines your score range—roughly speaking, the "ceiling" and "floor" of your potential Quantitative or Verbal score. Ultimately, your score will be determined by two factors: (1) the difficulty of the questions you receive and (2) the number of questions you get correct.

It is important to do as well as possible on the first section, since that will put you in the best position to achieve a great score. That said, your performance on the second section is still a crucial determinant of your ultimate score. (Note that the test only adapts within a given subject. In other words, your performance on the Verbal section will not affect the difficulty of a subsequent Quantitative section.) Overall, your goal will be to get as many questions right as possible, but knowing the structure can help you to understand how your score will be calculated.

GRE Study Tips

CREATE A STUDY PLAN

Think about how many hours you can consistently devote to GRE study. Then, build a schedule. We have found that most students have success with about three months of committed preparation before Test Day. Schedule time for study, practice, and review. It works best for many people to block out short, frequent periods of study time throughout the week. Check in with yourself frequently to make sure you're not falling behind your plan or forgetting about any of your resources. One of the most frequent mistakes in approaching study is to practice questions but not review them thoroughly—review time is your best chance to gain points.

LEARN AND PRACTICE

Know that you are going to make mistakes as you practice. It's normal. Consider this: every wrong answer you choose, and then learn from, reduces the chance that you'll get a similar question wrong on Test Day, the one and only day when wrong answers matter. So make mistakes willingly now, while they don't count, and resolve to learn from every one of them.

Stick with the new approaches you'll be learning. You will be assimilating many new techniques and strategies as you practice. The more consistently you practice these, the more they will become second nature, thereby eliminating uncertainty and saving you valuable time on Test Day. When you are starting out, however, new techniques often take longer or feel more cumbersome than the way you might otherwise have approached the question. Resist the temptation to dwell on short-term trends; focus instead on practicing well. Aim for consistency and accuracy at first, then emphasize pacing as you get closer to Test Day and grow more confident with applying the methods.

TAKE CONTROL OF THE TEST

In addition to learning test content, you must also devote time to building the right mentality and attitude that will help you succeed on Test Day. Take time to understand and incorporate these basic principles of good test mentality:

- Be aware of test timing and keep your composure even if you are struggling with a difficult question; missing one question won't ruin your score for a section.
- Be confident; you are already well on your way to a great score!
- Stay positive; consider the GRE an opportunity rather than an obstacle.

Chapter 2

Verbal Reasoning

GRE Verbal Section Overview

GRE Verbal Reasoning assesses your reading comprehension skills and your understanding and usage of vocabulary. The exam tests vocabulary contextually, and the reading passages are both dense and written with a sophisticated level of diction. The goal of the test's content and emphasis on analytical skills is to provide an accurate indication of your ability to understand what you're reading and to apply reasoning skills to the text's premises and arguments. These are skills you'll need at the graduate level.

The GRE contains two Verbal Reasoning sections with approximately 20 questions each. Each section will last 30 minutes and will be composed of a selection of the following question types:

- Text Completion
- Reading Comprehension
- Sentence Equivalence

Within each Verbal Reasoning section on the GRE, you will see an assortment of question types.

	Reading Comprehension	Text Completion	Sentence Equivalence
Number of Questions	approx. 10 questions (associated with 5 passages)	approx. 6	approx. 4
Time per Question	1–3 minutes to read passage and approx. 1 minute per question	1–1.5 minutes	1 minute

With so many question types and formats, it's a good idea to practice each type of question as much as possible so you don't make any careless mistakes on Test Day, like selecting only one answer choice when you must select two.

Introduction to Reading Comprehension

The GRE includes roughly ten reading comprehension passages spread between the two Verbal Reasoning sections of the test. Many of these passages are one paragraph in length, although a few are longer. Each passage is followed by one to six questions that relate to that passage. Reading Comprehension questions require strategic reading and paraphrasing skills. These questions will test your ability to determine the author's purpose and meaning, to consider what inferences can properly be drawn from the passage, to research details in the text, and to understand the meaning of words and the function of sentences in context. The GRE typically takes its topics from four disciplines: social sciences, biological sciences, physical sciences, and the arts and humanities.

You should aim to spend an average of 1–3 minutes to work through a passage and 1 minute per question. Some questions will be standard multiple choice, with five possible answer choices and one correct answer. Other questions will give you three answer choices, and one, two, or all three of the answer choices could be correct. If you omit any of the correct answer choices or add any incorrect answer choices, you will get the question wrong. There is no partial credit. The final type of reading comprehension question you'll see is called Select-in-Passage. You will have to select a sentence in the passage (by clicking on it) that meets a given criteria. If you are taking the paper-based test, you will not see this question type.

Reading Comprehension Practice

PASSAGE I

The daughter of Jewish emigrants, Nadine Gordimer was born in 1923, twenty-five years prior to apartheid, the institutional segregation and classification of race in South Africa. Gordimer focused her life's work on authentic portrayals of black African culture and the social issues and injustices surrounding race, class, and the landscape of her home country. It has been suggested that Gordimer's tone as a writer reflects South African race relations and violence prior to, during, and after apartheid; many suggest her literature informally serves as the historical text of a nation. As many black African authors were banned (1948–1990), Gordimer stepped outside of her own writing and questioned the stifling of the African "creative imagination" and the negative role it would have on the nation, its voice, and its literature. Just shy of 90, Gordimer still stands her ground; refusing to react to the increased violence surrounding her community in Johannesburg, she rejects hiding behind the barbed-wire walls that surround her neighbors' homes.

1. The author of the passage is primarily concerned with
   - (A) informing the reader of Gordimer's personal life.
   - (B) illustrating the role Gordimer played in literature and social protest.
   - (C) persuading the reader to read Gordimer's novels as historical texts.
   - (D) discussing the irony in Gordimer's past endeavors and present challenges.
   - (E) criticizing Gordimer's role in South African literature and apartheid.

2. The passage supplies information for answering which of the following questions?
   - (A) Gordimer's parents emigrated from which country?
   - (B) What is apartheid?
   - (C) What year was Gordimer's last book published?
   - (D) How has South African crime changed in the past 50 years?
   - (E) With whom did Gordimer fight, regarding the banning of books in her home country?

3. It can be inferred from the passage that Gordimer's narratives and tone reflect the pendulum of

    (A) her personal relationships.

    (B) the racial institutionalization and evolution of crime in her home country.

    (C) the racial segregation of literary figures in South Africa and the banning of black African literature.

    (D) the evolution of crime in South Africa.

    (E) the racial tensions of apartheid.

4. A conclusion can be drawn from the passage that South Africa in 2009 was

    (A) more dangerous than it was when Gordimer first started publishing.

    (B) equally dangerous compared to the apartheid years.

    (C) a society with continued racial and criminal concerns.

    (D) a society that continues to ban the works of black African authors.

    (E) a nation with increased security and racial solidarity.

PASSAGE II

In her 1977 novel *Egalia's Daughters*, Gerd Brantenberg creates a fictional matriarchy in which the *wim* (women) wield the social, political, and economic power, while the *menwim* (men) are assigned the housekeeping and child-rearing roles. The narrative's denouement is a gender revolution that seems virtually predestined but may, in fact, be based on a questionable assumption. While disadvantage has historically preceded both political and social rebellion, the idea that such an outcome is inevitable is not borne out by sociological research.

System Justification Theory (SJT) posits that even those disadvantaged by a social system have a tendency to defend and support it, contributing to the stasis of the status quo. If one's relative societal position is sufficiently internalized, it is ultimately seen as something that is fixed and immutable. People "know their place" and resist any cultural vision that suggests that it can, or even should, be changed. Research has shown that, in an environment that generally perceives women to be poor math students, the math performance of all female students declines, even among women who claim not to accept the stereotype. The mere existence of the stereotype would seem to be enough to ensure that it becomes, and remains, a self-fulfilling prophecy.

What cannot be known is whether or not this form of stereotype exposure would hold true for historically advantaged groups as well. Group consciousness studies to date have focused on the minority perspective, and any attempt to create, or even simulate, a sudden recasting of the advantaged majority as a target of discrimination would necessarily provide an artificial result. In small-scale individual testing, however, where men have perceived a specific experience to be discriminatory in nature, this has actually resulted in an increase in self-esteem related to their assumed disadvantage.

5. Which of the following, if true, would most weaken the study in sentence 4 of paragraph 2?

   (A) Female students who believe women are poor math students tend to study harder than those who don't.

   (B) Math teachers are more lenient when grading female students.

   (C) Math scores for men and women tend to be comparable in environments in which women are perceived to be weak in math.

   (D) In environments in which women are perceived to be weak in math, men's math scores tend to improve.

   (E) In environments in which there is no perception that women are weak in math, women's math scores tend to be comparable to men's.

6. Consider each of the three choices separately and select all that apply.

   It can be inferred from the passage that the author believes which of the following about Social Justification Theory?

   [A] It gives an incomplete picture of how individuals react to stereotyping.

   [B] It states that social reform can be repudiated by those who would most benefit from it.

   [C] It is used primarily to understand gender relations.

7. Select the sentence in either the second or third paragraph that supports the following argument: members of advantaged groups may react differently to perceived discrimination than do members of disadvantaged groups.

PASSAGE III

Though Martha Graham is better remembered in the dance community as a pioneer of modern dance choreography, it was her desire to create immortal dance performances. She danced first as a member of the Denishawn Company, put on solo performances in New York, and later danced at Radio City Music Hall. She gave lessons in movement and modeled coats to fund her own dance company. It was with this company that her eclectic and radical technique made its mark on modern dance history.

Graham was by no means the first dancer to deviate from the strict classical ballet techniques of the early 20th century. Many young American women were also making variations on the standard dance style. But Graham's alterations of sharp, jagged movements and sweeping floor work reformed the whole of modern dance theory and the very notion of what a dancer was. Her signature style continues to permeate the work of contemporary dance and influence modern choreographers, although some, such as Taylor and Cunningham, both former members of Graham's company, have disowned her intense manner of teaching and technique.

8. The passage states that Graham made a living as all of the following EXCEPT:
   - (A) model
   - (B) set designer
   - (C) professional dancer
   - (D) teacher
   - (E) choreographer

9. Consider each of the three choices separately and select all that apply.
   Which of the following statements is supported by the passage?
   - [A] Graham was at the forefront of the changing paradigm about acceptable forms of dance.
   - [B] Graham was better at dancing than at directing her company.
   - [C] Graham's spirit still lives on in the modern dance genre.

10. The author suggests that Taylor and Cunningham did not
    - (A) understand the style of Graham's technique.
    - (B) keep up with the other dancers in Graham's company.
    - (C) think Graham was very powerful as a teacher.
    - (D) like the immense vigor Graham used in her manner of teaching.
    - (E) think Graham was innovative in her choreography.

PASSAGE IV

Many aspects of coral reefs remain puzzling to scientists. One mystery concerns the relationship between *Scleractinia*, the coral type whose colonization produces reefs, and its symbiotic partner, a unicellular alga present in the coral's endodermic tissues. It is known that both organisms play an integral part in the formation of a reef's foundation by secreting and depositing calcium carbonate, which reacts with sea salt to form a hard limestone underlay. Scientists also know that, because of algal photosynthesis, the reef environment is oxygen rich, as similarly high amounts of carbon dioxide are rapidly removed. All of this accounts for the amazing renewability of coral reefs despite the erosion caused by waves. The precise manner in which one symbiotic organism stimulates the secretion of calcium carbonate by the other, however, remains unclear.

In addition to the unanswered question above, scientists have proposed various theories to explain the transformation of "fringing reefs" (those connected above sea level to land masses), into "barrier reefs" (those separated from shorelines by lagoons), and finally into island atolls. Although Darwin's view of the transformation is considered partially correct, some scientists feel that the creation of reef formations has more to do with the rise in sea level that occurred at the end of the last Ice Age than with a gradual submergence of the volcanic islands to which fringing reefs were originally attached. However, recent drillings at one atoll have revealed a substantial underlay of volcanic rock, which suggests that Darwin's explanation may be largely correct.

The term "coral reef" is something of a misnomer. The *Scleractinia* themselves generally comprise only 10 percent of the total mass of life forms of an average reef community. Algae, along with foraminifera, annelid worms, and assorted mollusks, can account for up to 90 percent of the reef mass. Moreover, the conditions under which reef growth occurs are determined by the needs of the algae, not those of the coral. Reefs flourish only in shallow, highly saline waters above 70 degrees Fahrenheit, because the algae require such an environment. Non-reef-building coral, meanwhile, occur worldwide.

11. The author suggests that coral reefs are able to survive the process of erosion
    - Ⓐ primarily through the activities of algae.
    - Ⓑ despite the high oxygen content of the reef environment.
    - Ⓒ as a result of the combined relations of coral and algae.
    - Ⓓ only if they have an above-surface connection to the shoreline.
    - Ⓔ because of the volcanic rock at their base.

12. It can be inferred from the passage that Darwin
    (A) believed that reefs became atolls through the sinking of volcanoes.
    (B) should have expanded his studies of reefs to include those found at atolls.
    (C) theorized that each reef formation was formed by an entirely different process.
    (D) is less persuasive on the topic of reef formation in light of recent discoveries.
    (E) was more interested in algae and coral than in other organisms living at reefs.

13. The passage does NOT discuss the relationship between
    (A) algal photosynthesis and high oxygen content.
    (B) Darwin's views and evidence supplied by recent research.
    (C) volcanic rock and the life forms found at reefs.
    (D) sea salt and calcium carbonate.
    (E) wave action and the renewal of reefs.

14. Which of the following questions is most completely answered by the passage?
    (A) What percentage of coral worldwide is of the reef-building type?
    (B) How do rises in sea level affect reef formation?
    (C) What are the requisite environmental conditions for coral reef formation?
    (D) How does coral stimulate the calcareous secretions of symbiotic algae?
    (E) What is the principal reason for the transformation of fringing reefs into atolls?

15. It can be inferred that the author would agree with all of the following statements EXCEPT:
    (A) Coral cannot produce reefs without algae.
    (B) The water around a coral reef contains high levels of oxygen.
    (C) Darwin's theory about the causes of reef formation is at least partly accurate.
    (D) The term "coral reef" should be abandoned by scientists.
    (E) Coral are more resistant to cold temperatures than the algae that live in their tissues.

PASSAGE V

Having rejected Catholicism, English society after the Protestant Reformation felt compelled to impose new order on an uncertain universe. Claiming knowledge of a divine plan which linked the celestial and natural worlds into one "great chain of being," some English thinkers depicted humans as the highest link on that portion of the chain belonging to the natural world, and human society, in turn, as comprising a series of vertical political hierarchies. Echoing the assertion of Elizabeth to a rebellious Parliament that "the feet do not rule the head," Edward Forset in 1606 elaborated one hierarchy in which the body was topped, literally and morally, by head and soul. In Forset's scheme, both soul and monarchy possessed "unity" or "indivisibility," each uniting and reigning over subordinate links contained in their respective segments of the worldly chain. Given popular acceptance of the idea of stability as God's will, Elizabeth and her immediate successors possessed a potent, though short lived, ideological restraint.

16. The passage suggests that, in the years following the Protestant Reformation, English monarchs were able to maintain their political influence primarily because

    (A) popular opinion was tightly controlled by a small group of thinkers.

    (B) English society accepted that a hierarchical society was consistent with divine will.

    (C) monarchs accepted a social position basically equal to that of most other people.

    (D) Parliament was politically passive and offered no significant resistance.

    (E) English society traditionally supported a strong monarchical authority.

17. The passage suggests that the idea of a new social order was seen by many English people as

    (A) necessary in order to fill a vacuum created by the decline of the monarchy.

    (B) an idiosyncratic viewpoint advocated by a few eccentric thinkers.

    (C) an amusing but not terribly urgent social issue.

    (D) a disguised attempt by the Catholic Church to restore its lost influence in English affairs.

    (E) unavoidable because an older order that had provided them with structure and security no longer existed.

18. Which of the following sentences would most logically follow the last sentence of this passage?

    Ⓐ Subsequently, popular acceptance of a divinely ordered social structure continued to shape English politics for an unusually lengthy period.

    Ⓑ However, because Forset's ideas were judged to be too radical, they initially failed to make a substantial impact on the balance of power in English government.

    Ⓒ Forset's arguments for a strict, hierarchically ordered society found especially enthusiastic support among many members of the English Parliament.

    Ⓓ This acceptance undoubtedly helped check growing assertiveness of those social classes that spoke through Parliament.

    Ⓔ Thus, freed of her problems with Parliament, Elizabeth was able to focus on the threat to social stability posed by the thinking of men like Forset.

PASSAGE VI

A theorist has defined modernization in underdeveloped countries as passing from "traditional authority," derived from long-standing custom and the authority of kinship leaders, to "legal-rational authority," based on procedures specifically established for particular goals. No doubt this scheme works well enough in categorizing some societies, but how is one to classify the Ibo society of south-eastern Nigeria? In precolonial Ibo society, village decisions were reached in general meetings, and formalized by striking the ground with an *ofo*, which is a staff possessed by the head of a kinship group. This might seem to fit the theorist's model, but the Ibo altered this procedure whenever appropriate—for instance, if the senior kinship head forgot his *ofo*, any other *ofo* could be used. The Ibo, too, freely revised any customary procedures in order to pursue trade—a flexibility that served them well in the new capitalist economy introduced by colonialism. If this theorist is to be consistent, he must concede that the Ibo were "modern" before the first colonist stepped ashore.

19. The author's primary concern in this passage is to
     A describe a Nigerian society.
     B reveal a shortcoming in a theory.
     C show how one form of authority gives way to another.
     D explain the interplay of colonialism and capitalism.
     E prove that Ibo society is modern.

20. Consider each of the three choices separately and select all that apply.

     Which of the following is consistent with the conception of "legal-rational authority," as defined in this passage?
     A A procedure is acceptable if it is not forbidden by law and is suited to a specified purpose.
     B A leader has unlimited authority within an area determined by custom.
     C A practice is correct if is one that has always been used in the past.

21. The author would agree that the categorization used by the theorist of modernization is
     A applicable in some cases.
     B totally without merit.
     C universally valid.
     D incapable of being empirically tested.
     E relevant only to societies that were never colonized.

PASSAGE VII

Mark Twain is "first and last and all the time, so far as he is anything, a humourist and nothing more." So writes Harry Thurston Peck, a book critic and contemporary of Twain, in rejecting the possibility that Twain's darker works of fiction and non-fictive social commentary will maintain any lasting presence in the canon of American literature. Twain's early body of work is certainly a splendid monument to the 19th-century American sense of humor, and Peck cites *The Celebrated Jumping Frog of Calaveras County*, *Roughing It,* and *Innocents Abroad* as examples of Twain's finest-meaning, funniest efforts. Similarly, as Peck points out, Twain built his reputation as a lecturer on his humorous descriptions of travels abroad and in the Western Territories.

Of course, a century of literary criticism has proven Peck's cavalier pigeon-holing far too limiting. Even Peck himself lauds Huckleberry Finn, whose strengths include an unfailing eye for hypocrisy and a deadly serious moral judgment, as a definitively American character who leaps real from the printed page. Twain certainly uses humor throughout all his works, but not as an end in itself. Twain's humor sweetens the sterner medicine that his unparalleled commentaries on life deliver.

22. The author mentions Huckleberry Finn in order to illustrate
    - (A) Twain's reputation for writing humorous novels.
    - (B) Twain's skill in creating hypocritical characters.
    - (C) Peck's error in considering Twain to be a humorist at all.
    - (D) Twain's ability to craft characters of multiple dimensions.
    - (E) Peck's insight into Twain's moral judgment.

23. The author of the passage is chiefly concerned with
    - (A) demonstrating that Twain was not a humorist.
    - (B) arguing that Peck's judgment of Twain is too limited.
    - (C) documenting Peck's contribution to literary criticism.
    - (D) concluding that Twain was better as a serious writer than as a humorist.
    - (E) pointing out the importance of serious themes in good writing.

PASSAGE VIII

The following passage was written in 2008.

Replacing gasoline-powered automobile engines with engines powered by hydrogen is a popular topic on late-night talk radio; the common public notions seem to be that hydrogen is already available as an inexpensive source of fuel and that hydrogen automobile engines will operate free of pollution. In fact, hydrogen is currently four times more expensive than gasoline to produce, and while a hydrogen fuel-cell engine creates water as its only by-product, there are no manufacturing processes for hydrogen that do not produce their own serious forms of pollution.

In 2003, President Bush announced the $1.2 billion Hydrogen Initiative, which calls for the commercial use of hydrogen fuel cells in automobile transportation by 2012. Yet science must first overcome tremendous obstacles to the production, transportation, and storage of vast quantities of hydrogen as well as to the development of an adequate hydrogen fuel cell engine. Increased research funding provides no guarantee that these obstacles will be overcome in time to meet the president's goals, if ever. For now, automobile manufacturers should content themselves with the continued development of conventional hybrid-fuel technologies and of more fuel-efficient, internal-combustion gasoline engines.

24. The primary purpose of the passage is to
    - (A) criticize people who listen to late-night talk radio.
    - (B) advocate the use of efficient gasoline-powered engines as a practical short-term expedient.
    - (C) demonstrate that the production of hydrogen generates pollution.
    - (D) argue that Congress should fund more research into hydrogen fuel cells.
    - (E) describe obstacles to the development of more fuel-efficient gasoline engines.

25. It can be inferred from the passage that the author believes which of the following about the current state of public awareness concerning hydrogen fuels?
    - (A) It is incomplete and inaccurate.
    - (B) It is entirely based on information gleaned from talk radio.
    - (C) It is deliberately distorted by talk radio.
    - (D) It is the driving force behind the president's Hydrogen Initiative.
    - (E) It would improve with more funding for hydrogen research.

26. The passage provides information that would answer which of the following questions?

    (A) Which fuel is more efficient in producing energy, hydrogen, or gasoline?

    (B) Will hybrid gasoline-electric automobiles outsell traditional gasoline-powered automobiles by 2012?

    (C) Have scientists already created a commercially adequate engine powered by hydrogen fuel cells?

    (D) Does the production of gasoline create more pollution than does the production of hydrogen?

    (E) Will the president's Hydrogen Initiative eventually lead to hydrogen-powered automobiles?

PASSAGE IX

The clubhouse model is one approach for assisting clients with mental illness in securing permanent employment. Typically, clients first practice job activities in the clubhouses from which the model derives its name. Having presumably honed their job skills, they then choose from a list of transitional jobs—part-time, temporary jobs obtained by the clubhouse staff in partnership with private employers. In these jobs, clients not only build further work experience, but also learn what kind of work they prefer. Generally speaking, only then are they steered toward permanent employment.

One criticism of this model focuses on the central importance of client choice. Many clients are reluctant to leave transitional jobs after growing accustomed to them. In addition, clients indicate strong preferences about their optimal jobs without exposure to clubhouses or transitional employment, and typically prefer jobs of their choice to those selected by others.

Supported employment, an alternative model, addresses these limitations by encouraging clients to immediately seek competitive employment. While it may seem intuitively improbable that the mentally ill can compete for mainstream jobs without special preparation, the evidence shows that supported employment leads to higher rates of competitive employment than the clubhouse model.

27. The passage suggests that the author believes which of the following about the clubhouse model?

    (A) It guides all clients through a three-step process to obtain competitive employment.

    (B) It does not give clients choices about the employment they obtain.

    (C) It is diametrically opposed to supported employment.

    (D) Its ultimate goal matches that of supported employment.

    (E) It emphasizes that clients should seek competitive employment as soon as possible.

28. According to the passage, the clubhouse model involves all of the following activities by clients EXCEPT:

    (A) making a list of temporary jobs for transitional employment

    (B) working at clubhouses

    (C) finding permanent work

    (D) making choices about the tasks they perform

    (E) working at temporary jobs for companies

29. The primary purpose of the passage is to

    (A) describe the methodology of the clubhouse model.

    (B) argue that supported employment is superior to the clubhouse model in every way.

    (C) show that the clubhouse model, while promising in theory, is essentially flawed in practice.

    (D) discuss the clubhouse model and supported employment.

    (E) present new research regarding the optimal treatment of the mentally ill.

PASSAGE X

Neurologists and biological psychologists have witnessed an exponential increase in the knowledge and understanding of particular structures of the brain over the past two decades. As technology becomes ever more advanced, scientists are able to isolate the functions of even small regions of the human brain. One noteworthy discovery is the role of the amygdala in human fear and aggression. The amygdala, a small, almond-shaped conglomerate, is just one part of the limbic system. Located at the very center of the brain, the limbic system is the core of our "emotional brain"; each individual structure in the limbic system is somehow connected to an aspect of human emotion.

Scientists have found that electrode stimulation of the amygdala can elicit extreme aggressive acts. Patients or experimental subjects who experience this utter rage and fearlessness have no rational foundation for their reaction. In other words, this aggression is wholly attributable to electrode stimulation. On the other hand, patients with trauma or damage to this structure exhibit a complete absence of aggression. Typically temperamental rhesus monkeys with amygdala damage are completely imperturbable. Researchers find that no amount of poking, prodding, or harassment will evoke even remotely aggressive responses from these subjects.

30. The passage is primarily concerned with
    - (A) emotional outcomes of amygdala damage in rhesus monkeys.
    - (B) technological advances that have occurred within the past two decades.
    - (C) scientists' recent and thorough understanding of all brain functions.
    - (D) the regulation of human emotion within the limbic system.
    - (E) the impact of technology on understanding the functions of certain brain structures.

31. The author suggests that persistent passivity and imperturbability may be a direct result of which of the following?
    - (A) drug-induced stimulation of the amygdala
    - (B) a stroke that resulted in severe tissue damage in the limbic system
    - (C) encephalitis as a result of head trauma
    - (D) activation of a strategically implanted electrode in a patient's amygdala
    - (E) damage to emotion-regulating structures in the frontal lobes

PASSAGE XI

Social scientists interested in gender differences often refer to two widely accepted theories of gender identity formation. Proposed by behaviorist Albert Bandura, social learning theory suggests that children adopt gender identities by observing and modeling others. Rewards and punishments teach these children what behaviors are appropriate for their given gender. For instance, a girl who is applauded for playing with dolls will continue to engage in this behavior in the future. On the other hand, a boy who is scolded for playing with dolls is taught that this behavior is not acceptable for his gender role. While this theory is intriguing, another theory provides a more thorough explanation of individual conceptualizations of gender.

Gender schema theory suggests that men and women develop mental proto-types, or "schemas," of what it means to be male or female. This prototype is socially constructed; influenced by, among other things, parents, peers, and media. This theory, unlike the broad social learning theory, accounts for more variance in gender identities; individuals can incorporate into their prototype's traits and behaviors that they deem characteristic to their gender. Gender schema theory is superior, as it goes beyond simple observation and reward by taking a more complex cognitive perspective.

32. The author mentions a girl and boy playing with dolls in order to
    - (A) put the passage in terms with which the reader can relate.
    - (B) demonstrate the unrealistic simplicity of social learning theory.
    - (C) convince the reader that social learning theory is the most accurate theory for how children learn gender differences.
    - (D) illustrate the use of punishment and reward as supported by social learning theory.
    - (E) endorse social learning theory with by providing research-based evidence.

33. According to the author, which of the following best summarizes the superiority of gender schema theory over social learning theory?

   Ⓐ Social learning theory focuses too much on children's play-related activities.

   Ⓑ Gender schema theory would better account for differing gender identities across a group of brothers.

   Ⓒ Social learning theory neglects to take overt behaviors into consideration.

   Ⓓ Both theories are convincing, but gender schema theory is better because it is more complicated.

   Ⓔ Gender schema theory provides more polarized differences between men and women.

34. The author's primary purpose in the passage is to

   Ⓐ explain theories of gender identity formation.

   Ⓑ challenge the theoretical bases of two opposing ideas of gender formation.

   Ⓒ advocate one theory of gender identity formation.

   Ⓓ describe ways in which people establish gender roles.

   Ⓔ identify areas for further exploration in gender formation.

PASSAGE XII

Often the only discernible evidence an ornithologist has of the presence of certain birds is their song. This is also true for the birds themselves. Bird song serves as a means to mark nesting territory. The nature of bird song is influenced by the habitat. Low-pitched sounds travel better in areas of dense vegetation than high-pitched sounds, which are common among birds nesting in open habitats. The timing and frequency of bird song are controlled by hormones, and thus are linked to the breeding season. In some species, only the male birds sing. The song of a male bird is thought to convey his experience to female birds. A female bird may in turn use that information to select a worthy mate.

35. Which of the following statements could most logically follow the last sentence of the passage?

Ⓐ If birds were to use plumage to attract their mates, they would not need to use song for that purpose.

Ⓑ Female birds of one species are aware of the song of male birds of another species.

Ⓒ Therefore, bird song is not simply a matter of survival; it also provides entertainment.

Ⓓ Therefore, bird song carries many essential meanings among birds.

Ⓔ Therefore, when birds with high-pitched sounds sing in the forest, it signifies an open habitat or mating information.

36. The author states that bird song does all of the following EXCEPT:

Ⓐ demarcate territory

Ⓑ express level of experience

Ⓒ facilitate breeding

Ⓓ reflect habitat

Ⓔ provide entertainment

PASSAGE XIII

Who is the true "Father of Aviation?" The answer depends on both the criteria one uses to define flight, and on the credit one is willing to give to those who laid the foundation for it. Brazilians point to their own Alberto Santos Dumont, who, in 1906, after becoming a world-famous pilot of dirigibles, was the first to take off, fly, and land a motor-driven airplane without the use of wind power. To most Americans, the answer seems obvious: Orville and Wilbur Wright flew three years prior in 1903 at Kitty Hawk, North Carolina, albeit with the assistance of its strong and steady winds. A definitive answer may never be reached, as nationalism sometimes sways opinion. Germans argue in favor of Otto Lilenthal, considered to be the first hang glider pilot, who made hundreds of flights before his death in 1896. The Montgolfiers of France popularized dirigibles via their balloon flights in the late 18th century. Their compatriot Henri Giffard flew a dirigible powered by a steam engine in 1852. And what of supposed earlier attempts made by more primitive cultures? Little or no record has been left of any such attempts, perhaps precluding the possibility of assigning proper credit to who may have actually been the "Father of Aviation."

37. The primary purpose of the passage is to

    (A) propose further investigation into a mystery.

    (B) discuss various opinions about a controversy.

    (C) present two hypotheses concerning the origins of flight.

    (D) describe reasons why the origins of flight are mysterious.

    (E) argue that the first aviator may have actually been a caveman.

38. The author implies that the use of dirigibles

    (A) was popularized by Santos Dumont.

    (B) involved technology not unlike that of a hang glider.

    (C) was probably employed by more primitive cultures.

    (D) was not well-known prior to the work of the Montgolfiers.

    (E) cannot effectively be considered early flight.

39. It can be inferred that the author would find the possibility mentioned in the last sentence of the passage more plausible if it were true that

Ⓐ Henri Giffard had not left a record of his flight history.

Ⓑ Santos Dumont had flown in Brazil, instead of Paris.

Ⓒ more people believed that primitive cultures were capable of creating flying machines.

Ⓓ primitive cultures were more capable of creating dirigibles than hang gliders.

Ⓔ primitive cultures left blueprints detailing a flight machine.

PASSAGE XIV

In his best-selling book *Hiroshima*, John Hershey does not overtly moralize on the use of atomic weapons by the United States during World War II; rather, he tells a straightforward account of the Hiroshima bombing and its immediate aftermath, as a journalist would describe any natural calamity. But by their very nature, the people and scenes he describes are so powerful, so compelling, and so fraught with moral implications that the reader cannot escape confronting fundamental issues of how human beings treat one another, during time of war and otherwise. Many critics regard *Hiroshima* as the greatest single piece of journalism produced in the 20th century for the specific reason that its story so effectively demands moral engagement, even as it astounds with its objectivity. Today's journalists need not assign their stories a heavy load of moral baggage in order to strike a significant blow for the betterment of the world. They need only to recognize the universal elements contained in any story of consequence and to describe those elements in a style that is vivid, truthful and within the bounds of objectivity.

40. The author's primary purpose in the passage is to
   - Ⓐ propose an alternative to traditional styles of journalism.
   - Ⓑ criticize the lack of moral pronouncements in most journalism.
   - Ⓒ describe how one author revolutionized journalism.
   - Ⓓ emphasize the importance of first-person narrative in good journalism.
   - Ⓔ suggest that objectivity can be valuable in contemporary journalism.

41. The author of the passage would probably consider which of the following stories to be most similar in style to the story Hershey wrote in *Hiroshima*?
   - Ⓐ An author pleads for a prisoner's freedom by condemning his imprisonment from a religious standpoint.
   - Ⓑ An author conveys the ferocity of a battle through first-hand accounts of what soldiers heard and said, and saw, felt, tasted, and smelled during the fighting.
   - Ⓒ An author inspires donations to fund a wildlife preserve by attributing charismatic personalities to animals.
   - Ⓓ An author endorses a course of political action by satirizing opponents as blundering imbeciles.
   - Ⓔ An author recounts a personal tragedy by repeatedly blaming others for the misfortune.

PASSAGE XV

The vertical zonation of sessile marine species in the intertidal zone is a long-examined phenomenon. This particular tide-cycle study examined the incidence of two sessile animal species, the common mussel (*Mytilus edulis*), and the acorn barnacle (*Semibalanus balanoides*), in plots of increasing altitude in the intertidal zone of a beach preserve in coastal Massachusetts. Results showed that incidence of *Mytilus* increased in frequency as height decreased, and incidence of *Semibalanus* increased in frequency as height increased, up to the high-tide line or "barnacle line." This distribution suggests competition between the two species, with the mussel successfully out-competing the barnacle for more time underwater and the barnacle evincing more ability than the mussel to reside in less ideal conditions. The transitional conclusion indicates that barnacles display numerous adaptations that equip them for life in the upper tide zone.

42. If the information provided in the passage is accurate, which of the following must also be true?

Ⓐ Some sessile species do not live in coastal areas.

Ⓑ *Semibalanus* would prefer by nature to live below the water level than above it.

Ⓒ The main food source of *Semibalanus* inhabits coastal areas at the level of the high-tide line.

Ⓓ Sessile species thrive in cold Atlantic waters better than in temperate tropical waters.

Ⓔ *Semibalanus* cannot survive in the upper tide zone.

43. Which of the following, if true, best strengthens the author's conclusion?

Ⓐ In tropical waters where there are no mussels, barnacles live predominantly close to the high-tide line.

Ⓑ Barnacle concentration decreases as the high-tide mark decreases.

Ⓒ Mussels can survive in air-only environments three times longer than barnacles.

Ⓓ Barnacles are able to feed on land-based flora, while mussels can only gain nutrition from underwater species.

Ⓔ When a larger geographical area is studied, the incidence of mussels matches that of barnacles.

44. The primary purpose of the passage is to
    Ⓐ dispute the findings of other, less thorough studies.
    Ⓑ assert the greater adaptability of one species over that of another.
    Ⓒ report the results and implications of a scientific study.
    Ⓓ argue for the superiority of one species over another.
    Ⓔ provide a conclusion about the interaction of two species.

PASSAGE XVI

No doubt the principle that punishment ought to have a reforming effect upon the criminal survives as a rudimentary organ in nearly all the schools which concern themselves with crime. But this is only a secondary principle, and as it were the indirect object of punishment; and besides, the observations of anthropology, psychology, and criminal statistics have finally disposed of it, having established the fact that, under any system of punishment, with the most severe or the most indulgent methods, there are always certain types of criminals, representing a large number of individuals, in regard to whom amendment is simply impossible, or very transitory, on account of their organic and moral degeneration. Nor must we forget that, since the natural roots of crime spring not only from the individual organism, but also, in large measure, from its physical and social environment, correction of the individual is not sufficient to prevent relapse if we do not also, to the best of our ability, reform the social environment. The utility and the duty of reformation none the less survive, even for the positive school, whenever it is possible, and for certain classes of criminals; but, as a fundamental principle of a scientific theory, it has passed away.

(Criminal Sociology by Enrico Ferri)

45. The author's use of the term "organic and moral degeneration" evokes an image of _____ on the part of the criminals.
    Ⓐ violent behavior
    Ⓑ qualified predictability
    Ⓒ inherent turpitude
    Ⓓ begrudged reformability
    Ⓔ inevitable relapse

46. The highlighted section refers to
    - (A) the inclusion and exclusion of reformation.
    - (B) the application and functionality of reformation.
    - (C) the usefulness and desirability of reformation.
    - (D) the righteousness and profitability of reformation.
    - (E) the practicality and obligation of reformation.

47. Select the phrase that describes the scope of the passage.
    - (A) all the schools which concern themselves with crime
    - (B) but this is only a secondary principle, and as it were the indirect object of punishment
    - (C) there are always certain types of criminals, representing a large number of individuals, in regard to whom amendment is simply impossible
    - (D) the natural roots of crime spring not only from the individual organism, but also, in large measure, from its physical and social environment
    - (E) as a fundamental principle of a scientific theory, it has passed away

PASSAGE XVII

Order of precedence is a sequential hierarchy of people of nominal—some even say symbolic—importance, practiced by sundry organizations and governments. One's position in an order of precedence does not unequivocally indicate one's responsibilities; rather, it reflects ceremonial or historic relevance. For instance, order of precedence may dictate where a host seats dignitaries at formal dinners. Moreover, order of precedence potentially determines the order of succession for heads of state removed from office or incapacitated, although the two terms are not often interchangeable. Universities and the professions frequently have their own rules of precedence, applied parochially and based on professional rank, with each rank being ordered within itself by seniority, meaning the date one attains that rank.

48. Consider each of the three choices separately and select all that apply.

    The author of this passage would agree with which of the following statements about order of precedence?

    [A] A country's order of precedence may have no official status but may be a symbolic hierarchy used to direct protocol.

    [B] General orders of precedence may be regarded as default rules on which almost all orders of precedence for events or institutions are based.

    [C] A university's specific order of precedence is based on merit and has no official status.

49. In the context of this passage, "parochially" most nearly means:
    - Ⓐ divisively
    - Ⓑ pertinaciously
    - Ⓒ dispassionately
    - Ⓓ provincially
    - Ⓔ indelibly

PASSAGE XVIII

The accusation that a particular critical remark is "irrelevant" to its object is one of the most frequently heard in discussion and debate among critics. It is frequently heard because it's frequently correct: there has never been a dearth of criticism that carelessly relates a work to an artist's biography, or employs point-less historic speculation, or invokes inappropriate creative standards, or describes the critic's own fuzzy reveries to misdirect our attention and obscure the essential significance of the object before us. Relevance and precision are critical to criticism. This fact underscores our concern to find a correct method for constructing criticism, a concern that has generated more controversy than any single commentator might hope to obfuscate with footnotes.

50. Consider each of the three choices separately and select all that apply.

The passage suggests that the author would agree with which of the following statements?

A Critics can take many paths to making irrelevant critical remarks.

B Pointless historical speculation can lead to irrelevant comments about critics.

C The concern for defining a correct method of relevant criticism has engendered enormous controversy.

51. In the context in which it appears, "dearth" most nearly means:

Ⓐ sufficiency

Ⓑ enigma

Ⓒ depredation

Ⓓ scarcity

Ⓔ inadequacy

PASSAGE XIX

Because of the lack of a comprehensive rail system in the United States, shipping relies greatly on the trucking industry, and hence on diesel fuel. Diesel consumption is therefore a major issue to be addressed in regards to not only air quality but also American dependence on foreign sources of oil. One proposed solution involves biofuels, which produce cleaner emissions than fossil fuels, but the use of corn and soy, traditionally food stocks, for production of biofuels has sparked a high rate of inflation in food prices around the world. Algae have also been proposed as a possible solution to this problem. Because half of algae's weight is lipid oil, and extraction is a simple process, it could serve as a more efficient alternative to corn- and soy-based oils. Given the successful use of algae for fuel production, the US government should begin production of algae biofuel plants to offset the detrimental effects of diesel fuel consumption by the trucking industry.

52. Which of the following statements, if true, casts the most doubt on the conclusion that the government should begin production of algae biofuel plants?

    Ⓐ Oil prices have been rising at a steady rate for more than 10 years.

    Ⓑ The high cost of algae-based biofuels will discourage the trucking industry from embracing the new fuel.

    Ⓒ Increased domestic oil production would offset dependence on foreign oil and reduce prices.

    Ⓓ Many types of algae cannot be used for biofuel production.

    Ⓔ Many farmers strongly support the use of corn and soy biofuels.

PASSAGE XX

The marks of a great leader are charm, confidence, and charisma—all traits related to an extroverted personality. It has long been held that great corporate leaders who are extroverted inspire and motivate their employees to be great as well, but researchers have discovered evidence to the contrary. There seems to be an inversely proportional relationship between the performance of an extroverted leader and the passivity of his or her team—leaders with the most passive team members tend to have the worst performance, while high-performing extroverted leaders owe their success to the innovative nature of their staffs. Whether it is due to arrogance, self-importance, or fear, outgoing leaders are less likely to take suggestions from enterprising staff and more likely to surround themselves with more reserved team members.

53. Consider each of the three choices separately and select all that apply.

    The passage implies which of the following about leadership?

    A Great leaders often exhibit attractive personal qualities.

    B If a leader accepts and implements suggestions from staff, he or she will improve as a leader.

    C Some long-held beliefs about the nature of leadership may be misguided.

54. In the context in which it appears, "enterprising" most nearly means:

    Ⓐ audacious

    Ⓑ hardworking

    Ⓒ intelligent

    Ⓓ assertive

    Ⓔ reckless

PASSAGE XXI

Cinematic renditions of historic pieces of literature provide an informative glimpse into the cultural and social context in which the films are made. Shakespeare's *Henry V* is a prime example, as it has been in circulation within the English-speaking world for over 400 years and has been interpreted in a number of different milieus. Since the source material has not changed, the way in which different artists and directors treat the play indicates not only the predispositions of the interpreter, but also the prevailing social and political views of the audience. This is acutely noticeable in a play like *Henry V,* which is highly charged with nationalistic concerns.

The play was written during the reign of Elizabeth I, when English national identity (and the modern English language) had begun to crystallize, and the language and culture we know today approached their present form. It is a historical biography of King Henry V of England, who waged a bloody campaign during the Hundred Years' War with the aim of conquering France. The introduction of the play features an adviser to the King explaining, in a confusing and nearly incomprehensible fashion, the justification for Henry's claim to the French throne. The text of the play itself has been interpreted as being ambiguous in its treatment of Henry's character. Henry has a number of rousing, heroic speeches, but he is also shown to be coldly unmerciful, as in the case of his refusal to pardon the petty thieves.

Shakespeare's play has been adapted in two famous film versions. The first, directed by Laurence Olivier, was made during the Second World War, immediately before the invasion of Normandy in 1944. Critics of the film have emphasized the pageantry, bravado, and nationalistic undertones of this version. The battle scenes in the film are understated and tame, with little of the carnage that would be expected of a medieval melee. They are shot in beautiful weather, and the actors are clad in radiant colors. The scene with Henry's harsh justice is omitted. The film was funded, in part, by the British government and is widely understood to have been intended as a propaganda film, made in anticipation of D-Day. The second version, directed by Kenneth Branagh, was made in 1989, only a few years after the Falklands War, and was much harsher in tone. The battle scenes are gory and are shot in gray, dismal weather. The actors wear muddy, blood-smeared costumes reflective of the period. The scene with Henry's harsh justice is included.

55. It can be inferred that the author
    - (A) regards texts as being open to interpretation.
    - (B) believes directors should remain as faithful to the original as possible.
    - (C) prefers the Olivier version.
    - (D) dislikes Henry.
    - (E) prefers Branagh's version.

56. The primary purpose of the passage is to
    - (A) describe Shakespeare's *Henry V.*
    - (B) denounce the intrusion of government involvement with the arts.
    - (C) describe cinematic interpretations of literature.
    - (D) teach the reader about cinematic versions of theatre.
    - (E) discuss the effect of contemporary situations upon interpretation of literature.

57. Consider each of the three choices separately and select all that apply.

    The author would be most likely to agree with which of the following?
    - [A] Original works of art are more reflective of their societal context than are cinematic adaptations of such works.
    - [B] Contemporary events influence the adaptation of historical source material.
    - [C] War is likely to produce good cinema.

58. Which of the following most accurately describes the relationship between the first sentence of paragraph 1 (Cinematic . . .) and sentence 7 of paragraph 3 (The film was . . .)?
    - (A) The first is an example of an argument; the second is a counterexample.
    - (B) The first is a synthesis of disparate ideas; the second is one of the components of that synthesis.
    - (C) The first is the topic of the passage; the second is an argument in support of it.
    - (D) The first presents an assertion; the second provides an example to support that assertion.
    - (E) The first is a thesis; the second is the antithesis.

PASSAGE XXII

The Security Council, the executive body of the United Nations, was created to grapple with issues of international security. Its unique structure of fifteen members, including five permanent members with veto power—the United Kingdom, the United States, China, Russia, and France—reflects the world's concentration of power circa 1945. The veto power is the most powerful tool in the United Nations: no binding resolution will pass unless it receives support from a majority of the Security Council members and has no vetoes against it. However, after sixty years, many members are aggressively suggesting an expansion of the permanent veto powers to better reflect today's world.

While most countries agree that the veto power is unfairly concentrated in the hands of a select few, no agreement exists on which countries should be given permanent seats. If states were picked based on population, then India and Indonesia should be added. If economic power were the deciding factor, then Japan and Germany would deserve seats. If those countries with proven leadership were chosen, South Africa and Brazil could receive veto power. Others have suggested that each continent deserves a permanent representative; others believe that each major religion should be bestowed a seat. The permutations suggested for the Security Council's expansion are endless, yet not one of them has garnered enough support to establish a consensus.

The current Security Council will need to approve any new permanent members with veto power. Such a measure would dilute the power of vetoes, a result current permanent members would be unlikely to approve. But the true conundrum facing the Security Council is that regardless of the specific method used to choose new permanent members, there is no guarantee that this new Security Council structure will not be outdated in sixty years. The expansion of the Security Council's veto powers is only a temporary fix to the current imbalance in Security Council power and should not be considered an enduring solution.

59. According to the passage, the current permanent members of the United Nations Security Council were selected because they

   Ⓐ had the largest populations in 1945.

   Ⓑ were the victorious powers in World War II.

   Ⓒ were the most powerful countries politically and economically in 1945.

   Ⓓ demonstrated their leadership ability in the United Nations' predecessor, the League of Nations.

   Ⓔ committed themselves to protecting international security after experiencing the atrocities of World War II.

60. Consider each of the three choices separately and select all that apply.

     According to the passage, countries have suggested which of the following as methods of choosing new Security Council permanent members?

     [A] financial buying and spending power

     [B] military size and strength

     [C] government affiliation with religion

61. The author suggests that the main issue with Security Council expansion is that

     Ⓐ the current members will approve any proposed expansion of permanent veto members.

     Ⓑ regardless of what new permanent member configuration is selected, it will likely have to be reorganized in the future.

     Ⓒ populations and financial power changes so quickly that it is difficult to tell which countries should be new members.

     Ⓓ many countries disagree that South Africa is a strong leader for the African bloc.

     Ⓔ developing countries want to expand the number of permanent members, while developed countries don't want to enlarge the Council.

62. Consider each of the three choices separately and select all that apply.

     The passage suggests that Security Council expansion is unlikely to occur for which of the following reasons?

     [A] Veto power countries are reluctant to share their veto power with other members.

     [B] Passing resolutions without incurring a veto from a newly added permanent member would become significantly more difficult.

     [C] Reaching a consensus on the proper method of selecting new permanent members is unlikely to occur.

63. As used in the passage, "conundrum" can best be defined as:

     Ⓐ revision

     Ⓑ paradox

     Ⓒ principle

     Ⓓ recommendation

     Ⓔ goal

PASSAGE XXIII

Adapted from *Pioneers of Science*, by Oliver Lodge

Young Galileo, with all the energy and imprudence of youth (what a blessing that youth has a little imprudence and disregard of consequences in pursuing a high ideal!), as soon as he perceived that his instructors were wrong on the subject of falling bodies, instantly informed them of the fact. Whether he expected them to be pleased or not is a question. Anyhow, they were not pleased, but were much annoyed by his impertinent arrogance.

The learned of those times had a crystallized system of truth, perfect, symmetrical—it wanted no novelty, no additions; every addition or growth was an imperfection, an excrescence, a deformity. Progress was unnecessary and undesired. In such an atmosphere true science was impossible. The life-blood of science is growth, expansion, freedom, development. Before it could appear it must throw off these old shackles of centuries. It must burst its old skin, and emerge, worn with the struggle, weakly and unprotected, but free and able to grow and to expand. The conflict was inevitable, and it was severe.

Now, Aristotle had said that bodies fell at rates depending on their weight. A 5 lb. weight would fall five times as quickly as a 1 lb. weight; a 50 lb. weight fifty times as quickly, and so on. Why he said so nobody knows. He cannot have tried. Probably it never occurred to him to doubt the fact. It seems so natural that a heavy body should fall quicker than a light one, and perhaps he thought of a stone and a feather, and was satisfied.

Galileo, however, asserted that the weight did not matter a bit, that everything fell at the same rate (even a stone and a feather, but for the resistance of the air), and would reach the ground in the same time. So one morning, before the assembled University, he ascended the famous leaning tower, taking with him a 100 lb. shot and a 1 lb. shot. He balanced them on the edge of the tower, and let them drop together. Together they fell, and together they struck the ground. The simultaneous clang of those two weights sounded the death-knell of the old system of philosophy, and heralded the birth of the new.

But was the change sudden? Were his opponents convinced? Not a bit. They saw that if they gave way on this one point they would be letting go their anchorage, and henceforward would be liable to drift along with the tide, not knowing whither. They dared not do this. No; they must cling to the old traditions; they could not cast away their rotting ropes and sail out on to the free ocean of God's truth in a spirit of fearless faith.

Yet they had received a shock: as by a breath of fresh salt breeze and a dash of spray in their faces, they had been awakened out of their comfortable lethargy. They felt the approach of a new era.

64. Consider each of the three choices separately and select all that apply.

   The passage implies which of the following about young Galileo's instructors?

   A They were extremely open-minded to his ideas.

   B They were shaken by Galileo's demonstration of weight's impact on falling bodies.

   C They were correct in agreeing with Aristotle's statements on weight and the speed of a falling body.

65. According to the passage, the "imprudence and disregard of consequences in pursuing a high ideal" that Galileo displayed can best be described as

   Ⓐ an example of Galileo's arrogance.

   Ⓑ a justifiable reason for his instructors disliking him.

   Ⓒ a blessing, in that it allowed for scientific progress.

   Ⓓ a personality flaw that Galileo later grew out of.

   Ⓔ an ultimately fatal flaw.

66. Select the sentence from the passage that suggests that Aristotle's statements on falling bodies were not verified by any valid experimentation.

   Ⓐ It seems so natural . . .

   Ⓑ He cannot have tried.

   Ⓒ Galileo, however, asserted . . .

   Ⓓ Now, Aristotle had said . . .

   Ⓔ The learned of those had . . .

67. Consider each of the three choices separately and select all that apply.

   Which of the following questions is/are answered by the passage?

   A How did Aristotle explore his theories on falling bodies?

   B When did Galileo's instructors finally come over to his way of thinking?

   C Do items of different weights fall at the same rate?

68. Information in the passage supports the inference that if a stone and a feather were dropped from a considerable height at the same time

   Ⓐ they would land at the same time.

   Ⓑ they would not land at the same time.

   Ⓒ the feather would land before the stone.

   Ⓓ the feather might not land at all if it were windy.

   Ⓔ the stone could hurt anyone standing below, but the feather could not.

PASSAGE XXIV

Adapted from *Daughters of the Puritans*, by Seth Curtis Beach

Louisa May Alcott has been called, perhaps truly, the most popular story-teller for children in her generation. She came up through great tribulation, paying dearly in labor and privation for her successes, but one must pronounce her life happy and fortunate, since she lived to enjoy her fame and fortune twenty years, to witness the sale of a million volumes of her writings, to receive more than two hundred thousand dollars from her publishers, and thereby to accomplish the great purpose upon which as a girl she had set her heart, which was to see her father and mother comfortable in their declining years.

Successful as Alcott was as a writer, she was greater as a woman, and the story of her life is as interesting, as full of tragedy and comedy, as the careers of her heroes and heroines. In fact, we have reason to believe that the adventures of her characters are often not so much invented as remembered, the pranks and frolics of her boys and girls being episodes from her own youthful experience. The happy girlhood which she portrays was her own, in spite of forbidding conditions. The struggle, in which her cheerful nature extorted happiness from unwilling fortune, gives a dramatic interest to her youthful experiences, as her literary disappointments and successes do to the years of her maturity.

Alcott's first story to see the light was printed in a newspaper when she was twenty, in 1852, though it had been written at sixteen. She received $5.00 for it, and the event is interesting as the beginning of her fortune. This little encouragement came at a period of considerable trial for the family. The following is from her journal of 1853: "In January, I started a little school of about a dozen in our parlor. In May, my school closed and I went to L. as second girl. I needed the change, could do the wash, and was glad to earn my $2.00 a week."

The picture of Jo in a garret in "Little Women," planning and writing stories, is drawn from Louisa's experiences of the following winter. A frequent entry in her journal for this period is "$5.00 for a story" and her winter's earnings are summed up, "school, one quarter, $50, sewing $50, stories, $20." In December we read, "Got five dollars for a tale and twelve for sewing." Teaching, writing, and sewing alternate in her life for the next five years, and, for a year or two yet, the needle is mightier than the pen; but in 1856, she began to be paid $10 for a story, and, in 1859, the Atlantic accepted a story and paid her $50.

69. Consider each of the three choices separately and select all that apply.

    The passage implies that the children portrayed in Alcott's fiction had

    A far more money than than Alcott had as a child.

    B happy childhoods, with pranks, frolics, and adventures.

    C lives that were not very different from that of Alcott as a child.

70. Consider each of the three choices separately and select all that apply.

    The author believes that the financial difficulties faced by Alcott at the beginning of her career

    A make her later years more dramatically interesting than they would otherwise be.

    B made it difficult for her to fulfill her life's wish of ensuring her parents' financial security.

    C were the inspiration for the travails that her literary heroines and heroes faced.

71. Consider each of the three choices separately and select all that apply.

    Which of the following statements regarding Alcott's early writing is supported by the passage?

    A Sewing was more profitable than writing during the early years of her career.

    B Her earliest ambition was to write novels for children.

    C Her first published story was written while she was a teenager.

72. It can be inferred from the passage that the author would support which of the following statements regarding the pursuit of happiness?

    Ⓐ Money is unimportant to reaching true happiness.

    Ⓑ Material success can be a factor in one's long-term happiness.

    Ⓒ The key to real happiness is marriage and children.

    Ⓓ Only a well-rounded life can bring one happiness.

    Ⓔ Happiness is an illusion created by works of fiction.

73. With which of the following sentences could the author most logically conclude this passage?

   Ⓐ Alcott's success was only short-lived, however.

   Ⓑ Thus did the myriad hardships endured by Alcott begin to lead into the attainment of her goals, both personal and professional.

   Ⓒ We can see from this that when pursuing a dream like writing, it's wise to have a backup plan.

   Ⓓ Many talented writers got their first big breaks from the Atlantic.

   Ⓔ Magazine and newspaper publications paved the way for Alcott's instant success as a novelist.

PASSAGE XXV

A box girder bridge, an evolution of the plate girder bridge, is fabricated from either post-stressed concrete or sheet steel plate and is commonly built for roadway flyovers and light rail transport. Some modern steel trestles, for example, are composed of a number of girder bridge segments. Concrete girder bridges are typically cast in place (using falsework supports that can be removed later), while the steel-plate type may be preassembled at a fabrication yard and then placed using cranes. The latter method is often used in situations where access for construction is limited due to traffic, which may be detoured around the work area, utilizing a limited number of lanes.

74. The passage is primarily concerned with
    - (A) the construction of modern steel bridges called box girder bridges.
    - (B) box girder bridge construction methods where access to construction is limited.
    - (C) how the box girder bridge is related to segmental bridges, such as trestles.
    - (D) why the plate girder bridge is considered the ancestor of the box girder bridge.
    - (E) the fabrication and construction methods of the box girder bridge.

75. According to the author, the girder bridge construction method employed where access for construction is limited to periods of light traffic is the
    - (A) cast-in-place method.
    - (B) post-stressed method.
    - (C) preassembled method.
    - (D) method using falsework supports.
    - (E) steel-plate method.

Answer Key

READING COMPREHENSION PRACTICE

1.	B	25.	A	52.	B
2.	B	26.	C	53.	A, B, C
3.	B	27.	D	54.	D
4.	C	28.	A	55.	A
5.	C	29.	D	56.	E
6.	A, B	30.	E	57.	B
7.	In small-scale individual testing . . .	31.	B	58.	D
		32.	D	59.	C
		33.	B	60.	A, C
		34.	C	61.	B
8.	B	35.	D	62.	A, C
9.	A, C	36.	E	63.	B
10.	D	37.	B	64.	B
11.	C	38.	D	65.	C
12.	A	39.	E	66.	He cannot have tried.
13.	C	40.	E		
14.	C	41.	B	67.	C
15.	D	42.	B	68.	B
16.	B	43.	D	69.	B, C
17.	E	44.	C	70.	A
18.	D	45.	C	71.	A, C
19.	B	46.	E	72.	B
20.	A	47.	B	73.	B
21.	A	48.	A	74.	E
22.	D	49.	D	75.	C
23.	B	50.	A, C		
24.	B	51.	D		

Answers and Explanations

READING COMPREHENSION PRACTICE

Passage I

1. B

Prior to answering any of the passage's questions, you should always consider the purpose of the passage. How would you summarize the passage? Does the author's tone suggest anything about the subject? What would you define as the purpose of the text? The answers to these questions will help when you get to the passage's questions. (B) is the credited response. This passage is a summary of Gordimer's role as a literary figure in South Africa and her use of literature as a reflection of South African society's race relations and violence.

(A) is not the credited response. This passage only touches on Gordimer's personal life; it is not the focus. (C) is not correct. Although it has been suggested that Gordimer's works informally illustrate the history of South Africa, the purpose of this passage is not to persuade you of this. (D) is incorrect because although the passage hints at irony, this is not the purpose or the author's primary concern in writing the text. (E) is not the credited response. The purpose of this passage is not to criticize Gordimer but rather to illustrate the roles she played in literary and social protest.

2. B

Read each question and ask yourself: using only the information provided in the passage, can I answer this question? Remember that partially complete answers do not mean that you *can* answer the question. The information in the text states that apartheid is "the institutional segregation and classification of race in South Africa." This allows you to answer the question "What is apartheid," which is choice (B).

3. B

This question asks you to draw a conclusion using information provided in the passage about Nadine Gordimer. (B) is correct. Gordimer's work runs parallel to and reflects the changing society within which she has lived since birth, specifically touching upon race and violence.

4. C

This question asks you to draw a conclusion using information provided in the passage about Nadine Gordimer. If Gordimer was born in 1923, then she must have been "just shy of 90" around 2009. (C) is correct. It is fair to infer that South Africa in 2009 is a society with continued racial and criminal concerns. The passage provides enough evidence for a reader to come to this conclusion.

(A) is not the credited response. There's not enough information in the passage to compare the violence then and now. (B) is difficult to infer from the passage; there is mention of crime today, but only hints of what crime was like in the past. There is not enough information for the reader to compare the two. (D) is not correct. The passage clearly states the years during which black African literature was banned in South Africa: 1948–1990. (E) is incorrect. The passage makes it clear that security is still a concern. Racial solidarity is not discussed in this passage, and there doesn't seem to be enough information for a reader to infer something about it.

Passage II

5. C

The stereotype referenced in the cited line is that women are poor math students; the passage says that, in environments in which this stereotype is prevalent, the math performance of all female students declines, even those who believe the stereotype is incorrect. If, as stated in choice (C), the female math students' declining performance was matched by similar declines among the male students, this would weaken the position that the women's performance declines resulted from the stereotype.

(A) would have no effect on the position, which attaches blame for the falling grades to the stereotype and doesn't mention study habits. (B) would not affect the female students' actual performances, merely the grades that are assigned to them. (D) would not have any necessary effect on the scores of female students. (E) would actually strengthen the argument, since it would support the idea that the stereotype was affecting women's grades in math.

6. A, B

The question asks us to infer what the author believes about Social Justification Theory (SJT). Since multiple choices could be correct, it may be harder to make a prediction, but we should start by paraphrasing a basic understanding of SJT. Our interpretation of paragraph 2 indicates that SJT posits that an oppressed group actually defends the very social system that disadvantages it. With that broad understanding, we can assess the answer choices.

To understand (A), we must go to paragraph 3, which discusses the limitations of SJT—strategic readers should notice that the paragraph begins "What cannot be known..."

According to this paragraph, studies to date have been limited in scope, and attempts to discriminate against the majority in a study would generate artificial results. This indicates that the picture provided by SJT is incomplete, so choice (A) is supported by the passage.

Choice (B) is also correct, because it is essentially a paraphrase of the statement in the passage that "even those disadvantaged by a social system have a tendency to defend and support it."

Choice (C) may be tempting because the author does discuss SJT through the prism of gender stereotyping, but this does not mean that SJT is primarily used in the field of gender relations. Perhaps scholars employ the theory just as often to analyze race or class. Since the author does not weigh in on this issue, choice (C) lacks adequate support. Thus, only choices (A) and (B) are correct.

7. In small-scale individual testing . . .

The question asks us to find evidence that members of advantaged groups may behave differently from members of disadvantaged groups when confronted with perceived discrimination. Based on our understanding of the passage, we know that members of advantaged groups are discussed in paragraph 3, so we can search there.

The final sentence states, "In small-scale individual testing, however, where men have perceived a specific experience to be discriminatory in nature, this has actually resulted in an increase in self-esteem related to their assumed disadvantage." The keyword "actually" helps indicate that men's increase in self-esteem contrasts with women's reaction to a similar situation (Paragraph 2 tells us that discrimination led women to doubt their own abilities and perform worse). Thus, choice (H), the final sentence of the passage, is the correct answer.

Passage III

8. B

This is a Detail EXCEPT question that is asking you to determine the one answer choice that is not in the passage. The best way to tackle Detail EXCEPT questions is to compare each answer choice to the passage and eliminate those discussed. All the answer choices are jobs Graham had (except one), and all of them can be found in the first paragraph. (B) is correct, because the passage doesn't mention anything about Graham designing sets for her productions. (E) is incorrect because the main idea of the passage is that Graham's choreography changed dance theory. The third sentence mentions three places where Graham danced professionally, which eliminates (C). The next sentence says she funded her own company by giving lessons and modeling coats, so both (A) and (D) can be ruled out as well.

9. A, C

The author discusses different aspects of Graham's career and her role in the dance community. The third sentence of the second paragraph, states that Graham's unique interpretation of dance movement "reformed the whole of modern dance theory and the very notion of what a dancer was." This statement supports the idea that she had a role in changing the way people thought about dance, so (A) is correct. The final sentence states, "Her signature style continues to permeate the work of contemporary dance and influence modern choreographers," which supports the conclusion in (C). The statement in (B), however, is a distortion. In the first paragraph, you learn that Graham wanted to be remembered for her dancing skills, but the fact that she is best remembered as a choreographer supports the idea that she was as strong a director as a dancer. The correct answers are (A) and (C).

10. D

The author writes that Taylor and Cunningham rejected Graham's "intense manner of teaching and technique." This is best reflected in (D). (A), (B), and (E) are out of scope; the author doesn't provide any evidence to suggest that Taylor and Cunningham didn't understand Graham's style, excel in her dance company, or consider her choreography innovative. (C) is a distortion. While Taylor and Cunningham did not adopt Graham's intense teaching style, the passage does not offer an assessment of whether or not it was "powerful." Taylor and Cunningham could have rejected the style for a number of other reasons.

Passage IV

11. C

The answer to this question appears in the first paragraph. The paragraph's next-to-last sentence states that "All of this accounts for . . . renewability . . . despite . . . erosion." Thus, the answer must appear in the previous sentences. These sentences discuss the symbiotic relationship between coral and algae, so the correct answer is (C). (A) might have been tempting because the sentence before ("All of this accounts . . .") refers to algae, but the focus of the first paragraph is on symbiosis, so the correct answer must include both coral and algae. (B) distorts the logic of the passage—oxygen contributes to renewability; "despite" is not appropriate here. (D) and (E) come from the wrong part of the passage.

12. A

Darwin is discussed in the second paragraph of the passage. This paragraph mentions his theory of reef transformation: the theory of gradual submergence of volcanic islands. That makes (A) correct. (B), (C), and (D) are contradictory choices. (E) is outside the scope of the passage. The parts of the reef that most interested Darwin are not mentioned in the text.

13. C

The relationships in (D), (A), and (E) are discussed in the third, fourth, and fifth sentences of the first paragraph, respectively. (B) is mentioned in the second paragraph. (C), however, connects items that are not associated with each other in the passage. Volcanic rock is discussed in the second paragraph, while life at reefs is brought up in the third. (C) is the correct answer.

14. C

(A) is tempting because it tries to get you to look at the third paragraph and see "10 percent." This percentage, however, refers to a particular type of reef life form; no percentage is given for reef-building coral worldwide. (B) appears promising since sea level and reefs appear in the second paragraph, but the mechanism by which sea level contributes to reef-building is never explained. (C) looks good: The second-to-last sentence provides considerable detail about where reefs can form. Checking the last two choices, (D) can be eliminated because the author specifies in the last sentence of the first paragraph that the answer to this question is unknown. Likewise, (E), the transformation of reefs, is never resolved. Two theories are presented and the author leans towards one of them, but never gives a definitive answer.

15. D

It might seem that the author would agree with statement (D), since the term "coral reef" is described as "something of a misnomer." However, the author does not indicate or imply that people need to stop using "coral reef." Therefore, (D) is correct.

Passage V

16. B

(B) is correct. This choice puts together the idea of hierarchy, as found in Forset and other thinkers, with the statement in the last sentence that people accepted stability as God's will. The implication is that Elizabeth and her successors maintained their influence and power because English society accepted the idea of a divinely prescribed social structure in which the monarch occupied the top of the social heap.

17. E

(E) is a fairly direct paraphrase of the idea stated in the passage's opening sentence, with the added (but straightforward) inference that the Catholic Church formerly provided structure and stability to English society, so (E) is the correct answer.

18. D

Choice (D) is supported by two references in the passage. The first is the reference to a "rebellious Parliament"; the second is the veiled suggestion in the last sentence that there were restive elements in English society that had to be held down or kept in check by the monarchy, and that the English public's interim acceptance of a divine hierarchical scheme aided the monarchy in this situation. This choice completes the thought by adding the plausible idea that Parliament represented these rebellious interests. The other choices all fail, in one way or another, to follow the logic of the passage's ideas.

Passage VI

19. B

The passage as a whole demonstrates that the theory of modernization outlined at the beginning of the passage fails to apply to at least one society.

Choice (B) best expresses this idea.

The passage does describe Ibo society, as (A) says, and proves that in some respects it should be classed as modern, as (E) suggests; but it does these things to support the larger point that the theory under discussion is flawed. The passage does not do the things indicated in (C) and (D).

20. A

This question asks us to find which answer choice(s) is/are consistent with the concept of "legal-rational authority." The concept of "legal-rational authority" is defined in the first sentence. The emphasis is on specificity and intentionality in establishing rules or procedures. Choice (A), which describes a pragmatic approach, much like that ascribed to the Ibo in the passage, isn't a direct illustration of "legal-rational authority," but it is consistent with the concept, as required by the question. Choices (B) and (C) embody the idea of the constancy of tradition; this is closer to the conception of traditional authority, and inconsistent with the idea of legal-rational authority. Thus, only choice (A) is correct.

21. A

The main point of the passage is to question the theorist's ideas, but this question doesn't ask for the main point—it asks for a point the author would assert. The second sentence states, "No doubt this scheme works well

enough in categorizing some societies," so the author agrees with choice (A). This rules out (B), but (C) is ruled out by the case of the Ibo. So is (D)—Ibo society is an empirical test. (E) distorts the reference to the Ibos' adapting to the post-colonization world, in the next-to-last sentence. Since the theorist's categorization doesn't apply to the Ibo before colonization either, (E) should be ruled out.

Passage VII

22. D

The author mentions Huckleberry Finn in the second paragraph. He says, "Even Peck himself lauds Huckleberry Finn, whose strengths include an unfailing eye for hypocrisy and a deadly serious moral judgment, as a definitively American character who leaps real from the printed page." The author concludes that Peck's assessment of Twain as strictly a humorist is too narrow because Huckleberry Finn is more than just a funny character; he is a serious and richly-drawn character, and he illustrates Twain's ability to craft characters of multiple dimensions. Therefore, choice (D) is correct.

(A) is a 180. Peck cites three literary works as examples of Twain's humorous writings. However, in the second paragraph, the author cites the character Huckleberry Finn as an example of Twain's ability to write well beyond humor. (B) is a misused detail. The author says that Finn knows hypocrisy when he sees it. He does not say that Huckleberry Finn is a hypocritical character. (C) is too extreme. The author agrees with Peck that Twain is a remarkable humorist but disagrees that Twain is only a humorist. (E) is a 180. The author believes that Peck lacks insight into Twain's use of writing to express moral judgment.

23. B

Since this is a global question, be sure that the answer you choose reflects the passage as a whole. In the first paragraph, the author introduces you to Peck's analysis of Twain: Peck believes that Twain is strictly a humorist. In the second paragraph, the author disagrees and points to Huckleberry Finn as evidence that Twain was also an extraordinary writer of broader, more serious works. He ultimately disagrees with Peck. Looking over the answer choices:

(A) is too extreme. The author clearly agrees in the first paragraph that Twain was an exemplary humorist; however, in the second paragraph, the author argues that Twain was much more than that.

(B) is correct. In the second paragraph, the author concludes that Peck was incorrect in his assessment that Twain was only a humorist. The author's purpose in writing the passage is to show how Peck was mistaken; Twain is much more than a humorist.

(C) is too broad in scope. The author does not document Peck's entire contribution to literary criticism. In the passage, the author evaluates one narrow aspect of Peck's contribution to literary criticism: his limited analysis of Twain.

(D) is a distortion. The author does state that Twain used humor to relay a serious message; however, he never says that he is better at serious writing than at humor. He only says that Twain was both a serious writer and a humorist.

(E) is too broad in scope. You may infer from the passage that the author agrees that serious themes can be important in good writing. But that's not the main point of the passage. The author's purpose in writing the passage is to show how Peck's assessment of

Twain was too limited; Twain is much more than a humorist.

Passage VIII

24. B

In the last sentence of the passage, the author says "automobile manufacturers should content themselves with the continued development of conventional hybrid-fuel technologies and of more fuel-efficient, internal-combustion gasoline engines." Choice (B) nicely sums up that conclusion. Choice (A) is too narrow in scope. The passage does mention that late-night talk radio listeners are wrong in their understanding of hydrogen fuel, but the main purpose of the passage is not to criticize them. The purpose is to advocate a policy. Choice (C) is a misused detail. The passage does say that the production of hydrogen generates pollution, but that is just evidence for the author's main conclusion. Choice (D) is a distortion. The author argues that automobile manufacturers, not Congress, should fund research into conventional fuel cells, not hydrogen fuel cells. Regardless, this is not the main idea of the passage. Choice (E) is a distortion. The author describes obstacles to the development of hydrogen engines, not gasoline engines.

25. A

Even though this is an Inference question, remember that the correct answer will not stray too far from the facts given in the passage. The author talks about public awareness of hydrogen fuels in the first sentence: "the common public notions seem to be that hydrogen is already available as an inexpensive source of fuel and that hydrogen automobile engines will operate free of pollution." The author goes on to provide evidence that these notions are incomplete (hydrogen fuel cells do produce only water, but manufacturing the hydrogen creates pollution) and inaccurate (hydrogen is four times more expensive than gasoline to produce). Therefore, choice (A) is the correct answer.

Choice (B) is the opposite of what's true. The author says people express their erroneous opinions on talk radio, not that they get those opinions from talk radio. Choice (C) is too extreme: The word "deliberately" brings up motive, which takes the answer far outside the author's intent. Nowhere does the author go so far as to state that talk radio deliberately distorts the facts surrounding hydrogen fuels. Choice (D) is a distortion and a misused detail. The author says the public's awareness of the technological issues behind hydrogen fuels is incomplete and inaccurate, but nowhere suggests a connection between that unawareness and the president's initiative. Choice (E) is outside the scope of the passage. While this conclusion may sound sensible to the reader, there is no evidence for this idea anywhere in the passage.

26.   C

The author suggests that scientists have not already created a commercially adequate engine powered by hydrogen fuel cells when she states that the president has called for the commercial use of fuel cells in transportation but that there are serious obstacles to getting it done. That strongly suggests it has not yet been done, so Choice (C) is the correct response. The rest of the questions are incorrect because the passage cannot answer them.

Passage IX

27.   D

The uncertain language ("suggests") tells us that this is an Inference question. Unlike most question types, these questions are usually not predictable, so we don't waste limited time trying to make a prediction. Instead, we go through the question choices and eliminate the ones that don't work. Watching for extreme language and other common traps can be a real time-saver here. Let's start from the bottom.

Choice (E) is a 180; the clubhouse model encourages a gradual approach to employment. Choice (D) sounds good; both models are paths to competitive employment. Since there is only one right answer, we can stop there and bank the time for other questions.

Just to learn to recognize the characteristics of wrong answers, though, we can review the other answer choices. Choice (C) contains extreme language; "diametrically opposed" means "completely opposite," and is strong language that is rarely supported by any passage, and certainly not by this one. Choice (B), similarly, distorts the second paragraph. While clients may not have enough choice under the clubhouse model, they do choose their transitional jobs from a list. Choice (A) is a distortion of the first paragraph. Although clients "typically" start by practicing for real jobs, and "generally speaking" go through these three steps, the passage never states that all clients go through the same steps.

28.   A

First, make sure you know right off the bat what the question is asking. We want to pick the answer that *doesn't* fit, so four of the answers will make sense and one of them will not. This question just asks for facts—what the clubhouse model involves—so it is a Detail question. We should use keywords and our understanding of the passage to find and reread the relevant text. The author describes the clubhouse model in paragraph 1, so review the list of activities there. Normally, we would make a prediction on a Detail question, but the question asks which activity clients *don't* do, so we can't make a prediction.

Let's look at the list, starting from the bottom because this is a "which of the following" question. Clients certainly work at transitional jobs, so we cross (E) off. (D) is a tricky one, since critics of the clubhouse model say it limits client choice, but the clients do get to choose which transitional jobs to work at, so (D) is out. The whole point of the clubhouse model is to build toward permanent work, so we can rule out choice (C). The model is named for the clubhouses where clients start out working, so (B) is out, which means the answer should be (A). It's easy to misread something and eliminate the wrong answer, however, so we'll check (A) just to be sure. The staff work with companies to make the list, not the clients—so (A) is false, making it the right answer.

29. D

The phrase "primary purpose" is a classic clue that this is a global question. We should make a prediction before looking at the answer choices and do a vertical scan of the verbs to find the answer quickly. We can predict something like, "describe or compare two models for helping the mentally ill find work, and give one reason the second model is better."

A vertical scan could eliminate choice (B), as "argue" is too strong for the tone of the passage. Choice (A) is the primary purpose for the first paragraph, but not the whole passage. Often, wrong answers on global questions are too narrowly focused like this. If the author didn't have to write the whole

passage to get a point across, it isn't the main point.

Choice (C) only focuses on the clubhouse model, and saying that this model is "essentially flawed" is too extreme. The author merely points out that the model has one weakness. Choice (D) seems to be a match from our prediction. Choice (E) is outside of scope; the passage is concerned with helping the mentally ill find jobs, not treating them. The answer is (D).

Passage X

30. E

Choice (A) is too narrow in scope. While the author does address emotional responses of rhesus monkeys with amygdala damage, he only mentions them in the second paragraph. Therefore, this is not the focus of the passage as a whole. Choice (B) is too broad in scope. The author does discuss technological advances but not all of the advances that have been made in the last two decades. He only talks about technological advances in reference to understanding the brain. Choice (C) is too extreme. The author discusses exponential advances in understanding of the brain, but never states that scientists' understanding is either thorough or entirely recent. Choice (D) is too narrow in scope. The author mentions the role of the limbic system in human emotion but this is not the focus of the passage. Choice (E) is the correct answer. In the passage, the author attributes advances in understanding the brain to technological advances within the past two decades. The author cites research on the amygdala as an example of this progress.

31. B

The author states that "patients with trauma or damage to this structure [the amygdala] exhibit a complete absence of aggression." Earlier in the passage the author indicates that the amygdala is located centrally in the brain's limbic system, which is responsible for emotional regulation. Choice (B) is the correct answer.

Passage XI

32. D
The author explains that the two key components of social learning theory are 1) observation and modeling, and 2) punishment and reward. In the example presented, a girl is being praised and rewarded for her behavior and, therefore encouraged to engage in that behavior in the future—thus contributing to her gender identity. The boy, however, is scolded for playing with dolls (a punishment). This, in turn, discourages him from playing with dolls in the future and also teaches him that playing with dolls does not fit in with his appropriate gender identity. Therefore, the author uses this example to help illustrate how social learning theory works. (D) is the correct answer.

33. B
In paragraph 2, the author states, "This theory, unlike the broad social learning theory, accounts for more variance in gender identities; individuals can incorporate into their prototypes traits and behaviors that they deem characteristic to their gender." In other words, individuals draw on their own experiences and mental concepts to form their personal notion of gender. Therefore, variance in gender roles among a group of brothers is better explained by gender schema theory. (B) is the correct answer.

34. C
The author presents social learning theory, then suggests, "another theory [gender schema theory] provides a more thorough explanation of individual conceptualizations of gender." In the final sentence of the passage, the author asserts, "Gender schema theory is superior, as it goes beyond simple observation and reward by taking a more complex cognitive perspective." For purpose questions, do a vertical scan to help you quickly eliminate choices. In this question, look for verbs like "support" or "advocate." Choice (A) is incorrect. In the passage, the author does not merely explain two theories of gender identity formation, but more specifically, endorses one over the other. Choice (B) is incorrect. While the author does endorse one theory over the other, the author does not challenge the theoretical basis of either theory. Choice (D) is incorrect and a misused detail. While the author does describe two theories of gender identity formation, the author also advocates one over the other. In addition, the author presents two theories of gender *identity* formation, NOT gender formation. Choice (E) is outside the scope of the passage. The author never discusses "further exploration" of either gender formation or gender identity formation. Choice (C) is the correct answer.

Passage XII

35. D
This is a variation on the classic GRE Inference question. You are asked to complete the passage with a logical conclusion or inference. You must consider what follows from the preceding sentence, but a question such as this also requires that you choose an answer that is within the scope of the passage. Because it primarily tests your grasp of the whole passage, it has global question type implications as well. (D) is correct, as it summarizes the main idea of the paragraph.

36. E

This is a Detail question, so you can expect that the correct answer will be stated in the actual text. However, notice that it is an EXCEPT question. In this case, the correct answer is the one that is NOT stated in the text. Choice (E) is correct. The entertainment of bird song is never mentioned.

Choice (A) is stated in the second sentence: "Bird song serves as a means to mark nesting territory." Choice (B) is stated in the second-to-last sentence: "The song of a male bird is thought to convey his experience to female birds." Choice (C) is stated in the fifth sentence: "The timing and frequency of bird song are controlled by hormones, and thus are linked to the breeding season," and the last sentence: "A female bird may in turn use that information to select a worthy mate." Choice (D) is stated in both the third sentence: "The nature of bird song is influenced by the habitat," and the fourth sentence: "Low-pitched sounds travel better in areas of dense vegetation than do high-pitched ones, which are common among birds nesting in open habitats."

Passage XIII

37. B

This is a Global question, and asks about the "big picture"—why the author wrote the passage. The author of the passage does not argue in favor of one theory concerning the "Father of Aviation," but instead touches on various theories. The purpose is to suggest that the answer is difficult to determine, and that it depends on the criteria and perspective employed by anyone trying to answer the question posed at the beginning of the passage. This passage is descriptive or explanatory, rather than argumentative.

Look for a choice that reflects these observations. A verb scan eliminates (A), "propose," (C), "present," and (E), "argue." The verbs that lead off choices (B), and (D), "discuss" and "describe," match your prediction. Then the question is: does the paragraph offer "various opinions" or "reasons"? The passage describes various opinions, so choice (B) is correct.

38. D

Inference questions often require you to read between the lines of the passage. Think carefully about the stated text of the passage and look to possibly combine or connect different pieces of the text. Answers to Inference questions are often difficult to predict, so you may need to select the correct choice by elimination of choices which contradict the passage.

Choice (A) is a distortion. Santos Dumont flew dirigibles, but there is no evidence or implication that he popularized them. Choice (B) is also a distortion. No connection was made between the hang-glider flights of Lilenthal and flights in dirigibles. Choice (C) is too extreme. The author suggests that primitive cultures may have found ways to fly, but does not go so far as to say that they did so, let alone that they did so using dirigibles. The phrase "probably employed" makes this answer choice too extreme and therefore wrong. The correct answer to an Inference question does not stray too far from the passage. Choice (D) is correct. The author says that the Montgolfiers popularized the use of balloons, which is another word for dirigibles. You can infer that before they became popular, the use of dirigibles was not well-known. Choice (E) is a 180. The author suggests the opposite, that the use of dirigibles was one of several viable means of early flight.

39. E

The possibility mentioned in the last sentence concerns whether primitive cultures achieved human flight. The author states that because little or no evidence exists, we may never know the truth. Therefore, the existence of evidence might make this possibility more plausible.

Choice (A) is a misused detail. Henri Giffard is mentioned earlier and has nothing to do with the idea mentioned in the last sentence. Choice (B) is out of scope. The sentence does not refer to Santos Dumont or where he flew. Also, the passage does not say where he flew. Choice (C) is a distortion. The author suggests that the lack of evidence is the problem, not people's disbelief. Choice (D) is out of scope. The issue is not which method the early cultures may have used to fly. Choice (E) is correct. The author states that the lack of records precludes knowing what primitive cultures may have done. Blueprints would be evidence that would fix this problem.

Passage XIV

40. E

This Global question asks you to determine *why* the author created the passage. The passage begins with the declaration that the book *Hiroshima* leads to important moral considerations even though it remains objective and does not overtly moralize. At the end, the author reinforces this when she says modern journalists should create their stories in the same objective way if they want to effect change. That is the author's opinion. Persuading readers of the validity of that opinion is the *why* of the passage, and it is summed up by Choice (E). Choice (A) falls beyond the scope of the passage. Nowhere in the passage do you read about alternatives to traditional journalism. The contrast in the passage is between objectivity and moralizing, rather than traditional and alternative. Choice (B) contradicts the passage. The author argues that the most effective stories present the facts without bias and let readers draw their own conclusions about morality. Choice (C) distorts a detail. The author cites Hershey as an example of a good journalist, but does not claim that Hershey revolutionized anything. Choice (D) is out of scope. The passage does not discuss first-person narrative.

41. B

How does the author describe the writing style of *Hiroshima*? According to the passage, "John Hershey does not overtly moralize on the use of atomic weapons by the United States during World War II; rather, he tells a straightforward account of the Hiroshima bombing and its immediate aftermath, as would a journalist describing any natural calamity." Hershey's journalism is later describes as "vivid, truthful and within the bounds of objectivity."

Choice (B) best fits that description. The author reports as a neutral observer who lets readers draw their own conclusions. Choices (A) and (E) defy objectivity by assigning blame—they overtly moralize. Choice (C) defies objectivity by assigning personalities to the animals. Choice (D) also clearly takes a side, which removes it from the bounds of objectivity.

Passage XV

42. B

Inference questions often ask you to determine what else would be supported by the passage. The passage states that the study finds mussels "successfully out-competing the barnacle for more time underwater," and that the barnacle resides in "less ideal" conditions in the upper-tide zone. Therefore, it must be desirable for these species to live underwater. Choice (B) is correct. Choice (A) is out of scope. The passage does not discuss the location of sessile species in these broader terms. Choices (C) and (D) are also out of scope. The food source is not discussed, nor is the temperature of the water. Choice (E) is a 180, since the passage states directly that the *Semibalanus* sessile species is found in the upper-tide zone.

43. D

In a Strengthen question, pre-phrase a prediction and use it to eliminate incorrect answer choices. The conclusion is that barnacles adapt to living above water better than mussels do. The correct answer will strengthen that idea. Choice (D) provides a match. It suggests a way barnacles have adapted to living above the water level.

44. C

A good prediction would be *give the basic details of an experiment*, which matches choice (C).

Choice (A) is out of scope, because the author does not mention other studies. Choice (B) is a distortion; while the author does conclude that the barnacle adapts in this particular scenario, he does not assert that it has greater adaptability. Choice (D) is extreme. The author does not claim the superiority of one species over the other. Finally, the passage also does not describe the interaction of the two species, and so choice (E) is also a distortion.

For a question like this, you can also use your understanding of the passage's overall tone to eliminate obviously wrong answer choices. If the answer choices begin with verbs, use the vertical scan method to rule out any choices

with verbs that contradict the primary purpose. In this case, the author presents a straightforward account without strong language, so you can eliminate highly negative or highly positive verb choices such as choices (A), (B), and (D).

Passage XVI

45. C

The sentence states that for some criminals, "amendment is simply not possible . . . on account of their organic and moral degeneration." The author uses the phrase to show that certain criminals are inherently evil, and to point out that one's nature cannot fundamentally be altered. The answer is (C).

46. E

The "utility and the duty of reformation" can be rephrased as the "functionality and the obligation of reformation." For this Definition question, look for the best synonym for the underlined section. The answer is (E).

47. B

The scope of the passage provides us with the particular focus of the passage. The topic is the principle of reformation, as introduced in the first sentence. Look for the answer choice that limits this topic to the level at which it's discussed in the passage. (B) is correct. This limits the discussion of the principle of reformation to its value as a principle for punishment and sets the tone for what follows.

Passage XVII

48. A

In this question, choice (A) is the only answer that applies.

"A country's order of precedence may have no official status but may be a symbolic hierarchy used to direct protocol," as in answer choice

(A): the example in the passage is where dignitaries sit at state dinners. Choice (B) is outside the scope of the passage; it doesn't state that orders of precedence are regarded as default rules. Finally, the author states that universities often have their own rules of precedence, which are "based on professional rank" and on "seniority," not merit, refuting choice (C).

49. D

In this passage, "parochially" most nearly means (D), "provincially," which in context includes both of the word's meanings, "locally or regionally" and "narrow in scope." The clue to the word's contextual meaning lies in the clause "Universities and the professions frequently have their own rules of precedence," and the sentence continues to cite two hierarchies specific to a university: professional rank and seniority within that rank.

The other four choices don't reflect the meaning of this passage: (A), "divisively," means "causing disagreement or dissension"; (B), "pertinaciously," means "holding firmly to some purpose or belief"; (C), "dispassionately," means "calmly" or "objectively"; and (E), "indelibly," means "permanently" or "strongly."

Passage XVIII

50. A, C

The author would agree with choice (A) , since she lists various ways that critical remarks can be irrelevant: carelessly relating an artist's work to his biography, using pointless historic speculation, invoking inappropriate standards, and taking off on reveries that misdirect attention and obscure the significance of an object. Moreover, the author claims that legitimate or relevant criticism is a topic of much "discussion and debate among critics," and that the concern for finding a correct method of constructing valid criticism "has generated more controversy than any single commentator might . . . obfuscate [confuse] with footnotes," so choice (C) is also correct. Choice (B) is correct up to the last phrase, "comments about critics." The passage is about artistic works that critics comment on, not the critics themselves.

51. D

In the context in which it appears, "dearth" most nearly means "shortage," or (D), "scarcity." According to the passage, no scarcity of irrelevant criticism exists; the passage goes on to define four types of such criticism. Choice (A), "sufficiency," is an antonym of "dearth"; it means "abundance" or "surplus." Choice (B), "enigma," means "puzzle" or "mystery." Choice (C), "depredation," means "the act of preying upon or plundering." Choice (E), "inadequacy," is close in meaning to "dearth," but it doesn't refer to a shortage but rather to a lack of suitability.

Passage XIX

52. B

The question asks for the answer that casts the most doubt on the conclusion stated in the final sentence of the passage: "Given the successful use of algae for fuel production, the US government should begin production of algae biofuel plants to offset the detrimental effects of diesel fuel consumption by the trucking industry." The passage cites evidence that algae biofuels are cleaner than traditional diesel fuels and would not lead to the inflation of food prices that is caused by the use of corn and soy biofuels. This argument makes one assumption that is common to many arguments that propose a future course of action: that there are no significant reasons why the plan would be ineffective at achieving the desired goal. In this case, if an answer choice cited a reason why the diesel trucking industry would be unwilling or unable to use algae biofuel, the argument would be significantly weakened. Thus, Choice (B) is the correct answer because it states that the cost of algae biofuel would discourage the trucking industry from using this new fuel. If this were true, then it would not be prudent for the government to invest in algae biofuel plants.

Choice (A) is a 180 because it actually adds urgency to, and thus supports, the conclusion that the government should invest in producing a new type of fuel. Choice (C) addresses the issue of foreign dependence on oil, but it does not address the air-quality issue arising from diesel-fuel consumption. Investing in algae biofuel could still be a good idea because it helps address the issue of air quality. Choice (D) does not give enough information to cast doubt on the argument because, even though some types of algae could not be used to produce biofuel, this implies that other types of algae *could* be used for this purpose. Thus, this information would not threaten the viability of the government's effort to produce algae-based biofuels. Choice (E) is irrelevant because it addresses the desires of certain farmers. Even if these farmers were unhappy about the switch to algae, this does not mean that investing in algae biofuel is a bad idea for the government or the trucking industry.

Passage XX

53. A, B, C

This question asks us to identify which statements about leadership are implied by the passage. In other words, we must select the statements that may not appear directly in the passage but are supported by the details or assertions in the passage. We can evaluate each answer choice individually to determine its viability as a correct answer.

Choice (A) is intimated in the first sentence, which states that great leaders are typically extroverted, exuding charm, confidence, and charisma. These three traits are all "attractive personal qualities." Choice (B) is suggested in the third and fourth sentences, which, when taken together, imply a direct relationship between openness to employee suggestions and leadership performance. The more passive the staff, the worse the leadership, and the reverse is true. Encouraging employees by listening and implementing their suggestions can improve performance of the leader. Choice (C) is a valid inference that emerges from the second sentence, which provides an example of a long-held view that researchers have recently challenged.

Answer choices (A), (B), and (C) are correct.

54. D

We can use the context of the passage, particularly its final sentence, to predict the meaning of the word "enterprising." The passage uses "enterprising" to describe workers who would make suggestions, in contrast to those who are more "reserved." Finally, we can tell from the context of the passage that the author thinks that these employees are worth listening to. Given these clues, we can predict that the answer will be one of the positively charged terms. "Forthright" or another word that describes someone who confidently takes initiative, would work here.

Choice (D), "assertive," matches our prediction, and it is positively charged. Choice (D) also contrasts to "reserved" and describes the kind of employee who would make suggestions. Choice (A), "audacious," which means "fearless" or "bold," has a slightly negative connotation. Audacity is not necessarily an attractive trait in a corporate setting, so the author would not use such a word to describe employees who submit invaluable input. We can eliminate choice (A). Choice (B), "hard-working," which means "dedicated," has a positive connotation, but it does not strongly contrast to "reserved." Passive or reserved employees can be extremely hard workers, so we can eliminate that choice, too. Likewise, choice (C), "intelligent," which means "smart," does not provide a suitable contrast to "reserved." Passive employees can be quite intelligent. Choice (E), "reckless," which means "irresponsible," is a negatively charged word. It would be quite imprudent to take advice from reckless staff members if you want to improve your performance as a leader.

The correct answer is choice (D).

Passage XXI

55. A

This is a question that asks you to put yourself in the author's shoes and try to reason from his perspective. The tone of the passage is neutral; even when describing Henry's darker moments, the author passes no judgement. (A) is correct. It matches the author's purpose for the passage. In order for cultural events to influence the interpretation of classical literature, such literature must be interpretable. (B) is incorrect. The author states no preference for cinematic versions that maintain greater fidelity to the source material. (C) and (E) are incorrect. The author states no preference for either of the film versions he describes. (D) is incorrect. The author is not doing a character study of Henry.

56. E

The correct answer to a Primary Purpose question summarizes what the author is trying to do in the passage. Here, the author uses cinematic depictions of *Henry V* to illustrate how contemporary culture influences the interpretation of art. Choice (E) cites the effect of contemporary situations on the interpretation of literature, striking at the heart of what the author explores in the passage. Choice (A) misses the point; the author uses Shakespeare's *Henry V* as an illustration, not for the purposes of describing the play itself. Choice (B) distorts the author's purpose, which is to illustrate the cultural influence, not judge which influences are positive or negative. Choice (C) is too broad; the passage isn't about cinematic interpretations of literature writ large. Choice (D) is also too general.

57. B

Questions of this type have three options, but any or all of them can be correct. Don't stop when you come across one correct answer. Additionally, evaluate each choice in light of the author's scope and purpose. (A) makes an irrelevant comparison. The author discusses the influence of historical and societal context on both Shakespeare's play and the later film adaptations of it, but never implies that one is more reflective of its social context than the other. (B) is correct: it paraphrases the author's primary purpose, so he's certain to agree with it. (C) is incorrect. The author makes no effort to argue about what makes *good* cinema, only what influences it when it's involved in interpreting classic literary works.

58. D

Questions like this reward you for understanding the logic of a passage. In this case, the first sentence is an assertion that lays out the topic and the scope of the passage. The other sentence is a specific example that the author offers in order to illustrate his main point. (D) is correct as it hits the prediction squarely.

Passage XXII

59. C

The first paragraph notes that the five permanent members were chosen because world power was concentrated in their hands in 1945. This answer is best reflected in (C).

(A), (B), and (D) are out of scope; the countries' populations in 1945, their victory in World War II (while true), and membership in the League of Nations were never discussed in the passage. (E) is tempting because by becoming the permanent veto powers of the Security Council, the members of the security council assumed stewardship for international peace and security. However, the question asks why they were chosen, not what purpose they served.

60. A, C

This Detail question asks us to determine which criteria had been suggested as grounds for determining which nations should receive veto power. The methods detailed in paragraph 2 were economic power, population, regional leadership, geographic representation, and religious affiliation.

Military size and strength was not mentioned in the passage, so (B) is incorrect. Economic power and religious affiliation are both mentioned, so (A) and (C) are both correct.

61. B

In paragraph 2, the author explains the disagreement over what method should be used to choose new permanent members, which might lead to a prediction that this is the main

issue with expansion. However, in paragraph 3, the author states that the "true conundrum" is that the expansion would only be temporary and this debate will resurface in the future. (B) summarizes this idea.

(A) is a 180; the author states that current Security Council members might veto new members, not approve them. (C) is a distortion. Population and financial status were mentioned as one method of selection in paragraph 2, but problems with fluctuations were not mentioned. (D) is out of scope. The author states that South Africa would be a new member if the selection were based on leadership. However, the author does not mention or imply that there is disagreement over whether South Africa is a strong leader of the African bloc. (E) is also out of scope because the author does not mention any conflict between developing and developed countries.

62. A, C

The beginning of paragraph 3 discusses how expanding the number of veto powers would dilute the powers of the current permanent members. Therefore, countries that currently possess veto power would be reluctant to approve such an expansion. This is one of the reasons the author gives to support her view that Security Council expansion appears unlikely, so (A) is correct.

Choice (B) is incorrect. The increased difficultly of passing resolutions would likely be the result of security council expansion, but the author does not cite this as a reason why expansion is unlikely.

Choice (C), the inability of members to decide which countries should be the new permanent members, is the focus of paragraph 2 and strongly reflects one of the reasons the author believes expansion is unlikely. Therefore, choices (A) and (C) are correct.

63. B

"Conundrum" is used in paragraph 3 to articulate that reforming the Security Council now does not mean that it will not have to be reformed in the future to achieve the desired reflection of the global political situation. (B), "paradox," which means "a puzzle or difficult problem," comes closest to capturing this meaning.

Choice (C) doesn't work because the threat of having to re-reform the Security Council is not certain yet, so it cannot be a fundamental rule.

Choice (A) is also incorrect because revision doesn't fit well in this sentence; we are looking for a word that means "problem" or "puzzle," not one that provides a solution to such an issue.

Choices (D) and (E) are the exact opposite of the author's sentiment. Her tone demonstrates that she hopes the Security Council won't have to endure such contentious debates about expansion in the future as are currently happening. It wouldn't make sense that she'd recommend future restructuring or want it to be a goal.

Passage XXIII

64. B

Choice (B) is correct, since it is supported by statements in the final paragraph.

Choice (A) directly contradicts information throughout the passage, and Choice (C) is false, since the passage shows clearly that Aristotle's statements were incorrect.

65. C

The quote referenced here comes from the first sentence of the passage. Look there for an answer.

(C) is correct. The passage opens by referring to the "imprudence and disregard of consequences in pursuing a high ideal" of youth as

"a blessing," and later in the passage shows how Galileo's behavior led to scientific progress.

(A) is incorrect. While the author does refer to Galileo as arrogant, the quote at issue is not used to describe that arrogance.

(B) is incorrect. The relevant quote is mentioned in the context of Galileo's behavior and his instructors' reactions to that behavior, but the passage does not indicate that those reactions were "justifiable."

(D) is incorrect. The behavior is described as a "blessing," and the passage never mentions whether Galileo grew out of this sort of behavior.

(E) is incorrect. The behavior is described as a "blessing," not a flaw. Although his instructors were "annoyed," it is shown later in the passage how Galileo's behavior led to scientific progress.

66. He cannot have tried.

Aristotle is discussed in paragraph 3. Look there for content that relates to experimentation.

In paragraph 3, the author says of Aristotle's statements about falling bodies, "Why he said so nobody knows. He cannot have tried."

67. C

Evaluate each question in turn, looking for an answer in the passage. Be wary of questions that are too far outside the scope of the passage. (C) is the only correct choice. Paragraph 4 answers this question and then proceeds to give an example of the answer.

(A) The passage specifically says that no one knows what Aristotle did to attempt to verify his theories on falling bodies.

(B) The passage ends by explaining that Galileo's instructors were not convinced but did feel "the approach of a new era."

68. B

The stone and the feather are discussed in paragraphs 3 and 4. Both of those references imply that the stone and the feather do not fall at the same rate.

(B) is the answer. The passage implies that the stone and the feather are the exception to the usual rule that everything falls at the same rate.

(A) is incorrect. The general rule stated by Galileo is that weight doesn't have an impact on speed of falling, but the passage indicates that because of air resistance, the stone and the feather do not follow this pattern. (C) is incorrect. The passage does not indicate that a feather would fall faster than a stone.

(D) is incorrect. The passage does not indicate that a feather might not land at all. (E) is incorrect. Common sense tells us that this might be true, but it is never mentioned in the passage.

Passage XXIV

69. B, C

Alcott's fiction is discussed in the most detail in the second paragraph of the passage. Use the information in that paragraph to evaluate each answer choice.

(B) is correct. Paragraph 2 talks about Alcott's characters and their pranks, frolics, adventures, and happy childhoods.

(C) is also correct. Paragraph 2 tells us that the lives of Alcott's characters were similar in substantial ways to her own.

(A) is incorrect. There is no information in the passage about whether or not Alcott's fictional characters were wealthy.

70. A

You may have to scan a few different parts of the passage to find the relevant quote that backs up the answer to this question. Remember that, as with most Reading Comprehension questions, the answer to this question does have clear textual support.

(A) is correct. In paragraph 2, the passage says that "her literary disappointments and successes" gave a "dramatic interest" to the "years of her maturity."

(B) is incorrect. The passage indicates that she did accomplish this goal.

(C) is incorrect. The passage does liken Alcott's literary struggles to those of her heroine Jo March, but never addresses any "heroes," nor says that Jo's experiences were so difficult as to be "travails."

71. A, C

The financial figures mentioned in paragraph 4 support choice (A), and choice (C) is indicated in paragraph 3. Choice (B) is not mentioned in the passage; Alcott's earliest ambitions are not discussed.

72. B

Even though this question is asking you to draw an inference about the author's attitude, the correct answer will still have direct textual support.

(B) is correct. The first paragraph supports this choice: "One must pronounce her life happy and fortunate, since she lived to enjoy her fame and fortune twenty years, to witness the sale of a million volumes of her writings, to receive more than two hundred thousand dollars from her publishers . . . " From this, we can conclude that the author believes that material success in some way contributed to Alcott's happiness.

73. B

When evaluating the answer choices here, keep in mind the overall tone and main idea of the passage; the correct sentence must not only be factually true, but also consistent with the passage as a whole.

(B) echoes previous statements in the passage about how Alcott had to overcome obstacles to become a successful author. This sentence also has a nice conclusory feel. (B) is the correct choice.

(A) is contrary to the passage, which indicates that Alcott had a long and successful career.

(C) doesn't mention Alcott at all, and she's the main point of the passage. Also, the tone here is not consistent with the rest of the passage.

(D) is not relevant to the rest of the passage.

(E) conflicts with the details of the passage, which indicate that Alcott "came up through great tribulation, paying dearly in labor and privation for her successes."

Passage XXV

74. E

The passage covers types of box girder bridge fabrication (post-stressed concrete and sheet steel plate) and construction of girder bridge sections. That's encompassed by choice (E). Choice (A), the construction of modern steel bridges called box girder bridges, is incorrect because the passage includes concrete versions of this bridge type as well. The passage touches on choice (B), but limited construction access is merely a detail in, not the main idea of, the passage. While the passage does say that some trestles are composed of girder bridge segments, choice (C) is again not the main idea of the passage. Answer choices such as (B) and (C) are of the Faulty Use of Detail wrong answer type, as they mention a detail in the passage that nevertheless is not the answer to the question. Finally, the passage does say that the plate girder bridge is considered the ancestor of the box girder bridge, but it

doesn't say why, so choice (D) is incorrect as well.

75. C

According to the author, the construction method commonly used in limited-access sites is preassembled steel plates, making (C) the correct choice. The cast-in-place method, choice (A), is used with concrete forms with falsework supports, choice (D), and is the former, not the latter, of the two methods mentioned in that sentence. Concerning choices (B) and (E), "post-stressed" (a kind of concrete) and "steel-plate" are described as kinds of fabrication, not construction methods.

Introduction to Text Completion

You will encounter approximately six Text Completion questions in each verbal section. You must select one entry for each blank from the corresponding column of choices. Variations include 1-, 2-, and 3-blank questions. Text Completion questions test your ability to recognize the point of a sentence and find the best word(s) to fit its meaning.

You should aim to complete each Text Completion question in an average of 1–1.5 minutes on Test Day. To master these, you'll need to work on building your vocabulary. However, Text Completion questions do not merely test vocabulary. By omitting a critical word (or two or three), they force you to read actively and strategically. Use context clues from the sentence to make predictions for the blanks.

Text Completion Practice

> For each blank select one entry from the corresponding column of choices. Fill all blanks in the way that best completes the text.

1. Recent dramatic (i) _____ in the economic landscape have made investment decisions difficult, as it is much harder for an analyst to foresee which businesses will (ii) _____ the demands of stockholders. Consequently, analysts have had to become more (iii) _____ in their predictions.

Blank (i)		Blank (ii)		Blank (iii)	
A	shifts	D	undermine	G	circumspect
B	accommodation	E	satisfy	H	sanguine
C	treatises	F	sever	I	tantamount

2. A (i) _____ orator, Margaret earned consistent acclaim and exaltation from critics and attracted an ardent fan base, many of whom particularly enjoyed her (ii) _____ wit, thoroughly dissimilar to that of her peers.

Blank (i)		Blank (ii)	
A	plainspoken	D	abrasive
B	timorous	E	pedestrian
C	nonpareil	F	singular

3. Aronson speaks both from personal experience and with the support of empirical research in assessing the root cause of school violence. He points out that we have created a school system in which bullying, rejection, and social ostracism are not only ignored but also (i) _____. The hierarchy of the high-school scene and the prevalence of cliques foster the in-group minority/out-group majority mentality, and create an atmosphere that is not just (ii) _____ to learning, but actually is often the source of severe teenage trauma. Aronson (iii) _____ that by addressing these root causes preemptively and intervening in the emotional education of the nation's youth, school violence can be curbed and the high-school experience can be improved.

Blank (i)		Blank (ii)		Blank (iii)	
A	disdained	D	not conducive	G	posits
B	institutionalized	E	fairly ubiquitous	H	controverts
C	upbraided	F	extremely serendipitous	I	misapprehends

4. The dog (i) _____ took the steaks from the grill and returned to his cage. The owners could not (ii) _____ what could have happened to them, unaware that they had left the latch open.

Blank (i)	**Blank (ii)**
A stolidly	**D** usurp
B surreptitiously	**E** vex
C tacitly	**F** surmise

5. The brand's simple yet sleek and sophisticated packaging of the perfume in the magazine advertisement communicates a specific image to the viewer. (i) _____ brand such as this one tries to sell the idea that a certain lifestyle and (ii) _____ will be achieved if the consumer purchases the product. Although logic tells us that perfume cannot make life wonderful, people everywhere are taken in by the (iii) _____.

Blank (i)	**Blank (ii)**	**Blank (iii)**
A An urbane	**D** authority	**G** umbrage
B An affable	**E** turpitude	**H** calumny
C A sanguine	**F** prestige	**I** ruse

6. It is easy to dismiss "flash mobs" as being composed of mere tricksters, acting out in harmony in order to express their unruly natures; however, there is an art and a measure of social commentary present in their controlled _____.

Ⓐ celebration

Ⓑ complacency

Ⓒ consternation

Ⓓ conformity

Ⓔ chaos

7. As she prepared to leave America, Edith looked forward to the smoking Vesuvius, a (i) _____, and Pompeii, the city which lay buried under (ii) _____ for centuries, which would be the most wonderful parts of her journey.

Blank (i)	**Blank (ii)**
A cordillera	**D** timber
B volcano	**E** ashes
C massif	**F** mud

8. In the past few decades, the importance of the primaries in terms of the overall election has increased significantly. As states have fought to increase their impact in deciding the presidential nominations, the process of front-loading has pushed the primary dates forward, and media coverage of candidates in this (i) _____ process has proved decisive in both the party nominations and the election itself. In part, the media (ii) _____ the growing importance of the presidential primaries by saturating media outlets with news of potential candidates and their fight to (iii) _____ the nomination. In the case of presidential primaries, it is increasingly the case that it is not the voters, but the media, that decide which candidates will advance and which will not.

Blank (i)		Blank (ii)		Blank (iii)	
A	curtailed	D	hinders	G	impede
B	protracted	E	stupefies	H	laud
C	hackneyed	F	perpetuates	I	clinch

9. The determined bicyclist practiced (i) _____ in preparation for the race, relying on her coach to (ii) _____ her level of performance and offer constructive criticism of her technique and her strategy. She realized that one's overall skill level is determined not only by physical prowess but also by the (iii) _____ aspect of racing.

Blank (i)		Blank (ii)		Blank (iii)	
A	assiduously	D	excoriate	G	somatic
B	perspicaciously	E	appraise	H	cerebral
C	vicariously	F	requite	I	corporeal

10. False modesty only emphasizes the arrogance of the one who proffers it; the attempt to repress one's high opinion of oneself instead _____ it.

Ⓐ withdraws

Ⓑ explains

Ⓒ accentuates

Ⓓ hides

Ⓔ condemns

11. The insurgents' bid to (i) _____ the citadel and the power it symbolized was eventually (ii) _____; consequently, the popular movement lost its momentum, and its leaders entered into a fitful but unavoidable treaty with the despised government. Nevertheless, over the years that followed, certain (iii) _____ were introduced that made the revolution's expenditure of blood and effort worthwhile.

Blank (i)		Blank (ii)		Blank (iii)	
A	probe	D	conclusive	G	innovations
B	seize	E	thwarted	H	individuals
C	sanction	F	vigorous	I	reforms

12. Tadeusz Kosciuszko not only fought against Russian and German hegemony in his native country of Poland, but also served under Washington's army during the War of Independence, abiding by his conviction that the struggle for freedom in one country does not _____ an active interest in the affairs of others.

   Ⓐ fail to limit

   Ⓑ mask

   Ⓒ entangle one in

   Ⓓ sanction

   Ⓔ preclude

13. Dwight's writing was considered (i) _____ by the editors. While his bland style might not have been a problem for someone writing encyclopedia entries, it was (ii) _____ for the work of a tabloid journalist, whose writing required sensationalism.

Blank (i)	Blank (ii)
A provocative	D unsuitable
B incendiary	E indispensable
C prosaic	F advantageous

14. No one can argue that the Roman arch did not solve the architectural problems that (i) _____ traditional post and beam construction. However, what can be debated is whether this architectural (ii) _____ was Roman in origin; archaeological findings show that it dated back to the Greeks and possibly to even more (iii) _____ cultures.

Blank (i)	Blank (ii)	Blank (iii)
A galvanize	D transformation	G superannuated
B succored	E alteration	H ancient
C beset	F innovation	I obsolete

15. Thomas was _____ child; at the age of eight, he had already begun mastering Shakespearean dramas.

   Ⓐ an impetuous

   Ⓑ a gifted

   Ⓒ an inchoate

   Ⓓ an experienced

   Ⓔ a guileless

16. Ava, a peripatetic day laborer, never failed to make _____ decisions; she believed in neither deliberation nor prudence when confronted with various choices.

    Ⓐ paradoxical

    Ⓑ ignoble

    Ⓒ headlong

    Ⓓ undemonstrative

    Ⓔ unctuous

17. Though the candidate insisted that his comments were (i) _____, many of his supporters were offended by his attitude, which they considered not only demeaning but (ii) _____ to their party's political (iii) _____, and called for him to step down as the party's candidate.

Blank (i)	Blank (ii)	Blank (iii)
A circumspect	D complementary	G platform
B innocuous	E immaterial	H stereotype
C pernicious	F deleterious	I label

18. A curious loophole in the increasingly vast body of intellectual property law is the _____ of protection for perfumes; although many people would agree that the creation of a scent can be an art, there are no legal repercussions for copying a perfume.

    Ⓐ audacity

    Ⓑ wealth

    Ⓒ dearth

    Ⓓ consummation

    Ⓔ insularity

19. The tour guide enjoyed bringing groups of ecotourists to mingle with the indigenous people on the isolated island, but she worried that although her motives were (i) _____, the presence of so many visitors was actually disruptive and was having a (ii) _____ effect on the (iii) _____ of the native community.

Blank (i)	Blank (ii)	Blank (iii)
A admirable	D beneficial	G economy
B ulterior	E cumulative	H welfare
C unethical	F injurious	I aesthetics

20. In Robert Rotberg's article, "The Failure and Collapse of Nation-States: Breakdown, Prevention, and Repair," he outlines a pattern of state (i) _____ that fundamentally hampers the ability of the state to provide its citizens with services. He notes that failing states often have informally privatized health-care systems, and that the result is a "hodgepodge" of questionable health clinics with limited funding and (ii) _____ facilities. Failing states' inability to provide for their citizens' health needs can be accounted for by a combination of institutional ineffectiveness and corruption. Not only is it difficult for such instable governments to find the resources necessary to manage a state-run disease (iii) _____ effort, any effort is also hampered by the sticky fingers of corrupt officials and perhaps institutionalized corruption.

Blank (i)	Blank (ii)	Blank (iii)
A inefficacy	D noxious	G eradication
B surfeit	E neglected	H probity
C rectitude	F covert	I philanthropy

21. The U.S. macro-culture, or the predominant culture that influences the majority of its people, is constantly shifting. One example is the change from the commonly held melting pot view to the cultural democracy view. Whereas before the macro-cultural belief was that all the different cultures that come to the United States are thrown together and combined to create one (i) _____ society, this belief is shifting towards a multicultural society in which the different cultures each bring a unique (ii) _____ that contributes to the common culture. The U.S. macro-culture is becoming less dominated by European-Americans and more influenced by minority groups. Especially in culturally diverse states such as California, Caucasians will soon be in the minority in the United States, and consequently the macro-culture will shift along with these demographic (iii) _____.

Blank (i)	Blank (ii)	Blank (iii)
A analogous	D temperament	G hierarchies
B disparate	E apotheosis	H vicissitudes
C homogeneous	F quintessence	I compressions

22. The new administration chose to emphasize a well-rounded experimental curriculum in which arts and trades were emphasized; by doing so, they essentially furthered the transition from traditional subjects to those that had previously been considered _____ as the foundation of an education.

Ⓐ crucial

Ⓑ compulsory

Ⓒ massive

Ⓓ dominant

Ⓔ inappropriate

23. Recent reports of significant progress in the global fight to (i) _____ malaria have been unfortunately accompanied by a critical response to the World Health Organization's questionable new methodology. Critics say that a new counting system may be responsible for the reported drop in malaria cases. While this directly calls into question the effectiveness of the WHO, it also brings issues of state effectiveness to light. The areas hardest hit—notably Africa, which accounts for (ii) _____ majority of the malaria-related deaths each year—are also notorious for weak states. While malaria may be the least of Africa's (iii) _____ worries, the UN malaria summit draws global attention to the problem of disease control. Within the context of the global political scene, this problem raises the issue of the state's ability to effectively combat disease.

Blank (i)	Blank (ii)	Blank (iii)
A ramify	D an incommensurate	G bureaucratic
B extirpate	E a profligate	H epidemiological
C redress	F a tantamount	I sanctimonious

24. The human visual experience is defined by a (i) _____. One important component of this visual experience is our ability to use visual information to create a (ii) _____ of three-dimensional space. This three-dimensionality depends heavily on the concepts of binocular disparity and stereopsis. Binocular disparity refers to the discrepancy between the visual information of the two retinas, and stereopsis is responsible for our ability to (iii) _____ depth from this disparity.

Blank (i)	Blank (ii)	Blank (iii)
A sequence of basic processes	D representation	G extricate
B series of complex processing mechanisms	E memory	H abrogate
C trio of simultaneous events	F replica	I discern

25. The value of the Internet start-up's stock (i) _____ what even the most optimistic of analysts had predicted; the company's overnight success soon (ii) _____ the interest of many more investors, and the original investors saw (iii) _____ return on their money.

Blank (i)	Blank (ii)	Blank (iii)
A exceeded	D inflamed	G a magnanimous
B averaged out to	E distracted	H a staggering
C burdened	F escaped	I an innocuous

26. His (i) _____ stunned everyone in the room, especially because the hostess had (ii) _____ his virtues to all of the guests before his arrival.

Blank (i)	Blank (ii)
A perspicacity	**D** extolled
B obsequiousness	**E** refuted
C effrontery	**F** regaled

27. As a result of poor planning and disorganization, the young team (i) _____ attacking the root of the problem. This went on until there was no other recourse left to them. They were obliged to (ii) _____ a (iii) _____, last-minute solution to the problem.

Blank (i)	Blank (ii)	Blank (iii)
A expedited	**D** implement	**G** measured
B postponed	**E** envision	**H** premeditated
C accelerated	**F** reject	**I** desperate

28. Connoisseurs gather _____ knowledge on a single subject.

Ⓐ scant

Ⓑ copious

Ⓒ spurious

Ⓓ peculiar

Ⓔ arcane

29. The (i) _____ hikers had been traveling by foot for twelve hours with no food or water. Samantha feared that she would become dangerously (ii) _____ if she had to continue any longer.

Blank (i)	Blank (ii)
A enervated	**D** timorous
B morose	**E** parched
C imperious	**F** lugubrious

30. In contrast to instances where size is commensurate with potency of flavor, smaller peppers tend to be far more _____ than larger peppers.

Ⓐ banal

Ⓑ piquant

Ⓒ acrid

Ⓓ unique

Ⓔ diverse

31. The town council preferred him to be modest about his exploits, and his present fits of hubris were met with resounding _____.

    Ⓐ encomium

    Ⓑ perspicacity

    Ⓒ obloquy

    Ⓓ pastiche

    Ⓔ panegyric

32. A dedicated gourmand, Franklin's expression became (i) _____ when the doctor delivered her advice. Though he would not have to be completely (ii) _____, his physician did warn him to cut down on decadent confections.

Blank (i)		Blank (ii)	
A	effervescent	**D**	ascetic
B	dour	**E**	temperate
C	wrathful	**F**	sanctimonious

33. It was (i) _____ portent when the speaker tripped on his way to the dais. Fortuitously, however, an immediate droll remark (ii) _____ the speaker's rapport with the crowd.

Blank (i)		Blank (ii)	
A	an augural	**D**	buoyed
B	a pernicious	**E**	severed
C	an inauspicious	**F**	alleviated

34. Mrs. Haddo never prided herself on any special gift, but she was well aware of the fact that she could read character with _____ instinct.

    Ⓐ adverse

    Ⓑ paranormal

    Ⓒ imperfect

    Ⓓ unerring

    Ⓔ blemished

35. Paradigmatic upheavals often occur after a period of increasing (i) _____, which creates quandaries for the scientific or cultural status quo. As the dominant theoretical models are questioned and (ii) _____, new models are proposed that may ultimately alter the perceptions of the entire population.

Blank (i)		Blank (ii)	
A	concatenation	**D**	impugned
B	aberration	**E**	emblematized
C	inculcation	**F**	approbated

36. Physiologically, the consequences of loneliness and social isolation are glaringly evident. Solitary behavior and social isolation have been linked to higher rates of (i) _____ and mortality. The stress response is hyper-activated in lonely individuals, which (ii) _____ a faster decline. Sleep, which is one of the body's greatest mechanisms of (iii) _____ physiological repair, is less efficient in lonely individuals, with lonely individuals much more likely to have "micro-awakenings" in the night, leading to daytime fatigue. Even fruit flies have shorter life spans when they are isolated.

Blank (i)	Blank (ii)	Blank (iii)
A fatality	**D** palliates	**G** aerobic
B morbidity	**E** promotes	**H** anabolic
C recuperation	**F** transmutes into	**I** diaphanous

37. Experts believe that as a result of global warming, many of the areas that were once lush and (i) _____ farmland will eventually become arid, (ii) _____ deserts, uninhabitable by any human being.

Blank (i)	Blank (ii)
A fertile	**D** rich
B desiccated	**E** barren
C parched	**F** moist

38. Olivia's reputation as a (i) _____ child continued well into adulthood; her friends were continually astounded at her tendency to (ii) _____ even the most dangerous of situations.

Blank (i)	Blank (ii)
A feckless	**D** embrace
B dauntless	**E** undermine
C guileless	**F** shun

39. Democracies around the world have found themselves struggling to tailor domestic security policies to fit the bill for both tight security and public approval ratings. This brings to light what political theorist Larry Diamond calls a fundamental paradox of democracy: the conflicting need for both (i) _____ and consent. Democratic governments, because they are popularly elected, are inclined to adjust to popular opinion regardless of the actual merit of policies. Following 9/11, there was a significant public outcry for more stringent national security measures. However, as the jarring impact of the 9/11 attack becomes more muted with time, more people are (ii) _____ having their own privacy compromised for the sake of (iii) _____ goal.

Blank (i)	Blank (ii)	Blank (iii)
A effectiveness	**D** repudiating	**G** an ebullient
B serendipity	**E** redressing	**H** a discursive
C aspersion	**F** jeopardizing	**I** an abstract

40. With the development of the Internet into a multi-access point news source for a wide variety of voices and data sources, it seems that newspapers have become nearly (i) _____. It is surprising that, nonetheless, subscriptions to certain major flagship papers, and even some hometown journals, have (ii) _____ in the last few years.

Blank (i)		Blank (ii)	
A	bombastic	D	proliferated
B	capricious	E	metamorphosed
C	obsolete	F	reeled

41. Michalewski's text indubitably serves as the _____ of his discipline; it surpassed all previous models of excellence and has replaced them with the rigor of heretofore unmatched academic standards.

(A) validation

(B) vainglory

(C) apotheosis

(D) munificence

(E) beneficence

42. It is (i) _____ to describe what precisely defines the literary quality of any written work during its time. Although many attempts have been made, any contemporary and (ii) _____ definition is ultimately impossible, because one cannot enumerate a work's style, originality, or influence. Indeed, many works that are now considered "classics" were widely (iii) _____ or even simply ignored in their time.

Blank (i)		Blank (ii)		Blank (iii)	
A	inane	D	quantitative	G	extolled
B	feasible	E	analytical	H	acclaimed
C	hopeless	F	subjective	I	criticized

43. James's (i) _____ disposition seemed irresistibly to infect those around him, taking wavering hope and turning it into robust optimism. It was as if his very presence made the silver lining of every cloud (ii) _____.

Blank (i)		Blank (ii)	
A	sanguinary	D	manifest
B	ruddy	E	tangible
C	sanguine	F	coruscate

44. Ryan is paralyzed by his own _____: he imagines having elaborate conversations with various people, but he fails to engage in conversations with them when opportunities arise.

    Ⓐ diffidence

    Ⓑ sycophancy

    Ⓒ imagination

    Ⓓ convalescence

    Ⓔ rectitude

45. The eminent sociobiologist demonstrated a relationship between social status and (i) _____ to infectious disease in male macaque monkeys: he then suggested that wealthy humans are also less prone to (ii) _____.

Blank (i)	Blank (ii)
A susceptibility	D compensation
B impartiality	E sickness
C dominance	F mobility

46. Demonstrating the contradictory relationship between the demeanor of the artists and their reception by the media, the artist who was the least _____ in interviews was also the most sought after.

    Ⓐ curt

    Ⓑ specific

    Ⓒ cordial

    Ⓓ aloof

    Ⓔ evasive

47. The study seems to have a high degree of internal validity. It sought to measure the effect of Muslim headgear, race, and affect on shooter bias, and the correlations are statistically significant and valid. The external validity is harder to evaluate. It seems unlikely that the (i) _____ would be true in a literal sense for all groups, but it may indicate a subtle form of stereotyping and racism (ii) _____ our mental processes that can have wide implications. These results, insofar as they indicate a subtle, largely-subconscious aggression towards Muslims, may well be (iii) _____ to the general population.

Blank (i)	Blank (ii)	Blank (iii)
A paradigm	D insular to	G generalized
B aspersion	E hindmost in	H postulated
C treachery	F intrinsic to	I acceded

48. The seemingly _____ community of retirees was actually a hotbed of controversy, as issues ranging from lawn care to shuffleboard sparked fierce debates.

    Ⓐ chivalrous

    Ⓑ cynical

    Ⓒ sincere

    Ⓓ fervid

    Ⓔ placid

49. Oxygen is an absolute _____ for human beings to survive, just as the availability of carbon dioxide is an indispensable condition for plant life.

    Ⓐ enhancement

    Ⓑ advancement

    Ⓒ luxury

    Ⓓ necessity

    Ⓔ compulsion

50. The country was in crisis: the article reported a large percentage of the population living in (i) _____, high unemployment rates, and a growing (ii) _____ between the quality of life of the upper and lower classes. Additionally, a growing percentage of the population did not have access to affordable health care, housing, or (iii) _____ education.

Blank (i)	Blank (ii)	Blank (iii)
A acrimony	D disparity	G a commensurate
B indigence	E plethora	H an adequate
C sumptuousness	F rancor	I a quixotic

51. The facade of the house was _____, making the interior even more disappointing to prospective buyers.

    Ⓐ ostentatious

    Ⓑ dilapidated

    Ⓒ august

    Ⓓ diminutive

    Ⓔ gloomy

52. The fastidious guest was so _____ while dining that it diminished the hostess' estimation of her.

   Ⓐ finicky

   Ⓑ boorish

   Ⓒ loquacious

   Ⓓ stolid

   Ⓔ curt

53. Although some people dismiss etiquette as merely (i) _____ rituals, it is actually one of the cornerstones of civilization, and is increasingly (ii) _____ by our informal society.

Blank (i)	Blank (ii)
A superficial	D embraced
B overwhelming	E threatened
C cherished	F integrated

54. Two of the most illustrious composers of the Baroque period—Johann Sebastian Bach and George Frideric Handel—were close (i) _____. Both were born in Germany in 1685; Bach died in 1750, still in Germany, while Handel died in 1759 in England, having (ii) _____ from Germany after spending time in Italy mastering the operatic form.

Blank (i)	Blank (ii)
A competitors	D disaffected
B contemporaries	E absconded
C contestants	F emigrated

55. Importing water hundreds of miles south is quite an operation, and the costs are reflected in the prices. This (i) _____, especially in the context of the current financial crisis, is a motivation for decreasing importation. Additionally, importation from this source is unreliable: the water supply could be cut off at any time for any number of reasons, which would leave the region devastated if it does not prepare for that (ii) _____. One reason for the potential of this water supply to be cut off is the susceptibility of the levees to damage. There is an extensive levee system in the northern region's delta, and if something like an earthquake were to (iii) _____ the levees, the resulting salinization of the source would leave the region cut off for over a year.

Blank (i)	Blank (ii)	Blank (iii)
A subsistence	D pathos	G expunge
B expenditure	E contingency	H rupture
C opulence	F conflagration	I protuberate

56. The two explorers could scarcely believe their (i) _____ fortune; they had gone deep into the rain forest in quest of medicinal plants and found not only the healing herb but also the ruins of (ii) _____ city. Consequent to their incredible discovery, both previously unknown men went on to enjoy great (iii) _____.

Blank (i)	Blank (ii)	Blank (iii)
A adverse	**D** an unexceptional	**G** rejection
B calamitous	**E** a clandestine	**H** prominence
C propitious	**F** an unillustrious	**I** affluence

57. Psychologists now believe that the likeliest sources of procrastination are not laziness and lack of willpower, but rather (i) _____ such as unclear goals, fear of failure, indecision, fatigue, and distraction—all problems that students and workers (ii) _____ facing a daunting task can target and solve.

Blank (i)	Blank (ii)
A hedges	**D** adeptly
B fixtures	**E** diffidently
C culprits	**F** collaboratively

58. In contrast with her later (i) _____, Allison was very (ii) _____ during her teen and young adult years, despite the fact that her parents held very traditional political views.

Blank (i)	Blank (ii)
A militance	**D** gregarious
B alacrity	**E** inexorable
C conservatism	**F** liberal

59. While there may still be some law firms that nurture a young attorney and help her develop the skills needed in the legal world, the _____ on billable hours makes such career development opportunities scarce.

Ⓐ scrutiny
Ⓑ turmoil
Ⓒ emphasis
Ⓓ decimation
Ⓔ intrusion

60. The prince was so (i) _____ that he sat for a full half-hour foolishly staring before him, without an (ii) _____ to move a muscle or to stir from his seat.

Blank (i)	Blank (ii)
A vitalized	**D** aspirin
B exhilarated	**E** interest
C stupefied	**F** effort

61. Connecting new information to English language learners' cultural backgrounds can be valuable when English learners have a different (i) _____ with which they view the world due to the environment they grew up in. However, it may be difficult even for a teacher who has done research to know the exact perspective the student can relate to because there may be (ii) _____ a specific culture's immigrant neighborhoods across the United States. Those that believe that students are more affected by popular "adolescent" American influences may be correct some of the time, especially with older students who may have been in America longer. Another merit of this approach is that many students may wish to (iii) _____ American culture so they may not respond to attempts to connect the material with their native culture. This may be especially true of English learners born in the United States who have never lived in their native cultural setting, but their family and community may have their own set of structures and beliefs.

Blank (i)	Blank (ii)	Blank (iii)
A perspicacity	D divergences between	G acculturate to
B platitude	E aberrations in	H systematize
C schema	F ineffability in	I ingratiate with

62. The body's response to sharply reduced caloric intake is to slow the metabolism; contrary to what some dieters may think, though, this reaction (i) _____ as a way to aid survival, not merely as a means to (ii) _____ modern attempts at weight loss. Restricting caloric intake too (iii) _____ is therefore not the best dieting strategy.

Blank (i)	Blank (ii)	Blank (iii)
A promoted	D enhance	G severely
B reiterated	E foil	H ambivalently
C evolved	F plunder	I immutably

63. The reclusive author lived in a (i) _____ atmosphere; her house was ornamented with black lace curtains on every window and (ii) _____ antique coffins in place of beds.

Blank (i)	Blank (ii)
A dilettantish	D ornate
B garrulous	E amiable
C macabre	F innocuous

64. Photographs and toys lend credence to a widespread belief that the panda bear is (i) _____ animal; however, this (ii) _____ belief has led to numerous attacks on people attempting to approach pandas in zoos.

Blank (i)	Blank (ii)
A an endangered	D pessimistic
B a docile	E comical
C an elusive	F spurious

65. Among the _____ books on culinary science in circulation, a few have dealt with the particular constraints of the kosher kitchen.

   Ⓐ negligible

   Ⓑ scarce

   Ⓒ copious

   Ⓓ scant

   Ⓔ noisome

66. Samuel Langhorne Clemens spent three years in the (i) _____ office of the little local paper; similar to others on the list of American authors that stretches from Benjamin Franklin to William Dean Howells, he began his connection with literature by setting (ii) _____.

Blank (i)	Blank (ii)
A printing	D polish
B dentist's	E type
C janitorial	F opinions

67. The packaging of the revitalization supplement (i) _____ that the user would feel an increase in energy within a week of taking it, but the bodybuilder actually felt more (ii) _____ than usual. After he stopped taking the supplement, he felt normal again, leading him to (iii) _____ that he was allergic to something in the vitamins.

Blank (i)	Blank (ii)	Blank (iii)
A dissembled	D innervated	G postulate
B adumbrated	E enervated	H contravene
C averred	F quickened	I exult

68. Maurice more than admired his mentor; it could be fairly said that he (i) _____ her, following her advice with a kind of slavish (ii) _____ that some might find unsettling. His co-workers called him a (iii) _____ behind his back.

Blank (i)	Blank (ii)	Blank (iii)
A suppressed	D petulance	G sycophant
B idolized	E dismay	H malefactor
C criticized	F devotion	I reprobate

69. The subject matter of Henrik Ibsen's plays seems mundane when compared to present-day plays, but when first performed, Ibsen's work was considered _____ and caused a palpable commotion in his native Norway.

    Ⓐ banal

    Ⓑ incendiary

    Ⓒ bombastic

    Ⓓ taciturn

    Ⓔ luminous

70. All televisions sold new today come with the V-chip, which parents can program to (i) _____ their children from watching certain programs. While some may argue that too many parents are not aware of how to operate the V-chip for this to be a (ii) _____ for cutting out indecency from television, if the parents are concerned enough, they should make the effort to learn how to work this useful device.

Blank (i)	Blank (ii)
A reduce	D feasible hindrance
B discriminate	E possible impediment
C preclude	F viable option

71. It was nearly impossible for Timothy to make an accounting error; he used a _____ system which guaranteed that all of the relevant figures were checked on three separate occasions.

    Ⓐ powerful

    Ⓑ meticulous

    Ⓒ credulous

    Ⓓ pedantic

    Ⓔ perfunctory

72. Just as the Elizabethan _____ thought little of Shakespeare because he failed to follow in the footsteps of the great Greeks, some modern critics dislike the best work of the dramatists of our own time, because they are not cast in the Shakespearean mold.

    Ⓐ experts

    Ⓑ audiences

    Ⓒ reviewers

    Ⓓ directors

    Ⓔ pundits

73. In every work of art there are at least four elements, which we may separate to _____ them individually: technique, observation, imagination, philosophy.

    Ⓐ interrogate

    Ⓑ consider

    Ⓒ neglect

    Ⓓ berate

    Ⓔ sketch

74. Whether as permanent fixtures in cathedrals or as (i) _____ shrines, reliquaries were objects of devotion, not because of their beautiful exteriors but because of what they held: a relic of a saint. These memorial objects often pose mysteries for historians, who (ii) _____ their external images to ascertain for which saint's relics the (iii) _____ container was created.

Blank (i)	Blank (ii)	Blank (iii)
A personal	D peruse	G commemorative
B perennial	E reify	H immense
C conveyable	F exculpate	I utilitarian

Answer Key

TEXT COMPLETION PRACTICE

1.	A, E, G	**26.**	C, D	**51.**	C
2.	C, F	**27.**	B, D, I	**52.**	A
3.	B, D, G	**28.**	B	**53.**	A, E
4.	B, F	**29.**	A, E	**54.**	B, F
5.	A, F, I	**30.**	B	**55.**	B, E, H
6.	E	**31.**	C	**56.**	C, E, H
7.	B, E	**32.**	B, D	**57.**	C, E
8.	B, F, I	**33.**	C, D	**58.**	C, F
9.	A, E, H	**34.**	D	**59.**	C
10.	C	**35.**	B, D	**60.**	C, F
11.	B, E, I	**36.**	B, E, H	**61.**	C, D, G
12.	E	**37.**	A, E	**62.**	C, E, G
13.	C, D	**38.**	B, D	**63.**	C, D
14.	C, F, H	**39.**	A, D, I	**64.**	B, F
15.	B	**40.**	C, D	**65.**	C
16.	C	**41.**	C	**66.**	A, E
17.	B, F, G	**42.**	C, D, I	**67.**	C, E, G
18.	C	**43.**	C, F	**68.**	B, F, G
19.	A, F, H	**44.**	A	**69.**	B
20.	A, E, G	**45.**	A, E	**70.**	C, F
21.	C, F, H	**46.**	C	**71.**	B
22.	E	**47.**	A, F, G	**72.**	C
23.	B, D, H	**48.**	E	**73.**	B
24.	B, D, I	**49.**	D	**74.**	C, D, G
25.	A, D, H	**50.**	B, D, H		

Answers and Explanations

TEXT COMPLETION PRACTICE

1. A, E, G

If it is harder for analysts to make predictions, the economic landscape is likely to be tricky or unstable; the word for the first blank should address that, with something like "fluctuations." Choice (A) *shifts* matches our prediction, while choices (B) *accommodation* ("anything that supplies a need or want") and (C) *treatises* ("a lengthy, formal exposition of a subject") are unsupported by context.

The second blank hinges on idiom: what do you do to "demands?" The credited answer is choice (E) *satisfy*. Choices (D) *undermine* ("attack by indirect methods") and (F) *sever* ("divide into parts") make no sense in this context.

The third blank should describe how analysts have become in light of the recent changes that have made investment decisions more difficult. Look for a word like "cautious." Choice (G) *circumspect* ("showing unwillingness to act without first weighing the risks or consequences") is a good match because it is logical that analysts would weigh the risks and consequences of their predictions more heavily if there have been recent dramatic shifts in the economic landscape. Choice (H) is wrong because it is not likely that analysts would become s*anguine*, or "cheerfully optimistic," in the face of possible economic upheaval. Choice (I) *tantamount*, or "equivalent," does not make sense here.

The credited choices are (A), (E), and (G).

2. C, F

Let's begin with the easier blank, which in this case is the second. The sentence states that Margaret impressed critics and fans with her wit, which was dissimilar to that of her peers. We can predict that her wit was "unique." Choice (F) *singular*, which means "distinctive" or "unique," matches that prediction and is the correct answer. Choice (D) *abrasive*, or "tending to annoy," and choice (E) *pedestrian*, or "lacking in imagination," both have negative connotations and do not explain why Margaret attracts so many fans and earns so much praise.

For the first blank, we need a word with a positive connotation, because critics and fans are impressed with Margaret's skills as an orator. We might predict that she is an "excellent" orator. This blank is tricky, though, because there is no exact synonym for "excellent." Choice (C) *nonpareil*, however, means "unequaled," which is a very positive characterization for an orator. This is the correct answer. Choice (A) *plainspoken* indicates a speaker who uses simple and direct language. Since we're told that Margaret is acclaimed for her wit, it is not an appropriate term to describe her and is therefore incorrect. Choice (B) *timorous*, or "timid," is not a desirable quality in an orator and is also incorrect.

The credited answers are (C) and (F).

3. B, D, G

For blank (i), we learn that the school system has ignored bullying, a stance that implies the school system accepts the behavior. Choice (B) *institutionalized* refers to "a behavior established and accepted as a fundamental part of culture" and is the credited choice. The tone of both choice (A) *disdained* ("looked upon or treated with contempt") and choice (C) *upbraided* ("to have found fault with") are negative, which is opposite to the current relationship.

Blank (ii) is part of a phrase describing the first effect of cliques on schools, the second of which is very negative ("severe teenage trauma"), so this effect should be too. Therefore, we should say that the clique atmosphere is choice (D) *not conducive*, or "not helpful," to learning. Choice (E) *fairly ubiquitous* means "existing everywhere, especially at the same time." Cliques might be ubiquitous in schools, but it does not make sense to say that cliques create an atmosphere that is omnipresent to learning. Choice (F) *extremely serendipitous* refers to "something good or desirable found by chance." Since cliques are presented in a very negative light, serendipitous is opposite to what we need here.

The last sentence gives the final conclusion Aronson makes on this topic, so the best choice for the verb is choice (G) *posits*, or "lays down as principle." Neither choice (H) *controverts* ("argues against") or choice (I) *misapprehends* ("misunderstands") makes sense in this context.

The credited choices are (B), (D), and (G).

4. B, F

We can first predict the meaning of Blank (ii) to be something like "figure out." Choice (F) *surmise*, or "infer with little evidence," fits this blank the best. Choices (D) *usurp* ("to seize by force or take possession of without right") and (E) *vex* ("to confuse or annoy") make no sense in context.

Since its owners did not know they left the dog's cage open and are puzzled by the steaks' disappearance, we can infer that the dog took the steaks stealthily, or choice (B) *surreptitiously*. Choice (A) *stolid* means "unemotional" or "impassive" and is incorrect. There is no information in the sentences that

addresses the dog's emotional expression. Choice (C) is also incorrect. *Tacit* is defined as "expressed without words." A dog's action of taking steaks is not an expression.

The credited choices are (B) and (F) .

5. A, F, I

The adjectives in the first sentence provide clues as to the word for blank (i). We're told that the packaging is "sleek and sophisticated," so look for a complementary word. Choice (A) *urbane* is the best fit. Choices (B) *affable* ("friendly and good-natured") and (C) *sanguine* ("optimistic" or "cheery") do not work in this context.

Blank (ii) refers to the idea the brand is selling, so choose a word to accompany a "certain [sophisticated] lifestyle." Choice (D) is not the credited response; we have no support for the idea that consumers are seeking *authority* or "power," or that they think a perfume could help them achieve it. Choice (E) is also not the credited response. *Turpitude* is defined as "depravity and moral corruption," and this is not an idea that the makers of the perfume would want to sell. Choice (F), though, matches our prediction. *Prestige* means "high status," and a consumer who is attracted to the perfume's sleek and sophisticated packaging would likely be interested in gaining prestige.

Finally, since the author feels that perfume cannot in fact fulfill these promises, he feels that the advertisement is a "deception," so that's our prediction for blank (iii). Choice (I) *ruse,* or a "trick," is the credited choice. The magazine ad tricks consumers into buying perfume because they believe it will change their image and lifestyle, when in fact it will not. Choices (G) *umbrage* ("resentment") and (H) *calumny* ("a false or malicious statement designed to ruin another's reputation") make no sense in this context.

The correct choices are (A), (F), and (I).

6. E

The sentence says that flash mobs consist of "tricksters" who "express their unruly nature," so the word should somehow indicate the idea of acting out or playing tricks. Choice (E) *chaos* is the only choice that adequately describes this situation. "Tricksters" with "unruly natures" "acting out in harmony" might very well create "controlled *chaos*." Choice (A) *celebration* does not ordinarily suggest "unruly natures." Choices (B) *complacency*, "smug satisfaction with an existing situation," and (C) *consternation*, "a sudden, alarming amazement or dread that results in utter dismay," do not fit in this context, while choice (D) "controlled *conformity*" does not properly imply that their actions are organized practical jokes.

Choice (E) is the credited response.

7. B, E

The first blank must be a term that would describe something "smoking." Of the three choices, only (B) *volcano*, produces smoke. Neither choice (A) *cordillera*, a "system or group of parallel mountain ranges together with the intervening plateaus," nor choice (C) *massif*, "a compact group of mountains," would ordinarily produce smoke.

The second blank will describe something a volcano produces that could bury a city. Volcanoes produce neither choice (F) *mud* nor choice (D) *timber*, but they can spew choice (E) *ash*, which is the credited choice.

Choices (B) and (E) are the credited responses.

8. B, F, I

The sentence with blank (i) emphasizes that primary dates have been moved forward in time, which would (B) *protract*, or "lengthen," the period of the election process. Choice (A) *curtailed*, or "shortened," has the opposite meaning needed here while choice (C) *hackneyed*, or "unoriginal," deals with a different issue.

Blank (ii)'s sentence tells us that the media "saturates" outlets with news of potential candidates, so we can predict that the blank should mean "makes continue." Choice (F) *perpetuates* ("to make something continue, usually for a very long time") fits this definition, while choice (D) *hinders* gives the phrase the opposite meaning, and choice (E) *stupefies*, or "astonishes," is illogical.

Blank (iii) should say what candidates fight to do during the primaries, which is choice (I) *clinch*, or "reach the goal," of obtaining the nomination. Neither choice (G) *impede*, or "interfere with the progress of," nor choice (H) *laud*, or "praise," make sense in this context.

The correct choices are (B), (F), and (I).

9. A, E, H

To fill the first blank, we need an adverb describing the way a "determined" bicyclist would practice. Determination requires time and effort, so we can predict that we need a word such as "diligently." Choice (A) *assiduously*, which means "persistently," matches our prediction and is the first correct answer. Choice (B) *perspicaciously*, which means "shrewdly" or "astutely," might describe a way to practice, but it does not convey the great effort that the word "determined" demands, so it is incorrect. Choice (C) *vicariously*, "felt as if taking part in the experiences of someone else," does not accurately describe the act of practicing to better one's own performance. Instead, practicing vicariously would suggest sitting down and watching someone else do the cycling. Hence, (C) is incorrect.

The second missing word refers to what a coach does with an athlete's "level of performance." "Measure" is a good prediction here and choice (E) *appraise,* or "evaluate," matches our prediction. The coach evaluates the cyclist's skill level and offers constructive criticism as feedback. Choice (D) *excoriate* means "criticize harshly" or "condemn," which is too strong a word for this context, so (D) is incorrect. Choice (F) *requite* means "repay" or "return" and does not make sense in this context, so it is likewise incorrect.

The detour road sign formed by the words "not only" and "but also" in the last part of the second sentence helps us fill the third blank. There will be a contrast between the two things that are important to determining the bicyclist's skill level. One part of the formula is "physical prowess," so we are looking for a word that names the other, contrasting aspect of performance. Furthermore, we can predict that because the coach is analyzing the bicyclist's "strategy," the other aspect will have to do with the mind. Choice (H) *cerebral,* meaning "intellectual," describes the mental part of the bicyclist's task and offers a contrast with "physical"; thus, (H) is the third correct answer. Choices (G) *somatic* and (I) *corporeal* both relate to a physical rather than a mental aspect, so they are incorrect.

The correct answers are answer choices (A), (E), and (H).

10. C

The semicolon in this sentence indicates that the second clause will be related to the first one. "False modesty" is the pretense of modesty, and is typically meant to present the appearance of a lack of boastfulness. An attempt to repress one's high opinion of

oneself will draw attention to it instead, so look for a word like "emphasize" in order to fill in the blank. Choice (C) *accentuates,* or "highlights," matches our prediction. None of choices (A) *withdraws,* (B) *explains,* (D) *hides,* or (E) *explains* makes sense in this context. Choice (C) is the credited response.

11. B, E, I

The straight-ahead road sign "consequently" tells us that the second clause of the first sentence follows logically from the first. The context of the second clause provides clues as to the nature of the noun in Blank (i), so this is the best place to start. The phrases "popular movement" and "negotiated a fitful but unavoidable treaty with the despised government" suggest people fighting the government, so a good prediction would be "capture." Choice (B) *seize,* which means "to take hold of," fits our prediction and is correct. Choice (A) *probe,* or "investigate," is incorrect because the context clues indicate that the insurgents wanted to take power away, not explore it. Choice (C) *sanction,* or "authorize," is the opposite of what we need.

For Blank (ii), the phrase "lost its momentum" suggests that the efforts to take the citadel were unsuccessful, so choice (E) *thwarted,* or "stopped," is correct. Choice (D) *conclusive,* or "decisive," would imply success in taking the citadel and so is incorrect. While the attack may have been *vigorous,* or "done with great force and energy," the second part of the sentence indicates that in the end it must have failed, so choice (F) is insufficient.

As for blank (iii), the word "nevertheless" is a detour road sign that suggests eventually worthwhile advancements were made. Choice (I) *reforms,* meaning "changes made to correct wrongs," fits this prediction and is correct. Choice (G) *innovations,* or "new ideas or methods," is incorrect because we're looking for improvements, not just changes. While it's true that (H) *individuals*, or "persons," may be "introduced," this choice does not describe a specific reward for the insurgents' tribulations, so (H) is incorrect.

The correct answers are (B), (E), and (I).

12. E

This sentence contains many details and so it is important to focus on what is most important by paraphrasing the sentence: Kosciuszko fought in both his native country and in the US, and he believed that fighting for freedom in one country did not stop him from fighting in other countries. Therefore, choice (E) *preclude*, or "prevent," fits.

Choice (A) *fail to limit* creates a double negative and is the opposite of the prediction. Choices (C) *entangle one in*, or "involve," and (D) *sanction*, or "permit," are also opposite to the prediction. Lastly, choice (B) *mask*, or "conceal," is an out of scope choice—the sentence does not mention hiding.

Choice (E) is the credited response.

13. C, D

Let's start with the second blank. The second sentence starts with the detour road sign "while," which means the second clause in the sentence will depart in meaning from the first. Dwight's writing style would not be a problem for someone writing encyclopedia entries, but we can predict that it would be "problematic" for a tabloid journalist, whose writing must be "sensational."

Choice (D) *unsuitable*, or "inappropriate," is the closest match to our prediction of "problematic." This is the correct answer. Choices (E) *indispensable*, or "essential," and (F) *advantageous*, or "beneficial," are both the opposite of what we're looking for and are therefore incorrect.

Now we can go back to the first blank. The second sentence states that Dwight had a "bland" style, and we know from the work we did filling in the second blank that it was the opposite of "sensational." A word such as "unexciting" would make a good prediction. Choice (C) *prosaic* means "straightforward" or "unimaginative," matches our prediction, and is correct. Choice (A) *provocative*, or "provoking," is the opposite of what we need, and choice (B) *incendiary*, meaning "fiery," is too strong a term for encyclopedia entries, so both these choices are incorrect.

The credited choices are (C) and (D).

14. C, F, H

The first missing word describes the relationship of "problems" to "traditional post and beam construction" before those problems were "solved." We can predict that the first blank holds a word meaning "affected in a negative way," such as "troubled" or "plagued." Choice (C) *beset*, which can mean "to trouble," matches our prediction and is correct. Choice (A) *galvanize* can mean "provoke into sudden activity," which does not logically describe how problems would affect post and beam construction, so this choice is incorrect. Choice (B) *succored* means "aided," which is the opposite of our prediction, so this choice is also incorrect.

The second blank will be filled by a word that describes the Roman arch. Because we know it solved problems that beset traditional post and beam construction, we can predict that the second missing word will mean something like "advance." Choice (F) *innovation*, a "new idea or method," matches our prediction and is correct. Choices (D) *transformation* and (E) *alteration* both mean "change," but are lacking. The Roman arch was not merely a change but an improvement, and the correct answer must reflect that fact. Hence, (D) and (E) are incorrect.

In the second sentence, the author is asserting that a development attributed to the Romans was actually developed in an earlier time period. The clues "dated back to" and "even more" indicate that the third missing word will simply mean "very old." All three choices for the third blank have similar meanings, but choice (H) *ancient*, is neutral in tone, so it is correct. Choices (G) *superannuated* and (I) *obsolete* also mean "old," but they connote the idea of being "out of use" or "out of date." The idea of a culture no longer being trendy or fashionable makes no sense in the context of the sentence, so (G) and (I) are incorrect.

Answer choices (C), (F), and (H) are the correct answers.

15.   B

The clue in this sentence is Thomas's mastery of Shakespeare at the age of eight. A prediction might be that he was an *advanced* child. Choice (B) *gifted* matches this prediction.

Thomas's decisions and development were not characterized in the sentence, so choices (A) *impetuous*, "rash,"(C) *inchoate*, "not fully developed," and (E) *guileless*, "sincere or straightforward," are all out of scope. Choice (D) *experienced* is also out of scope since it suggests mastery through a great number of experiences. Since Thomas is only eight, he is too young to be greatly experienced at anything.

16.   C

In the sentence, the word "peripatetic," or "wandering," is not vital to the blank. The final clause of the sentence is the clue that that Ava was not *wise* or *careful* when it came to making decisions. Choice (C), *headlong*, or "hastily," fits the meaning of "not wise."

Choice (B) *ignoble*, "dishonorable or base," is too extreme and negative to fit in this sentence. Choices (D) *undemonstrative*, "emotionless," and (E) *unctuous*, "excessively pious" or "smug," are out of scope since we know neither Ava's emotional state or interaction with others. "Deliberate" and "prudent" are similar in meaning—therefore, choice (A) is an opposite wrong answer choice since *paradoxical* would require opposing or conflicting events.

Choice (C) is the credited response.

17.   B, F, G

In this sentence, the detour road sign "though" points to a contrast between the two ideas in the sentence. The second idea is that the supporters were offended. They must have found the candidate's words somehow damaging, even though he said they were not. Thus, we can predict a world like "harmless" for the first blank. Choice (B) *innocuous* means "harmless" and is thus the correct answer. Choice (A) *circumspect* means "cautious," which does not adequately convey the contrast, so this choice is incorrect. Choice (C) *pernicious* means "harmful" and is the opposite of what we need, so it is likewise incorrect.

Because we know that the supporters were offended and called for the candidate to pull out of the race, we know that they believed that the candidate's behavior was "harmful" to their political cause. Therefore, choice (F) *deleterious* is correct because it means "damaging." Choice (D) *complementary* means "in accordance with," so this choice is the exact opposite of what we're looking for and is incorrect. Choice (E) *immaterial* means "irrelevant," which does not carry the negative connotation of harm that we need here, so this choice is also incorrect.

Knowing the effect of the candidate's words also clues us to the meaning of the word in the third blank. Supporters wanted the candidate to step down as the party's nominee, so they must have believed his behavior was damaging to the political beliefs of the party. The correct answer will have something to do with "beliefs" or "ideas." Choice (G) *platform*, "the set of principles to which a political party adheres," matches this prediction and is correct. Choice (H) *stereotype*, or "generalization," is not the kind of thing that supporters would mind being harmed, so this choice is incorrect. Choice (I) *label*, or "title," is insufficient because the candidate is presumably harming more than just the name of the party, so this choice is also incorrect.

Choices (B), (F), and (G) are correct.

18. C

If there is an "increasingly vast body of intellectual property law," a loophole would have to be a lack of legal regulation. Choice (C) *dearth*, or "lack," fits well here. Choices (A) *audacity* ("boldness or insolence"), (B) *wealth* ("abundance"), (D) *consummation* ("the bringing of something to a satisfying conclusion"), and (E) *insularity* ("narrow-mindedness" or "isolation") do not fit in this context.

Choice (C) is the credited response.

19. A, F, H

Let's start with the second blank. The key phrase "actually disruptive" suggests that the second missing word will reflect a negative effect that tourists are having on the native population. Choice (F) *deleterious*, or "harmful," fits this prediction and is correct. Choice (D) *beneficial*, or "helpful," is the opposite of the meaning we seek. Choice (E) *cumulative*, meaning "increasing over time," is appealing in that the effect can be com-

pounded with repeated visits, but the choice does not convey the negative meaning indicated by "disruptive."

Proceeding to the third blank, we are looking for a word that summarizes an aspect of the native community that is being negatively affected by tourism. Since there are no specific clues about what the tourists are negatively affecting, we need a general word like "livelihood." Choice (H) *welfare*, or "state of well-being," is definitely an aspect of native life that could be negatively affected by disruptive tourists, so this is the correct answer. Choice (G) *economy* relates to one aspect of the native community, but there are no clues to indicate how the economy would be affected—positively or negatively. Therefore, choice (G) is incorrect. Choice (I) *aesthetics*, or "beliefs about the nature of beauty," is wrong for the same reason. Without specific clues to guide us, we cannot conclude that such beliefs would be affected by the intrusion of tourists.

Going back to the first blank, the detour road sign "although" lets us know that the tour guide's motives contrast with the negative effect the tourists are having on the native population. We can predict a word with positive connotations such as "noble." Choice (A) *admirable*, or "commendable," fulfills this expectation and is correct. Choice (B) *ulterior*, meaning "hidden," is often used to describe motives that are negative, so this choice is incorrect. Choice (C) *unethical*, or "morally bad," is also negative, so this choice is incorrect as well.

The correct answer choices are (A), (F), and (H).

20. A, E, G

The pattern of the state in blank (i) is one that "fundamentally hampers the ability of the state to provide its citizens with services." This tells us that the word should be negative. We can predict something like "weakness" or "inefficiency" here. Choice (A) *inefficacy*, or "the state of not producing the desired effect or result," is a good fit here. Neither choice (B) *surfeit* ("an overabundant supply or indulgence") nor (C) *rectitude* ("uprightness or extreme morality") work in this context.

An adjective in blank (ii) describing the health clinic facilities of these states should therefore also be negative. Look for something that would describe a clinic impeded by "limited funding." Choice (E) *neglected* is suitable in this context. Choice (D) *noxious* means "harmful, poisonous, or lethal." While it is possible that "questionable health clinics with limited funding" could have harmful, poisonous, or lethal facilities, we cannot assume that this is the case. A less extreme adjective should be used. The definition of choice (F) *covert* is "hidden or undercover." Although the health clinics are questionable, the author does not suggest that they are hidden.

For blank (iii), we can predict that the state would want to get rid of disease, so our prediction here is "elimination." Choice (G) *eradication* is a suitable synonym for elimination. Choice (H) *probity* means "virtue or integrity." A state-run disease virtue effort does not make sense. As for choice (I), it is unlikely that states struggling with health-care systems would be running *philanthropy*, or "charity," efforts.

The correct choices are (A), (E), and (G).

21. C, F, H

In a melting pot, different cultures are "thrown together" and blended to create one *homogeneous* society, a society that is "composed of parts or elements that are all of the same kind," so choice (C) is the credited response. Choice (A) *analogous* ("corresponding in some particular") is somewhat similar in

meaning but does not create the most fluid and coherent sentence, while choice (B) *disparate*, or "dissimilar," is the opposite in meaning, so neither is a good fit for blank (i).

As for blank (ii), the new view on society is that different cultures bring their unique *quintessence*, or "essence," to the common culture. Choice (F) is the credited choice. Choice (D) *temperament* is "the combination of mental, physical, and emotional traits of a person." A culture is made up of many people, so it could not be said to have one type of temperament. Choice (E) *apotheosis* is defined as "the elevation or exaltation of a person to the rank of god." This noun does not fit this context.

The closing of the passage indicates that soon minority groups will become the majority in the United States, leading to demographic *vicissitudes*, or "changes," that will affect the macro-culture. Choice (H) is the credited response for blank (iii). Choice (G) *hierarchies* are "systems of ranking." Though population could be a system for ranking, hierarchies typically are based on power and seniority, which is not addressed here. Choice (I) *compression* refers to "the state of being compressed, or pressed together." Although this is a type of change, it is too specific to fit this context.

The correct choices are (C), (F), and (H).

22. E

Since the "arts and trades" are now emphasized in this new "experimental curriculum," we can infer that they were previously not emphasized, and the word in the blank should indicate that they were not considered the proper foundation of an education. Choice (E) *inappropriate* works in this context. None of choices (A) *crucial* ("critical"), (B) *compulsory* ("required"), (C) *massive* ("bulky and heavy"), or (D) *dominant* ("commanding, influential") are suitable.

Choice (E) is the credited response.

23. B, D, H

This paragraph describes the global fight against malaria, particularly in Africa. Malaria is a fatal disease, so the fight is choice (B) to *extirpate*, or "destroy," malaria, which is the word for blank (i). Choice (A) to *ramify* means "to subdivide into branches or subdivisions" which is not the aim of the global fight against malaria. Choice (C) to *redress* is "to provide compensation for a loss or wrong experienced." The global fight is to destroy malaria, not provide it compensation.

The sentence with blank (ii) tells us that Africa is notable among the areas hardest hit by malaria, so logically it would have choice (D) *an incommensurate*, or "disproportionate," number of malaria-related deaths each year. Choice (E) *a profligate* means "extremely extravagant or immoral" and makes no sense in context. Choice (F) *a tantamount* makes no sense; while "tantamount" means "equivalent in significance," it can't be parsed grammatically here. Furthermore, since we have learned that Africa is notable among the areas hardest hit by malaria, it would not have an equivalent majority of malaria-related deaths.

For blank (iii), malaria falls under Africa's *epidemiological* worries, which are those "dealing with the incidence and cause of disease in large populations," so choice (H) is the credited response here. Choice (G) *bureaucratic* describes "government by many administrators and minor officials" and can also mean "arbitrary and routine," so it is not the best fit here. Choice (I) *sanctimonious* means "giving a hypocritical appearance of piety" and does not have anything to do with the issue of malaria.

The credited choices are (B), (D), and (H).

24. B, D, I

Since the first sentence is a broad introductory sentence, we should focus first on the rest of the passage and then return to blank (i). The second sentence tells us that one part of the visual experience is our ability to use visual information to create something. We can predict that blank (ii) should be filled with a word similar in meaning to "image." Choice (D) *representation* works well here. Choice (E) is not the credited response. This paragraph describes the human visual experience as it occurs. While people can have *memories* of three-dimensional space, the visual information that we receive originally creates a representation of that three-dimensional space. As for choice (F), when we receive visual information, we do not create a *replica*, or "copy," of it. The processes of binocular disparity and stereopsis allow us to create a representation, or image, of a three-dimensional space.

Blank (iii) should contain a verb meaning "tell the difference between," since we must process depth from the information received from the two retinas to create three-dimensionality. Choice (I) *discern* is the best choice. Choice (G) *extricate* is "to release somebody or something with difficulty from a physical constraint or an unpleasant situation." During the visual experience, we do not try to remove depth from binocular disparity. Choice (H) *abrogate* is "to abolish, usually by authority." We want to distinguish depth from our binocular disparity; we would not want to abolish depth, since it is a key component of the human visual experience.

Based on this information, we can now return to blank (i) and pick choice (B) *series of complex processing mechanisms* to define the human visual experience. Clearly the mechanisms involved in vision are complex and involve processing information received by the retinas. Choice (A), *sequence of basic processes* is not the credited response. After reading the rest of the paragraph, it becomes clear that the processes involved in the human visual experience are complex, not *basic*. And since this paragraph describes two mechanisms that help create three-dimensionality in vision, choice (C) *trio of simultaneous events* is not the credited choice because there are not *three* distinct events mentioned in the paragraph.

The correct choices are (B), (D), and (I).

25.   A, D, H

In the first part of this sentence, we're looking for a verb that will work with the phrase "what even the most optimistic of analysts had predicted"; we can assume that it's something that would be positive. "Surpass" would work here, so that's our prediction. Choice (A) *exceeded* works well with the superlative "most optimistic." The most optimistic investors would have higher predictions than the average, so choice (B) *averaged out to* wouldn't work here. Choice (C) *burdened* is nonsensical in the first blank.

The second blank needs to be something that shows an increase in interest. "Excited" is a good prediction. Choice (D) *inflamed* means "kindled or excited feelings" and makes sense here since investors would be likely to become even more interested in a successful company. Neither of choices (E) and (F) are suitable here. "*Distracted* the interest of many more investors" makes no sense, while there is no reason that "overnight success" would "*escape* the interest" of investors.

The third blank should describe the type of return investors would see after an overnight success, so our prediction will be something like "rapid" or "impressive." Choice (H) is the

credited response. It makes sense that the original investors would see a *staggering*, or "overwhelming," return on their money from an overnight success. As for choice (G), a return on an investment could not be described as *magnanimous*, or "generous and noble in spirit." Finally, it does not make sense that investors would see an *innocuous*, or "harmless," return on their money after an overnight success, so choice (I) is incorrect.

The correct choices are (A), (D), and (H).

26.   C, D

It is helpful to start with blank (ii) here. Virtues are positive attributes that would typically be praised, revered, or choice (D) *extolled*. Choice (E) *refuted* is "disproved." The guests would not be stunned by his behavior if the hostess had already tried to disprove his virtue. As for choice (F), it is illogical to say the hostess had *regaled*, or "entertained," his virtues.

Regarding blank (i), because the hostess extolled his virtues before he arrived, we can infer that the guests were shocked by poor behavior. Choice (C) *effrontery*, or "impudence or insolence," is the most negative choice given. Choice (A) *perspicacity* ("shrewdness or perceptiveness") is firmly positive. Choice (B) *obsequiousness* is "excessive compliance or submissiveness." While obsequiousness might not be a desirable trait, it would not stun a room full of guests.

The credited responses are choices (C) and (D).

27.   B, D, I

The sentences provide context clues to the missing words. You learn that the young team did something until only one option remained open to them, something consistent with "last-minute solution." You're also told that the team was disorganized and that they planned poorly. Since the solution was last-minute, predict that they must have "put off their work" until they had no other recourse than to "attempt a frantic" last-minute solution, so those are our predictions respectively for the three blanks.

Regarding blank (i), choice (B) *postponed* means "put off or delayed." This explains the need for a last-minute solution and matches our prediction. Choice (A) *expedited* means "accomplished promptly" and is inconsistent with requiring a last-minute solution. As for choice (C), the team did not *accelerate* or "hasten" attacking the root of the problem; otherwise, they would not logically require a last-minute solution. This is opposite to what we need here.

As for blank (ii), choice (D) is the credited response. The team needed to *implement* or "carry out" a last-minute solution. Regarding choice (E), if all the team had to do was *envision*, or "mentally picture" a solution, it doesn't seem that time would have been an issue. And since they waited until the last minute, it isn't likely they would *reject* or "discard" a solution, so we can eliminate choice (F).

Finally, consider blank (iii). Choice (I) *desperate* means "reckless because of an urgent need" and accurately describes a "last-minute solution to the problem" brought on by poor planning and organization. It is the credited response. Choice (G) *measured* means "steady or deliberate" and is inconsistent with waiting until the last minute to find a solution, while choice (H) *premeditated* means "done deliberately or planned in advance" and is the opposite of last minute. Neither fits here.

The correct choices are (B), (D), and (I).

28. B

By definition a connoisseur is an expert, and thus knows very much about a subject. You can predict "a large amount." Choice (B) *copious* is the credited response. None of choices (A) *scant* ("meager"), (C) *spurious* ("false or fake") (D) *peculiar* ("strange or odd") or (E) *arcane* ("mysterious and obscure") are as well fitted.

Choice (B) is the credited response.

29. A, E

The word that fills the first blank should describe people who have been traveling for a long time. They would likely be very tired. Choice (A) *enervated* ("weakened or exhausted") is just what we're looking for. While the hikers might also be choice (B) *morose*, or "gloomy," because they are tired, one cannot necessarily assume this from the context of the sentence. Choice (C) *imperious* means "superior and domineering" and makes no sense in context.

For the second blank, since the hikers have been traveling without food or water, it is logical that Samantha would worry about becoming "dangerously dehydrated" or choice (E) *parched*. Choice (D) *timorous* means "timid" or "hesitant." This sentence focuses on Samantha's physical state, not her mental one and so this is not a credited response. Likewise, choice (F) *lugubrious*, which "means extremely sad or mournful," should be eliminated. The context tells us that this blank refers to Samantha's physical, not mental, state.

The credited choices are (A) and (E).

30. B

The road sign is "in contrast." Therefore, instead of size being "commensurate," or proportional, to potency, it must be disproportional. Predict *flavorful* for the blank.

Choice (B) *piquant* means "spicy," and reads well into the sentence.

Choice (C) might be tempting since it also refers to a strong flavor, but *acrid* is associated with acidity, not spiciness. Choice (A) *banal* is opposite, since the small peppers are not "bland." Choices (D) *unique* ("one of a kind") and (E) *diverse* ("multiform") are out of scope.

Choice (B) is the credited response.

31. C

If the council prefers modesty, then fits of "hubris" or excessive arrogance would be criticized. "Criticize" is a great prediction and choice (C) *obloquy* ("censure" or "blame") matches.

Both choices (A) *encomium* and (E) *panegyric* mean "praise" and are opposite wrong answer choices. Moreover, since they mean more or less the same thing, how can one be right and the other not? Choices (B) and (D) are out of scope: *perspicacity* is astuteness, while a *pastiche* is a piece of artwork that consciously borrows from other pieces.

One way to bypass difficult vocabulary is to eliminate by using word charge. The prediction above, *criticize*, is negative. Choices (A), (B), and (E) have a positive word charge while (D) is nonsensical in this context. Eliminate them in order to increase your odds of getting the correct answer.

Choice (C) is the credited response.

32. B, D

Because we don't know what the doctor's advice is, we have to go to the second sentence, and complete the second blank first. The word "gourmand" indicates that Franklin is "excessively fond of food and drink." The detour road sign "though" at the beginning of the second sentence signals a contrast between the first and second clauses of that sentence. Franklin's doctor tells him to cut down on confections (desserts), but cutting down would mean Franklin does not have to completely eliminate desserts from his diet. Let's predict: "Though he would not have to be totally free of indulgence, his doctor did warn him to cut down on decadent confections."

Choice (D) *ascetic* means "self-denying" or "austere," which fits our prediction and is correct. Choice (E) *temperate*, meaning "moderate," is incorrect, as being "completely moderate" is a contradiction in terms, and choice (F) *sanctimonious*, meaning "excessively preachy," may be a contrast to decadence in general, but does not relate to reining in one's diet. Hence, both (E) and (F) are incorrect.

Moving back to the first blank, remember that we now know Franklin is being ordered to cut back on sweets, and that he is a gourmand, which means "lover of food." Because this is likely to make him unhappy, let's predict: "A dedicated gourmand, Franklin's expression became sad when the doctor delivered her advice."

Choice (B) *dour* means "gloomy," which matches our prediction perfectly and is correct. Choice (A) *effervescent* means "bubbly," which has a happy connotation, so this choice is incorrect. Choice (C) *wrathful* has a negative meaning but is far too strongly charged; wrathful is more violent than sad. Hence, this choice is also incorrect.

The correct answers are choices (B) and (D).

33. C, D

The detour road sign "however" signals a contrast between the first and second sentence. "Fortuitously" means "fortunately" or "luckily," so the first sentence must be about an "unlucky" event. Choice (C) *an inauspicious*, meaning "unfavorable," matches our prediction and is correct. Choice (A) *an augural* refers to a formal opening or induction, which might make sense if things ended poorly for the speaker, but "fortuitously" makes this answer choice incorrect. Choice (B) *a pernicious* means "very harmful," which has a negative connotation, but in the end no actual harm was done here, so this choice is also incorrect.

The second blank also follows from the word "fortuitously," and it describes what happened to the speaker's rapport with the crowd. "Rapport" means "positive connection," so a strong prediction would be that the speaker's "droll" (or humorous) remark "elevated" or "repaired" the rapport with the audience. Choice (D) *buoyed*, or "raised," matches this prediction perfectly and is correct. Choice (E) *severed* is the opposite of what we're looking for because "severed" means "cut off completely," and cutting off rapport would not have been a fortuitous result. Hence, this choice is incorrect. Choice (F) *alleviated* means "to relieve," which makes no sense when applied to rapport, so (F) is incorrect.

Choices (C) and (D) are the correct answers.

34. D

"But" indicates that although Mrs. Haddo didn't take pride in "any special gifts," she acknowledged something similar, her ability for reading character. Look for a positively-charged modifier. Choice (D) *unerring*, or "lacking flaws or error," is the most positive of the choices and works well here. As for the other choices, all are unsuitable. Choice (A) *adverse* is a negative word, and would not describe a "special gift." Choice (B) *paranormal* means "magical, outside the scope of scientific understanding" and is inappropriate for the ability to read another's character.

Choices (C) *imperfect* and (E) *blemished* mean "flawed" or "sullied"; this is the opposite of what you would expect from a special gift. Choice (D) is the credited response.

35. B, D

The word that goes in the first blank creates "quandaries," or difficulties, for the "status quo." We might look for a word like "disturbance." Choice (B) *aberration*, or "departure from what is normal," matches our prediction and is correct. Choice (A) *concatenation*, or "sequence," identifies a neutral or normal progression, rather than a disturbance that would lead to an upheaval, so this choice is incorrect. Choice (C) *inculcation*, or "indoctrination," is not the kind of activity that creates quandaries or challenges for the status quo; rather, indoctrination typically maintains the status quo. Hence, this choice is also incorrect.

Now we can move on to the second blank. Something is happening to the old theoretical models that is causing them to be thrown out and replaced by new ones. A word such as "criticized" would make a good prediction. Choice (D) *impugned*, or "challenged," matches our prediction perfectly and is correct. Choice (E) *emblematized*, or "served as a symbol," implies that the old models are becoming even more firmly entrenched, so this choice is incorrect. Choice (F) *approbated*, or "authorized," similarly implies that the old models are staying around, so this choice is also incorrect.

The correct answers are (B) and (D).

36. B, E, H

Blank (i) is another result of social isolation other than higher rates of mortality. Illness would also likely be at a higher rate since illness leads to death, so "illness" or something similar would be a good prediction here. Choice (B) *morbidity* is defined as "the presence of illness or disease." It is logical that the same characteristics that cause higher rates of mortality, or death, would also cause higher rates of illness or disease, so this is the credited choice. Think carefully about choice (A). Both *fatality* and *mortality* refer to death, so including both would be redundant. Choice (C) *recuperation* is "recovery from an illness or injury." Since solitary behavior and social isolation have been linked to higher rates of mortality, they are more likely to also be correlated to illness than to recovery. This is opposite to what we need here.

Similarly, in blank (ii) we can infer that the stress response would lead to a faster decline in health, so we can predict "encourages" or "advances." Choice (E) *promotes* means "encourages growth or development." The stress response encourages the development of a faster decline in a lonely individual's health. This is the credited response. Choice (D) *palliates* means "relieves or alleviates." A "stress response" would lead to a rapid decline, not reduce the severity of a rapid decline, so this is not the correct response. Choice (F) *transmutes into* means "to change or alter in form." The "stress response" does not *change into* a faster decline, but rather *leads to* a faster decline in overall health.

Finally, if some of the choices in Blank (iii) are unfamiliar, try to use process of elimination. Choice (G) *aerobic* means "living or taking place only in the presence of oxygen." Oxygen is not mentioned elsewhere in the passage, so this choice can be eliminated. Choice (I) *diaphanous* means "light, airy, or transparent" and would not fit as part of this physiological term. This leaves us with the best choice, (H) *anabolic*, which refers to "metabolic processes in which energy is used to construct complex molecules from simpler ones." This is a beneficial function of the body, so it is logical that it

would be connected to sleep, a vital component of good health.

The correct choices are (B), (E), and (H).

37. A, E

This sentence gives you a couple of clues: there is a transition from what areas once were to what they may eventually become, and the comparison words should be similar to "lush" for the first blank and "arid" for the second.

Looking at blank (i), choice (A) *fertile*, or "crop-bearing," has positive connotations and fits well with "lush." Choice (B) *desiccated* means "dried up," and would make sense as an adjective to describe a desert, not lush farmland. Choice (C) *parched*, meaning "dry," would make sense in the second blank, not in the first.

Regarding blank (ii), choice (E) *barren*, or "unable to produce," is a good word to describe a desert here. Neither choice (D) nor (F) is appropriate here. *Rich* would be better in the first blank than in the second, and an "arid desert" would not be *moist*.

Choices (A) and (E) are the credited responses.

38. B, D

The key to this question is the semicolon between the two blanks. It is a straight-ahead road sign that indicates the two parts of the sentence will support one another. We'll start with the easier blank, which is the second one in this case. We're told that Olivia's friends were astounded at how she handled dangerous situations. Because most people would be expected to avoid or fear dangerous situations, Olivia must be astounding in that she faces them head-on. We can make "accept" our prediction and check the answer choices. Choice (D) *embrace*, or "willingly accept," matches our prediction. Choice (E) *undermine*, which means "destroy" or "subvert," does not fit the context. Choice (F) *shun*, meaning "to keep away from," has the opposite meaning of the word we need.

For the first blank, remember that the semi-colon is a straight-ahead road sign, so the first part of the sentence will support the meaning of the second. If Olivia faces danger head-on, a good prediction would be "fearless." Choice (B) *dauntless* means just that. Choice (A) *feckless*, meaning "ineffectual," does not make sense, nor does (C) *guileless*, meaning "honest."

The answers are (B) and (D).

39. A, D, I

This paragraph focuses on the government's struggle between providing effective national security and not upsetting the public. The second sentence lists these two conflicting needs as consent, consistent with "public approval ratings," and blank (i), which should relate to providing tight national security. Since none of the choices relates directly to "security," look for a word which somehow corresponds with it.

The first sentence outlines the two needs democracies must fulfill: security and public approval. Since consent of the public is already listed, the other blank should have to do with tight security. (A) effectiveness, corresponds with tight security and is the credited choice. On the other hand, choice (B) is not suitable here. While *serendipity*, or "luck," would be great for the government to have, it is based on chance, so it would not be a realistic goal to strive for. Choice (C) *aspersion* is a "derogatory remark or expression of ill-will." A democracy would not need or want aspersion.

Later in the paragraph, the author mentions that the public wanted more stringent security after 9/11. However, the next sentence says that peoples' feelings began to change when their memories of 9/11 faded. The verb in blank (ii) should express peoples' reaction of having their privacy compromised for security measures. "Rejecting" or "refusing" would be a good prediction here. Choice (D) *repudiating* is "rejecting" or "refusing to accept" and matches perfectly. The previous sentence says that people wanted higher national security measures after the 9/11 attack. The "however" in the next sentence tells us that more recently people's feelings have changed—they are rejecting having their privacy compromised by these national security measures.

Neither choice (E) nor (F) is suitable here. *Redressing* means "putting right something that was wrong." While the general idea of this word fits this sentence, it is awkward and incorrectly used in this blank. And *jeopardizing* means "putting at risk or endangering." People could not jeopardize having their own privacy compromised by the government. It would only be logical to say that the government jeopardized the privacy of the people.

Blank (iii) should describe this more recent view of the government's security goals. As the impact of 9/11 becomes muted over time, security threats become less concrete or immediate. Because there have not been any instances of threatened security in the recent past, and it is unknown when the next tragedy will occur, look for a word that indicates that security concerns are indefinite or uncertain. Choice (I) fits well here. *Abstract* means "based on general principles or theories rather than on specific instances." Because the horror of 9/11 is not as fresh on their minds, people do not want their privacy taken away for some vague future unknown. The definition of choice (G) *an ebullient* is "extremely lively or enthusiastic." Some government officials might be extremely enthusiastic about their security goals, but this adjective should relate to the peoples' perspective of these goals. Finally, choice (H) *a discursive* can mean "rambling or lacking order." Though some people might view the government's security goals as lacking order, this is not the aspect of the goals people are concerned about that is discussed in this paragraph.

The correct choices are (A), (D), and (I).

40. C, D

Let's start with the first blank, which describes the state of newspapers now that the Internet has developed into an advanced news source. A good prediction here might be "antiquated." Choice (C) *obsolete* means "outdated" and matches our prediction, so this is the first correct answer. Choice (A) *bombastic* means "characterized by unnecessarily high-sounding language." This choice does not match our prediction, nor does it fit the context of the sentence, so it is incorrect. Choice (B) *capricious*, which means "impulsive" or "unpredictable," is unsupported by any context clues and is therefore incorrect.

In the second sentence, the words "nonetheless" and "surprising" indicate contrast and paradox. In other words, although newspapers might seem antiquated in comparison to modern alternatives, subscriptions are not behaving the way the trend would suggest. Thus, a good prediction for blank (ii) would be that subscriptions have "increased." Choice (D) *proliferated* means "increased rapidly," which matches our prediction and is the second correct answer. Choice (E) *metamorphosed* means "changed," but since it gives no indication whether the change is positive or negative, it is too vague and thus incorrect. Choice (F) *reeled* can mean "faltered." Since

newspaper subscriptions have increased, not declined, it is also incorrect.

The correct answers are choices (C) and (D).

41. C

The clues in the sentence indicate that Michalewski's text is impressive and important. A quick scan of the answer choices, however, reveals that almost every single one of the answer choices carries a positive charge. The only one with a negative charge is choice (B) *vainglory*, or "excessive boastfulness," so it can be eliminated. A good prediction might be *model*, based on the use of the same word later in the sentence. Choice (C) *apotheosis*, or "highest point in development," fits this prediction.

Choice (A) *validation*, or "confirmation," doesn't fit the prediction. Choices (D) and (E), *munificence* and *beneficence*, both mean "generosity," so they can be eliminated since they can't both be the answer. Remember to eliminate synonyms in the answer choices.

Choice (C) is the credited response.

42. C, D, I

Let us begin with the first blank, which refers to the overall point of the passage: the inability to determine the precise quality of a literary work. We can predict that the first missing word will be synonymous with "impossible." Choice (C) *hopeless* matches our prediction and is correct. Choice (A) *inane*, or "meaningless," is off the mark because we're told about the insurmountable difficulties of the task, not the lack of meaning. Choice (B) *feasible*, meaning "possible to accomplish," is the opposite of what we're looking for and is thus incorrect.

For the second blank, the key word in the passage is "enumerate," to list or count. Choice (D) *quantitative*, "measurable," is the correct answer because it matches the mathematical sense of "enumerate." Choice (E) *analytical*, "by logical process," might seem tempting, but it fails to capture the quantitative aspect of "enumerate," so it is incorrect. A choice (F) *subjective* definition, a "personal" or "individual" one, would be impossible to measure by definition, so this choice is the opposite of what we need and is also incorrect.

Finally, the third blank requires a negatively charged word. The straight-ahead road sign "Indeed" indicates that the final sentence will continue the logic of the previous ones. The first two sentences have stated that it is impossible to measure the literary quality of a work during the time it was written. The final sentence underscores this point by contrasting the high esteem nowadays granted to "literary classics" with the way in which they were viewed during their time. A good prediction would be "not highly regarded." Choice (I) *criticized* signifies a negative reaction during their time to works now considered "classics," so this is the correct answer. Choices (G) *extolled* and (H) *acclaimed*, which both mean "praised," are both too positive to be correct.

The correct answers are choices (C), (D), and (I).

43. C, F

Here we can begin with the first blank, an adjective describing James's disposition, which must be strongly optimistic if it "infects" others and makes them optimistic as well. Choice (C) *sanguine* can mean "reddish" (in regard to complexion) but also "confident" or "optimistic" (in reference to disposition, as is the case here). This second meaning matches our prediction, so choice (C) is the correct response. Choice (B) *ruddy*, "healthily red," refers strictly to someone's complexion

and is incorrect. While choice (A) *sanguinary* may look similar to *sanguine*, it actually means "bloody" or "bloodthirsty," which is unsupported by the context and is thus incorrect.

For the second blank, the context refers to the saying "every cloud has a silver lining," which means that one should always look on the bright side of things or see the best in even bad situations. The key to selecting the correct answer here is in the previous sentence; James takes "wavering hope" and turns it into "robust optimism." He makes optimism stronger, and our answer will reflect this. Choice (F) *coruscate*, meaning "gleam" or "radiate," completes the image of the silver lining growing brighter, so this is the correct choice. Choice (D) *manifest*, meaning "apparent" or "visible," is tempting, but we see from the context that hope—the silver lining—is already present, and what James's presence does is to make it stronger; thus, we can reject (D) as incorrect. Choice (E) *tangible*, "corporeal" or "touchable," makes little sense because the silver lining is figurative, not literal, so (E) can also be eliminated.

Choices (C) and (F) are the correct answers.

44. A

Since Ryan does not have conversations, our prediction is that Ryan is *timid* or *quiet*. Choice (A) matches this prediction, since *diffidence* is the quality of being reserved because of shyness or insecurity.

Choice (C) *imagination* may seem like a possibility because Ryan imagines these conversations. However, it is not his imagination that paralyzes him, but his failure to engage in conversations. Choices (B) *sycophancy*, (D) *convalescence*, and (E) *rectitude* are all out of scope, since the sentence does not mention Ryan's relationship with his superiors, an illness, or his goodness.

Choice (A) is the credited response.

45. A, E

The key here is that the sociobiologist made some sort of observation about social status and infectious diseases regarding macaque monkeys, and that he tried to suggest that this relationship holds true for humans as well. To remain consistent, the second blank should match "disease" so choice (E) *sickness* is a good match. Choices (D) *compensation* ("something given in return for services or injury") and (F) *mobility* ("the ability to be moved") are both out of scope.

Next, turn to the first blank. Choice (A) *susceptibility*, which can mean "especially liable to illness," makes sense in reference to disease, while choices (B) *impartiality* ("the state of being unbiased") and (C) *dominance* ("state of authority") do not.

Choices (A) and (E) are the credited choices.

46. C

The first clue in the sentence is "contradictory," and this is used in reference to the relationship between demeanor (of the artists) and reception (by the media). Thus, you can conclude an artist with an unpleasant demeanor is paradoxically well received by the media. Since the word "least" comes before the blank, you can predict *pleasant* or *cooperative*. Choice (C), *cordial*, or "friendly," matches. Even if you didn't know what *cordial* meant, you could still eliminate choices (A) *curt* ("rudely brief"), (B) *specific* ("detailed"), (D) *aloof* ("unfriendly"), and (E) *evasive* ("not direct") based on word charge. They all have a negative or neutral charge and the correct answer is a positive word. By narrowing your choices in this way you can guess strategically.

47. A, F, G

The beginning of the paragraph establishes that this study has found an internally valid correlation. Next the author evaluates the external validity of this correlation. Since studies have to be performed with some kind of group, we can call the findings a *paradigm*, or a "typical example of something or an example that serves as a model or pattern," especially one that forms the basis of a methodology or theory, that the study's author hopes to apply to a larger population. The sentence questions whether the example of the correlations from the study would apply to a more general population, so (A) is the credited choice for blank (i).

Neither of the other choices are suitable. The example presented in the study is not (B) an *aspersion*, or "a curse or expression of ill-will." Choice (C) *treachery* means "violation of allegiance, confidence, or plighted faith." While some of the issues brought up in the study could be seen as treachery, this noun represents one point of view. A more general noun meaning a typical example should be used.

For blank (ii), we need to describe the relationship between "a subtle form of stereotyping and racism" and our mental processes. "Subtle" provides a clue that the best choice to show this relationship is choice (F) *intrinsic to*, or "inherent to." Often elements of our mental processes, such as our tendency to stereotype others, are innate. Choice (D) *insular to* can mean "pertaining to an island," "isolated," or "narrow-minded." None of these definitions fits this sentence. Choice (E) is also unsuitable. *Hindmost* is defined "as farthest from the front." Although a subtle mental process could be thought of as in the back of one's mind, there is no direct evidence in the paragraph that the author believes that stereotyping and racism are the mental processes farthest from the front of peoples' minds.

All three choices for blank (iii) correctly show a positive relationship between the results of the study and the general population, but choices (H) and (I) do not quite fit in meaning or fluency. The definition of *postulated* is "suggested or assumed the existence, fact, or truth of something as a basis for reasoning, discussion, or belief." The author does not wish to say that the results of the study could be assumed to represent the general population. While this verb is similar in meaning to generalize, it implies that the study results are interacting with the general population and is incorrect idiomatically here. And although we do want to show a positive relationship between the results and the general population here, it is illogical to say that the results may well be *acceded*, or "agreed," to the general population. On the other hand, choice (G) *generalized* shows that the author believes the study results may be able to be applied to the general population. The author told us earlier that the external validity, or ability to generalize the example, is difficult to evaluate. She has stated already that this example might not be true for all in a literal sense, and now the author presents the other side: that perhaps the results may be able to be generalized to all citizens.

The correct answers are (A), (F), and (G).

48. E
The word "seemingly" and its partner, "actually," shows us that there's a contrast here. We need a word that is in contrast to a "hotbed" in which there are "fierce debates." Choice (E) *placid* means "peaceful," and fits well in this context.

Choice (A) *chivalrous*, meaning "courteous and loyal, especially to women," is too specific and less appropriate. A community that was choice (B) *cynical* or "distrusting" would not be at odds with this situation. Neither choice (C) *sincere*, meaning "earnest," nor choice (D) *fervid*, meaning "feverish," are suitable here either.

Choice (E) is the credited response.

49. D
The words "just as" in this sentence indicate that the two parts of the sentence convey similar ideas. Carbon dioxide is indispensable, therefore you can predict that oxygen is "necessary" or "essential." Choice (D) *necessity* is correct.

Choice (A) *enhancement* ("improvement"), choice (B) *advancement* ("development"), choice (C) *luxury* ("lavish"), and choice (E) *compulsion* ("impulse") do not work in this context.

Choice (D) is the credited response.

50. B, D, H
The first sentence tells us that the subject of the paragraph is a country with high unemployment rates. We can infer that the country's population would be mostly living in "poverty," so that's our prediction. The definition of choice (B) *indigence* is "extreme poverty in which the basic necessities of life are lacking." This matches our prediction and is the correct answer. Choice (A) *acrimony* means "bitterness or discord." This paragraph discusses the socioeconomic conditions in a country but does not mention any discord between citizens, so this is not the credited choice. Choice (C) *sumptuousness* is defined as "great wealth." Since the country has high unemployment rates and a growing disparity between the quality of life of the upper and lower classes, most of its citizens would not

live in sumptuousness, so this is also not the credited choice.

Blank (ii) refers to the quality of life of the upper and lower classes, so we need a word like "difference" or "gap." Choice (D) *disparity* means "inequality," and is the credited choice. There is a lack of equality between the quality of life of the upper and lower classes in a country in economic crisis. Choice (E) *plethora* does not fit in this context. It would not make sense to say that there is a growing *plethora*, or "abundance," between the quality of life of the upper and lower classes. Choice (F) *rancor* is a "deep, bitter resentment." A nonhuman thing such as "the quality of life" cannot have rancor.

Blank (iii) describes the type of education the country is lacking: "sufficient" would be a good prediction here. Choice (H) *adequate* means "sufficient in quantity or quality to meet a need" and matches our prediction. Because of the country's economic crisis, we can assume that the schools are not able to provide education that meets the needs of the students. Neither of the other choices works. The definition of choice (G) *commensurate* is "corresponding in size or degree, or in proportion." There is nothing for education to correspond to in this sentence. Choice (I) *quixotic*, or "extravagantly romantic or idealistic," is not an appropriate adjective to describe the education system of a country in economic crisis.

The correct choices are (B), (D), and (H).

51. C

The blank must cause the interior to be "even more" disappointing to buyers. We can predict that an attractive or impressive facade would make the sight of an unsatisfactory interior greater.

Choice (B) is tempting in that *dilapidation, or "state of disrepair,"* can be disappointing to buyers. However, the interior was disappointing, not the state of the facade, which makes it an opposite wrong answer choice. Choice (A) *ostentatious* is also tempting, but since it means "pretentious or vulgar," it is not a term that would make the house "even more" disappointing. Both choice (D) *diminutive* ("extremely small") and choice (E) *gloomy* ("depressing") are decidedly negative when it comes to real estate. A positive term is needed here and choice (C) *august*, or "impressive," matches.

52. A

There are two clues: the hostess had a diminished opinion of the guest, and the guest was "fastidious," or picky. A synonym like "fussy" is a good prediction and choice (A) *finicky* matches it.

Although choices (B) *boorish* ("bad-mannered"), (C) *loquacious* ("talkative"), (D) *stolid* ("impassive"), and (E) *curt* ("rudely brief") are words that might describe how a poor dinner guest acts, there are no clues in the sentence to suggest that she was any of these.

Choice (A) is the credited response.

53. A, E

This sentence's use of "although" and "actually" shows us that there is a contrast between the first and second parts of the sentence. The first blank must be something that could be preceded by the adverb "merely," and it must contrast with "one of the cornerstones of civilization." Choice (A) *superficial*, "relating merely to the surfaces of things," is a good contrast and is the credited response. Both choice (B) *overwhelming* ("overpowering") and choice (C) *cherished* ("cared for tenderly") don't sound right when preceded by "merely" and are wrong in context.

Since the second blank should describe what our informal society is doing to etiquette, choice (E) is correct. It makes sense that etiquette would be *threatened* or "endangered" by an informal society. The other choices don't make sense in this context. An informal society would neither (D) *embrace* ("receive gladly") nor (F) *integrate* ("combine") etiquette.

Choices (A) and (E) are the credited responses.

54. B, F

To fill the first blank, we note that the two composers shared the same birth years and died nine years apart. We need a word that describes people who live at the same time. Choice (B) *contemporaries* means "people who lived during the same time period" and is the first credited answer. If we were unsure of the meaning, we still might recognize the root *tempor*, which means "time." Choice (A) *competitors*, meaning "rivals" or "opponents," is not supported by the context, which says nothing about a rivalry between Bach and Handel. Therefore, (A) is incorrect. Choice (C) *contestants*, meaning "those taking part in a contest," is similarly unsupported by any context and is therefore incorrect.

The second blank needs a verb to complete the verb phrase. Because Handel was born in Germany but died in England, we can predict that the verb will describe the action of moving from one nation to another. Choice (F) *emigrated* means "left one's birth nation to live elsewhere" and matches our prediction perfectly. This is the second correct answer. Choice (D) *disaffected* is incorrect because it means "discontented" or "resentful" and does not fit the context at all. It is a trap because it can be confused with "defected," meaning

"deserted" or "abandoned." While choice (E) *absconded*, meaning "left in secret" or "escaped," does describe the action of leaving one place for another, it makes no sense here because there is no suggestion that Handel left Germany secretly nor is there a reason given for why he might have done so.

The correct answers are choices (B) and (F).

55. B, E, H

For blank (i), we need a reason for decreasing the importing of water from the north. Since we're told the costs are reflected in the prices and that there's a currently financial crisis, we can predict that the word we need will relate to "expense." Choice (B) *expenditure* is defined as "the act of using up or of paying out" and is exactly what we're looking for here. The expenditure here is the cost of importing water hundreds of miles south. Choice (A) *subsistence* is "the condition of being or managing to stay alive, especially when there is barely enough food or money for survival." Although the region is in a financial crisis, the word we need refers to the purchase of water from the north, so this is not the credited response. Choice (C) *opulence*, or "wealth or abundance," should not be used to refer to a region that is in a financial crisis.

The next sentence gives another matter of concern: the water source is unreliable and could be cut off at any time. Blank (ii) refers to something that needs preparation. We can predict "situation" or "uncertainty" here. Choice (E) *contingency* is an "event that may occur in the future, especially a problem, emergency, or expense that might rise unexpectedly, and therefore needs preparation," and is the credited response. The region must prepare for the contingency that its water supply could be cut off at any time. The definition of choice (D) *pathos* is "pity or sympathy" and makes no sense in this context. Choice (F) is also unsuitable here. *Conflagration* means a "destructive fire." The region needs to prepare for the possibility that its water supply might be cut off, not for a conflagration.

Finally, we're told a specific reason the water supply could be cut off. For blank (iii), we need a word to describe what damage an earthquake could do to a levee, like "fracture." Choice (H) to *rupture* means "to break, tear, or burst something." In this case, the levees would be ruptured by a natural catastrophe such as an earthquake, so this is what we're looking for. Choice (G) to *expunge* is "to obliterate or eradicate." An earthquake would most likely damage the levees but not completely obliterate them. Choice (I) to *protuberate* means "to swell or bulge" beyond the surrounding surface. An earthquake would cause a break, not swelling, in the levees.

The correct answers are (B), (E), and (H).

56. C, E, H

The clues in the first sentence make the first blank easiest to predict. The two explorers found "not only" what they had come to find "but also" the ruins of a city. Therefore we can predict a positive word for the first blank. Choice (C) *propitious*, which means "favorable," has a positive word charge and is correct. Choice (A) *adverse*, meaning "harmful" or "unfavorable," and choice (B) *calamitous*, or "disastrous," both have negative meanings and are therefore incorrect.

Because the city described by the second blank was found by the two explorers "deep" in the rain forest, we can predict that the city was "difficult to find" or "previously unseen." Choice (E) *clandestine*, which means "hidden," matches our prediction and is the correct answer. Choices (D) *unexceptional*, or "ordi-

nary," and (F) *unillustrious*, or "not memorable," would both indicate that the city's discovery was unremarkable, a reality that contradicts the idea that the explorers' discovery was "incredible." Both (D) and (F) are therefore incorrect.

Since the two explorers were "previously unknown" prior to their discoveries, we can predict that the men "went on to enjoy" a state that contrasts positively with their previous anonymity. Choice (H) *prominence*, which means "importance" or "distinction," fulfills this prediction and is correct. Choice (G) *rejection* is a negative word that means the men were "refused" in some way, which is not supported by the context. Choice (I) *affluence* or "wealth" is a tempting choice; however, we do not have any clues in the sentence to indicate that the men profited financially from their discovery.

The correct answers are (C), (E), and (H).

57. C, E

The road sign "not [this], but [that]" in the first part of the sentence tells us that we need to fill the first blank with a word that is roughly synonymous with "sources"; the sentence lists two sets of sources, one incorrect and one correct. Choice (C) *culprits* means "those responsible for a fault" and fits this context by personifying the causes of procrastination. This is the correct answer. Choice (A) *hedges* means "evasions" or "excuses," which might be offered by procrastinators, but it is not synonymous with "sources," so it is incorrect. Choice (B) *fixtures* are "features so common to a situation that they are expected to be present." *Fixtures* is not a synonym for "sources," so this choice is also incorrect.

The second blank asks for a word that describes a person "facing a daunting task" who is likely to procrastinate rather than starting right away. Choice (E) *diffidently* means "reluctantly" or "lacking confidence" and describes a person in this situation, so this is the correct response. Choice (D) *adeptly*, which means "capably" or "ably," is not supported by the sentence's context, which describes a situation in which failure seems more likely than success. Hence, choice (D) is incorrect. Choice (F) *collaboratively* means "acting in coordinated effort with others"; the sentence does not suggest that a person should face a daunting task with others, so this choice is also incorrect.

The correct answers are (C) and (E).

58. C, F

The phrase "despite . . . views" implies that the two blanks will deal with Allison's political views, and "in contrast" tells us that the two words will be opposites. "Traditional political views" is the concrete term we're given, so work backwards from it. The "despite" lets us know that Allison initially went against her parents' traditional political views; therefore, the second blank is best filled with choice (F) *liberal.* Choice (D) *gregarious* means "drawn to the company of others, or sociable." This sentence discusses Allison's political preferences, not her personality traits. Choice (E) *inexorable* means unyielding. Although it is possible that Allison was inexorable during her teen and young adult years, a word that better expresses Allison's political viewpoint fits better with this sentence. Neither (D) or (E) fits in this context.

Returning to the first blank, we want to find the choice that describes the opposite of liberalism, since her younger years are "in contrast" with the later ones. Choice (C) *conservatism* fits here. Choice (A) *militance* is defined as "a combative aggressiveness." Some governments can be described as militant, but this blank should be filled with a word that more specifically describes one typical political perspective. Choice (B) *alacrity* is eagerness or speed. Key words in the sentence tell us that the subject is Allison's political leanings, and this choice is not directly related to politics.

Choices (C) and (F) are the credited responses.

59. C

We need to find a word that shows that the law firms are concerned more with billing hours than supporting their attorneys. Choice (C) is what we're looking for. It makes sense that an *emphasis* on billable hours would make career development a lower priority. None of the other choices work. It's idiomatically incorrect to say that there would be "*scrutiny* on" something; the correct phrase would be "scrutiny of." "*Turmoil* on billable hours" doesn't make sense, since *turmoil* is "a state of great commotion or disturbance." *Decimation* means "the act of destroying something," and that doesn't make any sense here. And "*intrusion* on billable hours" also doesn't make sense. Who's doing the intruding?

Choice (C) is the credited response.

60. C, F

Since the prince can only sit and stare, the word chosen to complete the sentence's first blank must be the state of being (an emotion or physical condition, for instance) that caused that condition. Choice (C) *stupefied* means "astonished or shocked" or "made (someone) unable to think or feel properly" and fits perfectly here. Choice (A) *vitalized* or "animated" does not correspond with the prince sitting down and staring and is opposite to what we're looking for. Choice (B) is similarly incorrect. *Exhilarated* does not describe the Prince's reaction since it means "to be happy, animated, or elated."

The second blank follows the contrast word "without," so the correct answer must refer to moving a muscle. Choice (F) is the credited response. Someone who is sitting for a full half-hour staring foolishly is not making an *effort* to move. Choice (D) is incorrect; there is no logical connection between sitting staring foolishly for a half hour and not taking an "aspirin." Finally, choice (E) *interest* is not idiomatically correct here.

61. C, D, G

This passage discusses the relevance of teachers relating to the perspective of a non-native English speaker, which may come from his or her cultural background and American influences. Choice (C) *schema* appropriately describes the structure of knowledge and assumptions we use to interpret the world and is the credited choice for blank (i). *Schema* can be deeply influenced by background and affects the way people view the world. Choice (A) *perspicacity* means "shrewdness or perceptiveness." A more general term meaning plan or theory should be used instead. Choice (B) is also incorrect. A *platitude* is an "uninspired remark or cliche," and thus not a mental structure from which people view the world.

We can predict that blank (ii) will be a synonym for differences (between different immigrant neighborhoods from the same culture), since these would account for a teacher's inability to know a student's cultural perspective based on general research. Choice (D) *divergences between*, or "differences between two or more things," is the choice that best matches this prediction. Perspectives of English learners could diverge because of differences in immigrant neighborhoods across the United States. Neither

of the other choices works here. Choice (E) *aberrations in* are "departures from what is normal or desirable." The passage does not state that there are abnormal aspects of immigrant neighborhoods. The definition of choice (F) *ineffability in* is "the quality of being unspeakable or incapable of being expressed through words." This makes no sense in context.

The sentence before the one containing blank (iii) discusses English learners who identify less with their native cultures and are instead more influenced by popular American culture. These students show a desire to (G) *acculturate to*, or "absorb and assimilate the culture of another group." This is the credited choice. Choice (H) is incorrect. To *systematize* is "to arrange something or be arranged according to a system." While a culture could be described as a type of system, *acculturate* more specifically conveys how some students absorb American culture. Choice (I) also does not work in this context. *To ingratiate* means "to try to enter somebody's favor, especially in order to gain an advantage." Although some English learners may wish to gain favor from citizens of their new culture, they would not be gaining favor with the culture itself.

The correct choices are (C), (D), and (G).

62. C, E, G

The sentence suggests that dieters are frustrated when they reduce caloric intake: instead of losing weight, their metabolism slows. The first blank relates to slow metabolism as a "reaction" to something. Look for a word that means something like "developed." Choice (C) *evolved* shows that slow metabolism is a reaction that the body has "developed over time" and is the credited response. Choice (A) *promoted* or "advanced" does not work in context. Neither does choice (B). *Reit-*

erate means "repeat" and that doesn't make sense in the first blank.

Since slowing metabolism interferes with weight loss, look for a word that is a synonym for "hamper" for the second blank. Used as a verb, choice (E) To *foil* means "to keep a person from succeeding" and matches our prediction. A slow metabolism can foil or frustrate weight loss plans. Choice (D) is not the credited response. A slow metabolism doesn't *enhance* or "intensify" weight loss; rather it impedes it. Choice (F) *plunder* means "to steal" and makes no sense in context.

The third blank should be a synonym for "sharply" in the first sentence. Choice (G) is the credited response. *Severely*, or "extremely," makes sense here since the first sentence tells us that "the body's response to sharply reduced caloric intake is to slow the metabolism." Neither of the other choices work. Choice (H) *ambivalently* describes a manner that is "unsure" or "mixed" and is not an appropriate modifier to describe "restricting" here. Choice (I) *Immutably* means "unchangeably." Restricting caloric intake would definitely vary day to day and over time, so it could not be described as unchangeable.

Choices (C), (E), and (G) are the credited responses.

63.   C, D

Because the author likes black lace curtains on her windows and coffins for sleeping, the first missing word will relate to the author's fascination with creepy things. Choice (C) *macabre* means "gruesome" or "having to do with death," and this is the correct answer. Choice (A) *dilettantish* means "amateurish," and because we don't know anything about the author's writing ability, there are no clues in the sentence to support this choice. Choice (B) *garrulous* means "talkative." Again, there

are no clues in the sentence to support this idea that the author has a talkative disposition.

Next, turn to blank (ii). Since the home is "ornamented," the coffins will likely have some sort of decorative quality. Something relevant to the appearance of the coffins would fit. Choice (D) *ornate*, which means "elaborately decorated," fits as a descriptor of the coffins and is the correct answer. Choice (E) *amiable* means "friendly" and is not a logical adjective to use to describe a coffin. Choice (F) *innocuous* means "harmless," and though there is no reason to assume the coffins are harmful, there isn't any information in the sentence declaring them harmless, either. It should be noted that a prediction such as "creepy" might also make sense, but there are no words meaning anything close to "creepy" among the choices.

Choices (C) and (D) are the credited responses.

64.   B, F

The detour road sign "however" tells us that there is a contrast between "photographs and toys" and "numerous attacks." The photos and toys suggest that pandas would not attack, so we can predict "gentle" for our first blank. Choice (B) *docile*, or "easily managed," matches this perfectly. Choice (A) *endangered*, or "threatened," might be a true description of the panda, but nothing in this passage suggests this. Likewise, pandas may be (C) *elusive* or "cleverly evasive," but even if they are, that word does not match the context clues of our sentence.

The second blank, which modifies "belief," will relate to the "widespread belief" that the panda is docile. Since pandas attack people when approached, they are not peaceful or docile, so we can predict this belief is "false." Choice (F) *spurious* means just this and is a great match. Choice (D) *pessimistic* is a trap that a test taker might pair with *endangered*, but it means "gloomy" and doesn't fit here. Choice (E) *comical* is a distortion; while it's possible to view an incorrect belief as "funny," nothing in the sentence supports this. In fact, it is inappropriate in the context.

Choices (B) and (F) are correct.

65. C

The blank provides a general category defining a quantity that is *larger* than the "few" books on cooking in the kosher kitchen. Choices (A) *negligible*, (B) *scarce*, and (D) *scant* are opposite wrong answer choices, since they are synonymous with "few." Choice (C) *copious*, or "abundant," matches our prediction. Choice (E) *noisome*, or "offensive," is out of scope.

Choice (C) is the credited response.

66. A, E

These terms have a work:tool relationship. What would be "set" at a "little local paper," and in what kind of office would that take place?

It might be useful to start with blank (ii). Choice (E) is the credited response. In old newspaper offices, the pages were laid out by *type*. Choice (D) is out of scope: *polish* is not related to either literature or newspapers. Choice (F) is also not the credited response. The phrase "setting *opinions*" is awkward; there's a better answer among the choices.

Turning now to blank (i), choice (A) is the credited response. In old *printing* offices, newspapers were laid out by "type." Choices (B) and (C) are both out of scope. There is no logic in a small newspaper having its own *dentist's* office and there is no relationship between a *janitorial* office and "setting type."

Choices (A) and (E) are the credited responses.

67. C, E, G

We can begin by examining the first blank. We can assume that this blank will make a connection between the supplement packaging and the claim that the user will feel an increase in energy. Since it is a revitalization supplement, we can infer that the package "claimed" that the user would get an energy boost. Choice (C) *averred*, or "claimed confidently," makes sense in the first blank because the package is simply making a statement or claim. It makes sense that the package made a convincing claim that the bodybuilder believed. Choice (A) *dissembled*, meaning "misleading" or "concealed," is incorrect because nothing in the sentence suggests that the supplement package is making deceptive claims. Choice (B) *adumbrated*, or "foreshadowed vaguely," is incorrect because the package would not be so subtle in claiming that the user would receive the desired effect from the revitalization supplement.

The second blank is set off by the detour road sign "but," indicating that the results of taking the supplement contrasted with the claim made by the packaging. A good prediction for this blank would be "exhausted," which contrasts with the claim that the supplement gives the user more energy. Choice (E) *enervated*, or "weakened" or "without force or strength," is suitable for the second blank because it contrasts with the package's claims and aptly describes how the bodybuilder felt despite taking the revitalizing supplement. Choice (D) *innervated*, meaning "furnished with nerves," might be tricky because it sounds like "enervate," but it means "stimulated through or furnished with nerves" and makes no sense in the sentence, so it is incorrect. Choice (F) *quickened*, or "enlivened," is incorrect because it agrees, rather than contrasts, with the package's claims.

In the last sentence, the bodybuilder stops taking the supplement and makes a conclusion based on the fact that he felt weakened by it. A good prediction for the third blank would be "assume." Choice (G) *postulate*, or "assume without proof," makes sense in the last blank because the bodybuilder makes a guess about why the supplement makes him tired without actually having any medical tests done to confirm his idea. Choice (H) *contravene*, or "deny," is the opposite of what we need. The sentence suggests the bodybuilder believed he was allergic to the supplement. Choice (I) *exult*, or "express joy," is incorrect because the sentence does not indicate that the bodybuilder is excited that he is allergic to the energy-draining supplement.

The correct answers are (C), (E), and (G).

68.   B, F, G

We need a word for the first blank that will indicated "more than admiration." Choice (B) *idolized* communicates the idea of something more extreme than mere admiration and is the credited response. Choice (A) *suppressed* means "vanquished or withheld," which doesn't make sense in the first blank. Choice (C) *criticized* is the opposite of the kind of word we want for the first blank since Maurice is not "finding fault" with his mentor.

The second blank will be filled a with a word that goes well with the concept of so slavishly following someone's advice that others find it unsettling. "Adoration" is a good prediction. Choice (F) "slavish *devotion*" is the kind of strong attachment that others would find unsettling and is the credited response. Choice (D) *petulance* ("impatient irritation")

and choice (E) *dismay* ("disillusioned alarm") do not make sense in the second blank.

The third blank should be a name Maurice's co-workers might call him for his over-the-top commitment to his mentor. Since they use the word behind his back, we can predict something insulting like "lackey" or "minion." Choice (G) matches our prediction. It makes sense that his co-workers would call him a *sycophant*, or "someone who servilely flatters a powerful person for personal gain." Choice (H) is not is not the credited response. A *malefactor* is an "evildoer or culprit." While we are looking for a negative term, there is no support for something so extreme. Finally, choice (I) is also not the credited response. A *reprobate* is "a morally unprincipled person." There is no support for such a harsh term for the person described here.

The correct choices are (B), (F), and (G).

69.   B

The word "but" is a detour or contrast road sign, so the blank must contrast "mundane." Also, the answer choice must describe an event that would cause a "palpable commotion." Based on this, we can predict "exciting" or "revolutionary" for the blank. Choice (B) *incendiary* ("inflammatory or provocative") matches this best. None of choices (A) *banal* ("stale" or "unoriginal"), (C) *bombastic* ("pretentious, pompous"), (D) *taciturn* ("silent" or "dour"), or (E) *luminous* ("shining or bright") work in this context.

Choice (B) is the credited response.

70.   C, F

The second sentence tells us about parents concerned about "indecent" television, so the first blank will be a synonym for "prevent." Choice (C) *preclude* means "to prevent someone from doing something" and fits perfectly. Neither of the other choices work as well. Choice (A) is nonsensical in this context. While parents may want to *reduce*, or "lessen," their children's viewing of certain programming, parents do not want to reduce their actual children, which this wording implies. Choice (B) *discriminate* means "recognize or identify a difference." The sentence implies that the V-chip would prevent children from watching indecent programs, not identify them.

Since blank (ii) is followed by the prepositional phrase "for cutting out indecency from television," we are looking for a positive noun phrase. Read the choices carefully. Choice (F) *viable option* is the only positive response. Parents would want the V-chip to be a *viable* or "practical" option for cutting out indecency from television. Choices (D) and (E) both refer to "potential obstacles." *Feasible hindrance* and *possible impediment* would work if they were followed by the prepositional phrase "to children watching indecent television." As it is, they are very similar in meaning, but both can't be right.

Choices (C) and (F) are the credited responses.

71.   B

One clue in this sentence is that it is "nearly impossible" to make an error. A prediction might be that it is a *thorough* or *foolproof* system. Choice (B) *meticulous* matches the prediction.

Choice (A) *powerful* suggests that the accounting system was successful, but does not account for accuracy. Choice (C) *credulous* means "gullible or trusting." One way to figure out the meaning is to use the root CRED: to believe or to trust. Choice (D) *pedantic* is a word associated with attention to detail. However, *pedantic* is an adjective used to describe a person, rather than a

system, who shows off what he knows and emphasizes detail when explaining. Choice (E) *perfunctory* means "done in a routine or indifferent way." This is the opposite of the correct answer.

72.   C

The sentence sets up parallelism with the words "just as." Therefore, the word should be a synonym for *critics*, who share the same role in two different eras. Choice (C) *reviewers* matches our prediction. Choices (A) *experts* and (E) *pundits* are both tempting since critics know much about their fields. However, they are synonyms, so neither can be correct. Choices (B) *audiences* and (D) *directors* are both out of scope because even though they are related to plays, they do not fit the situation in the sentence.

Choice (C) is the credited response.

73.   B

The sentence tells us that there are four elements of art and that we must deal with them separately. Look for a word that suggests we "study," "investigate," or "think about" these elements. Choice (B) *consider* means to "contemplate" and matches our prediction. When someone views art, they contemplate its meaning and its individual elements.

None of the other responses is appropriate. Choice (A) *interrogate*, or "question," makes no sense in this context. Choice (C) *neglect* means "not pay attention to" and is contrary to the logic of the sentence. Choice (D) *berate* means "scold" and is an illogical choice. Finally, this sentence discusses considering the four elements that make up a piece of art, not actually creating one, so choice (E) *sketch* is not correct.

Choice (B) is the credited response.

74. C, D, G

To fill the first blank, we note the detour road sign "Whether . . . or," which indicates a contrast to "permanent fixtures." The first missing word must mean something like "not permanent." Choice (C) *conveyable* means "portable," and so describes a shrine that is not fixed in one place, as in a cathedral, but rather on the move. Thus, it is the correct answer. Choice (A) *personal*, "made for or belonging to an individual," is unsupported. There is no evidence for the notion that a reliquary was a "personal" shrine. Choice (B) *perennial* means "recurrent" or "constant" and is too close in meaning to "permanent" to be correct.

Context clues help us fill the second blank. We read that the images on reliquaries "pose mysteries," and we can deduce that the mysteries concern whose relics the container was made to hold. What must historians be doing with the images on a reliquary to solve the mystery? We can predict that they "examine" those images and try to match them to the saint the reliquary is associated with. Choice (D) *peruse*, "examine closely," describes this action and is correct. Choice (E) *reify*, or "treat something as if it had material existence," does not make sense in this context as the images already clearly exist as material things. Choice (E) is thus incorrect. Nor does choice (F) *exculpate*, "to pardon," make sense when applied to images. Hence, choice (F) is also incorrect.

The third blank is an adjective that describes the container. We know that a reliquary held the "relic of a saint" and that it was a "memorial object." Hence, we need a word that pertains to preserving the saint's memory. Answer choice (G) *commemorative*, meaning "serving as a memorial or reminder," describes the function of reliquaries well and is the correct answer. A *commemorative* container would honor the memory of a saint. Choice (H) *immense*, "very large," is incorrect because no clues in the passage indicate that the reliquaries were particularly large. In fact, those that were "conveyable" were probably not. Finally, choice (I) *utilitarian*, meaning "practical" or "down-to-earth," describes reliquaries in one sense—they had a practical use—but the word connotes a no-frills solution; reliquaries were ornate and beautiful. Hence, it cannot be correct.

Choices (C), (D), and (G) are the credited responses.

Introduction to Sentence Equivalence

You will encounter approximately four Sentence Equivalence questions in each verbal section. One word will be missing, and you must identify two correct words to complete the sentence. The correct answer choices, when used in the sentence, will fit the meaning of the sentence as a whole and create complete sentences that are similar in meaning. This question type tests your ability to figure out how a sentence should be completed by using the meaning of the entire sentence.

Aim to complete each Sentence Equivalence question in an average of 1 minute on Test Day. In order to build your skills on this question type, you must work on building your vocabulary and identifying context clues. One important thing to keep in mind when you're answering a Sentence Equivalence question on the GRE is that the correct choices are often, but are not necessarily, synonyms.

Sentence Equivalence Practice

Select the two answer choices that, when used to complete the sentence, fit the meaning of the sentence as a whole and produce completed sentences that are alike in meaning.

1. Even though many literature buffs attest to the intelligibility of Thomas Pynchon, most uninitiated readers are _____ by his novels' complex narrative structure and nonlinear chronology.

   A infuriated

   B enticed

   C undaunted

   D deterred

   E confounded

   F bewildered

2. To the viewer uneducated in the tenets of cubism, Pablo Picasso's brush strokes may seem _____, without discernible purpose or reason.

   A arbitrary

   B incalculable

   C whimsical

   D superfluous

   E deliberate

   F meticulous

3. Establishing the validity of one's authority is an important but difficult part of management; one undeserved _____ may well negate the credibility built up over a long period of time.

   A panegyric

   B censure

   C reprimand

   D catechization

   E depredation

   F spoliation

4. Workers greeted the announcement of reduced sick day allowances
_____; they were accustomed to management's capricious adoption and
abandonment of new policies.

  A disgustedly

  B impassively

  C stoically

  D enigmatically

  E pompously

  F blithely

5. In the past, dogs with similar conditions responded _____ to the
unorthodox treatment, so the veterinarian claimed it was her only viable
option.

  A naturally

  B favorably

  C rapidly

  D positively

  E poorly

  F slowly

6. Art critic Clement Greenberg was sometimes ridiculed for his dogmatic
elitism, yet despite such affronts, his theories were largely _____ by
modernists.

  A lambasted

  B extolled

  C accepted

  D understood

  E commended

  F emulated

7. The detective story that Poe invented sharply _____ itself from the
    earlier tales of mystery, and also from the later narratives in which actual
    detectives figure incidentally.

    A carves

    B compares

    C defines

    D distinguishes

    E differentiates

    F hatches

8. Since she was still _____ from her illness, Jamie was ordered by her
    physician to stay home and rest for several more days in order to prevent a
    relapse of her symptoms.

    A convalescing

    B disparaging

    C floundering

    D travailing

    E prevaricating

    F recuperating

9. It is to be expected that each generation has its own code of etiquette;
    however, the social behavior dictated by those codes can sometimes be
    _____.

    A imbecilic

    B surprising

    C deplorable

    D puerile

    E prudent

    F bewildering

10. The prisoner was noticeably agitated on the morning of his escape and, in retrospect, his fidgety movements and _____ glances should have alerted the guards to the impending foul play.

    A accusatory

    B dubious

    C surreptitious

    D objectionable

    E unsavory

    F furtive

11. After her coworkers discovered that she had attempted to blame them for the loss of trade secrets to a rival company, she was _____ completely; the resulting sense of isolation eventually forced her to find a job with a different firm.

    A apprised

    B shunned

    C esteemed

    D delineated

    E ostracized

    F attenuated

12. The reliability of meteorologists remains dubious to most people, because weather itself is _____; no matter how meticulously a prediction is researched or how certain it may initially appear, no one can portend with perfect accuracy something that is fundamentally mercurial.

    A unambiguous

    B homogeneous

    C transparent

    D capricious

    E erratic

    F laconic

13. She had _____ about going to the amusement park during the busiest part of the summer, since she was unhappy with the prospect of crowded midways and long waits on line for rides.

   A provisions

   B qualms

   C conniptions

   D nescience

   E misgivings

   F transgressions

14. Jon was a skilled chef and had learned many techniques from various ethnic traditions that he incorporated into his cuisine, creating a _____ of flavors.

   A division

   B mélange

   C quagmire

   D fusion

   E morass

   F myriad

15. Eleanor knew that she had to confront her students about the poor performance of the entire class on the last examination; realizing, though, that after her remonstration they would undoubtedly be glum or resentful, she took a final moment to enjoy their _____ chatter before she began to speak.

   A dogmatic

   B blithe

   C erudite

   D beguiling

   E mirthful

   F innocuous

16. Unaccustomed to the _____ conditions near the top of the peak, John felt unwell and was forced to take a break.

    A vertiginous

    B soporific

    C exacting

    D placid

    E excruciating

    F nauseating

17. After being bedridden for months, James found that his muscles had atrophied, which initially _____ his ability to walk or lift heavy objects.

    A belittled

    B castigated

    C hampered

    D bolstered

    E curtailed

    F improved

18. _____ regimes were commonplace in the ancient world; even the philosophies of Plato, which inspired many aspects of the US Constitution, espoused the idea of a dictatorship, albeit benign, as the ideal form of government.

    A Institutional

    B Autocratic

    C Oligarchic

    D Despotic

    E Anarchist

    F Celestial

19. The symphony, which critics regarded as self-indulgent, inconsistent, and technically clumsy, reflected the young composer's real but still _____ talents.

    A pedestrian

    B exceptional

    C underdeveloped

    D egregious

    E immature

    F ordinary

20. Pundits were quick to say that the mayor's stance on environmental reform was far too _____; she easily relinquished her already minimal resolve to avoid confrontation.

    A temperate

    B craven

    C timid

    D moderate

    E self-serving

    F radical

21. By the fifth sequel, the director had become _____ in his delivery; even the most die-hard fans of the series lost interest.

    A convoluted

    B cautious

    C remedial

    D perfunctory

    E unpleasant

    F mundane

22. Throughout the contemporary composer's most famous symphony, the tempos and chord progressions seemed _____, unpredictably changing without reason.

    A erratic

    B saturnine

    C irascible

    D spontaneous

    E inimitable

    F mercurial

23. After the accident, the patient initially made rapid progress; unfortunately, his injuries retarded the recovery of his muscular coordination and _____ his ability to speak, frustrating his caregivers.

    A animated

    B dispelled

    C unsettled

    D inhibited

    E impaired

    F augmented

24. After a 12-year imprisonment under false treason charges, Alfred Dreyfus was justly _____, effectively putting an end to the French political scandal known as the Dreyfus Affair.

    A abrogated

    B exonerated

    C acquitted

    D interred

    E assassinated

    F shunned

25. North America prior to 1500 was home to hundreds of distinct cultural groups, and each one was characterized by its own language, mythology, and social mores; the idea of a single "Native American" culture is _____ by that diversity.

    A implicated

    B belittled

    C proven

    D contradicted

    E demonstrated

    F negated

26. Although his association with Olivia Wharton has brought his ideas into the mainstream, some of Dr. Stephen Garner's more _____ theories are still not accepted by all of his peers.

    A controversial

    B demanding

    C famous

    D divisive

    E endemic

    F conducive

27. When my health began to _____, I started keeping a journal in which I chronicled my increasingly labored breathing and ever-present fatigue.

   A degenerate

   B deride

   C develop

   D diminish

   E distribute

   F daunt

28. Because she was famed for her objectivity and temperate attitude, the _____ offered by the news anchor at the protest rally seemed especially uncharacteristic.

   A account

   B accolades

   C invective

   D diatribe

   E perspective

   F insinuations

29. After receiving _____ welcome from the engineering team, the new employee thought this potentially daunting vocational transition turned out to be quite pleasant.

   A an intimidating

   B a comforting

   C a stolid

   D an impassioned

   E a reassuring

   F a discouraging

30. It was easy to explain the haughty teenager's impertinent behavior and limitless desires; she was _____ throughout her childhood, and no whim was ever denied her.

   A tolerated

   B cosseted

   C borne

   D exculpated

   E dandled

   F moderated

31. Even after repeated viewings, the narrative details in Ingmar Bergman's films remain _____, never restricted to univocal interpretations.

    A desultory

    B disjointed

    C multitudinous

    D unequivocal

    E polysemous

    F ambiguous

32. The event planner did not see planning parties as the _____ of her job; those occasions were merely one component of her work, which included client and vendor relations as well.

    A highlight

    B disadvantage

    C sum

    D irony

    E totality

    F incentive

33. No matter how justified the usually mild and considerate Ms. Branson was in her comments, given the predicament she found herself in due to the committee's incompetence, her _____ remarks were out of character.

    A bemused

    B discerning

    C portentous

    D vitriolic

    E discriminating

    F rancorous

34. Onomatopoeia, the formation of words that are _____ of their referents, is sometimes used in advertising to evoke specific associations; one well-known example is the "Plop, plop, fizz, fizz" jingle used by Alka-Seltzer.

    A reminiscent

    B verbose

    C evocative

    D garrulous

    E latent

    F tractable

35. The protest at the capital yesterday was an absolute _____; while the activists had the best of intentions, the demonstration showed a complete lack of organization and was actually counterproductive to their cause.

   A stalemate

   B debacle

   C impasse

   D fiasco

   E obstacle

   F enigma

36. Some music historians believe that American jazz played such a vital role in the development of amorphous musical structure because of the possibility of _____ resulting from jazz musicians' ability to form endless combinations of improvised solos and chord progressions.

   A uniformity

   B diversity

   C mellifluousness

   D variety

   E harmony

   F aggregations

37. While Mr. Hamilton's extensive support for the victims of the flood seemed _____, his motives were likely rooted in his need for publicity, since he is a candidate for mayor.

   A miserly

   B abashed

   C altruistic

   D solemn

   E outlandish

   F philanthropic

38. As my musical ability began to _____, I logged my progress in my journal, describing the mellifluous melodies and harmonies that seemed to spontaneously flow from my fingertips.

    [A] wither

    [B] advance

    [C] deteriorate

    [D] erupt

    [E] subside

    [F] improve

39. Though it seems to propagandize a communist ideology, upon close inspection, the philosopher's 1909 treatise _____ his notorious involvement in Leninist communism.

    [A] belied

    [B] antedated

    [C] catalyzed

    [D] adumbrated

    [E] delineated

    [F] predated

40. Rarely aggressive, Sheila often avoids conflict, but once somebody attacks her beliefs, she becomes a noble warrior, channeling a latent _____.

    [A] passivity

    [B] pugnacity

    [C] rancor

    [D] assertiveness

    [E] docility

    [F] bellicosity

41. Far from _____ the more belligerent parties involved in the delicate negotiation, the mayor's most recent proposal incensed even the more moderate members of the negotiating teams.

    [A] mollifying

    [B] acknowledging

    [C] appeasing

    [D] aggravating

    [E] aggrieving

    [F] ejecting

42. Only by refusing to acknowledge years of overspending and exorbitant bonuses could experts reason that a cash bailout would result in anything other than _____ solution to the corporation's economic crisis.

    Ⓐ a permanent

    Ⓑ a haphazard

    Ⓒ a fleeting

    Ⓓ an efficacious

    Ⓔ a futile

    Ⓕ a transitory

43. The Supreme Court has found that certain guarantees in the Bill of Rights have a _____ that extends those rights beyond the limits of the text and creates a degree of uncertainty about how far Constitutional protection extends.

    Ⓐ curtailment

    Ⓑ distortion

    Ⓒ significance

    Ⓓ hypocorism

    Ⓔ penumbra

    Ⓕ vagueness

44. Some experts argue that the diagnostic criteria used by psychiatrists and psychologists to identify borderline personality disorder do not sufficiently describe the pathological moods that accompany the condition, which can range from misery to ecstasy; they claim that because the sufferer's erratic emotions could be underestimated and mistaken for a mere _____ spirit, misdiagnosis is common.

    Ⓐ pompous

    Ⓑ capricious

    Ⓒ perplexing

    Ⓓ evident

    Ⓔ mercurial

    Ⓕ depressive

45. Critics felt that the candidate was far too _____; he did not easily concede a point and relished the chance to be drawn into confrontation.
    - A temperate
    - B feisty
    - C meek
    - D pugnacious
    - E stalwart
    - F doughty

46. Not only was his braggadocio boring, but his claims were _____; he obviously lacked the intellectual savvy to serve on the judiciary committee, and I suspected that he lacked the credentials as well.
    - A incoherent
    - B spurious
    - C flippant
    - D conversant
    - E bogus
    - F blasphemous

47. Known for their devotion to their masters, dogs were often used as symbols of _____ in Medieval and Renaissance paintings.
    - A treachery
    - B opulence
    - C allegiance
    - D fidelity
    - E antiquity
    - F valor

48. Due to the low voter turnout, reporters described the storm's effect as _____ to both campaigns.
    - A harmful
    - B benign
    - C inconsequential
    - D calamitous
    - E deleterious
    - F beneficial

49. Considering the surfeit of information churned out by news websites, we have to turn to _____ accounts in order to stay abreast of current events.

    A downplayed

    B arresting

    C lyrical

    D synoptic

    E abundant

    F abbreviated

50. The girl's composure was astounding given her youthfulness; _____ and self-possessed, she clearly had no predilection for confusing exhilaration with contentment.

    A nonplussed

    B demure

    C contrite

    D decorous

    E lethargic

    F apathetic

51. Public transportation offers an environmentally friendly and cost-efficient alternative to driving, particularly in crowded urban areas; however, the _____ schedules of the buses and trains makes them an undesirable option to many commuters.

    A malevolent

    B saturnine

    C viscous

    D inconsistent

    E fluctuant

    F vicious

52. Although her friends dreaded the onset of tax season, Jane's _____ nature forced her to keep carefully organized records throughout the year, and she was able to quickly and easily fill out the complex forms.

    A assiduous

    B mathematical

    C fastidious

    D chary

    E punctilious

    F calculating

53. He worked on his presentation all night without sleeping, and felt that his energy was completely _____; nonetheless, he went to the gym before work in the morning, just as he always did.

    A wretched

    B depleted

    C exhausted

    D buttressed

    E desiccated

    F irascible

54. Only one thing could _____ Dan's ability to get to the meeting on time: the terrible traffic on the freeway.

    A augment

    B antecede

    C augur

    D venerate

    E hinder

    F impede

55. Joel's _____ demeanor toward the boss should not be interpreted as sycophancy; he is just as warm and friendly with everybody else in the office.

    A indifferent

    B professional

    C amicable

    D boorish

    E obsequious

    F affable

56. The formerly flexible and adaptable New Deal economic strategies underwent a slow _____ as bureaucracy transformed them into rigid policies.

- [A] deterioration
- [B] resurrection
- [C] ossification
- [D] calibration
- [E] preservation
- [F] obsolescence

57. It was the CEO's view that her corporation's reputation would be _____ by the proposed ad campaign, so she elected to fire the current advertising company and bring in a new one.

- [A] sullied
- [B] augmented
- [C] enhanced
- [D] transformed
- [E] altered
- [F] marred

58. While the physicist's argument does contain some innovative notions, we can hardly characterize his work as _____.

- [A] conventional
- [B] novel
- [C] pioneering
- [D] commonplace
- [E] frivolous
- [F] unoriginal

59. Our government's commitment to democracy encourages many of the country's leaders to _____ despotic regimes in public pronouncements; however, some of these same regimes have privately received aid from our government in the interest of national security.

- [A] disparage
- [B] castigate
- [C] obviate
- [D] eulogize
- [E] espouse
- [F] ameliorate

60. Jarring, subversive, and experimental, the films of director Jean-Luc Godard shook the foundation of classical Hollywood style with a thoroughly _____ approach to cinema.

    A revolutionary

    B unusual

    C conventional

    D fascinating

    E conservative

    F radical

61. He now carefully _____ the tail from the body of the kite, being very particular to undo all the tangles near the tassel.

    A crumpled

    B unfolded

    C pleated

    D attached

    E uncreased

    F twisted

62. The speed with which an Internet user can now communicate with people all over the world has led to _____ advances in information management.

    A antediluvian

    B obsolescent

    C revolutionary

    D eclectic

    E innovative

    F inchoate

63. Many people see the 1980s as the apex of greed and decadence, and point to the stereotypical "yuppie" as the _____ of that decade.

    A transmutation

    B constitution

    C anachronism

    D justification

    E personification

    F embodiment

64. Although the researcher knew that her claims might be viewed as audacious and would be difficult to corroborate, their _____ was sufficient to motivate her continued work in the field.

   A adulteration

   B enigma

   C verisimilitude

   D laudability

   E erudition

   F authenticity

65. While the path leading to the lake was no longer open to the public, the trampled undergrowth was a _____ the plethora of hikers who had passed through the formerly pristine forest over the years.

   A deference to

   B repercussion of

   C precursor to

   D consequence of

   E harbinger of

   F souvenir from

66. Though now considered a linchpin of conservative politics, the speech was originally intended to _____ socially and economically liberal ideals.

   A crystallize

   B disseminate

   C obscure

   D promulgate

   E castigate

   F placate

67. Hannah and Louise appear to refute the hypothesis that the shared genetic code of identical twins creates duplicate personalities, as Hannah has never been inclined to stray far from her small farming town in Nebraska, while Louise has a _____ for travel and often derides her sister's provincialism.

    A premonition

    B penance

    C precedent

    D prerogative

    E penchant

    F proclivity

68. Although the couch had appeared imposing in the furniture store, once it was installed in the living room it seemed _____ by the grandeur of that room's high ceiling and sumptuous décor.

    A absconded

    B minimized

    C obviated

    D rarefied

    E diminished

    F depicted

69. Marilyn never had any _____ attracting attention with her good looks, but in the company of intellectuals, she was often overlooked and ignored, despite her sharp wit and interesting ideas.

    A trouble

    B luck

    C pleasure in

    D damage from

    E difficulty

    F reservations about

70. Our gracious host was _____ of hospitality, even though she had been raised by notoriously asocial parents who were far more likely to retreat to the privacy of their home than to entertain their neighbors with kindness and home-cooked meals.

    A the antithesis

    B the personification

    C a champion

    D a maverick

    E the bane

    F the epitome

71. Maria had successfully navigated complex literary tomes that would have intimidated some scholars, yet she had difficulty following the incoherent plot of this particular book, as, in her opinion, it was far too _____ to be readable.

    A monotonous

    B fallacious

    C chaotic

    D disjointed

    E erroneous

    F complicated

72. Advances in medical genetics have been largely successful in diagnosing and alleviating genetic disorders, yet despite such progress, deadly diseases like cystic fibrosis and Huntington's disease claim _____ number of lives each year.

    A a staggering

    B a considerable

    C a substantial

    D an inconsequential

    E a minuscule

    F a negligible

73. When my mental acuity began to _____, I took up crossword puzzles and brainteasers, hoping the cerebral exercise would delay the onset of senility.

   A atrophy

   B regress

   C enervate

   D wane

   E acquiesce

   F digress

74. Nigel was usually a model of equanimity, so his _____ demeanor during the attorney's cross-examination left many surprised.

   A staid

   B sedate

   C testy

   D placid

   E discomposed

   F jubilant

Answers and explanations begin on the next page.

Answer Key

SENTENCE EQUIVALENCE PRACTICE

1.	E, F	**26.**	A, D	**51.**	D, E
2.	A, C	**27.**	A, D	**52.**	C, E
3.	B, C	**28.**	C, D	**53.**	B, C
4.	B, C	**29.**	B, E	**54.**	E, F
5.	B, D	**30.**	B, E	**55.**	C, F
6.	B, E	**31.**	E, F	**56.**	C, F
7.	D, E	**32.**	C, E	**57.**	A, F
8.	A, F	**33.**	D, F	**58.**	B, C
9.	B, F	**34.**	A, C	**59.**	A, B
10.	C, F	**35.**	B, D	**60.**	A, F
11.	B, E	**36.**	B, D	**61.**	B, E
12.	D, E	**37.**	C, F	**62.**	C, E
13.	B, E	**38.**	B, F	**63.**	E, F
14.	B, D	**39.**	B, F	**64.**	C, F
15.	B, E	**40.**	B, F	**65.**	B, D
16.	A, F	**41.**	A, C	**66.**	B, D
17.	C, E	**42.**	C, F	**67.**	E, F
18.	B, D	**43.**	E, F	**68.**	B, E
19.	C, E	**44.**	B, E	**69.**	A, E
20.	B, C	**45.**	B, D	**70.**	B, F
21.	D, F	**46.**	B, E	**71.**	C, D
22.	A, F	**47.**	C, D	**72.**	B, C
23.	D, E	**48.**	A, E	**73.**	A, D
24.	B, C	**49.**	D, F	**74.**	C, E
25.	D, F	**50.**	B, D		

Answers and Explanations

SENTENCE EQUIVALENCE PRACTICE

1. E, F

The use of "even though" signals a contrast between the blank—which describes how uninitiated readers feel about Pynchon's complexity—and the opinion that his fiction is "intelligible," or comprehensible. Thus, we must assume that the uninitiated readers find Pynchon's novels to be difficult, intimidating, or confusing. (E) *confounded* and (F) *bewildered* mean "confused."

2. A, C

If Picasso's brush strokes may seem to be "without discernible purpose or reason," then we need a word that encapsulates this phrase, which elaborates on (and thus defines) our blank. Words like "capricious" or "impulsive" are good predictions for the correct choices. *Arbitrary* means "based on random choice or whim, without reason." *Whimsical* means "determined by chance or impulse." (A) and (C) are correct.

3. B, C

This question is tough on two levels: the vocabulary is difficult and the sentence's structure doesn't really tell you if the words for the blank will have a positive or negative charge. A good first step is to try to figure out which words among the answer choices are synonyms. (B) *censure* is an expression of disapproval or rebuke, and is synonymous with (C) *reprimand* in this context. (F) *spoliation* is a synonym for (E) *depredation*, an act of plundering, robbing, or ravaging. This is too strong for the present context.

4. B, C

Reduced sick day allowances are likely to be considered a bad thing, but the workers here know that management has impulsive or changeable (capricious) tendencies when it comes to adopting or abandoning policies. Therefore, we'd expect them to show little reaction. *Impassively* means "without emotion," and is a good word to describe the employees here. *Stoically* means "accepting of what happens without complaining or showing emotion." Since they were accustomed to the unfair policies of their management, they were used to accepting these changes. (B) and (C) are correct.

5. B, D

If the veterinarian claimed that the unorthodox treatment was her only "viable option," meaning it was her only chance for a successful treatment, we can infer that dogs in similar conditions responded "well" to the treatment. Look for words that indicate a positive response to the treatment. Responding *favorably* to the treatment suggests that the dogs' conditions improved. Like *favorably*, *positively* suggests that the dogs' conditions improved with treatment. (B) and (D) are correct.

6. B, E

The use of "despite" signals a contrast between the blank (which describes how modernists viewed Greenberg) and the ridicule he received from others. Thus, we need our blank to mean the opposite of "ridiculed." We should look for a work that means close to "praised." *Commended*, a close synonym of *extolled*, means "praised."

Commended and *extolled* produce sentences alike in meaning. (B) and (E) are correct.

7. D, E

There's a clue here in the word "from," used soon after the blank. Do you attach, support, or do other "positive" actions "from" something? No. You separate, *distinguish*, or depart "from" things. *Differentiate* means to "distinguish or make/draw a distinction." Note that the sentence compares Poe's detective tales with earlier mystery stories and later detective narratives. (D) and (E) are correct.

8. A, F

The word "still" tells us that Jamie's illness has already begun; she is either still suffering from it or is recovering. We see from the phrase "prevent a relapse of her symptoms" that the symptoms have abated; therefore, we can conclude that Jamie is getting over her illness. Look for words that describe that for the blank. *Recuperating* means "recovering from sickness," and has the same meaning in this sentence as *convalescing*. (A) and (F) are correct.

9. B, F

By using the word "however," this sentence sets up a contrast between "expected" and the word that fills in the blank. Look for a word that means the opposite of "expected." Something *surprising* would be in contrast to something expected. *Bewildering* is an antonym for "expected." (B) and (F) are correct.

10. C, F

In the second part of the sentence, "in retrospect" combined with "should have" is a straight-ahead road sign that tells us that the second idea in this clause should logically follow from the first idea. We can assume that the prisoner's agitation had looked suspicious and that, like his fidgety movements, his glances conveyed guilt. Therefore, we can predict that the missing word has a meaning similar to "sly" or "sneaky."

Next, we must review the answer choices to see which two match our prediction. Choices (C) *surreptitious* and (F) *furtive*, which mean "secretive" or "sneaky," fit our prediction well and are the correct answers.

11. B, E

In this sentence, context is key; the unnamed "she" here did something bad—trying to blame something on her coworkers—and the outcome was similarly bad, resulting in a "sense of isolation." Whatever words go in the blank, they will indicate that something negative happened to her that made her feel isolated. *Ostracized* is synonymous with *shunned*, which fits well in this sentence. (B) and (E) are correct.

12. D, E

There are two important clues here. The reliability of meteorologists is *dubious*, or questionable, and that is because weather can't be predicted with perfect accuracy. Weather is fundamentally *mercurial*, or changeable. Therefore, the words for the blank will indicate that weather is unpredictable or changeable. *Capricious* means "fickle" or "changeable," which are synonyms of *erratic*. (D) and (E) are correct.

13. B, E

The key here is the word "unhappy," because the structure and meaning of the sentence suggest that the words for the blank will echo that term. Logically, she wouldn't have joy or pleasure about something that made her unhappy, so we know that we're looking for words that suggest a negative perspective. Synonymous with *qualms*, *misgivings* are feelings of apprehension or doubt. (B) and (E) are correct.

14. B, D

Since Jon was a skilled chef, it seems likely that his food would be tasty; therefore, we know that the words in the blank will be positive. Moreover, since he's incorporating many different styles of cooking, his flavors would be made up of different components. A *mélange* is a blending or *fusion*, and is a word that is often used in the context of food. (B) and (D) are correct.

15. B, E

Note the contrast in this sentence: after Eleanor remonstrates ("scolds") her class, they will be glum and resentful. These negative words indicate that the words for the blank will be positive, and will also have to plausibly describe "chatter." *Mirthful* is a synonym for *blithe*, meaning "extremely joyous," and its positive connotations work well in this sentence. Choices (B) and (E) are correct.

16. A, F

Remember that for Sentence Equivalence questions the correct answers are not necessarily exact synonyms of one another. This particular sentence states that John wasn't used to the conditions at the top of the peak, and, consequently, he was feeling ill. So we know that the conditions at the high altitude of the peak make people feel sick. Let's predict "sickening" for the blank.

Looking at the choices, we notice choices (A) *vertiginous*, which means "dizzying," and (F) *nauseating*, which means "sickening." While not exact synonyms, they create similar sentences; therefore, these are the correct answers.

17. C, E

Knowing the meaning of the challenging word within the sentence itself makes all the difference here, although context could supply sufficient clues. Muscles that have *atrophied* have wasted away, which makes sense after someone was stuck in bed for months. Wasted muscles would make physical action tough. Look for words that mean "to limit or interfere" with the ability to walk or lift heavy objects. Something that is *curtailed* is limited, and that's equivalent to being *hampered* in this context. (C) and (E) are correct.

18. B, D

The semicolon functions as a straight-ahead road sign indicating that the missing word will describe a form of government similar to the dictatorship described in the second half of the sentence. A dictator is a single ruler who is the focus of power in a political structure. We can predict a word like "dictatorial" for the blank, so we should look for descriptions of political structures that concentrate power in a single figure.

Choice (B) *Autocratic*, or "governed by a single ruler," matches our prediction and is correct. Choice (D) *Despotic*, or "ruled by a single person with absolute power," is also a good description of a dictatorship, so this is the second correct answer.

19. C, E

Because critics thought the symphony was "self-indulgent, inconsistent, and technically clumsy," we can assume that the symphony revealed the composer's unsatisfactory or inadequate talents. And further, the word "still" tells us that these "real" talents have room to grow, but at the moment, they are "still" inadequate. In this context, *immature*—like *underdeveloped*—means "not yet fully developed," and so it denotes both the inadequacy of the composer's talents and the potential to improve. (C) and (E) are correct.

20. B, C

This sentence's straight-ahead road sign, the semicolon, indicates that the theme in one clause is mirrored in the other. You can see that pundits considered the mayor's stance on environmental reform on a par with her "minimal resolve" and desire to "avoid confrontation." The synonyms you're looking for need to reflect that weakness, and the choices that best fit the sentence are (B) *craven* and (C) *timid*, meaning "cowardly" or "easily frightened."

21. D, F

Use the key phrase "lost interest" to determine the tone of the word in the blank. The semicolon between the two phrases acts as a straight-ahead road sign. You need a negative word to describe the director's work as "rote" or "boring." *Perfunctory* means "lacking in interest or enthusiasm," which makes sense here. *Mundane* means "in a routine manner." (D) and (F) are correct.

22. A, F

If the tempos and chord progressions were "unpredictably changing without reason," we need a word that suggests "unpredictable change." Words like "fickle" or "volatile" are good predictions. *Mercurial* means "changing often; very changeable," and so it means the same thing as *erratic* in this context. (A) and (F) are correct.

23. D, E

The detour road sign "unfortunately" indicates that the second clause will have a contrasting meaning to the first clause. Since the first clause deals with the patient's "rapid progress," the detour road sign leads us to predict that the patient's condition will

worsen. In addition, the fact that his recovery was "retarded," or "slowed down," tells us to look for a negative word to describe the effect of the injury on his ability to speak. We can predict that the patient's ability to speak was "damaged" or "constrained."

Answer choices (D) *inhibited*, meaning "hindered," and (E) *impaired*, meaning "damaged," both mean something similar to "constrained" and are therefore correct.

24. B, C

The key phrase "imprisonment under false charges" and keyword "justly" indicate that Dreyfus was likely released from prison. A good prediction would be that Dreyfus was justly "freed." *Exonerated* means "freed from guilt," and a*cquitted* means "found not guilty." (B) and (C) are correct.

25. D, F

This sentence compares the "idea of a single . . . culture," to the reality of "hundreds of distinct cultural groups." We need to find a word that explains that the reality disproved the idea. Reality was in opposition to, or *contradicted*, the idea of a single culture. Diversity would *negate* the "idea of a single . . . culture." (D) and (F) are correct.

26. A, D

Look for a word that would describe something not accepted by one's peers, and in contrast to "mainstream," as the word "although" indicates. *Controversial* means "causing dispute or debate," and would describe theories of the kind mentioned in the sentence. *Divisive* means "causing disagreement or hostility within a group," and would describe ideas that are accepted by some but rejected by others. (A) and (D) are correct.

27. A, D

Pay attention to the second part of this sentence to decode the first part. "Increasingly labored breathing" and "ever-present fatigue" would indicate that someone is unwell and becoming more so. Therefore, we need to look for words that mean "decrease" or something similar. *Diminish* means "lessen or decrease," and has a meaning similar to that of *degenerate* in this context. (A) and (D) are correct.

28. C, D

In this sentence, a contrast exists between the news anchor's usual attitude, described by keywords as "objective" and "temperate," and her "uncharacteristic" behavior. So you need synonyms for "a strong position" that also have a negative connotation. *Invective* means "violent or vehement denunciation", and is a suitable contrast to "objectivity" or "temperate attitude." A *diatribe* is a "bitter or abusive attack" and fits this context. (C) and (D) are correct.

29. B, E

If the employee's "vocational transition turned out to be quite pleasant," then we can assume that he received a warm welcome from the engineering team. Look for positive words that will reproduce the meaning of "warm welcome," especially words that suggest relief from anxiety (after all, transitioning to the new job was a "potentially daunting" experience). *Reassuring* means restoring confidence and relieving anxiety, so it has a similar meaning to *comforting* in this context. (B) and (E) are correct.

30. B, E

Note the straight-ahead road sign in the semicolon. It tells us that the thought expressed in the first part of the sentence, the teenager's haughty attitude, will be borne out in the second half. It also tells us that the negative charge in the first half of the sentence will continue in the second. So we're looking for a word that reflects poorly on the teenager. Based on these clues, we can infer that the teenager's "limitless desires" were a result of her being spoiled her whole life. One of our answer choices—(F) *dandled*—is a high-level vocabulary word whose meaning we may not know, so we need to examine the other choices carefully. Like *cosseted*, *dandled* means "pampered." Choices (B) and (E) are correct.

31. E, F

If the narrative details in Bergman's films are "never restricted to univocal (having one meaning) interpretations," then the word we are looking for must suggest "having more than one meaning." Look for a word that denotes the characteristic of having more than one meaning or interpretation. Formally speaking, *polysemous* describes words that have multiple meanings. Broadly speaking, it can also refer to a more general characteristic of having multiple meanings or interpretations. *Ambiguous* means "open to more than one interpretation." (E) and (F) are correct.

32. C, E

In this sentence, we need a word that is a contrast to "merely one component," since the placement of the semicolon indicates that the second part of the sentence elaborates on the idea in the first part. *Sum* contrasts with the idea of "merely one component," as does *totality*. (C) and (E) are correct.

33. D, F

The context clues "no matter how justified" and "out of character" signal a contrast in the tone of Branson's remarks with her customary demeanor, which is "temperate" and "considerate." Since Branson's comments were occasioned by "incompetence," we expect negative commentary. We anticipate that the missing word will be an antonym of "temperate" and "considerate," and predict words consistent with "hotheaded" or "scathing."

Choices (D) *vitriolic* and (F) *rancorous* both mean "vicious" or "bitter" and produce sentences with equivalent meanings. These are the correct answers.

34. A, C
This sentence might look intimidating at first if you don't know what onomatopoeia is, but the sentence gives you an example to illustrate the term. Focus on figuring out the way that the words "Plop, plop, fizz, fizz" evoke associations, and don't forget to eliminate any words that don't have a synonym among the choices. *Evocative* is synonymous with *reminiscent* here, in that it refers to something that brings something else to mind.

35. B, D
The semicolon indicates that the second part of the sentence defines the blank. Since the demonstration lacked organization and actually hurt the activists' cause, a good prediction for the blank would be "disaster." Choices (B) *debacle* and (D) *fiasco* both mean "disaster," and are therefore correct.

36. B, D
The key phrase here is "endless combinations." If jazz musicians are able to form "endless combinations" of solos and chord progressions, then we might expect the result to be the possibility of *variety*. *Diversity*, like *variety*, is a reasonable product of "endless combinations," so it gives us the meaning we are looking for. (B) and (D) are correct.

37. C, F
The detour road sign "while" tells us that there will be a contrast between the first and second clauses of the sentence. The second clause tells us that Mr. Hamilton helped others in order to generate good publicity for himself. Since this is a self-interested motive, the first half of the sentence will emphasize its opposite: the appearance of selflessness or generosity towards others.

Choice (C) *altruistic* means "generous," and choice (F) *philanthropic* means "charitable"; both convey a sense of generosity toward others. Therefore (C) and (F) are correct.

38. B, F
If the speaker began to execute mellifluous (sweet sounding) melodies and harmonies, then her musical ability must be getting better. We need a word that denotes progress. Choice (F) *improve* suggests that the speaker's ability began to progress, so *improve* functions in the same way as (B) *advance*. In context, *advance* suggests that our speaker's musical ability improved.

39. B, F
The use of "though" signals a contrast between the first and second clauses: if the first clause tells us that the philosopher's treatise may seem to be influenced by communism, the second clause must refute this observation. *Predated* means "preceded in time." *Antedated* means "to be earlier or older than something." In context, it suggests that, while the treatise did seem to reflect the philosopher's communist ideology, its publication actually preceded his involvement in communist politics. (B) and (F) are correct.

40. B, F
The phrase "but once" establishes a contrast between Sheila's regularly unaggressive

behavior and the way she behaves when "somebody attacks her beliefs." We can assume, then, that Sheila would channel a latent (i.e. present but not active) "aggression" when somebody attacks her beliefs; using the "noble warrior" detail as a further clue, we might expect the word to mean close to "belligerence" rather than simply "aggression." Choice (B) *pugnacity,* meaning "eagerness to fight" or "aggression," and (F) *bellicosity,* meaning "eagerness to argue or fight," are close to our prediction word, "belligerence." (B) and (F) are the correct answers.

41. A, C

"Far from" introduces a contrasting ideas question. The correct answers will starkly contrast what follows the comma, which is increased belligerence from even the moderate parties. *Appeasing,* like *mollifying,* means "pacifying or placating." Choices (A) and (C) are correct.

42. C, F

It's important to notice the phrases "only be refusing to acknowledge" and "would result in anything *other* than." Taken together, these phrases suggest that experts would have to overlook the obvious severity of the financial crisis if they were to predict that the cash bailout would provide *anything but* a weak, temporary, or ineffectual solution to the corporation's problems. Our answer must suggest that a bailout offers no substantial solution to the crisis. *Transitory* means "temporary," so it works in the same way as does *fleeting.* In context, this suggests that the bailout will only provide a solution that will not last. Choices (C) and (F) are correct.

43. E, F

This is a difficult question, but there are context clues that help us. Whatever those guarantees have, it "extends . . . beyond the limits of the text and creates . . . uncertainty." The correct choice will be consistent with those traits. A *penumbra* is "an area in which something exists to an uncertain degree." The term was originally used in astronomy, but has been brought into wider use and can indicate the idea that certain unstated rights are implied in or emanate from the Constitution. *Vagueness* is "the quality of being not clear in meaning or intention," which fits with the phrase "a degree of uncertainty." Choices (E) and (F) are correct.

44. B, E

The missing word will have some relationship to "erratic emotions." Because the clues from the previous sentence tell us that the sufferer experiences a range of moods, we can predict the word that belongs in the blank may be similar in meaning to "wild." However, the word "mere" indicates that the word we're looking for should have a more benign connotation. A good prediction for the blank might be "whimsical," "fanciful," or some other word that refers to rapidly changing moods without suggesting psychological pathology.

Both choice (B) *capricious* and choice (E) *mercurial* mean "quickly changing" and lack an overtly negative connotation. This matches our prediction.

45. B, D

This Sentence Equivalence question uses a semicolon as a straight-ahead road sign signifying that the words that go in the blank will characterize a candidate who is stubborn and enjoys arguments. Choices (B) *feisty* and (D) *pugnacious* both mean "easily provoked"; these match your prediction and are correct.

46. B, E

In this sentence, the semicolon indicates that the clause that follows it helps explain the clause that precedes it. Therefore, we know that the man was neither intelligent nor qualified to brag as he did, and we can assume that the claims he made were false. The missing word will thus have a meaning similar to "false." Answer choices (B) *spurious* and (E) *bogus* both mean "not genuine" or "false" and are the correct answers.

47. C, D

This is a straight-ahead definition. Here the keywords are "known for their devotion to their masters," so you might predict something like "devotedness" or "loyalty." (C) and (D)—*allegiance* and *fidelity* are both logical synonyms to complete the sentence.

48. A, E

Choice (A) *harmful* is a synonym for (D) *calamitous*, but it also complements (E) *deleterious*. Consider the tone; *calamitous* means "catastrophic," which is more severe in tone and meaning than either *harmful* or *deleterious*. In this sentence, *calamitous* has too strong a meaning—low voter turnout isn't ideal, but it's not disastrous, either. Therefore, (A) *harmful* and (E) *deleterious* are the best fit.

49. D, F

If there is a surfeit (overabundance) of information produced by news websites, we might reason that the only way we can stay abreast of (keep up with) current events would be to read "shortened" or "summarized" accounts—otherwise, there is simply too much information to sift through. We need words that suggest a brief account or an account reduced to its essential info. *Synoptic* means "summarized so as to extract the core information." Synoptic accounts would be preferable considering an overabundance of information. *Abbreviated* means "shortened"; in context, an abbreviated account is one that is shortened so as to provide a brief overview. Choices (D) and (F) are correct.

50. B, D

The semicolon serves as a straight-ahead road sign, indicating that the second clause clarifies (rather than contrasts with) the first clause. Therefore, like the word "self-possessed," the missing word would describe someone who demonstrated composure. We can predict that the correct answers will mean something like "poised" or "self-assured," both of which would be consistent with self-possession and composure.

Choices (B) *demure*, meaning "reserved" and (D) *decorous*, meaning "with propriety" and "appropriate to the situation," are consistent with self-possession and composure. Although *demure* and *decorous* may veer more toward the topic of etiquette than we expected, no other two choices are consistent with our prediction, so choices (B) and (D) are correct.

51. D, E

"However" here is a clue that there's a contrast between the first and second clauses of this sentence. The first part of the sentence mentions benefits of using public transportation, so the second part must talk about drawbacks, which would make public transportation "an undesirable option to many commuters." Logically, it's likely the schedules are irregular or sporadic. Choice (E) *fluctuant* means "fluctuating or varying," and is synonymous with (D) *inconsistent*. Choices (D) and (E) are correct.

52. C, E

Examining the sentence, we see that Jane keeps "carefully organized records," and this is what allows her to fill out the "complex forms." Hence, we can predict that our answers will describe Jane's nature as "meticulous."

Answer choices (C) *fastidious*, or "attentive to accuracy and detail," and (E) *punctilious*, or "concerned with details and precision," both describe the same set of traits illustrated in our prediction: that Jane is "meticulous." These are the correct answers.

53. B, C

Think about how someone would feel if he stayed up all night working and didn't sleep. We need words meaning "used up." The word "nonetheless" is another clue, because it tells us that in going to the gym, he did something one wouldn't have expected. Something that is *depleted* is used up or *exhausted*. Choices (B) and (C) are correct.

54. E, F

The road sign here is the colon. We know that we're looking for a consistent idea that shows Dan is trying to get to the meeting on time, but that he's stuck in traffic. It's likely the traffic will "prevent" him from getting to the meeting on time. That's the synonymous pair we're looking for. *Hinder* means "make difficult." *Impede* means "to slow progress." Choices (E) and (F) are correct.

55. C, F

The sentence suggests that one shouldn't interpret Joel's demeanor toward the boss as sycophantic ("characterized by flattery or sucking up") since he is "warm and friendly" with everybody else. We might expect Joel's demeanor toward his boss, then, to be "warm and friendly;" we need a word that encapsulates this friendly demeanor. *Affable* means "warm and friendly," which is the meaning we need, and is a close synonym of *amicable*. Choices (C) and (F) are correct.

56. C, F

The strategies used to be flexible and adaptable, but now they're rigid. Choose a word that describes a change of that kind. *Obsolescence* is "the condition of no longer being used or useful," which is nearly is the opposite of "flexible and new." *Ossification* is "the process of becoming rigid or inflexible." Choices (C) and (F) are correct.

57. A, F

If the CEO fired the advertising company and brought in a new one, you can logically infer that she believed the advertising campaign would have a negative impact upon her company's reputation. This is confirmed by the straight-ahead road sign "so" that begins the second clause, which indicates that both clauses share a negative charge. Choices (A) *sullied*, "stained or impure" and (F) *marred*, "made imperfect," are negatively charged words, and both make sense in the context of the sentence.

58. B, C

The use of "while" signals a contrast between each clause. The physicist's argument does have innovative ideas, *but* it still would be inaccurate to characterize his work as *innovative*. Thus, we should look for a word that means "new and groundbreaking." *Pioneering* means "being the first or original of one's kind," and in context, it suggests innovation. When used as an adjective, *novel* means "new and fresh." In this context, it suggests innovation. Choices (B) and (C) are correct.

59. A, B

The detour/contrast road sign "however" indicates that the private support of despotic regimes contrasts with the public treatment of those same entities. The key phrase "commitment to democracy" indicates an expected reaction to a despotic regime—a despot is a ruler with absolute power, so despotic regimes clash with democratic ideals. We can predict that the meaning of the word that belongs in the blank will be similar in meaning to "condemn."

Choices (A) *disparage* and (B) *castigate* both mean "to criticize," so both match our prediction; these are the correct answers.

60. A, F

The blank should summarize Godard's approach to filmmaking, so the answer should encapsulate the adjectives "jarring, subversive, and experimental" and address the fact that his films "shook the foundation of classical style." Thus, our answer choice should indicate a startling transformation from old to new. *Revolutionary* means "introducing fundamental change," so it properly summarizes Godard's approach to cinema. *Radical* means "introducing fundamental change," and so it is a close synonym of *revolutionary*. Choices (A) and (F) are correct.

61. B, E

The word that goes in the blank is a verb, describing what he does with the tail of the kite, and "undo all the tangles near the tassel" hints to the reader what the correct answer should be. *Unfolded* supports the idea of "being very particular to undo all the tangles near the tassel." *Uncrease*, or "get rid of lines, folds, or wrinkles" is appropriate to "undo all the tangles." (B) and (E) are correct.

62. C, E

"Advances" in this context indicates development or progress. Look for words that would describe dramatic, positive advances. *Revo-* *lutionary* advances would indicate that the progress being made is radically new or *innovative*. Choices (C) and (E) are correct.

63. E, F

We are talking about a yuppie being "stereotypical" of greed, so we need words that indicate a symbol of this. *Personification* is "the human representation or symbol of a thing." *Embodiment* means "a perfect representative," which fits this context. Choices (E) and (F) are correct.

64. C, F

In order for a researcher to continue working on projects that would be difficult to corroborate—which is to say, it would be hard to demonstrate their truthfulness—she would have to be convinced that there was something about them that was beneficial enough to make up for that negative issue. The demonstrable truthfulness of them would be such reason. *Verisimilitude*, like *authenticity*, is the "appearance of truth," and if the researcher were convinced that the claims were true, she might be willing to continue working on them. Choices (C) and (F) are correct.

65. B, D

Since the path is "no longer open to the public," we can conclude that whatever is left from the hikers passing through the forest is some kind of aftereffect. The contrast of "formerly pristine" to "trampled" is a clue that this effect is viewed as a negative thing. A *repercussion* is a "consequence, generally negative." That makes sense in this context. Choices (B) and (D) are correct.

66. B, D

The use of "though" signals a contrast between the first and second clauses: if the speech is now considered a linchpin (a central source of stability) of conservative politics, then the second clause must tell us that the speech was originally intended to support, express, or clarify liberal ideals (the opposite of conservatism). Our word must somehow suggest the speech was originally intended to communicate liberal values. Similar to *disseminate, promulgate* means "make widely known, often through formal declaration." (B) and (D) are the correct answers.

67. E, F

The second part of this sentence holds two clues to the meaning of the missing word. The word "as" is a straight-ahead road sign indicating that the idea in the second part of the sentence follows logically from the first, and the word "while" is a detour road sign that points to a contrast between Hannah and Louise. Hannah is characterized as "provincial," which can mean "unsophisticated" and "inclined toward the local," so we know that Louise is the opposite in that respect. Also, we know from the description of Hannah that she does not like to travel. Therefore, we can deduce that Louise does and predict that the missing word will have a meaning similar to "liking." Choices (E) *penchant* and (F) *proclivity* both mean "liking" or "inclination," so they are correct.

68. B, E

This sentence sets up a contrast by using the word "although" to show that there is a difference between "imposing" and the word that goes in the blank. We should look for a meaning like "smaller." *Diminished* means "made to seem smaller or less important," which fits the meaning we're looking for. To *minimize* is to "make smaller." The couch seemed smaller compared to the grandeur of the room after it was brought home. Choices (B) and (E) are correct.

69. A, E

Since the word "but" introduces the second part of this sentence, we know that the first part must be a contrast to being "overlooked and ignored." Therefore, she probably easily attracted attention with her good looks. "Never had any *trouble* attracting attention" is a good contrast to being "overlooked and ignored." Similarly, it makes sense to say that Marilyn never had *difficulty* attracting attention for her good looks, and contrasts with her wit being overlooked and ignored. Choices (A) and (E) are correct.

70. B, F

The phrase "even though" serves as a clue that suggests a contrast between the behavior of the host, outlined in the introductory clause, and that of her parents, described in the remainder of the sentence.

Because the host is described as "gracious" while her parents are described as having been the opposite of gracious, we can predict that the host was the embodiment of hospitality. We can then scan the answer choices for those that have meanings similar to our prediction. Choices (B) and (F) have meanings similar to "embodiment" and are therefore correct.

71. C, D

In this sentence the word "as" functions as a straight-ahead road sign that indicates that the clause that follows it helps explain the clause before it. The clause before the word "as" states that Maria had difficulty following the "incoherent" plot. Therefore, we should look for words that are similar in meaning to "incoherent," such as "disconnected." *Chaotic* means "completely confused or disordered" and is a good fit. *Disjointed* means "disconnected or incoherent" and works well in this context. Choices (C) and (D) are correct.

72. B, C

The word "despite" suggests that the "number of lives" lost is unexpectedly large considering the remarkable medicinal progress. We need a word that suggests a *significant* number of lives. *Substantial* is a close synonym of *considerable* and correctly denotes a significant number of deaths. (A) *Staggering* means "astonishing," and in context, it does correctly suggest a surprisingly high number. However, there are no other answer choices that match the extreme degree of "staggering," so it is incorrect. Choices (B) and (C) are correct.

73. A, D

If the speaker took up cerebral exercise as a means to delay "senility" (loss of mental capacity as a result of old age), we can expect that the speaker's mental acuity (sharpness of mind) had begim to "degenerate" or "worsen." *Atrophy* means "a weakening or degeneration, especially through lack of use." *Atrophy* is particularly appropriate, then, if we consider the speaker's attempt to reverse this degeneration with exercise. *Wane* means "to decrease in vigor or power," so it functions in the same way that *atrophy* functions. Though (B) *regress* can mean "get worse," it implies a return to a previous state or previous behavior. Our speaker's condition seems progressive rather than regressive because he fears senility; in addition, there is no other choice that gives us a sentence with the same meaning. Choices (A) and (D) are correct.

74. C, E

The key to this question is the context keyword "surprised." Since Nigel is typically a model of "equanimity" (calm), the correct answer choices, describing surprising behavior on his part, must mean something like "unsettled." Choices (C) *testy* (irritable) and (E) *discomposed* (out of sorts) create sentences that indicate that Nigel lost his equanimity and failed to remain calm. These are the correct answers.

Chapter 3

Quantitative Reasoning

GRE Quantitative Section Overview

The Quantitative Reasoning sections of the GRE test your basic math skills, your knowledge of mathematical concepts, and your ability to reason logically. You will see questions related to arithmetic, algebra, and geometry. The emphasis in the Quantitative Reasoning section is on your ability to reason, using your knowledge of the various topics. The goal is to make the test an accurate indicator of your ability to apply given information, think logically, and draw conclusions. These are skills you will need at the graduate level of study.

The GRE contains two Quantitative Reasoning sections with approximately 20 questions each. Each section will last 35 minutes, and be composed of a selection of the following question types:

- Quantitative Comparison
- Problem Solving
- Data Interpretation

The Quantitative Reasoning portion of the GRE draws heavily upon your ability to combine your knowledge of mathematical concepts with your reasoning powers. Specifically, it evaluates your ability to:

- compare quantities using reasoning
- solve word problems
- interpret data presented in charts and graphs

Within each Quantitative Reasoning section on the GRE, you will see an assortment of question types.

	Quantitative Comparison	Problem Solving	Data Interpretation
Number of Questions	approx. 7–8	approx. 9–10	approx. 3
Time per Question	1.5 minutes	1.5–2 minutes	2 minutes

Try to keep these time estimates in mind as you prepare for the test. If you use them as you practice, you will be comfortable keeping to the same amounts of time on Test Day.

THE ONSCREEN CALCULATOR

An onscreen calculator will be available during the GRE, but there are several points to consider about its use. A calculator can be a time saver, and time is immensely important on the GRE. But while calculators can speed up computations, they can also foster dependence, making it hard for you to spot the shortcuts in GRE questions. Using the calculator to perform a long, involved computation to answer a question will use up your allotted time for that question—and perhaps for several more. You may even make a mistake in your computation, leading to an incorrect answer. Remember, this is a reasoning test. The quantitative questions on the GRE are not designed to require lengthy computations.

If that is the case, why is a calculator provided? A calculator can be an asset for the occasional computation that a few questions require. It may prevent an error caused by a freehand calculation. The onscreen calculator provided is a simple, four-function calculator. An image of the calculator is provided below, showing the function keys, including the square root key and change of sign key.

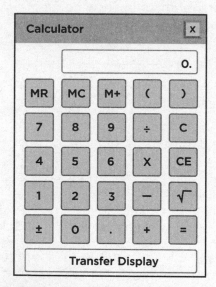

By not relying on the calculator, you will be free to focus on interpreting numbers and data and using your critical thinking skills. This is the intention of the GRE test makers. For example, Problem Solving questions often involve more algebra than calculating, and Quantitative Comparison questions will require more reasoning than calculating.

Introduction to Problem Solving

Problem Solving questions test several general mathematics categories: algebra, arithmetic, number properties, and geometry.

In a Problem Solving question, you may be asked to solve a pure math problem or a word problem involving a real-world situation. You will be asked to enter your answer into an onscreen box, select one answer, or select one or more options that correctly answer the problem.

The directions for a Problem Solving question requiring a single answer will look like this:

Directions: Click to select your choice.

A Problem Solving question requiring you to select a single answer will look like this:

Sample Question	Exit section	Review	Mark	Help ?	Back	Next

Sample Question

A health club charges $35 per month plus $2.50 for each aerobics class attended. How many aerobics classes were attended in a certain month if the total monthly charge was $52.50?

○ 7

○ 8

○ 9

○ 10

○ 11

Click to select your choice(s).

The directions for a Problem Solving question requiring you to select one or more answers will look like this:

Directions: Click to select your choice(s).

If a Problem Solving question asks you to select an exact number of choices, you must select that exact number of correct choices for the question to be counted as correct. Otherwise, you must select all the correct choices for the question to be counted as correct.

A Problem Solving question requiring you to select one or more answers will look like this:

Sample Question	Exit section	Review	Mark	Help ?	Back	Next

Sample Question

If $0<x<1$, which of the following *must* be true?

Choose <u>all</u> possible answers.

- [ ] $2x < x$
- [ ] $2x < 1$
- [ ] $2x > 1$
- [ ] $x^2 < x$
- [ ] $x^2 < 1$

Click to select your choice(s).

The directions for a Problem Solving question requiring you to make a Numeric Entry will look like this:

> **Directions:** Click in the box and type your numeric answer. Backspace to erase.

Enter your answer as an integer or decimal if there is one box or as a fraction if there are two boxes.

A Problem Solving question with Numeric Entry will look like this:

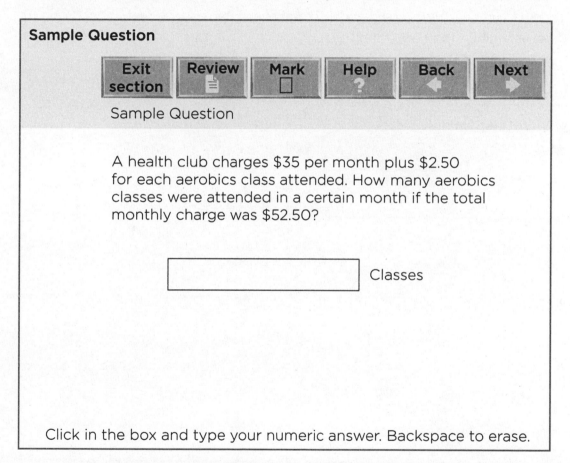

Arithmetic and Number Properties

Most of the problems on the GRE involve arithmetic to some extent. Among the most important topics are number properties, ratios, and percents. You should know most of the definitions such as what an integer is, what even numbers are, etc. Not only do arithmetic topics themselves appear on the GRE, they are also essential for understanding some of the more advanced topics tested.

Arithmetic topics tested on the GRE may include arithmetic operations, exponents and roots, properties and types of integers, such as divisibility, factorization, prime numbers, remainders and odd and even integers, and math concepts such as estimation, percent, ratio, rate, absolute value, decimal representation, and sequences of numbers.

Arithmetic and Number Properties Practice

Select one or more answer choices according to the specific question directions.

If the question does not specify how many answer choices to select, select all that apply.

The correct answer may be just one of the choices or as many as all of the choices, depending on the question.

No credit is given unless you select all of the correct choices and no others.

If the question specifies how many answer choices to select, select exactly that number of choices.

1. Which <u>two</u> of the following integers have a sum greater than 0?

   A –3
   B –4
   C –5
   D 4

2. Which <u>three</u> of the following integers have a product that is less than –85?

   A 7
   B 2
   C –6
   D –5
   E –4
   F –2

3. Which of the following are solutions to the following inequality?

   $x^2 + 17 - 7x < 5$

   Indicate <u>all</u> such solutions.

   A 3
   B 3.3
   C 3.7
   D 4

Enter your answer in the answer box(es) below the question.

Equivalent forms of the correct answer, such as 2.5 and 2.50, are all correct. Fractions do not need to be reduced to lowest terms.

Enter the exact answer unless the question asks you to round your answer.

4. A certain item is on sale for 85% of its original price of $60. The money saved from purchasing the item at the sale price over the original price is 12% of what amount, in dollars? (Ignore the $ symbol when entering your answer).

   $ [   ]

5. A magazine subscription first cost $50, but was then marked down 20%. The next month it was marked down another 10%. What is the percent by which the magazine has been reduced from its original price?

   [   ] %

$$2^{16} = 16^{n+3}$$

6. What is the value of n?

    ☐

7. If the ratio of $2a - b$ to $a + b$ is 2:5, what is the ratio of a to b? Express the ratio as a fraction.

$$4 < x < 7$$

$$9 < y < 12$$

8. If x and y are both integers that satisfy the inequalities, what is the lowest value of $\dfrac{x+y}{(-y)^2}$?

    Express your answer as a fraction.

9. A group of students has a ratio of 2 women to 3 men. After 6 more men join the group, the ratio changes to 1 woman to 2 men. How many men were originally in the group?

    ☐ men

10. Six percent of seven more than triple the product of forty-eight and twelve is what percent of three hundred and fourteen? Round your answer to the nearest hundredth.

    ☐

11. A certain store marks down a watch by 20% each month it isn't sold. If the watch costs $40 on January 1, what does the watch cost on June 1? Round to the nearest cent.

    $ ☐

12. Out of a total x games, a basketball team won 21 more than it lost. If the number of games lost is one-third of the total games played, how many games did the team win?

    ☐ games

13. What is x percent of 50, if 150 percent of x is 120?

    ☐

14. A certain integer x is a multiple of both 6 and 7. Which of the following must be true?

    I. x is a multiple of 21
    II. x is equal to 42
    III. x is an even number

    Ⓐ I
    Ⓑ I and II
    Ⓒ II and III
    Ⓓ I and III
    Ⓔ III

15. What is the remainder when 7^4 is divided by 6?

    Ⓐ 5
    Ⓑ 4
    Ⓒ 2
    Ⓓ 1
    Ⓔ 0

16. A ruler one meter in length is marked off in eighths of a centimeter. What is the distance, in centimeters, from the edge of the ruler to the 37th mark from the edge of the ruler?

    (A) $3\frac{1}{4}$

    (B) $4\frac{1}{2}$

    (C) $4\frac{5}{8}$

    (D) $37\frac{1}{8}$

    (E) 296

17. The number 5^7 must be divisible by all of the following EXCEPT:

    (A) 625
    (B) 125
    (C) 25
    (D) 15
    (E) 5

18.
$$\frac{\frac{4}{5} \cdot 10 \cdot \frac{3}{4} \cdot 12}{\frac{3}{10} \cdot 5 \cdot \frac{7}{8} \cdot 24} =$$

    (A) $\frac{2}{7}$

    (B) $2\frac{2}{7}$

    (C) 3

    (D) $16\frac{1}{7}$

    (E) 27

19. If membership in Club KrissKross increases from 175 to 225, what is the percent increase?

    (A) 21.3%
    (B) 28.6%
    (C) 33.3%
    (D) 50.0%
    (E) 53.5%

20. If c can have only the values 3, –4, and –12 and d can have only the values –5, 4, and 2, what is the greatest possible value for $3c + d^2$?

    (A) 13
    (B) 17
    (C) 25
    (D) 34
    (E) 37

21. If $\sqrt{c} = 25$, then $c =$

    (A) 5
    (B) 25
    (C) 50
    (D) 600
    (E) 625

22.
$$\frac{1}{\left(\frac{1}{2}\right)} + \frac{2}{\left(\frac{2}{3}\right)} + \frac{3}{\left(\frac{3}{4}\right)} =$$

    (A) $\frac{6}{13}$

    (B) $\frac{13}{6}$

    (C) $\frac{25}{12}$

    (D) 7

    (E) 9

23. The Ryder family traveled at an average rate of 60 miles per hour (mph) for 10 hours to complete their trip. If they traveled the first 4 of the hours of their trip at a constant speed of 70 mph, at what average speed did they travel for the remaining 6 hours to obtain the 60 mph average for the entire trip?

   Ⓐ 50

   Ⓑ $53\frac{1}{3}$

   Ⓒ 55

   Ⓓ $56\frac{1}{2}$

   Ⓔ 60

24. If the sales tax on a refrigerator priced at $400 is between 6% and 9%, then the total cost of the refrigerator could be

   Ⓐ $418

   Ⓑ $423

   Ⓒ $429

   Ⓓ $436

   Ⓔ $440

25. $\sqrt{(29 + 8)(13 + 24)} =$

   Ⓐ $\sqrt{(37)}$

   Ⓑ 37

   Ⓒ 74

   Ⓓ 1,369

   Ⓔ 1,874,161

26. $(7x)^3$ must be divisible by all of the following EXCEPT:

   Ⓐ 1

   Ⓑ $7x^2$

   Ⓒ 21

   Ⓓ $49x^3$

   Ⓔ $343x$

27. The price of Company A's stock fell by 20% two weeks ago and by another 25% last week to its current price. By what percent of the current price does the share price need to rise in order to return to its original price?

   Ⓐ 40%

   Ⓑ 45%

   Ⓒ $66\frac{2}{3}$%

   Ⓓ 75%

   Ⓔ 82%

28. Find the 50th term of the arithmetic sequence 13, 4, –5, –14, . . .

   ☐

29. What number yields $\frac{3}{7}$ when multiplied by $\frac{9}{7}$?

   Ⓐ $\frac{18}{49}$

   Ⓑ $\frac{1}{3}$

   Ⓒ $\frac{3}{7}$

   Ⓓ $\frac{7}{3}$

   Ⓔ 3

30. If $3^x = 81$, then $x^3 =$

   Ⓐ 12
   Ⓑ 16
   Ⓒ 64
   Ⓓ 81
   Ⓔ 128

31. Which of the following is equal to 8^5?
   Indicate *all* correct expressions.

   Ⓐ $2^5 \times 4^5$
   Ⓑ 2^{15}
   Ⓒ 2×4^7

32. The first term of a certain sequence is 5. If every term after the first term is 3 less than 2 times the term immediately preceding it, what is the positive difference between the third and fourth terms?

   Ⓐ 8
   Ⓑ 11
   Ⓒ 16
   Ⓓ 19
   Ⓔ 32

33. Which of the following is equivalent to $\frac{\sqrt{3} + 1}{\sqrt{3} - 1}$?

   Ⓐ $3 - \sqrt{3}$

   Ⓑ $2\sqrt{3} - 2$

   Ⓒ 3

   Ⓓ $2 + \sqrt{3}$

   Ⓔ $4 + 2\sqrt{3}$

34. In a class of 30 students, the ratio of males to females is 3 to 2. What is the number of females in the class?

   ⬚ females

35. On an elliptical trainer, a speed of 60 revolutions per minute is equivalent to 9 miles per hour. How many revolutions are equivalent to 1 mile?

   ⬚ revolutions

36. The total amount of rainfall in a city increased by 20% last month and then decreased by 5% this month. If this month's rainfall was 2.85 inches, what was the city's total rainfall, in inches, two months ago?

   Express your answer as a decimal.

   ⬚ inches

Select one or more answer choices according to the specific question directions.

If the question does not specify how many answer choices to select, select all that apply.

The correct answer may be just one of the choices or as many as all of the choices, depending on the question.

No credit is given unless you select all of the correct choices and no others.

If the question specifies how many answer choices to select, select exactly that number of choices.

37. Which of the following integers are multiples of 6, 9, and 12?

    Indicate all such integers.

    A 18
    B 24
    C 54
    D 72
    E 912
    F 972

38. If p is a positive prime number and q is a multiple of p, which of the following must be multiples of both p and q?

    Indicate all such numbers.

    A p
    B q
    C p^2
    D q^2

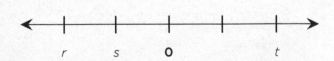

39. On the number line, each mark is an equally spaced integer. Which of the following could be true?

    Indicate all such statements.

    A $t^r > t^s$
    B $rst < 0$
    C $(r - s)^t > 0$

40. Let x be the units digit of an integer N, such that $x \geq 8$. Let y be the units digit of a different integer P, such that $y < 3$. Which of the following could be the units digit of NP?

    A 0
    B 1
    C 2
    D 3
    E 4
    F 5
    G 6
    H 7
    I 8
    J 9

41. q and r are two distinct prime numbers that are both greater than 20. Which of the following could be a multiple of q and r?

    Indicate all such values.

    A $q^3 r^2$
    B $16q$
    C $9r$
    D $52qr$

42. If q is an integer and also the square root of p, then which of the following must also be an integer?

Indicate all such integers.

A $\dfrac{p}{q}$

B $\dfrac{q}{p}$

C $\sqrt{q}$

D $\sqrt{p}$

43. If n is an integer and also a multiple of 3, which of the following must be a multiple of 12?

Indicate all such integers.

A $3n$

B $4n$

C $n^2 + 12$

D $12n$

44. The variable q is an integer and a perfect square. Which of the following is also an integer?

Indicate all such integers.

A $q^2 + \sqrt{q} + 1$

B $q^3 + \dfrac{q}{2} + 3$

C $\dfrac{\sqrt{q}}{2}$

D $q^2 + q + \sqrt{q}$

45. If n is an integer, and $n > 0$, which of the following could be the units digit of $1{,}572^n$?

Indicate all such numbers.

A 0

B 1

C 2

D 3

E 4

F 5

G 6

H 7

I 8

J 9

Enter your answer in the answer box(es) below the question.

Equivalent forms of the correct answer, such as 2.5 and 2.50, are all correct. Fractions do not need to be reduced to lowest terms.

Enter the exact answer unless the question asks you to round your answer.

---

46. The difference between the squares of two consecutive integers is 37. What is the larger of the two numbers?

Select one or more answer choices according to the specific question directions.

If the question does not specify how many answer choices to select, select all that apply.

The correct answer may be just one of the choices or as many as all of the choices, depending on the question.

No credit is given unless you select all of the correct choices and no others.

If the question specifies how many answer choices to select, select exactly that number of choices.

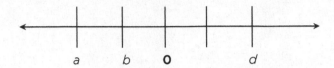

47. On the number line shown above, all the tick marks are equally spaced. Which of the following statements about numbers a, b, and d must be true?

Select all such statements.

A $ab + ad > 0$

B $b - a = d$

C $(ab)(bd)(ad) > 0$

D $\frac{a}{d} + \frac{b}{d} < 0$

48. If b is the square root of an integer, then which of the following numbers must be an integer?

Indicate all such numbers.

A $9b^4 - 3b^2 + 1$

B $\frac{b^2}{4} + 4$

C $b^2 + 2b + 1$

49. If integer v is a power of 3, which of the following numbers must also be a power of 3?

Indicate all such numbers.

A $9v + \frac{v}{3}$

B $\sqrt[3]{v}$

C v^2

50. Which of the following numbers has more than four factors?

Indicate all such numbers.

A 10

B 12

C 14

D 16

E 18

51. Which of the following numbers have exactly three factors?

Indicate all such numbers.

A 9

B 16

C 23

D 25

E 33

52. If whole number m has exactly three factors, which of the following statements must be true?

    Indicate <u>all</u> such statements.

    A m is a prime number

    B m is the square of another number

    C m is a composite number

    D $\sqrt{m}$ is a prime number

    E m is the cube of another number

    F m is odd

53. When x is divided by 4, there is a remainder of 3. What is the remainder when $x + 7$ is divided by 4?

    [   ]

54. If $4 < x < 7$ and $1 < y < 5$, which of the following represents all of the possible values of xy?

    (A) $1 < xy < 35$

    (B) $4 < xy < 35$

    (C) $1 < xy < 7$

    (D) $7 < xy < 35$

    (E) $5 < xy < 12$

55. If $x \neq 0$, which of the following must be greater than x?

    I. $3x$

    II. x^5

    III. $5 - x$

    (A) None

    (B) I only

    (C) II only

    (D) I and II

    (E) I and III

56. If the average (arithmetic mean) of 15, 19, and n is between 17 and 20, inclusive, what is the greatest possible value of n?

    (A) 60

    (B) 41

    (C) 26

    (D) 20

    (E) 17

57. A certain integer x is a multiple of both 5 and 8. Which of the following must be true?

    I. x is a multiple of 20

    II. x is equal to 40

    III. x is an even number

    (A) I only

    (B) I and II

    (C) II and III

    (D) III only

    (E) I and III

58. What is the remainder when 8^4 is divided by 3?

    (A) 0

    (B) 1

    (C) 2

    (D) 3

    (E) 4

59. If both x and y are positive odd integers, which of the following must be odd ?

    I. $(x + 1)^y$

    II. $x^{(y - 1)}$

    III. y^x

    (A) I only

    (B) I and II

    (C) II and III

    (D) I and III

    (E) III only

60. If a is an odd, positive integer and $b = 3a$, then which of the following expressions must result in an odd value?

    (A) $a + 3b$

    (B) $a^2 - 3a + 1$

    (C) $8 - 2b$

    (D) $a^2 + b^2 - 4$

    (E) $4(5a)$

61. If both the product and the sum of four integers are even, which of the following could be the number of even integers in the group?

Indicate *all* such numbers.

    A 0

    B 2

    C 4

62. $200 \leq x \leq 300$. How many values of x are divisible by both 5 and 8?

    (A) 2

    (B) 3

    (C) 4

    (D) 5

    (E) 8

63. Which of the following is NOT a factor of 168?

    (A) 21

    (B) 24

    (C) 28

    (D) 32

    (E) 42

64. A wire is cut into three equal parts. The resulting segments are then cut into 4, 6, and 8 equal parts, respectively. If each of the resulting segments has an integer length, what is the minimum length of the wire?

    (A) 24

    (B) 48

    (C) 72

    (D) 192

    (E) 576

65. Which of the following is a multiple of all three integers 2, 3, and 5?

    (A) 525

    (B) 560

    (C) 615

    (D) 620

    (E) 660

66. If the integer P is greater than 5 and leaves a remainder of 4 when divided by 9, all of the following must be true EXCEPT

    Ⓐ The number that is 4 less than P is a multiple of 9.

    Ⓑ The number that is 5 more than P is a multiple of 9

    Ⓒ The number that is 2 more than P is a multiple of 3.

    Ⓓ When divided by 3, P will leave a remainder of 1.

    Ⓔ When divided by 2, P will leave a remainder of 1.

67. How many positive integers between 21 and 59 are equal to the product of a multiple of 4 and an odd number?

    Ⓐ 0

    Ⓑ 4

    Ⓒ 8

    Ⓓ 9

    Ⓔ 12

68. How many positive integers are both multiples of 4 and divisors of 128?

    Ⓐ 3

    Ⓑ 4

    Ⓒ 5

    Ⓓ 6

    Ⓔ 7

69. How many different positive integer factors does $(2^7)(3^4)(7^3)(23^5)$ have?

    Ⓐ 420

    Ⓑ 630

    Ⓒ 960

    Ⓓ 1,075

    Ⓔ 1,280

70. The positive integer x is a multiple of 2, 4, and 7. Which of the following must be true?

Indicate *all* such statements.

    Ⓐ $x^2 + x$ is a multiple of 28.

    Ⓑ $2x$ is a multiple of 112.

    Ⓒ $\frac{x^2}{16}$ is a multiple of 49.

71. If a is even and b is odd, which of the following must be odd?

Indicate *all* such expressions.

    Ⓐ $3a + 4b$

    Ⓑ $(a^2 + 3)b$

    Ⓒ $a + 3b$

72. Which of the following numbers are prime?

Indicate *all* correct answer choices.

    Ⓐ 9

    Ⓑ 13

    Ⓒ 15

    Ⓓ 17

    Ⓔ 21

    Ⓕ 23

    Ⓖ 29

    Ⓗ 33

73. If the integer x is odd and the integer y is even, which of the following expressions must be even?

Indicate *all* possible correct answers.

    Ⓐ $x + y$

    Ⓑ $2x$

    Ⓒ xy

    Ⓓ $2y$

    Ⓔ $y - x$

74. If x is a positive integer and $x \div 9$ has a remainder of 3, which could be the value of x?

Indicate *two* possible values.

A. 265
B. 372
C. 573
D. 642
E. 817

Answers and explanations begin on the next page.

Answer Key

ARITHMETIC AND NUMBER PROPERTIES PRACTICE

1.	A, D	26.	C	51.	A, D
2.	C, D, E	27.	C	52.	B, C, D
3.	B, C	28.	−428	53.	2
4.	75	29.	B	54.	B
5.	28	30.	C	55.	A
6.	1	31.	A, B, C	56.	C
7.	$\frac{7}{8}$	32.	A	57.	E
8.	$\frac{16}{121}$	33.	D	58.	B
9.	18	34.	12	59.	C
10.	33.15	35.	400	60.	B
11.	13.11	36.	2.5	61.	B, C
12.	42	37.	D, F	62.	B
13.	40	38.	B, D	63.	D
14.	D	39.	C	64.	C
15.	D	40.	A, G, I, J	65.	E
16.	C	41.	A, D	66.	E
17.	D	42.	A, D	67.	D
18.	B	43.	B, D	68.	D
19.	B	44.	A, D	69.	C
20.	D	45.	C, E, G, I	70.	A, C
21.	E	46.	19	71.	B, C
22.	E	47.	C, D	72.	B, D, F, G
23.	B	48.	A	73.	B, C, D
24.	C	49.	C	74.	B, D
25.	B	50.	B, D, E		

Answers and Explanations

ARITHMETIC AND NUMBER PROPERTIES PRACTICE

1. A, D

For this kind of problem, it is sometimes convenient to eliminate some answer choices.

We know that we want a sum that is positive, or greater than 0.

We have only one positive number, so we know that answer choice (D) will need to be one of our answers.

Now we look at the sums of 4 and the other answer choices.

4 + –5 = –1: This is negative. Incorrect.

4 + –4 = 0: This is not greater than 0, but exactly 0. Also incorrect.

4 + –3 = 1: This is positive. Correct.

Thus, (A) and (D) are the correct answers.

2. C, D, E

For this question we must look at the properties of positive and negative integers.

We know that we want the product to be a negative integer, so we need to multiply a negative value with a positive value: in this case, the product will comprise either three negative numbers or one negative number and two positive numbers.

There are only two positive numbers, (A) and (B), or 7 and 2. Their product is 14.

If we multiply this by the negative number with the lowest value, (C), we find:

$$14 \times (-6) = -84.$$

–84 is still greater than –85, which tells us that neither (A) nor (B) can be correct. (Remember, "less" in this case means a higher negative number!)

There are 4 negative numbers remaining, (C), (D), (E) and (F). Let's try multiplying the 3 lowest numbers:

$$(-6) \times (-5) \times (-4) = -120$$

This gives us a value less than –85. On the other hand, if we used (F), –2, with any of the other choices, the product would still be greater than –85. For instance:

$$(-6) \times (-5) \times (-2) = -60$$

Thus (C), (D), and (E) are the correct answers, since their product is –120, which is less than –85.

3. B, C

This is a straightforward inequality question.

We must then move all numbers to one side of the inequality, and then combine like terms.

$$x^2 + 17 - 7x < 5$$

We subtract 5 from both sides and get:

$$x^2 - 7x + 12 < 0$$

Then we can factor:

$$(x - 3)(x - 4) < 0$$

The product of these factors will be negative (less than zero) only when *exactly* one of the factors is negative. So we must avoid the cases where either both factors are negative or both cases are positive.

Thus, if we pick a few numbers to see what makes the inequality true, we get:

$3 < x < 4$

So any value in between 3 and 4 is correct.

(B) and (C) are our correct answers.

4. 75

In order to solve this problem, let's translate the words into an equation.

First we have 85% of $60. So let's change 85% into a decimal and determine the sale price.

$$0.85 \times 60 = 51$$

We now know that the sale price is $51. The original price is $60, so the amount saved is $9.

Next we need to find the amount of money for which 12% of that amount is $9.

Set the unknown amount as the variable x and set up an equation.

$$9 = 0.12x$$

Divide both sides by 0.12:

$$x = 75$$

5. 28

In order to solve this problem, we first need to find how much the magazine subscription cost after the two markdowns.

If it started at $50 and then got marked down by 20%, the new price will be 80% of the original.

$$\$50 \times 0.8 = \$40$$

After that, however, it is marked down another 10%, or costs 90% of the *new* price.

$$\$40 \times 0.9 = \$36$$

To find the percent change, we can divide the total change by the original price and multiply that fraction by 100 % : $\frac{\text{(old price – new price)}}{\text{(old price)}100\,\%}$

$$\text{Total percentage change} = \frac{(\$50 - \$36)}{(\$50)(100\,\%)}$$

$$= \left(\frac{\$14}{\$50}\right)(100\,\%)$$

$$= (0.28)(100\,\%)$$

$$= 28\,\%$$

Thus, the price of the subscription dropped by 28%.

6. 1

To solve this problem, let's find a common base; i.e., convert 16 to a power of 2.

$$16 = 2^4$$

So we can substitute 2^4 for 16 in the original equation:

$$2^{16} = (2^4)^{n+3}$$

Now we can simplify: when we have a single base with an exponent raised to another exponent, we multiply the exponents (in this case, using the distributive property).

$$2^{16} = 2^{4n+12}$$

Because we now have the same base, and the results are equal, the exponents *must* be equal.

If we set the exponents equal to each other, we can solve for n as follows:

$$16 = 4n + 12$$

Subtract 12 from both sides:

$$4 = 4n$$

Divide both sides by 4:

$$n = 1$$

7. $\frac{7}{8}$

Set up a proportion using the given ratios and solve for $a + b$:

$$\frac{2a - b}{a + b} = \frac{2}{5}$$

Fraction equal to fraction—cross-multiply:

$$5(2a - b) = 2(a + b)$$
$$10a - 5b = 2a + 2b$$
$$10a - 2a = 2b + 5b$$
$$8a = 7b$$
$$a : b = 7 : 8$$

8. $\frac{16}{121}$

To get the lowest value of $\frac{(x+y)}{(-y)^2}$, we want to maximize the denominator and minimize the numerator. Let's start with the denominator.

Any negative number squared will always be a positive number. As mentioned above, we want to get the greatest possible denominator that satisfies the parameters of the inequality. Since y is an integer less than 12, the next greatest integer is 11. Therefore, y equals 11; we will substitute this into the problem.

Let's now move on to the numerator.

We already know that y equals 11, but we want to use the smallest value of x: x is an integer greater than 4; therefore x equals 5. Substitute 5 for the value of x before solving.

Numerator: 5 + 11

Denominator: $(-11)^2$

Numerator = 16

Denominator = 121

9. 18

To solve this problem, let's first set variables.

\# of women = x

\# of men originally = y

The first ratio is:

$$\frac{2}{3} = \frac{x}{y}$$

Then we can cross-multiply:

$$3x = 2y$$

After 6 more men join the group, the new ratio is:

$$\frac{1}{2} = \frac{x}{(y+6)}$$

Then cross-multiply:

$$y + 6 = 2x$$

We now have two equations, so we can set up a system of equations.

$$y + 6 = 2x$$
$$3x = 2y$$

Let's isolate the y in the first equation:

$$y = 2x - 6$$

Then substitute the y in the second equation:

$$3x = 2(2x - 6)$$
$$3x = 4x - 12$$
$$-x = -12$$
$$x = 12$$

If $x = 12$, and the original ratio was 2:3, then $y = 18$.

10. 33.15

Let's first translate this into an equation.

The product of forty-eight and twelve is $48 \times 12 = 576$.

Triple that is $576 \times 3 = 1{,}728$.

Seven more than that is $1{,}728 + 7 = 1{,}735$.

Now we can find six percent of that: $1{,}735 \times 0.06 = 104.1$

Now we need to find what percent 104.1 is of 314. We can set up a ratio to find the percent:

$$\frac{104.1}{314} = \frac{x}{100}$$
$$10{,}410 = 314x$$
$$x = 33.1528\ldots$$

Rounded to the nearest hundredth, the answer is 33.15 percent.

11. 13.11

In order to solve, we can use the equation for exponential growth/decay. In this case, because the cost is marked down, we use the decay equation.

The price after 5 months = $\$40 \times (0.8)^5$

We use (0.8) because the price is marked down 20% each month, so the total resulting price will be 80% of the starting price.

We raise this value to the power of 5 because we are finding the price after 5 months.

Evaluating the equation, we get:

Price = $40 × (0.32768)

Price = $13.1072

Since we are asked to round to the nearest cent, the answer is 13.11.

12. 42

To solve this problem, let's set up algebraic equations.

We know that we have a total of x games.

We can set up a variable, y, as being the number of games lost.

$$y + (y + 21) = x$$
$$2y + 21 = x$$

Next, we know that the number of games lost is one-third of the total games.

$$y = \frac{1}{3}x$$
$$3y = x$$

Now we can substitute to find the value of y.

$$2y + 21 = 3y$$
$$y = 21$$

Now we know that the team lost 21 games, which means it won 42 games total.

13. 40

To solve this problem, we need to split it into separate parts first.

To find x, we'll set up an algebraic equation by translating the second half of the question.

150 percent of x is 120:

$$1.5x = 120$$
$$x = 80$$

Now we can translate "what is x percent of 50?" to "what is 80 percent of 50?"

$$50 (0.8) = 40$$

14. D

To answer questions like this it is helpful to find the prime factors of 6 and 7, as well as their lowest common multiple.

6 has 2 and 3 as prime factors, and 7 is a prime number, so the least common multiple among these numbers is 2 × 3 × 7 = 42.

Any integer x, which is a common multiple of both of them, has to be a multiple of 42, such as 84, 126, or 168.

To answer I, we know that x must be some multiple of 42, or to put it another way, 21 × 2, which means that it will always be a multiple of 21. So I is true.

To answer II, we know that x could be 42, but it could also be 84, 126, 168, etc. So II cannot be true.

To answer III, we know that any odd × even or even × even is even so, x must be even. So III is true.

The correct answer is (D).

15. D

7^4 is equal to 7 × 7 × 7 × 7 = 2,401.

2,401 divided by 6 is 400, with a remainder of 1. (400 × 6 = 2,400, so 1 is the remainder).

The correct answer is (D).

16. C

There is a mark every $\frac{1}{8}$ of a centimeter, so the distance of the 37th mark is $37\frac{1}{8}$ or $\frac{37}{8}$ or $4\frac{5}{8}$ centimeters from the edge of the ruler.

The correct answer is (C).

17. D

The easiest way to solve this is to prime factor.

We are given 5^7. Its prime factors are $5 \times 5 \times 5 \times 5 \times 5 \times 5 \times 5$, so we know that 5^7 is divisible by any product of these numbers.

$$
\begin{aligned}
625 &= 5 \times 5 \times 5 \times 5 \\
125 &= 5 \times 5 \times 5 \\
25 &= 5 \times 5 \\
5 &= 5
\end{aligned}
$$

But the prime factors of 15 are 5×3. Because 5^7 does not have a factor of 3, 5^7 is not divisible by 15.

The correct answer to this "EXCEPT" problem is (D).

18. B

The best way to solve this complex fraction is to simplify the numerator and denominator by canceling what can be canceled out.

$$\frac{4}{5} \times 10 \times \frac{3}{4} \times 12 \Rightarrow \frac{4 \times 10}{5} \times \frac{3 \times 12}{4}$$

Considering the first product, note that $10 = 5 \times 2$, so the 5s cancel, resulting in a product of $4 \times 2 = 8$.

For the second product, $12 = 4 \times 3$, so the 4s cancel, resulting in a product of $3 \times 3 = 9$.

Combing these two products, the numerator becomes $4 \times 2 \times 3 \times 3 \Rightarrow 8 \times 9 \Rightarrow 72$.

Now, do the same to the terms in the denominator.

$$\frac{3}{10} \times 5 \times \frac{7}{8} \times 24 \Rightarrow \frac{3 \times 5}{10} \times \frac{7 \times 24}{8}$$

Again, $10 = 5 \times 2$ so the 5s cancel in the first product, resulting in $\frac{3}{2}$.

For the second product in the denominator, $24 = 8 \times 3$ so the 8s cancel, producing $7 \times 3 = 21$.

Combing these two products, the denominator becomes $\frac{3}{2} \times 21 \Rightarrow \frac{63}{2}$.

Now the original equation can be expressed as $\frac{72}{\left(\frac{63}{2}\right)}$. By applying the rules for dividing a number by a fraction $\left(\frac{a}{\left(\frac{b}{c}\right)} = a \times \left(\frac{c}{b}\right)\right)$, we can rearrange this fraction as $\frac{72 \times 2}{63}$ or $\frac{144}{63}$.

Once we have made it this far, we can simplify this fraction and find the answer. To do this, we must cancel out the common factors of 144 and 63. First look for 2, but as 63 is odd, that does not work. Next, 3 works, as both numbers are divisible by 3 (we know this because their digits sum to a number divisible by 3: $1 + 4 + 4 = 9$ and $6 + 3 = 9$).

After taking out the 3s, we get $\frac{48}{21}$, which is once again divisible by 3. Once more, we take the 3s out and get $\frac{16}{7}$. We can express this as $2\frac{2}{7}$.

The correct answer is (B).

19. B

The percent increase is calculated by the formula: $\frac{(\text{New} - \text{Old})}{(\text{Old})} \times 100\%$. If we substitute for this problem's values, we find $\frac{(225 - 175)}{175} \times 100\%$, which equals $\left(\frac{50}{175}\right) \times 100\%$, or $\left(\frac{2}{7}\right) \times 100\%$, or approximately 28.6%.

An easy way to get the approximate value of $\frac{2}{7}$ is to first divide 100 by 7, yielding some number between 14 and 15 (because $14 \times 7 = 98$ and $15 \times 7 = 105$). Therefore, $\frac{1}{7}$ is equal to something between .14 and .15. We have 2 sevenths, so multiply this number by 2 and we get (B) as the answer.

20. D

In order for $3c + d^2$ to have the greatest value, we want to assign values to both c and d that result in the largest positive values for each stem.

In order to obtain the largest possible value for $3c$, we assign 3. For d, we want to assign the largest absolute value of d, because squaring a negative number still results in a positive number. Therefore, the greatest result of these is equal to $3(3) + (-5)^2 = 34$.

The correct answer is (D).

21. E

To solve for c, we must square both sides of the equation, because we are given the square root of c.

$$\sqrt{c} = 25$$
$$\left(\sqrt{c}\right)^2 = (25)^2$$
$$c = 25^2 \text{ or } 625$$

Don't make the mistake here of taking the square root of 25 to find c.

The correct answer is (E).

22. E

First, let's simplify this expression by converting each complex fraction into a product of the numerator and the reciprocal of its denominator:

$$\frac{1}{\left(\frac{1}{2}\right)} = \frac{1 \times 2}{1} = 2$$

$$\frac{2}{\left(\frac{2}{3}\right)} = \frac{2 \times 3}{2} = 3$$

$$\frac{3}{\left(\frac{3}{4}\right)} = \frac{3 \times 4}{3} = 4$$

Now let's put it back together:

$$2 + 3 + 4 = 9$$

The correct answer is (E).

23. B

Use the distance formula: distance = rate × time.

Use the information on the entire trip to determine how many miles the Ryder family traveled: 60 mph × 10 hours = 600 miles.

Next, determine how many of the 600 miles were traveled at 70 mph: d = 70 mph × 4 hours = 280 miles.

Subtract 280 miles from the total distance traveled, 600 miles, to find the remaining number of miles traveled at an unknown speed: 600 – 280 = 320.

Now, use the rate formula to determine the miles per hour for the remainder of the trip:

$$\text{Rate} = \frac{\text{Distance}}{\text{Time}}.$$

In this case, mph = $\frac{320 \text{ miles}}{6 \text{ hours}}$ $53\frac{1}{3}$ mph, which is the rate for the Ryder family for the remaining 6 hours of the trip. The correct choice is (B).

24. C

The quickest way to solve this is to add 6% and 9% of $400 to $400 to get the range of the prices that the refrigerator could be.

6% of $400 is $24 and 9% of $400 is $36; therefore, the total price could be *between* $424 and $436 ($436 is *not* between $424 and $436). The only answer that falls in this range is (C).

25. B

First, we'll want to start by doing the operations in the parentheses. Here, (29 + 8) = 37 and (13 + 24) = 37

Now we have $\sqrt{(37)(37)}$.

We can now recognize that $(37)(37) = 37^2$ and the square root of any number squared is the number itself.

We could also multiply 37 times 37 to get 1,369 and then take the square root of that, but the first analysis is by far the simplest and quickest.

The correct answer is (B).

26. C

The easiest way to solve this "EXCEPT" problem is to prime factor the given expression.

We are given $(7x)^3$. Its prime factors are $7 \times 7 \times 7 \times x \times x \times x$, so we know that $(7x)^3$ is divisible by any product of these numbers. Because there is no 3 in this, we cannot get a factor of 3×7 or 21, so we know the answer is (C); $(7x)^3$ is not necessarily divisible by 21. $(7x)^3$ *is* divisible by any combination of its prime factors.

The correct answer is (C).

27. C

Pick a value for the price of the stock. Since this is a percent question, picking $100 will make the math more manageable. The first change in the price of the stock was a decrease of 20%, which when applied to our initial value of $100, or $20, makes the new price $100 - $20 = $80.

The price then fell by another 25%: 25% is the same as $\frac{1}{4}$, and $\frac{1}{4}$ of $80 is $20. Therefore, after the second decrease, the current price of the stock is $80 - $20 = $60. To return from $60 to its original price of $100 is an increase of $100 - $60, or $40. $40 is what percent of the current price, $60?

$\frac{\$40}{\$60}$ (100%) $= \frac{2}{3}$ (100%) $= 66\frac{2}{3}\%$. Answer choice (C) is correct.

28. −428

You could write out 50 terms to solve this problem, but there's a shortcut. You're told that this is an arithmetic sequence, and the value of the nth term in an arithmetic sequence is the first term in the sequence (a_1) added to the value of the common difference between each successive pair of terms (d) multiplied by 1 less than n

Here the common difference is −9. So:

$$\begin{aligned} a_n &= a_1 + (n - 1) \times d \\ a_{50} &= 13 + (50 - 1) \times (-9) \\ a_{50} &= 13 + (49) \times (-9) \\ a_{50} &= 13 + (-441) \\ a_{50} &= -428 \end{aligned}$$

29. B

Read this question carefully! The question is *not* asking for the product of $\frac{3}{7}$ and $\frac{9}{7}$. It is asking what number you must multiply by $\frac{9}{7}$ to get a result of $\frac{3}{7}$. To find the answer, divide $\frac{3}{7}$ by $\frac{9}{7}$. To divide fractions, multiply by the reciprocal:

$$\frac{3}{7} \times \frac{7}{9} = \frac{1\cancel{3}}{\cancel{7}_1} \times \frac{\cancel{7}^1}{\cancel{9}_3} = \frac{1}{3}$$

30. C

We first need a value for x. Let's try looking at some powers of 3.

$3^1 = 3$
$3^2 = 9$
$3^3 = 27$
$3^4 = 81$

Therefore, $x = 4$. Then we calculate:

$x^3 = 4^3 = 4 \times 4 \times 4 = 64$

31. A, B, C

When working with exponents, it helps to convert each number to a common base before comparing. The question is asking for equivalents of 8^5, so begin by converting that to $(2^3)^5 = 2^{15}$. Now convert each of the choices where necessary:

(A) $2^5 \times 4^5 = 2^5 \times (2^2)^5 = 2^5 \times 2^{10} = 2^{15}$

(B) 2^{15}

(C) $2 \times 4^7 = 2 \times (2^2)^7 = 2 \times 2^{14} = 2^{15}$

All three choices equal 2^{15}, so they are all correct.

32. A

For each number x in the sequence, the next number is $2x - 3$. The first four terms in the sequence are 5, 7, 11, and 19. The difference between 19 and 11 is 8, so (A) is correct.

33. D

Rather than undertaking long calculations, you may want to estimate the value of $\sqrt{3}$. (For this, you need to know that $\sqrt{3} = 1.7$)

$\frac{\sqrt{3} + 1}{\sqrt{3} - 1?}$ is approximately $\frac{1.7 + 1}{1.7 - 1} = \frac{2.7}{.7}$, which is just under 4. Now let's look for a match in the answer choices:

(A) $3 - \sqrt{3}$ is approximately $3 - 1.7$. Too small.

(B) $2\sqrt{3} - 2$ is approximately $3.4 - 2$. Too small.

(C) 3 is too small.

(D) $2 + \sqrt{3}$ is approximately $2 + 1.7$, which sounds pretty good!

(E) $4 + 2\sqrt{3}$ is much greater than 4. Too big.

The answer must be (D).

34. 12

The ratio of males to females is 3 to 2. So, the ratio of females (2) to the entire class (males and females = 3 + 2 = 5) is 2 to 5. Let f = number of females. Then, $\frac{2}{5} = \frac{f}{30}$. Cross-multiply to get $5f = 60$; $f = 12$.

The answer is 12.

35. 400

Let r be the number of revolutions per mile. Then $9r$ is the number of revolutions per hour, or 60 minutes. We can write and solve a proportion using ratios of revolutions to time:

$$\frac{60}{1} = \frac{9r}{60}$$
$$9r = 3,600$$
$$r = 400$$

The correct answer is 400.

36. 2.5

The question asks for an original amount given the final amount after two percent changes. We can work backwards and write an equation to find the total rainfall last month. Then we can use that amount to find the total rainfall two months ago. Let l equal the total rainfall last month (after the percent increase but before the percent decrease).

$$(1 - 0.05)l = 2.85$$
$$0.95l = 2.85$$
$$l = 3.00$$

Now, let r equal the total rainfall two months ago. Using last month's total rainfall, we can determine the rainfall two months ago.

$$(1 + 0.2)r = 3.00$$
$$1.2r = 3.00$$
$$r = 2.5$$

The total rainfall two months ago was 2.5 inches, so the answer is 2.5.

37. D, F

In order to solve a problem like this, we could start by seeing which answer choices are multiples of 6. Unfortunately, all of the answer choices are multiples of 6.

Let's use the next number in line. Answer choices (A), (C), (D), and (F) are all multiples of 9 and of 6. We can eliminate answer choices (B) and (E), which are not multiples of 9.

The next step is to see which of the remaining choices are also multiples of 12.

18 is not a multiple of 12, nor is 54. Therefore we can eliminate (A) and (C).

Choices (D) and (F) are both multiples of 12, as well as multiples of 9 and 6, so they are correct.

38. B, D

Let's pick numbers and plug them in, making sure we understand the properties of prime numbers.

q is a multiple of p, which is positive, so $q > p$.

We can pick a positive prime value for p:

$p = 7$
$q = 14$

Now let's plug these values into the answer choices:

(A) $p = 7$

(B) $q = 14$

(C) $p^2 = 49$

(D) $q^2 = 196$

Using these values, we can see that only (B) and (D) are multiples of both 7 and 14.

To check this, pick another set. If $p = 3$, and $q = 3$ also, for instance, all answer choices will be multiples of both p and q. But the question asks for which answer choices *must* be correct. Only (B) and (D) will work all the time.

39. C

In order to solve, we know that each mark is an equal distance apart.

This means we need to know number properties.

Let's allocate actual values for each variable:

$r = -2$
$s = -1$
$t = 2$

Then we can plug into each answer choice.

For (A), we have $2^{-2} > 2^{-1}$

$$\frac{1}{4} > \frac{1}{2}$$

This is false, so (A) is incorrect.

For (B), we have $(-2)(-1)(2) < 0$

$$4 < 0$$

This is also false, so (B) is incorrect.

For (C), we have $(-2-(-1))^2 > 0$

$$(-1)^2 > 0$$
$$1 > 0$$

This is true, so (C) is correct.

40. A, G, I, J

We know that the units digits of N is either 8 or 9.

We also know that the units digit of P is 2, 1, or 0.

We can set up a small table to show the possible units digits of their products.

	$x = 8$	$x = 9$
$y = 2$	6	8
$y = 1$	8	9
$y = 0$	0	0

The only results we get are 0, 6, 8, and 9. These are our answers.

41.   A, D

In order to solve this problem, we must first see which values are multiples of either q or r. Let's choose q.

(A), (B), and (D) are multiples of q, because we can see q in the number.

Next, we see which ones also include r. These are (A) and (D).

(B) and (C) are incorrect because although there are prime numbers that are factors of 16 and 9, we know that r cannot be one of them, as both q and r are greater than 20.

42.   A, D

We know that q is an integer, but also the square root of p, so $q^2 = p$.

Let's assign a value to plug in for q and for p.

  $p = 9$
  $q = 3$

Now we can plug the values into the answer choices:

(A) $\frac{9}{3} = 3$, an integer. This is correct.

(B) $\frac{3}{9}$, not an integer. This is incorrect.

(C) the square root of 3 is not an integer, so this is incorrect.

(D) the square root of 9 is 3, which is an integer. Correct.

(A) and (D) are our correct answers.

43.   B, D

We know that n is a multiple of 3. In order for any number to be a multiple of 12 as well, we must multiply n by any multiple of 4.

Thus, (B) is automatically a correct answer.

(D) is also correct since, regardless of what n is, multiplying it by 12 makes it a multiple of 12.

(A) is incorrect: multiplying a multiple of 3 by 3 does not necessarily make it a multiple of 12.

(C) is also incorrect. For $n = 9$, for instance, 81 + 12 = 93, which is not a multiple of 12.

So, the correct answers are (B) and (D).

44.   A, D

We know that q is an integer, and also a perfect square. This means the square root of q is also an integer.

(A) q is an integer, so q^2 is an integer as well. We know the square root of q is also an integer, and adding the two plus 1 will still leave us with an integer.

(B) We are not positive that q is an even integer, so it may not divide evenly by 2.

(C) Same issue as answer choice (B): the square root of q is an integer, but not necessarily an even one.

(D) All components, q^2, q, and the square root of q, are integers. When we add them together, we will get an integer.

Thus, (A) and (D) are our correct answers.

45.   C, E, G, I

The units digit of $1{,}572^n$ is the same as the units digits of 2^n. We are simply looking at the last digit in the number.

(To verify this, compute $1{,}572^2$, and 2^2. We get 2,471,184 and 4. The units digits are the same.)

Since we know that n is a positive integer, we can start with 1 and work up.

Note that because the question asks for what the units digit COULD be, we must include every possible result we see that comes up in our computations.

$2^1 = 2$: units digit is 2. (C) is a correct answer.

$2^2 = 4$: units digit is 4. (E) is a correct answer.

$2^3 = 8$: units digit is 8. (I) is a correct answer.

$2^4 = 16$: units digit is 6. (G) is a correct answer.

$2^5 = 32$. (C) again.

$2^6 = 64$. (E) again.

We see that the pattern of units digits repeats 2, 4, 6, and 8, so (C), (E), (G), and (I) are our correct answers.

46. 19

Let x be the smaller integer and $x + 1$ be the larger integer. We can then set up the following equation:

$$\begin{aligned}
(x+1)^2 - x^2 &= 37 \\
x^2 + 2x + 1 - x^2 &= 37 \\
2x + 1 &= 37 \\
2x &= 26 \\
x &= 18
\end{aligned}$$

So the larger integer is 19. We can verify this: $19^2 - 18^2 = 361 - 324 = 37$.

47. C, D

We don't know actual numeric values for a, b, or d, but we know that a and b are negative, while d is positive. And since the tick marks are equally spaced, we know that $a = 2b$, and that $d = -a$. Sometimes it'll be easier to solve these mathematically, but other times we can solve them graphically.

Since we need to select all true statements, we need to consider each one in turn.

(A) $ab + ad > 0$

At a quick glance, we know that ab is the product of two negative numbers, so it's positive, while ad is the product of a negative and a positive number, so it's negative. But which of those two terms has the greater absolute value? That will determine whether or not the sum is positive.

One approach is to simplify: $ab + ad = a(b + d)$. Since $d = -a = -2b$, we know that $b + d = b - 2b = -b$. Since b is negative, $-b$ is positive; since a is negative also, and $a(-b)$ is negative, so $ab + ad < 0$. This statement is false.

Another approach is just to eyeball it: the absolute value of ab is going to be smaller than the absolute value of ad, since b is a smaller number (in absolute value) than d. So ab, the positive term, is smaller than ad, the negative term, and the sum will be negative.

(B) $b - a = d$

Graphically, we can see $b - a$ yields a result that is one tick mark on the positive side of 0: since a is two tick marks on the negative side of 0, subtracting a will yield a result two tick marks to the right of b. Since d is two tick marks away from 0, though, this statement must be false.

Mathematically, since $a = 2b$, $b - a = b - 2b = -b$, but $d = -a = -2b$, so $b - a \neq d$.

(C) $(ab)(bd)(ad) > 0$

This term is equivalent to $(abd)^2$. Any number squared is greater than 0, so this statement is true.

(D) $\dfrac{a}{d} + \dfrac{b}{d} < 0$

Dividing a negative number by a positive number yields a negative number, so each of these terms are negative and so is their sum. This statement is true.

Choices (C) and (D) must be true.

An alternative method is to Pick Numbers. A scan of the answer choices tells you that you must have numbers that are easy to divide. Let's make $a = -4$, $b = -2$, and $d = 4$. Testing each answer choice with these values will again establish that only choices (C) and (D) must be true.

48. A

As few as one and as many as all of the answer choices might be correct, so let's examine each one in turn. What we know is that b is the square root of an integer, meaning that b^2 is an integer. b itself might not be, and in fact probably isn't, since the square roots of most integers are not themselves integers.

(A) $9b^4 - 3b^2 + 1$

Seeing an expression like this might tempt you to try to factor, but it's not necessary. We know that b^2 is an integer, and so squaring that will yield another integer, b^4. Thus this expression is just the addition and subtraction of terms that themselves are integers, so the result must also be an integer.

(B) $\frac{b^2}{4} + 4$

Although we know that b^2 is an integer, dividing it by 4 might no longer yield an integer. For example, if $b^2 = 9$, the result of this operation would be 6.25—not an integer. But it also might remain an integer when divided by 4, such as if $b^2 = 16$. So it's indeterminate whether or not this term itself is an integer.

(C) $b^2 + 2b + 1$

Although b^2 must be an integer, as we already noted, b is not necessarily an integer, nor is $2b$. Even if we factor this to $(b + 1)^2$, we are left unsure whether this is an integer. b could be 4, but it could also be $\sqrt{5}$.

49. C

If v is a power of 3, that means that $v = 3^n$ for some positive integer n. In other words, v could equal 3, 9, 27, 81, and so on.

Let's examine each answer choice to see whether it must be a power of 3.

(A) $9v + \frac{v}{3}$

$9v = 3^2 \times v = 3^2 \times 3^n = 3^{2+n}$ so $9v$ will also be a power of 3.

But $\frac{v}{3}$ is not necessarily a power of 3: for instance, suppose $v = 3$. More importantly, when these two terms are added together,

even if they are both powers of 3, the sum will not be. For example, let $v = 9$:

$$9(9) + 3 = 84$$

84 is divisible by 3 but not a power of 3. This statement is false.

(B) $\sqrt[3]{v}$

Don't be confused by seeing another 3: this is the cube root of 3, meaning 3 is in the exponent, not in the base. The fact that $v = 3^n$, where the base that is raised to the power n is 3, doesn't make it any more or less likely that v will have a cube root that is an integer.

What does it take for a number to have a cube root? It means that the number $= a^n$ for some integer a where n is divisible by 3. It doesn't matter whether a (the base) is divisible by 3, only whether n (the power) is. So if $n = 3, 6, 9$, etc, then $v = 3^n$ will have a cube root.

However, if v does in fact have a cube root, then that cube root will be a power of 3, since the only factors of v are powers of 3.

So the question here is just whether or not $\sqrt[3]{v}$ is an integer. If it is, it will be a power of 3 as well. But since it might not be an integer, this choice will not always yield a power of 3. For example, if $v = 3$ or 9, the cube root of v won't be an integer. But if $v = 27$, the cube root is 3, which is 3^1.

(C) v^2

If v is a power of 3, namely 3^n for some positive integer n, then $v^2 = (3^n)^2 = 3^{2n}$, which is also a power of 3 regardless of the value of n.

50. B, D, E

This is a multiple-choice question with one or more correct answers, so we have to take a close look at all the answer choices.

Any whole number is divisible by itself and 1, so that's two factors to begin with. If there is exactly one other pair of numbers that can be multiplied together to produce the number, there are four factors. If there are two or more other pairs, there are more than four factors.

Let's consider the various answer choices:

(A) 10 is divisible by 1, 2, 5, and 10: exactly four factors. Incorrect.

(B) 12 is divisible by 1, 2, 3, 4, 6, and 12: more than four factors. Correct.

(C) 14 is divisible by 1, 2, 7, and 14: exactly four factors. Incorrect.

(D) 16 is divisible by 1, 2, 4, 8, and 16: more than four factors. Correct.

(E) 18 is divisible by 1, 2, 3, 6, 9, and 18: more than four factors. Correct.

The correct answer choices are (B), (D), and (E).

51. A, D

This is a multiple-choice question with one or more correct answers, so we need to examine all the answer choices closely.

All whole numbers are divisible by 1 and themselves. For a number to have exactly three factors, it must also be a perfect square that is not divisible by any other whole numbers (in other words, its square root must be a prime number).

Let's examine the answer choices:

(A) 9 is a square number; its only factors are 1, 3, and 9. Correct.

(B) 16 is a square number, but it is also divisible by 2 and 8, so it has five factors. (The square root of 16 is 4, which is not a prime number: 4 is divisible by 2, which is why 16 has more than three factors).

(C) 23 is a prime number, so it only has two factors: 1 and 23.

(D) 25 is a square number; its only factors are 1, 5, and 25. Correct.

(E) 33 is divisible by 1, 3, 11, and 33; it has four factors.

The correct answer choices are (A) and (D).

52. B, C, D

This is a multiple-choice question with one or more correct answers.

If a whole number has exactly three factors, it is a perfect square number, and its square root is prime. In the case of a number like m, the only three factors will be 1, $\sqrt{m}$ (which itself has no further factors), and the number itself.

Let's examine the answer choices:

(A) m is a prime number

Prime numbers have exactly two factors: 1 and themselves. They never have three factors. This is not true.

(B) m is the square of another number

This must be true; otherwise, m would have an even number of factors. The only way to have an odd number of factors is for two of the factors to be the same—and this only happens in square numbers.

(C) m is a composite number

A composite number is a number that is not prime. Since we know that m is a square number, it cannot be prime, so it is indeed composite. True.

(D) $\sqrt{m}$ is a prime number

This must be true. We know that m has an integral square root, but if that square root were not prime then it itself would be factorable, and those factors would also be factors of m—yielding a total of more than three factors.

(E) m is the cube of another number

This cannot be true: if m were the cube of another number—let's call it x—then x^2 would be a factor of m as well, and there would be at least four total factors of m.

(F) *m* is odd

This might seem to be always true, now that we've established that *m* is the square of a prime whole number. We also know that the square of an odd number is also an odd number; the only square numbers that are even are the squares of even numbers. So are there any prime numbers that are not odd? Yes! 2 is the only even prime number, which means that *m* could equal 4. Because it's possible that *m* = 4, even if all other possible values of *m* are odd, we cannot categorically state that *m* is odd.

The correct answer choices are (B), (C), and (D).

53. 2

To solve this problem, it is best to pick a value of *x* that will satisfy the first set of conditions.

When *x* is divided by 4, there is a remainder of 3, which means to find possible values of *x* we can take multiples of 4 and add 3:

    4 + 3 = 7
    8 + 3 = 11
    12 + 3 = 15

etc.

Any of these will work for *x*, so let's pick 11.

The question asks for *x* + 7 divided by 4:

$$(11) + 7 = 18$$

$$\frac{18}{4} = 4\,R\,2$$

The remainder is 2, and will be so for any value that satisfies the first conditions for *x*.

54. B

To solve this, we must take the extremes and determine what is the lowest and greatest value of *xy*.

To do this, we must use 4 and 1 and 7 and 5. Even though *x* cannot be 4 or 7 and *y* cannot

be 1 or 5, using these will give us the minimum and maximum for *xy*.

Min: 4 × 1 = 4

Max: 7 × 5 = 35

So 4 < *xy* < 35

The correct answer is (B).

55. A

We know that *x* does not equal zero, so to test the results, we should pick both positive and negative numbers and evaluate the results. Since this is a "must be true" question, if we can find a counterexample, then the statement is not eligible.

Let's first start with a negative number, say –3. For statement I, we get 3(–3) = –9, so this is not greater than –3. For statement II, we get –3^5, which is equal to –243, so again this is not greater than –3. For statement III, we get 5 – (–3), which is 8, so it is greater than –3. An answer choice with statement III could work.

Next, we should try a positive number, such as 5. Testing statement III with *x* = 5, we have 5 – 5 = 0, and this is less than 5. Even though statement III worked with a negative number, it did not work with a positive number.

This rules out all answer choices but (A): none of the statements hold true for all nonzero numbers. The correct answer is (A).

56. C

We are given that the average of two given numbers and one unknown is between a range, and we must find the biggest possible value of *n*.

To determine *n*, we must find what the total of the numbers could be. To find this, we know that to calculate the arithmetic mean, we multiply the number of items times the average to get the total sum of the items:

average × total items = total sum

We are given that the average of the three items is between 17 and 20 inclusive, therefore we multiply 20 (the largest number) times the number of items to get 20 × 3 = 60. This gives us the largest possible total of the numbers.

Now, we simply subtract 15 and 19 from 60 to get the largest value of *n*.

60 – 15 – 19 = 26

57. E

To answer questions like this it is helpful to find the prime factors of 5 and 8, as well as their lowest common multiple.

The prime factors of 8 are 2 × 2 × 2, and 5 is a prime number, so their lowest common multiple is 2 × 2 × 2 × 5 = 40.

Any integer *x*, which is a common multiple of both of them, has to be a multiple of 40, such as 80, 120, or 160.

To analyze statement I, we know that *x* must be some multiple of 40, or to put it another way, 20 × 2, which means that it will always be a multiple of 20. So I must be true.

To analyze statement II, we know that *x* could be 40, but it could also be 80, 120, 160, etc. So II cannot be true.

To analyze statement III, we know that any product of odd × even or even × even is even, so *x* must be even. So III must be true.

The correct answer is (E).

58. B

8^4 is equal to 8 × 8 × 8 × 8 = 4,096.

4,096 divided by 3 is 1,365 with a remainder of 1. (1,365 × 3 = 4,095, so 1 is the remainder).

A way of testing if a number is divisible by 3 is to add the digits, and if that sum is divisible by 3, then the original number is divisible by 3. So here, we could move down one number and add the digits. 4,095 adds to 4 + 9 + 5 = 18, which is divisible by 3. Because 4,096 is one

more than 4,095, there must be a remainder of 1.

Also, when dividing by 3, it is impossible to have a remainder of 3 or 4, so (D) and (E) could be eliminated immediately.

The correct answer is (B).

59. C

Basic number properties are being tested here. Odd × odd = odd, but even × (odd or even) = even.

I. has an odd + 1 = even being multiplied by itself an odd number of times. So no matter what *y* is, it will always be even × even thus making this even. FALSE.

II. has an odd value *x* being multiplied by itself an even number of times. But this is still an odd × odd = odd. TRUE.

III. has an odd raised to an odd power (which does not matter) so the same odd × odd = odd applies. TRUE.

Statements II and III must be odd. The correct answer is (C).

60. B

Since *a* is odd, 3*a* must also be odd. This means that *b* is also odd.

(A) must be even, as it is the sum of two odd integers.

(B) must be odd. a^2 is odd and 3*a* is odd, so their difference must be even. When 1 is added to an even number, the result is odd. This must be the answer.

(C) must be even because 8 is even and 2*b* is even. The difference of two even numbers is always even.

(D) must be even. a^2 is odd and b^2 is odd, so their sum must be even. When 4 is subtracted from an even number, the result is always even.

(E) must be even. Any multiple of 4 is even.

The correct choice is (B).

61. B, C

The product of a set of numbers will be even if at least one number is even, and the sum of a set of numbers will be even if there is an even number of odd integers. If you forget this rule on Test Day, you can Backsolve:

(A) With 0 even integers, there would be 4 − 0 = 4 odd integers. For example, the integers could be 1, 3, 5, and 7. Then 1 + 3 + 5 + 7 = 16, which is even, but 1 × 3 × 5 × 7 = 105, which is odd. Eliminate this choice.

(B) With 2 even integers, there would be 4 − 2 = 2 odd integers. For example, the integers could be 1, 2, 3, and 4. Then 1 + 2 + 3 + 4 = 10 and 1 × 2 × 3 × 4 = 24. These are both even, so this choice works.

(C) With 4 even integers, there would be 4 − 4 = 0 odd integers. For example, the integers could be 2, 4, 6, and 8. Then 2 + 4 + 6 + 8 = 20 and 2 × 4 × 6 × 8 = 384. These are both even, so this choice works.

The correct answers are choices (B) and (C).

62. B

Any number divisible by 8 and 5 is divisible by 8 × 5, since 5 is prime and not a factor of 8. Also, 8 × 5 = 40 is a factor of 200, the smallest number in x's range. Add 40 to 200 to find the next number in the series, 240, then 40 again for 280. The next number that is a multiple of 40 after 280 is larger than 300, the top of the range. This means 200, 240, and 280 are the three values that are divisible by 8 and 5.

63. D

The key to our analysis is to first determine the prime factorization of 168. 168 = 8 × 21 = 2 × 2 × 2 × 3 × 7. Any number that is the product of any subgroup of the numbers in the list (2, 2, 2, 3, 7) will also be a factor of 168. Note

that 2 appears three times in the list because it occurs as a factor of 168 three times.

Now look at the answer choices. 21 is the product of 3 and 7. 24 is the product of 2, 2, 2, and 3. 28 is the product of 2, 2, and 7. 42 is the product of 2, 3, and 7. However, the prime factorization of 32 is 2 × 2 × 2 × 2 × 2. Thus the prime factor 2 occurs 5 times in 32. Since 168 only contains 3 factors of 2, 32 cannot be a factor of 168.

The correct answer is (D).

64. C

What concept is being tested here? We are dividing a wire into different segments, and all the resulting pieces have integer lengths. This means that each third of the wire has a length that is evenly divisible by 4, 6, and 8. So this problem is really testing divisibility.

The answer choices are actual numbers, so you could answer this problem by Backsolving. Now, because we are looking for a minimum length, more than one answer could potentially work: we should begin by plugging in the smallest answer choice, not the middle answer choice.

(A) 24. If we were to divide the wire into three equal pieces, each piece would have length 8. Although 8 is divisible by 4 and 8, it is not divisible by 6.

(B) 48. If we were to divide the wire into three equal pieces, each piece would have length 16. Again, 16 is divisible by 4 and 8, but not by 6.

(C) 72. If we were to divide the wire into three equal pieces, each piece would have length 24. 24 is divisible by 4, 6, and 8. This is the correct answer.

65. E

No odd number is a multiple of 2, so (A) and (C) are eliminated. The digits in numbers that are multiples of 3 add up to multiples of 3, which eliminates (B) and (D). Choice (E) must be correct. Note that all five choices are multiples of 5: each ends in either 5 or 0.

66. E

Pick a value for P and test each answer choice. To find a value that works, take any multiple of 9 and add 4 to it: 18 is a multiple of 9; P could be 22. Each of the answer choices works except (E). Note that, if you had selected $P = 27 + 4 = 31$, (E) would have worked. In that case, you would have to try the next possible value of P, 40, to see that choice (E) does not have to be true.

You can also reason your way through this problem. Choice (A) must be true because it is a paraphrase of the process by which you found a value of P. Choice (B) must be true since P equals 4 added to a multiple of 9, and adding 5 to that number results in adding 9 to a multiple of 9. Choice (C) must be true since any multiple of 9 is also a multiple of 3; 4 added to a multiple of 9, plus 2 more, results in a number 6 more than a multiple of 9 since the sum of two multiples of 3 must also be a multiple of 3. Choice (D) must be true because the remainder when 4 is divided by 3 is 1, and you already know that the rest of the number is divisible by 3. Choice (E) is not true when P is 4 more than an even multiple of 9, like 22 or 40.

67. D

The first few multiples of 4 are 4, 8, 12, 16, and 20. The multiples of 4 that are between 21 and 59 are 24, 28, 32, 36, 40, 44, 48, 52, and 56. These can each be written as the product of 4 and an odd number as follows:

24	=	3 × 8
28	=	4 × 7
32	=	32 × 1
36	=	3 × 12 (or 4 × 9)
40	=	8 × 5
44	=	4 × 11
48	=	3 × 16
52	=	4 × 13
56	=	8 × 7

The correct answer is choice (D).

68. D

We need to find positive integers that are both multiples of 4 and divisors (factors) of 128. The simplest method is to find the factors of 128, and then check to see which ones are also multiples of 4.

The positive integer factors of 128 are 1, 2, 4, 8, 16, 32, 64, and 128. Of these, 4, 8, 16, 32, 64, and 128 are multiples of 4.

There are six positive integers that are common to both lists, and so choice (D) is correct.

69. C

The bases 2, 3, 7, and 23 appearing in $(2^7)(3^4)(7^3)(23^5)$ are prime numbers. Now, any factor can be made up of any of the primes we have available to us. For instance, 9 is a factor of our number, using up two of our four available 3s, but zero 2s, zero 7s and zero 23s. Therefore the factors of $(2^7)(3^4)(7^3)(23^5)$ are of the form $(2^a)(3^b)(7^c)(23^d)$, where each of a, b, c, and d is a non-negative integer, and $0 \le a \le 7$, $0 \le b \le 4$, $0 \le c \le 3$, and $0 \le d \le 5$. The number of possible values of a is 8 because a can be 0 or any of the first 7 positive integers. The number of possible values of b is 5 because b can be 0 or any of the first 4 positive integers. The number of possible values of c is 4 because c can be 0 or any of the first 3 positive integers. The number of possible values of d is 6 because d can be 0 or any of the first 5 positive integers. The number of different positive integer factors of $(2^7)(3^4)(7^3)(23^5)$ is $8 \times 5 \times 4 \times 6 = 960$. Choice (C) is correct.

70.   A, C

Begin by finding the least common multiple of the three numbers. Do this by identifying their shared distinct prime factors. The numbers 2 and 7 are prime, but 4 can be factored into 2×2, so the least common multiple is $2 \times 2 \times 7 = 28$. As 28 is the least common multiple, every possible value of x will be a multiple of 28, so whatever works for $x = 28$ will always work.

(A) We could punch 28^2 into the calculator, but there's no need: This expression is basically $(28 \times 28) + 28$. Factor out a 28 and we have $28(28 + 1) = 28(29)$, which is certainly a multiple of 28.

(B) $2x = 2 \times 28 = 56$. This is NOT a multiple of 112, so eliminate this choice.

(C) This choice may seem daunting to test at first, but a bit of critical thinking can solve it easily: $28 = 4 \times 7$, so $28^2 = 4^2 \times 7^2$. We are dividing this numerator by 16, or 4^2, so we're left with 7^2 if $x = 28$. Since $7^2 = 49$, $\frac{x^2}{16}$ is definitely a multiple of 49.

The correct answers are choices (A) and (C).

71.   B, C

If number properties give you trouble on Test Day, remember that you can always fall back on Picking Numbers. As we are testing the properties of odd and even numbers, every permissible pair of numbers we pick will yield the same result. We are told that a is even and b is odd, so let's pick 2 for a and 3 for b.

(A) $3a + 4b = 3(2) + 4(3) = 6 + 12 = 18$. This is not odd.

(B) $(a^2 + 3)b = (2^2 + 3) \times 3 = 7 \times 3 = 21$. This is odd.

(C) $a + 3b = 2 + 3(3) = 2 + 9 = 11$. This is odd.

The correct answers are choices (B) and (C).

72.   B, D, F, G

A prime number is a number with only two distinct factors: 1 and itself. Hence, a number that is divisible by more than just 1 or itself is not prime. Of the choices, (A), (C), (E), and (H) are all divisible by 3, so we can eliminate them. Each of the remaining choices is only divisible by 1 and itself, so the correct answers are choices (B), (D), (F), and (G).

73.   B, C, D

With variables in the question stem and the answer choices, let us use Picking Numbers. Since x is odd and y is even, let us pick 3 for x and 2 for y:

(A) $x + y = 3 + 2 = 5$. This is odd. Eliminate.

(B) $2x = 2(3) = 6$. This is even.

(C) $xy = 3(2) = 6$. This is even.

(D) $2y = 2(2) = 4$. This is even.

(E) $y - x = 2 - 3 = -1$. This is odd. Eliminate.

Answer choices (B), (C), and (D) are the correct answers.

74.   B, D

We can divide each integer by 9 to determine which have remainders of 3:

(A) $265 \div 9 = 29$ R4

(B) $372 \div 9 = 41$ R3

(C) $573 \div 9 = 63$ R6

(D) $642 \div 9 = 71$ R3

(E) $817 \div 9 = 90$ R7

Answer choices (B) and (D) are correct.

Algebra and Properties of Sets

The use of variables to represent numbers is what differentiates algebra from arithmetic. Calculations in algebra may involve solving for a value of a variable that makes an equation true, or they may involve substituting different values for a variable in an expression. On the GRE, you will see some questions that are strictly algebra based, but you will also see questions that involve the use of algebra along with reasoning, problem solving, and data interpretation skills.

There are a variety of algebra topics tested on the GRE, including setting up equations to solve word problems, factoring and simplifying algebraic expressions, solving linear, quadratic, and simultaneous equations, and coordinate geometry.

The GRE will also test your ability to draw conclusions about sets of objects or data using statistics to describe the behavior of data, evaluating various presentations of data, and calculating the likelihood of events occurring. This includes concepts such as mean, median, mode, range, and standard deviation. Concepts like probability, combinations, and permutations are among the most challenging for many GRE students. Don't be afraid of these topics, but don't be afraid to focus on the fundamentals of statistics and graphics interpretation. You can come back to challenging combinatorics questions once you have the basics mastered.

Algebra & Properties of Sets Practice

Enter your answer in the answer box(es) below the question.

Equivalent forms of the correct answer, such as 2.5 and 2.50, are all correct. Fractions do not need to be reduced to lowest terms.

Enter the exact answer unless the question asks you to round your answer.

1. The average (arithmetic mean) of a set of five distinct positive integers is 20. What is the greatest possible value of the largest of these numbers?

   [ ]

2. What is the maximum y-value of the following function?

   $y = 8t - \dfrac{t^2}{2} - 24$

   [ ]

3. A factory uses two machines to produce widgets. The first can produce n widgets in 20 minutes. The second can produce n widgets in 30 minutes. If the machines are both operating consistently at the specified rates, how many minutes will it take to produce a total of $3n$ widgets?

   [ ] minutes

4. At a local clothing store, hats cost $6.20 a piece and shirts cost $15.50 a piece. If Luis spent a total of $74.40 on hats and shirts at this store, what is the greatest possible number of shirts that he bought?

   [ ] shirts

   $f(x) = 3x^{-3}$

5. What is the ratio of $f(3x)$ to $f(x)$?

   $\dfrac{[\quad]}{[\quad]}$

6. If x is an integer and $y = -12x^{-3}$, what value of x will result in the greatest possible value of y?

   [ ]

7. What is the slope of the line drawn from the intersection point of the lines $x - 6y = 14$ and $y = .25x - 12$ to the point (100, -15)?

   [ ]

Select one or more answer choices according to the specific question directions.

If the question does not specify how many answer choices to select, select all that apply.

The correct answer may be just one of the choices or as many as all of the choices, depending on the question.

No credit is given unless you select all of the correct choices and no others.

If the question specifies how many answer choices to select, select exactly that number of choices.

8. According to the following system of inequalities, which of the following points lie within the region of the solution set?

   $$2x + 3y \geq 6$$
   $$-x + y \geq -4$$

   Indicate all such points.

   A (6,1)

   B (4,1)

   C (2,1)

   D (2,–1)

Enter your answer in the answer box(es) below the question.

Equivalent forms of the correct answer, such as 2.5 and 2.50, are all correct. Fractions do not need to be reduced to lowest terms.

Enter the exact answer unless the question asks you to round your answer.

9. Dante buys shirts and pants from a local clothing store. Each pair of pants costs $21. Each shirt costs $15. If he spends $138 on 8 items, how many shirts did he buy?

   [   ] shirts

10. Anna buys apples and bananas. She spends the same amount on both, but she buys one more pound of apples than bananas. The price of bananas is $1 more per pound than the price of apples. If she purchased 4 pounds of apples, what is the price per pound of bananas?

    $ [   ]

Select one or more answer choices according to the specific question directions.

If the question does not specify how many answer choices to select, select all that apply.

The correct answer may be just one of the choices or as many as all of the choices, depending on the question.

No credit is given unless you select all of the correct choices and no others.

If the question specifies how many answer choices to select, select exactly that number of choices.

11. In Billy's first-grade class, the average height of the students is 110 cm. In his sister Andrea's fifth-grade class, the average height of the students is 140 cm. If the combined average height of all the students in the two classes is at least 130 cm, and there are 30 students in Andrea's class, what could be the total number of students in Billy's class?

Indicate all such possibilities.

A 5

B 10

C 12

D 15

E 30

F 60

12. Which points lie on the graph of $\frac{3y+xy}{x+3} = x - 2$?

Indicate all such points.

A (2,0)

B (−2,1)

C (−1,−3)

D $\left(\frac{4}{3}, \frac{1}{3}\right)$

E (1,3)

13. Which of the following points lie on or above the line whose equation is given by $12x + 16y = 8$?

Indicate all such points.

A (−2, 2)

B $\left(0, -\frac{1}{2}\right)$

C $\left(-4, \frac{9}{2}\right)$

D (6, −2)

E (16, −12)

14. If the ratio of x to $\frac{y}{3}$ is $\frac{1}{3}$ times the ratio of y to x, then which of the following could be the value of $\frac{y}{x}$?

Indicate all such values.

A −3

B −1

C $-\frac{1}{3}$

D $\frac{1}{3}$

E 1

F 3

15. If $1 < |a| < 3$ and $5 > b > 2$, then which of the following inequalities could be true?

    Indicate <u>all</u> such inequalities.

    A $-4 < ab < 0$

    B $-2 < ab < 2$

    C $2 < ab < 15$

    D $5 < ab < 6$

16. If $-1 < x < 0 < y < 1$, which of the following inequalities must be true?

    Indicate <u>all</u> such inequalities.

    A $x + y > 0$

    B $xy < 0$

    C $x^2 + y^2 > x + y$

    D $2x + x^2 < y$

17. Given that $3x^2 - 2x - 1 = 0$, which could be the *real* value of x?

    Indicate <u>all</u> such values.

    A 6

    B 1

    C $\frac{1}{3}$

    D $-\frac{1}{3}$

    E -3

    F There are no real solutions to the equation.

18. If $x \neq 0$, which of the following terms must be positive?

    Indicate <u>all</u> such terms.

    A x^{-2}

    B x^0

    C $\frac{1}{x^{-3}}$

    D $|x|$

    E $x^{-3} \times x^4$

    F $(x)^4 \times (-x)^4$

    G $(x^{-3})^4$

Enter your answer in the answer box(es) below the question.

Equivalent forms of the correct answer, such as 2.5 and 2.50, are all correct. Fractions do not need to be reduced to lowest terms.

Enter the exact answer unless the question asks you to round your answer.

19. After the following expression is simplified, to what power is x raised?

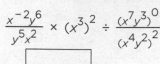

[answer box]

20. Nick drove from town A to town B in 1 hour and 15 minutes. Driving back the exact same route, he took 1 hour and 45 minutes. If the distance from town A to town B is 60 miles, what was the rate for the entire trip? Put your answer in miles per hour.

[answer box] miles per hour

21. Machine A produces 100 widgets in 75 minutes. Machine B produces 75 widgets every 50 minutes. How many widgets can both machines working together produce in one hour?

[answer box] widgets

22. Keren rode her moped from home to the beach at an average speed of 20 miles per hour. She rode back at an average speed of 30 miles per hour. What was her average speed for the entire trip, in miles per hour?

[answer box] miles per hour

23. If $12 - y = x$, then what is the value of $x^2 + 2xy + y^2 - 172$?

[answer box]

24. If $x \neq 0$, then $\dfrac{\left[x^2 x^4 \left(x^2\right)^3\right]}{x^4}$

Ⓐ x

Ⓑ x^2

Ⓒ x^7

Ⓓ x^8

Ⓔ x^{12}

25. The price per pair of brand A jeans is $45 and the price per pair of brand B jeans is $65. If there is no sales tax and Chris chooses only from among these two brands, what is the greatest number of pairs of jeans that he can buy with exactly $560?

Ⓐ 8

Ⓑ 10

Ⓒ 12

Ⓓ 14

Ⓔ 20

$$x - y + z = 0$$
$$4x + y + 5z = 0$$

26. If $z \neq 0$, then in the system of equations given, what is the ratio of x to z equal to?

    (A) $-\dfrac{6}{5}$

    (B) $-\dfrac{5}{6}$

    (C) $-\dfrac{1}{30}$

    (D) $-\dfrac{1}{5}$

    (E) $-\dfrac{1}{6}$

27. If Uma's company outfits all of its sales force with laptop computers for a total cost of $690,250, and each laptop costs $550, how many employees are in Uma's sales force?

    (A) 1,255
    (B) 1,355
    (C) 1,455
    (D) 1,534
    (E) 1,973

28. If $4x = -8$, then $3x^2 + 7x - 8 =$

    (A) -2
    (B) -10
    (C) 18
    (D) 28
    (E) 128

29. If x is an integer and $y = 4x + 12$, what is the greatest value of x for which y is less than 200?

    (A) 17
    (B) 25
    (C) 46
    (D) 47
    (E) 53

30. A clock gains 8 minutes and 17 seconds every 7 days. If the rate of gain does not change, how much does the clock gain in one day?

    (A) 1 minute 1 second
    (B) 1 minute 6 seconds
    (C) 1 minute 11 seconds
    (D) 1 minute 16 seconds
    (E) 1 minute 21 seconds

31. If $3d - 2r = 5r - 4d$, what is d in terms of r?

    (A) $\dfrac{r}{5}$

    (B) $\dfrac{r}{3}$

    (C) r

    (D) $2r$

    (E) $4r$

32. What is the least integer value of a such that $\dfrac{1}{(3)^a} < .01$?

    (A) 4
    (B) 5
    (C) 6
    (D) 34
    (E) There is no such least value.

33. If x exceeds y by 15 and y is half the value of x, what is the value of y?

    Ⓐ 7.5
    Ⓑ 10
    Ⓒ 15
    Ⓓ 30
    Ⓔ 60

34. A piece of licorice of length l inches is cut into two pieces, resulting in one of the two pieces having a length of two inches more than three times the length of the other piece. Which of the following is the length, in inches, of the longer piece?

    Ⓐ $\dfrac{(3l+2)}{4}$

    Ⓑ $\dfrac{(3l-2)}{4}$

    Ⓒ $\dfrac{(4l-2)}{3}$

    Ⓓ $\dfrac{(l-2)}{2}$

    Ⓔ $\dfrac{(l+2)}{2}$

35. If $a \geq 2$ and b is 3 less than the square of a, which of the following expresses a in terms of b?

    Ⓐ $a = b^2 - 3$

    Ⓑ $a = b^2 + 3$

    Ⓒ $a = 3 + \sqrt{b}$

    Ⓓ $a = \sqrt{(3-b)}$

    Ⓔ $a = \sqrt{(b+3)}$

36. If 7 cans of soda cost a total of $9.80, then what is the cost of 5 cans of soda at the same price per can?

    Ⓐ $1.40
    Ⓑ $5.00
    Ⓒ $7.00
    Ⓓ $7.40
    Ⓔ $9.80

37. At the rate of 6,000 revolutions per minute, how many revolutions will a wheel make in x seconds?

    Ⓐ $6,000x$

    Ⓑ $100x$

    Ⓒ $\dfrac{100}{x}$

    Ⓓ $\dfrac{6,000}{x}$

    Ⓔ $\dfrac{360,000}{x}$

38. If $5(x - 2) = x + 6$, then $x =$

    Ⓐ -4
    Ⓑ -1
    Ⓒ 1
    Ⓓ 2
    Ⓔ 4

39. If $x^2 + y^2 = 16 - 2xy$, then $(x + y)^4 =$

    Ⓐ 4
    Ⓑ 32
    Ⓒ 48
    Ⓓ 64
    Ⓔ 256

40. Celia has exactly 3 times as many French as non-French photographs in her collection. Which of the following CANNOT be the number of photographs in Celia's collection?

    (A) 100
    (B) 84
    (C) 76
    (D) 69
    (E) 32

41. A widow received $\frac{1}{3}$ of her husband's estate, and each of her three sons received $\frac{1}{3}$ of the balance. If the widow and one of her sons received a total of $120,000, what was the amount of the estate?

    (A) $180,000
    (B) $192,000
    (C) $216,000
    (D) $270,000
    (E) $275,000

42. If $\left|\frac{x}{4}\right| > 1$, which of the following must be true?

    (A) $x > 4$
    (B) $x < 4$
    (C) $x = 4$
    (D) $x \neq 4$
    (E) $x < -4$

43. If $|3x - 2 + 4x| > 7$, which of the following is a possible value for x?

    (A) $\frac{-2}{3}$
    (B) $\frac{-1}{2}$
    (C) $\frac{3}{4}$
    (D) $\frac{5}{4}$
    (E) $\frac{4}{3}$

44. If $z < 0$, then what is $\sqrt{-z|z|}$?

    (A) $\sqrt{z}$
    (B) $\sqrt{-z}$
    (C) z
    (D) $-z$
    (E) 0

45. If $|a| + |b| = |a + b|$, $a \neq 0$, and $b \neq 0$, then which of the following must be true?

    (A) $ab < 0$
    (B) $ab > 0$
    (C) $a - b > 0$
    (D) $a + b < 0$
    (E) $a + b > 0$

46. Let $x_1, x_2, x_3 \ldots x_n$ be a sequence of positive numbers where $x_1 = 1$, and $x_{n+1} = x_n + 4$. What represents the nth term in the sequence?

    Ⓐ $-3n$

    Ⓑ $3n - 4$

    Ⓒ $4n - 3$

    Ⓓ $4n - 4s$

    Ⓔ $5n$

$$a = 4(3 - 5) + 2$$

$$b = -4(5 - 3)$$

47. What is the value of $2|a| - |2b|$?

    Ⓐ -14

    Ⓑ -4

    Ⓒ 2

    Ⓓ 4

    Ⓔ 14

48. A picket fence is composed of x pickets, each of which is $\frac{1}{2}$ inch wide. If there are six inches of space between each pair of pickets, which of the following represents the length of the fence in feet?

    Ⓐ $\frac{13}{2}x$

    Ⓑ $\frac{13}{2}x - 6$

    Ⓒ $\frac{13}{24}x$

    Ⓓ $\frac{13x + 1}{24}$

    Ⓔ $\frac{13x - 12}{24}$

49. If a rocket can travel $\frac{x}{5}$ miles every y seconds, how many miles can it travel in z minutes?

    Ⓐ $\frac{xy}{5z}$

    Ⓑ $\frac{xz}{5y}$

    Ⓒ $\frac{xyz}{6}$

    Ⓓ $\frac{12xy}{z}$

    Ⓔ $\frac{12xz}{y}$

$$4x^2 - 16 = 0, \ x > 0.$$

50. What is the value of x?

    ☐

51. A group of x friends buys 20 T-shirts that cost $4 each. They spend $1 per T-shirt to print a design and a total of $5 to promote their T-shirt business. They sell all 20 shirts for $18 each and split the profit equally. If each friend's share of the profit is $51, how many friends are in the group?

    ☐ friends

52. Waiter A's compensation for any week is $500 plus 15 percent of the portion of A's total receipts above $600 for that week. Waiter B's compensation for any week is 25 percent of B's total receipts for that week. For what amount of total weekly receipts would both waiters earn the same compensation?

    (A) $12,200

    (B) $10,600

    (C) $8,900

    (D) $6,300

    (E) $4,100

53. A certain farmer planted x acres of corn at a cost of p dollars per acre. If y acres were destroyed by locusts and the farmer sold the rest of the crop for q dollars per acre, which of the following represents the farmer's gross profit on the sale of the corn?

    (A) $(x - y)q - xp$

    (B) $(x - y)p - yq$

    (C) $(q - p)y - xp$

    (D) $xp - yq$

    (E) $(x - y)(q - p)$

54. A supervisor has to select a three-member project team from among her 12 employees. Unfortunately, two of the employees cannot work together on the same team. With this restriction, how many different teams can she form?

    ⬚ teams

55. A school has a junior class of 312 students. Every student in the junior class must study at least one of three foreign languages offered by the school. If 190 students study Spanish, 83 study Italian, 72 study Russian, and no student takes all three classes, how many students are studying multiple languages?

    ⬚ students

56. In a shipment of 50 processors, on average, 5 will be defective. If two are pulled randomly from a shipment and tested, what is the probability that exactly one will be defective?

Select one or more answer choices according to the specific question directions.

If the question does not specify how many answer choices to select, select all that apply.

The correct answer may be just one of the choices, or as many as all of the choices, depending on the question.

No credit is given unless you select all of the correct choices and no others.

If the question specifies how many answer choices to select, select exactly that number of choices.

57. In a chemistry class, there are more than twice as many boys as there are girls. On the most recent test, the average grade for the girls was 92%, while the boys averaged 83%. Which of the following could be the average test score for the entire class combined?

Indicate all such scores.

[A] 82%

[B] 84%

[C] 85%

[D] 87%

[E] 90%

[F] 92%

58. Haruna and Rina went to a concert. Haruna drove there, averaging exactly 30 mph. After the concert, there was no traffic, so Rina drove back and averaged more than 60 mph. Which of the following could be the average speed for the entire trip?

Indicate all such speeds.

[A] 40 mph

[B] 45 mph

[C] 50 mph

[D] 55 mph

59. Which two of the following numbers have an average equal to 1?

[A] –7

[B] –5

[C] 6

[D] 7

When a group of boys and girls was placed in a corn maze, $\frac{2}{3}$ of the girls were able to find their way through the maze, and $\frac{1}{3}$ of the boys were able to find their way through the maze.

What is the chance that a child selected at random would find his or her way through the maze?

60. Which of the following statements individually provide(s) sufficient information to answer the question?

Indicate all such statements.

[A] There are four times as many girls as boys.

[B] Half of the group was under age 8, and they all found their way through the maze.

[C] 4 out of 10 children in the group did not find their way through the maze.

61. If *S* is the set containing all the positive factors of 24, and *T* is the set of all composite (non-prime) numbers, which of the following numbers could be in *S* ∩ *T*?

Indicate <u>all</u> such numbers.

[A] 2

[B] 3

[C] 6

[D] 24

[E] 48

Enter your answer in the answer box(es) below the question.

Equivalent forms of the correct answer, such as 2.5 and 2.50, are all correct. Fractions do not need to be reduced to lowest terms.

Enter the exact answer unless the question asks you to round your answer.

---

62. A long distance phone call costs $1.99 for the first minute and $0.34 for each additional minute. Simon called the same long distance number twice, once for 8 minutes and the next for 7 minutes. What is the average price in dollars per hour for Simon's long distance usage thus far?

$ [   ]

63. The average of 27 numbers is 8. If six numbers are added and the average does not change, what is the average of the 6 added numbers?

[   ]

64. *J* is the set of positive integers less than or equal to 50, and *K* is the set of squares of the integers in *J* that are also odd numbers. How many elements does the intersection of *J* and *K* contain?

(A) 4

(B) 7

(C) 15

(D) 54

(E) 57

65. In a puzzle game, Tran was given the word STRUM. How many unique three-letter arrangements are possible using the letters of the word?

(A) 15

(B) 60

(C) 90

(D) 120

(E) 240

66. A coin is tossed and a six-sided die is rolled in a game. If Marie gets heads and an even number, she will advance to the second round. In the second round, she will again toss the coin and roll the die. If she gets tails and an odd number, she will advance to the third round. What is the probability that she will NOT advance to the third round?

   Ⓐ $\frac{1}{32}$

   Ⓑ $\frac{1}{16}$

   Ⓒ $\frac{9}{16}$

   Ⓓ $\frac{15}{16}$

   Ⓔ It cannot be determined.

67. The average (arithmetic mean) of five numbers is $4x + 3$. If the sum of two of the numbers is $2x$, what is the average of the other three numbers?

   Ⓐ $6x + 5$

   Ⓑ $6x + 9$

   Ⓒ $12x + 9$

   Ⓓ $18x + 9$

   Ⓔ $18x + 15$

68. A certain board game is played by rolling a pair of six-sided dice and then moving one's piece the number of spaces indicated by the sum showing on the dice. A player is "frozen" if her opponent's piece comes to rest in the space already occupied by her piece. If player A is about to roll and is currently six spaces behind player B, what is the probability that player B will be frozen after player A rolls?

   Ⓐ $\frac{1}{12}$

   Ⓑ $\frac{5}{36}$

   Ⓒ $\frac{1}{6}$

   Ⓓ $\frac{1}{3}$

   Ⓔ $\frac{17}{36}$

69. A club has exactly 3 men and 7 women as members. If 2 members are selected at random to be president and vice-president respectively, and if no member can hold two offices simultaneously, what is the probability that a woman is selected for at least one of the positions?

   Ⓐ $\frac{14}{15}$

   Ⓑ $\frac{4}{5}$

   Ⓒ $\frac{8}{15}$

   Ⓓ $\frac{7}{15}$

   Ⓔ $\frac{1}{5}$

70. A certain company will issue four-letter identification codes to all of its employees. The codes will include only the letters A, C, F, H, K, Q and V. If all the letters of each code are distinct, how many such codes are possible?

    (A) 35

    (B) 70

    (C) 105

    (D) 840

    (E) 1,680

71. At a certain pet show, exactly 6 dogs are entered in the beagle division and exactly 6 are entered in the dalmatian division. If the top 3 dogs in each division receive first-, second-, and third-place ribbons respectively, with no other dogs receiving a prize, how many different ways can ribbons be awarded to winners in the two divisions together?

    (A) 28,800

    (B) 14,400

    (C) 720

    (D) 400

    (E) 36

72. A promoter is organizing an opera concert. Ten singers are available for the program: 3 sopranos, 3 mezzos, 2 tenors and 2 baritones. If the promoter intends every segment to be a duet by performers with different vocal ranges, how many pairings of performers are possible?

    (A) 6

    (B) 10

    (C) 24

    (D) 36

    (E) 37

73. The average (arithmetic mean) of 5 numbers is 35. After one of the numbers is removed, the average (arithmetic mean) of the remaining numbers is 39. What number has been removed?

    (A) 1

    (B) 5

    (C) 19

    (D) 34

    (E) It cannot be determined from the information given.

74. How many different 6-digit positive integers are there, where 3 of the digits are each one of the digits 5 or 7, and each of the other 3 digits are one of the digits 1, 4, 6, or 8?

    (A) 5,760

    (B) 7,290

    (C) 7,680

    (D) 8,640

    (E) 10,240

75. If a deck of 52 cards has 2 red jacks, 2 red queens, and 2 red kings, what is the probability of selecting 1 card that is a red jack, a red queen, or a red king?

    Express your answer as a fraction in its simplest terms.

Answer Key

ALGEBRA & PROPERTIES OF SETS PRACTICE

1.	90	**27.**	A	**53.**	A
2.	8	**28.**	B	**54.**	210
3.	36	**29.**	C	**55.**	33
4.	4	**30.**	C	**56.**	$\frac{9}{49}$
5.	$\frac{1}{27}$	**31.**	C	**57.**	B, C
6.	–1	**32.**	B	**58.**	B, C, D
7.	2	**33.**	C	**59.**	B, D
8.	B, C	**34.**	A	**60.**	A, C
9.	5	**35.**	E	**61.**	C, D
10.	4	**36.**	C	**62.**	33.60
11.	A, B, C, D	**37.**	B	**63.**	8
12.	A, C	**38.**	E	**64.**	A
13.	A, C, D	**39.**	E	**65.**	B
14.	A, F	**40.**	D	**66.**	D
15.	A, C, D	**41.**	C	**67.**	A
16.	B; D	**42.**	D	**68.**	B
17.	B, D	**43.**	E	**69.**	A
18.	A, B, D, F, G	**44.**	D	**70.**	D
19.	10	**45.**	B	**71.**	B
20.	40	**46.**	C	**72.**	E
21.	170	**47.**	B	**73.**	C
22.	24	**48.**	E	**74.**	E
23.	–28	**49.**	E	**75.**	$\frac{3}{26}$
24.	D	**50.**	2		
25.	C	**51.**	5		
26.	A	**52.**	E		

Answers and Explanations

ALGEBRA & PROPERTIES OF SETS PRACTICE

1. 90

The greatest possible value of the largest number in this set will require that every other number be as small as possible. Since the numbers are all distinct and positive, the smallest possible values that satisfy the conditions are 1, 2, 3, and 4. This gives us an equation as follows:

$$\frac{(1 + 2 + 3 + 4 + x)}{5} = 20$$
$$10 + x = 100$$
$$x = 90$$

2. 8

There are a couple of ways to solve this.

For one, since this quadratic can be factored, we can solve for its zeroes.

$$y = 8t - \frac{t^2}{2} - 24$$
$$0 = 8t - \frac{t^2}{2} - 24$$
$$0 = 16t - t^2 - 48$$
$$0 = t^2 - 16t + 48$$
$$0 = (t - 12)(t - 4)$$
$$t = 4, t = 12$$

Since parabolas are symmetric, the point in the middle of the zero values will be the maximum value of the parabola. Thus, the function will be at its maximum at the midpoint between 4 and 12.

$$t = \frac{(4 + 12)}{2} = \frac{16}{2} = 8$$

When $t = 8$, the y-value is: $8(8) - \frac{8^2}{2} - 24 = 64 - \left(\frac{64}{2}\right) - 24 = 64 - 32 - 24 = 8$.

Another way to approach this is to remember that since this parabola opens downwards (which we know because the lead coefficient is negative), the maximum will be at the vertex. We can find the t-coordinate of the vertex with the formula $t = \frac{-b}{2a}$.

In this case, $b = 8$ and $a = \frac{-1}{2}$. So we get:

$$\frac{-8}{\left(2 \times -\frac{1}{2}\right)} = \frac{-8}{-1} = 8.$$

3. 36

Combined rate problems first require that we convert each machine's work into a rate. The first machine can produce at a rate of $\frac{n}{20}$ widgets per minute; the second can produce $\frac{n}{30}$ widgets per minute. Finding a common denominator and adding the two rates together gives us:

$$\frac{3n}{60} + \frac{2n}{60} = \frac{5n}{60} = \frac{n \text{ widgets}}{12 \text{ minutes}}$$

The total amount of widgets produced is the rate multiplied by the time:

$$3n = \left(\frac{n}{12}\right)t$$
$$36 = t$$
$$t = 36 \text{ minutes}$$

4. 4

The question tells us that Luis spent exactly $74.40, so we must find the greatest number of shirts that could have been bought that would allow the remaining money to be divided evenly by the price of a hat ($6.20). We can start with the greatest number of shirts that could be bought for less than $74.40 and verify the remaining amount.

If we divide the total amount spent by the cost for one shirt, we get $\frac{74.40}{15.50} = 4.8$.

We can assume that Luis cannot buy a fraction of a shirt, so the answer can be no greater than 4.

Since $4 \times 15.50 = 62.00$, we subtract this amount from the total amount to get $74.40 - 62.00 = 12.40$.

$12.40 divides evenly by the price of a hat: $\frac{12.40}{6.20} = 2$.

Therefore, Luis can have bought 4 shirts and 2 hats, and our answer is 4. (We do not need to verify if Luis could have bought some other combination of shirts and hats for exactly $74.40, as the question asks us to find the *maximum* number of shirts.)

5. $\frac{1}{27}$

We can solve this problem by picking a value for x and generating values for $f(3x)$ and $f(x)$.

If we set $x = 1$:

$$f(3x) = f(3(1)) = f(3);$$

$$f(3) = 3(3)^{-3} = \frac{3}{(3^3)} = \frac{3}{27}.$$

$$f(x) = f(1) = 3(1)^{-3} = \frac{3}{(1^3)} = \frac{3}{1} = 3.$$

Since $f(3x) = \frac{3}{27}$ and $f(x) = 3$, the ratio of $f(3x)$ to $f(x)$ is $\frac{\left(\frac{3}{27}\right)}{3} = \frac{1}{27}$.

6. −1

We can rewrite y as $\frac{-12}{x^3}$.

The value of y will clearly be greatest if x^3 is negative. Since x is in the denominator of the expression, y will also be greatest if x is as

close to 0 as possible, while remaining negative. Since x must be an integer, y will thus be largest when $x = -1$.

This will give y a value of 12.

To see why this is the greatest possible value, consider the alternative possibilities:

If x is a smaller integer, y will be positive, but we'll be dividing 12 by larger numbers, making y smaller.

For example, if $x = -2$, $y = 1.5$.

x cannot equal 0, or y will be undefined.

If x is positive, y will be negative. For example, if $x = 1$, $y = -12$.

7. 2

Let's rearrange the terms of the two equations so that they're parallel in structure:

$$x - 6y = 14$$
$$-.25x + y = -12$$

If we multiply the second equation by 4, we get:

$$-x + 4y = -48$$

Adding the two equations gives us:

$$\begin{aligned} x - 6y &= 14 \\ +(-x + 4y &= -48) \\ \hline 0x - 2y &= -34 \\ -2y &= -34 \\ y &= 17 \end{aligned}$$

Plugging 17 back into one of our equations gives us $x - 6(17) = 14$.

$$x - 102 = 14$$
$$x = 116$$

The intersection point is (116,17).

The slope is given by:

$$\frac{17 - (-15)}{116 - 100} = \frac{32}{16}$$

The slope is 2.

8. B, C

In order to solve this problem, we can plug in the answer choices to see if they yield correct responses, or we can draw out the lines and see which region contains the correct responses. Because this is a timed test, it's likely quicker to take the answer choices and plug them in algebraically.

(A) (6, 1)

$2(6) + 3 (1) = 15 \geq 6$

$-(6) + (1) = -5 < -4$

This satisfies only the first inequality, not both, so it's incorrect.

(B) (4, 1)

$2(4) + 3(1) = 11 \geq 6$

$-(4) + (1) = -3 \geq -4$

This satisfies both inequalities, so it is a correct answer.

(C) (2, 1)

$2(2) + 3(1) = 7 \geq 6$

$-(2) + (1) = -1 \geq -4$

This satisfies both inequalities, so it is a correct answer.

(D) (2, -1)

$2(2) + 3(-1) = 1 < 6$

$-(2) + (-1) = -3 \geq -4$

This satisfies the second inequality only, so this is incorrect.

Thus, our correct answers are (B) and (C).

9. 5

We can use the information we are given to set up a system of equations. Let P be the number of pairs of pants Dante purchased and let S be the number of shirts. We know that:

$P + S = 8$

$21P + 15S = 138$

We can rewrite the first equation as $P = 8 - S$. We can then substitute this into the second equation:

$$21(8 - S) + 15S = 138$$
$$168 - 21S + 15S = 138$$
$$168 - 6S = 138$$
$$-6S = -30$$
$$S = 5$$

Dante purchased 5 shirts.

10. 4

Let's begin by establishing variables:

A = apples
B = bananas
P_a = price of apples
P_b = price of bananas

We can express the information in the following equations:

$A = B + 1$ [She buys one more pound of apples than bananas]

$P_b = P_a + 1$ [The price of bananas is $1 more than the price of apples]

$(A)(P_a) = (B)(P_b)$ [Expenditure on both items is equal]

$A = 4$

$B = 3$

$$(4)(P_a) = (3)(P_a + 1)$$
$$4P_a = 3P_a + 3$$
$$P_a = 3$$

If the price of apples is $3, then the price of bananas is $4.

11. A, B, C, D

Since we've got an inequality here (the overall average is *at least* 130 cm), let's begin by examining the border case: when the overall average is exactly 130 cm.

One way to solve this is in your head. If the average of two groups is $\frac{2}{3}$ of the way weighted towards one side, that means that $\frac{2}{3}$ of the total items being measured are located in the group on that side. Thus, if there are 30 students in Andrea's class, which is the $\frac{2}{3}$-weighted side, there must be $\frac{1}{3}$ of the students remaining, or 15 students, in Billy's class for the overall average to be exactly 130.

The other way is with a calculation. Let x be the number of students in Billy's class.

The sum of the students' heights in Billy's class is $110x$, and in Andrea's class $(140)(30)$, and the total number of students is $30 + x$. So the equation for the overall weighted average is:

$$130 = \frac{110x + 140 \times 30}{30 + x}$$

$$130 \times 30 + 130x = 110x + 140 \times 30$$

$$20x = 10 \times 30$$

$$x = 15$$

In either case, we now know that if the overall average height of all the students were exactly 130 cm, there would be 15 students in Billy's class. Since we are actually told that the overall average height is *at least* 130 cm, not necessarily exactly 130 cm, we know that Billy's class must contain 15 students or fewer. Why fewer? With fewer students in the shorter class, the overall average height would go up, but with more students in the shorter class the overall average would be further weighted towards the short end of things.

The first four answer choices are all less than or equal to 15, so they are all possibilities.

12. A, C

If a point lies on the graph of an equation, those values of x and y satisfy the equation.

Theoretically, you could just plug each coordinate pair into the equation to see if it yields a true statement; if so, the point does indeed lie on the graph of the given equation. However, before you jump to plugging in, it's worth taking a look to see if the equation can simplify easily. In fact, it does.

$$\frac{3y + xy}{x + 3} = x - 2$$

simplifies to:

$$\frac{y(x + 3)}{x + 3} = x - 2$$

$$y = x - 2$$

We've ended up with a much simpler equation, and from a glance we can identify the correct answer choices as those where x is 2 greater than y: choices (A) and (C), (2,0) and (–1,–3).

13. A, C, D

If a point in the coordinate system satisfies an equation, that point lies on the graph of that equation. In other words, if (x,y) satisfies the equation, then that point lies on the line given by the equation. And if (x,y) lies on the line and $z > y$, then (x,z) will lie above the line of the equation.

The first step here is simplifying the equation:

$12x + 16y = 8$ is equivalent to

$$3x + 4y = 2$$

$$4y = -3x + 2$$

$$y = \left(-\frac{3}{4}\right)x + \frac{1}{2}$$

To determine the answer, plug in the x-coordinate given in the answer choice into the above equation. If the result you get, which is the y-coordinate corresponding with that x-coordinate on the given line, is less than or equal to the y-coordinate in the answer choice, that point is on or above the line whose equation is given.

(A) $(-2,2)$:

$$\left(-\frac{3}{4}\right)(-2) + \frac{1}{2} = \frac{3}{2} + \frac{1}{2} = 2.$$

This point is on the line given. Check!

(B) $\left(0, -\frac{1}{2}\right)$:

$\left(-\frac{3}{4}\right)(0) + \frac{1}{2} = \frac{1}{2}$, which is greater than $-\frac{1}{2}$. This point lies below the line, not above it. No.

(C) $\left(-4, \frac{9}{2}\right)$:

$\left(\frac{-3}{4}\right)(-4) + \frac{1}{2} = 3 + \frac{1}{2} = \frac{7}{2}$,

so $\left(-4, \frac{7}{2}\right)$ lies on the line, which means $\left(-4, \frac{9}{2}\right)$ lies above the line. Check!

(D) $(6,-2)$:

$\left(-\frac{3}{4}\right)(6) + \frac{1}{2} = -\frac{9}{2} + \frac{1}{2} = -4$,

so $(6,-4)$ is on the line, and since $-2 > -4$, $(6,-2)$ is above the line. Check!

(E) $(16,-12)$:

$\left(-\frac{3}{4}\right)(16) + \frac{1}{2} = -12 + \frac{1}{2}$,

which is greater than -12, so this point lies below the line. No.

The correct answer choices are (A), (C), and (D).

14. A, F

This is a multiple-choice question with one or more correct answers, so let's take a close look at all the answer choices.

Begin by reading the question closely to set up the equation correctly.

The ratio of x to $\frac{y}{3}$ means x divided by $\frac{y}{3}$. Dividing by a fraction is the same as multiplying by the inverse of that fraction, so x divided by $\frac{y}{3} = \frac{3x}{y}$.

We're told that this ratio—that is, $\frac{3x}{y}$ —is $\frac{1}{3}$ times the ratio of y to x.

$\frac{1}{3} \times$ the ratio of y to $x = \frac{1}{3} \times \frac{y}{x} = \frac{y}{3x}$

Pulling it all together, our equation is: $\frac{3x}{y} = \frac{y}{3x}$

Cross-multiply: $y^2 = 9x^2$.

The question asks us about the value of $\frac{y}{x}$, so let's see what we know about that.

$$y^2 = 9x^2$$

$$\frac{y^2}{x^2} = 9$$

$$\frac{y}{x} = 3 \text{ or } -3$$

Looking at the answer choices, we see that (A) and (F) are correct.

15. A, C, D

This is a multiple-choice question with one or more correct answers, so be sure to consider all the answer choices.

The inequalities in the answer choices relate to the value of ab, so let's consider what ab could be.

Because our first inequality contains an absolute value, it's actually equivalent to two inequalities:

$1 < |a| < 3$ means that either $-3 < a < -1$ or $1 < a < 3$.

In order to determine the potential values of ab, we need to consider both of these options.

Let's start with the first option, $-3 < a < -1$. In this case, what could the value of ab be? Well, since a is negative and b is positive, ab will be negative, and the lower boundary will be the most negative value of a times the most positive value of b, namely $-3 \times 5 = -15 < ab$. And the upper boundary is the least negative product possible, namely the smallest value of a times the smallest value of b, $-1 \times 2 = -2 > ab$. Putting them together, we have $-15 < ab < -2$.

Now consider the second option, $1 < a < 3$. Now both a and b are positive, so ab is positive as well. The lower boundary for ab in this case is the smallest possible a times the smallest possible b, $1 \times 2 = 2 < ab$. The upper boundary for ab in this case is the biggest possible a times the biggest possible b, $3 \times 5 = 15 > ab$. Putting them together, we have $2 < ab < 15$.

So now we have an overall answer to the question "what could ab be?" Either $-15 < ab < -2$ or $2 < ab < 15$.

What does this mean? It means that ab could lie anywhere within those two ranges. Now let's examine the answer choices, keeping in mind that as long as ab can be a value somewhere in the range given, the answer will be a correct answer.

(A) $-4 < ab < 0$

This is probably the hardest of the answer choices. At first glance, you might reject it, since we know that ab can't equal -1, for example. But consider the matter more closely: the question asked which of the answer choices <u>could</u> be true. Given what we now know, is it possible that ab lies between -4 and -0? Certainly—for example, if $ab = -3$. We know that ab could equal -3, since that lies between -15 and -2. Since at least one possible value for ab lies between -4 and 0, ab could lie between -4 and 0, and this inequality could indeed be true.

(B) $-2 < ab < 2$

No. ab could not possibly fall into this range, since we know that ab is either less than -2 or greater than 2.

(C) $2 < ab < 15$

This could certainly be true; after all, we know that ab is either $-15 < ab < -2$ or $2 < ab < 15$.

(D) $5 < ab < 6$

This could certainly be true as well. Once we know that ab could be $2 < ab < 15$, it's also within the realm of possibility that ab falls within a narrower sub-range of that range, such as between 5 and 6.

16. B, D

This is a multiple-choice question with one or more correct answers, so let's consider all the answer choices carefully. Note that it is not enough for the answer choices to be possible for some values of x and y; the question stem asks only for inequalities which must always be true. One way to evaluate these quickly is to see if you can come up for some values for x and y that are inconsistent with the inequality; if you can do this, then the answer is incorrect.

(A) $x + y > 0$

x is negative and y is positive, but we don't know which one is more negative or more positive than the other—in other words, we don't know whether the absolute value of x is greater or less than the absolute value of y, so we don't know if this inequality is true.

For example, if $x = -\frac{1}{2}$ and $y = \frac{3}{4}$, then the statement would be true. On the other hand, if $x = -\frac{1}{2}$ and $y = \frac{1}{4}$, it would be false.

(B) $xy < 0$

Since x is negative and y is positive, their product must be negative. True.

(C) $x^2 + y^2 > x + y$

Since y is greater than 0 but less than 1, it is certainly the case that $y > y^2$. On the other hand, since x is negative, it's also the case that $x < x^2$. So we can't know whether the inequality in this answer choice is true or not: it depends on whether the difference between y and y^2 is greater than the difference between x and x^2.

For example: if $x = -\frac{1}{2}$ and $y = \frac{3}{4}$, then

$x^2 + y^2 = \frac{13}{16} > x + y = \frac{1}{4}$.

True.

But if $x = -\frac{1}{8}$ and $y = \frac{1}{2}$, then

$x^2 + y^2 = \frac{17}{64} < x + y = \frac{3}{8}$. False.

(D) $2x + x^2 < y$

This one becomes clearer when you factor the left-hand side: $x(2 + x) < y$

x is negative and $2 + x$ is positive. Therefore, $x(2 + x)$ will be negative, while y is positive. This statement is certainly true.

Answer choices (B) and (D) must be true.

17. B, D

The key here is realizing that by asking for "all such values," this is a multiple-choice question with one or more correct answers. It's a quadratic equation, which always has two solutions unless the equation can be factored into a single term squared—in which case there's just one double root. However, not every quadratic equation has solutions, which is what our question asks for: any imaginary solutions are to be excluded.

(Note: the GRE will never ask you to provide answers that are imaginary, complex, or non-real numbers. This question alludes to their existence, but does not ask you to manipulate them, understand them, or solve for them.)

In order to solve our equation, we need to factor it. It factors to $(3x + 1)(x - 1)$, but

you can also go ahead and use the quadratic equation:

$$x = \frac{-b \pm \sqrt{b^2 - 4ac}}{2a}$$

$$x = \frac{2 \pm \sqrt{4 - (-12)}}{6}$$

$$x = \frac{2 \pm 4}{6}$$

$$x = 1, -\frac{1}{3}$$

These are the two roots (both real), so select them wherever they appear in the answer choices.

The correct answer choices are (B) and (D).

18. A, B, D, F, G

This is a multiple-choice question with one or more correct answers. Look closely at all the answer choices to select the correct ones.

The first thing to note is that all the answer choices relate to a variable, x, about which we don't know anything. More to the point, we don't know whether it's positive or negative. The question asks which terms <u>must</u> be positive, meaning regardless of the value of x.

(A) x^{-2}

Don't be fooled by the negative sign: x^{-2} just means $\frac{1}{x^2}$. And x^2 must be positive, even if x is negative, so in fact x^{-2} does have to be positive. Correct.

(B) x^0

Any number raised to the power of 0 equals 1. Correct.

(C) $\frac{1}{x^{-3}}$

This is equivalent to x^3, which is positive if x is positive but negative if x is negative. Incorrect.

(D) $|x|$

The absolute value of a number is always positive. Correct.

(E) $x^{-3} \times x^4$

$x^{-3} \times x^4 = x^{-3+4} = x^1 = x$, which is positive if x is positive but negative if x is negative. Incorrect.

(F) $(x)^4 \times (-x)^4$

In general, $a^x \times b^x = (ab)^x$

So $(x)^4 \times (-x)^4 = (-x^2)^4$

Now $-x^2$ is always negative, but when raised to the power of 4 it yields a positive product. Correct.

(G) $(x^{-3})^4$

$(x^{-3})^4 = x^{-3 \times 4} = x^{-12}$

Any number raised to an even power, whether the power is positive or negative, yields a positive result. Correct.

The correct answer choices are (A), (B), (D), (F), and (G).

19. 10

In order to solve this problem, let's begin to simplify the expressions.

The negative exponent in the numerator of the first term can be changed to a positive exponent in the denominator, and the zero exponent in the numerator of the final term makes the numerator equal to 1. We can also change the division sign to a multiplication sign by inverting the numerator and denominator in the final term. After simplifying exponents and combining like terms, we are left with:

$$\frac{y}{x^4} \cdot x^6 \cdot \frac{x^8 y^4}{1}$$

Then we can combine all the like terms in the numerators and denominators:

$$\frac{x^{14} y^5}{x^4}$$

Lastly, we can simplify the x exponents:

$$x^{10} y^5$$

Thus, the exponent attached to the x is 10.

20. 40

In order to solve this problem, we'll use the distance formula: $d = rt$

Let d = distance, r = rate, and t = time.

We know the distance and the time, so we simply have to plug into the formula.

The distance from town A to town B is 60 miles, but we must multiply this by 2 because Nick made two trips—there and back.

So $d = 60 \times 2 = 120$ miles.

Next we need to figure out the time for the entire trip. We'll do this by adding the times together:

1 hour and 15 minutes + 1 hour and 45 minutes = 3 hours total.

So now we can plug into the formula.

120 miles = rate × (3 hours)

We divide both sides by 3 hours:

$$\text{rate} = \frac{120 \text{ miles}}{3 \text{ hours}}$$

$$\text{rate} = \frac{40 \text{ miles}}{\text{hour}}$$

21. 170

In order to solve this problem, we can set up a rate equality. We know we want the number of widgets made in one hour, so we can either convert 75 minutes to 1.25 hours or convert 1 hour to 60 minutes. This example shows the latter.

For machine A:

$$\frac{100 \text{ widgets}}{75 \text{ minutes}} = \frac{x \text{ widgets}}{60 \text{ minutes}}$$

Cross-multiply:

$$6,000 = 75x$$

Divide both sides by 75:

$$x = 80$$

Machine A produces 80 widgets per hour.

For Machine B:

$$\frac{75 \text{ widgets}}{50 \text{ minutes}} = \frac{x \text{ widgets}}{60 \text{ minutes}}$$

Cross-multiply:

$$4,500 = 50x$$

Divide both sides by 50:

$$x = 90$$

Machine B produces 90 widgets per hour.

So in one hour, the sum of both machines will be 80 + 90 = 170 widgets.

22. 24

Unfortunately, we cannot simply average the two speeds here. Keren will spend longer traveling at one speed than she will at the other speed, as it will take her longer to cover the distance at the slower speed; this means her average overall speed will be closer to that slower speed.

Fortunately, the question format (numeric entry) tells us that the answer must always be the same, no matter what the distance is that Keren is traveling. This means we can just pick a distance to help answer the question. We don't know how far her home is from the beach, but we can pick a value.

Let's say it's 60 miles from home to the beach. Knowing her average speeds both ways, we can figure out total travel time.

$$d = rt$$

Going to the beach:

$$60 \text{ miles} = 20 \text{ mph} \times t$$
$$t = \frac{60}{20} = 3 \text{ hours}$$

Return trip:

$$60 \text{ miles} = 30 \text{ mph} \times t$$
$$t = \frac{60}{30} = 2 \text{ hours}$$

Now we can solve for the entire trip.

Total distance = 120 (add the two 60-mile trips she took)

Total time = 5 hours (add the times for both trips)

$$d = rt$$
$$120 \text{ miles} = r \times 5 \text{ hours}$$
$$r = 24 \text{ mph}$$

23. –28

When we look at the last polynomial expression, we should spot $(x + y)^2$ lurking there in the form of $x^2 + 2xy + y^2$. The GRE loves using this pattern, and as a reflex we should factor it right away to $(x + y)^2 - 172$.

With this in mind, we can simplify the first part of the question:

$$12 - y = x$$
$$12 = x + y$$

. . . so we can substitute 12 in place of $(x + y)$ in the final expression.

To solve, then, we simply square 12 and subtract 172.

$$12^2 - 172 = 144 - 172 = -28.$$

24. D

It is easier to simplify this by adding the exponents where you can and multiplying the exponents where you can.

Remember that when multiplying two terms with the same base, you add the exponents: $x^2x^4 = x^6$.

$$\text{hint: } x^2x^4 = (xx)(xxxx)$$
$$= (xxxxxx)$$
$$= x^6$$

When there is a power to a number or variable in parentheses, the powers are multiplied: $(x^2)^3 = x^6$.

hint: $x^2 x^4$ = $(xx)(xx)(xx)$

= $xxxxxx$

= x^6

so now we have: $x^6 x^6 = x^{12}$.

Division works just the opposite, so we must subtract the exponents $12 - 4 = 8$, resulting in x^8.

The correct answer is (D).

25. C

There are two pairs of jeans with different prices. Because the question asks for the greatest number of pairs of jeans that can be bought, Chris wants to buy as many of the cheaper pairs as he can. The most pairs that can be bought with $560 would be $\frac{\$560}{45} = 12.44$, but the problem specifies that Chris spends exactly $560, and he can't buy .44 pairs of jeans, so we need to keep looking. See what would happen if he bought one less pair of $45 jeans, or $45 × 11. The total is $495. Deduct this from $560: do we get a multiple of $65? In fact, we have exactly $65 left over, so we have our answer: Chris can buy 11 pairs of $45 jeans and 1 pair of $65 jeans, for a total of 12 pairs.

The correct answer is (C).

26. A

We can determine the ratio of x to z (that is, $\frac{x}{z}$) if we can generate an equation from the system featuring only x and z.

We can do this by adding the two equations, as this eliminates y.

$$\begin{array}{r} x - y + z = 0 \\ +4x + y + 5z = 0 \\ \hline 5x + 6z = 0 \end{array} \Rightarrow \text{We can subtract } 6z$$

from both sides.

$5x = -6z \Rightarrow$ Now we can divide both sides by 5.

$x = -\frac{6z}{5} \Rightarrow$ Now we can divide both sides by z.

$\frac{x}{z} = -\frac{6}{5}$

Now we know that $\frac{x}{z}$ is equal to $-\frac{6}{5}$.

The correct answer is (A).

27. A

If we let x represent the number of employees, we know that $550 × x = 690{,}250$.

To solve for x, we need to divide both sides by 550:

$x = \frac{690{,}250}{550} = 1{,}255$.

The correct answer is (A).

28. B

The first part of this question gives us the ability to solve for x.

$4x = -8 \Rightarrow$ Divide each side by 4.

$x = -2$

With this information, plug -2 in for x in the other equation.

$3x^2 + 7x - 8$

$3(-2)^2 + 7(-2) - 8 \Rightarrow$ Do a little of the math.

$12 + (-14) - 8 = -10$

The correct answer is (B).

29. C

The easiest way to solve this is to plug in the value 200 for y and then solve the equation.

So $200 > 4x + 12 \Rightarrow$ Subtract 12 from both sides.

$188 > 4x \Rightarrow$ Divide both sides by 4.

$47 > x$

The greatest integer that x can be and still have $4x + 12 < 200$ is 46.

The correct answer is (C).

30. C

There are several ways to do this, but probably the easiest is to convert to seconds and then divide.

8 minutes 17 seconds is equal to 60(8) + 17 or 497.

Now divide $\frac{497}{7}$ to get the gain in one day.

$\frac{497}{7}$ is equal to 71, or 1 minute and 11 seconds.

The correct answer is (C).

31. C

In order to solve for d in terms of r, we must first get the r's and the d's on the same side of the equation, respectively.

$$3d - 2r = 5r - 4d$$
$$3d + 4d = 5r + 2r$$
$$7d = 7r$$

So $d = r$. Thus the correct answer is (C).

32. B

In simple terms, this question is asking what the lowest value of a is such that $\frac{1}{3^a} < .01$. This inequality holds true whenever the denominator is greater than 100.

Therefore, we are looking for the lowest integer that makes 3^a greater than 100. We know that 3^4 is equal to 81 and 3^5 is equal to 243; therefore, 5 is the lowest integer that satisfies the inequality. The correct answer is (B).

33. C

We need to set up the two equations and solve.

$$y + 15 = x$$
$$\frac{x}{2} = y$$

So if we replace y with $\frac{x}{2}$ in the first equation we get:

$$\frac{x}{2} + 15 = x$$
$$x + 30 = 2x$$
$$30 = x$$

Now that we have a value for x, we can substitute it back into one of the original equations to get y:

$$y = \frac{30}{2} = 15$$

The correct answer is (C).

34. A

We need to set up the equations in this question. Let's assign x and y to the the two cut pieces, where $x > y$.

The full length of the licorice, l, is the total of the two cut pieces, so:

$$l = x + y$$

Next, we must translate the fact that one piece is two inches longer than three times the length of the other piece. The first of these is clearly the longer piece, so x is two inches longer than three times y:

$$x = 3y + 2$$
$$x - 2 = 3y$$
$$\frac{(x-2)}{3} = y$$

Since the question asks us to provide x, let's replace y in the first equation and solve for x in terms of l.

$$l = x + \frac{(x-2)}{3}$$
$$3l = 3x + x - 2$$
$$3l + 2 = 4x$$
$$\frac{(3l+2)}{4} = x$$

The correct answer is (A).

35. E

This one is probably easiest to solve by plugging in numbers. Pick any two numbers for a and b that fit the statement, such as $a = 3$ and $b = 6$ (because 6 is 3 less than the square of 3). When we plug into the answer choices, we see that (E) is the only equation that returns $a = 3$ when we plug $b = 6$ into it:

$a = \sqrt{(6+3)}$, so a must be 3, so our answer is (E).

36. C

In order to answer this question, we must first solve for the price of one can of soda. Once we find this price, we can multiply by 5 to get the cost of 5 sodas.

Let x be the price of a soda.

$$7x = 9.80$$
$$x = \frac{9.80}{7}$$
$$x = 1.40$$

Now we must multiply this number by 5 to get the total price for 5 sodas.

$1.40 \times 5 = 7.00$

The correct answer is (C).

37. B

At first this question seems fairly difficult, but it is actually quite simple.

Because the question asks how many revolutions per second the wheel makes, It is easiest to divide 6,000 by 60 to get the number of revolutions per second.

$\frac{6,000}{60} = 100$; therefore, the wheel makes 100 revolutions per second and, consequently, will make $100x$ revolutions in x seconds.

The correct answer is (B).

38. E

We need to isolate x in this question. So

$5(x-2) = x + 6$ $\Rightarrow$	Multiply the 5 out.
$5x - 10 = x + 6$ $\Rightarrow$	Add a 10 to both sides.
$5x = x + 16$ $\Rightarrow$	Subtract an x from both.
$4x = 16$ $\Rightarrow$	Divide both sides by 4.
$x = 4$	

The correct answer is (E).

39. E

This is a great GRE example of things you should know. Knowing how to factor a quadratic equation quickly and identifying a frequently recurring pattern will serve you well. Also, knowing the squares of the first 20 or so numbers will save you time here.

The first step is to recognize that $x^2 + 2xy + y^2$, which factors to $(x + y)^2$, is lurking in the first equation:

$$x^2 + y^2 = 16 - 2xy$$
$$x^2 + 2xy + y^2 = 16$$
$$(x+y)(x+y)^2 = 16$$

Rewrite $(x + y)^4$ as $((x + y)^2)^2$ and replace the $(x + y)^2$ with 16:

$16^2 = 256$.

The correct answer is (E).

40. D

Since we know that 3 out of every 4 of Celia's photographs is a French photograph, and photographs do not come in fractions, we know that the amount of photographs in the collection must be evenly divisible by 4.

(A) $\frac{100}{4} = 25$ (This would mean 25 non-French photographs and 75 French photographs.)

(B) $\frac{84}{4} = 21$

(C) $\frac{76}{4} = 19$

(D) $\frac{69}{4}$ = 17.25 (This is the problematic one—it would mean 17.25 non-French photographs, which is impossible.)

(E) $\frac{32}{4}$ = 8

The correct answer is (D).

41. C

The best way to solve this is to convert the fractions into ones where we can add and create an equation.

"The balance", i.e., the amount of the estate left over after the widow took her share, is $\frac{2}{3}$ of the estate. Because her sons each received $\frac{1}{3}$ of that balance, we know that they each received one-third of $\frac{2}{3}$ of some amount, or $\frac{1}{3} \times \frac{2}{3} \times x$. Thus, each son received $\frac{2}{9} \times x$, or $\frac{2}{9}$ of the total estate.

Now we can add what the widow received to what one of the sons received (it doesn't matter which, as they all received the same amount) and equate it to 120,000.

$$\left(\tfrac{1}{3}\right)x + \left(\tfrac{2}{9}\right)x = 120,000$$

Find the LCD:

$$\left(\tfrac{3}{9}\right)x + \left(\tfrac{2}{9}\right)x = 120,000$$

$$\left(\tfrac{5}{9}\right)x = 120,000$$

$$x = 120,000 \times \left(\tfrac{9}{5}\right)$$

$$x = 216,000$$

The correct answer is (C).

42. D

We can begin by solving this absolute value by splitting it into two inequalities:

$$\tfrac{x}{4} > 1 \text{ and } \tfrac{x}{4} < -1$$

Remember that for the inequality that has the –1, we must also flip the direction of the inequality. Now we can solve for the two ranges of x:

$$x > 4 \text{ and } x < 4$$

x can be all numbers greater than 4 or less than –4.

This question asks what "must be true," so we need to find the answer choice that is true for ALL values of x. Note that the correct answer here ends up being the statement that is the least restrictive in its effect upon x, and so the most easily supported as something that "must be true." This will not always be the case, but it is worth watching out for.

43. E

Let's start by simplifying inside the absolute value:

$$|3x - 2 + 4x| > 7$$
$$|7x - 2| > 7$$

Now we can rewrite the absolute value as two inequalities (one greater than the positive value, one less than the negative) and solve each, starting with the first:

$$7x - 2 > 7$$
$$7x > 9$$
$$x > \tfrac{9}{7}$$

and now the other:

$$7x - 2 < -7$$
$$7x < -5$$
$$x < \tfrac{-5}{7}$$

Because an inequality is given, when we solve for x, there are technically an infinite amount of possible values that would meet the conditions. We get a range of values:

$$x < \frac{-5}{7} \text{ and } x > \frac{9}{7}.$$

Only one value among the choices, $\left(\frac{4}{3}\right)$, lives in either of these ranges for x.

44. D

If $z < 0$, then z can be any negative number. Let's choose a number and solve, and find the answer choice that produces the same value. If $z = -2$, then:

$$\sqrt{-z|z|}$$
$$\sqrt{-(-2)||-2||}$$
$$\sqrt{2 \times 2}$$
$$\sqrt{4}$$
$$2$$

Now let's substitute –2 for z in all the answer choices to see which ones produce a result of positive 2.

(A) $\sqrt{-2}$ ⇒ Incorrect (and an imaginary number!).

(B) $\sqrt{2}$ ⇒ Incorrect.

(C) –2 ⇒ Incorrect.

(D) 2 ⇒ This works!

(E) 0 ⇒ Incorrect.

Since we only found one answer choice that gave us the correct result, it must be the correct answer. Note: if we had found two answer choices that worked (this would have happened if we had set $z = -1$ at the start), we would just have to try another value for z on the two answer choices that worked the first time.

The correct answer is (D).

45. B

Because there are three different absolute value items, splitting this absolute value problem into multiple equations would take too long—it would produce eight different equations! Instead, let's take a look at the concept that's being tested.

If both a and b are positive (say $a = 1$ and $b = 2$ for example) then the equation is true.

If both a and b are negative (say $a = -1$ and $b = -2$), then the equation is true.

However if one variable is negative ($a = -1$) and the other is positive ($b = 2$), then the equation is *not* true.

a and b must always be the same sign, so their product will always be positive. The correct answer is (B).

46. C

Here we need to recall the formula for an arithmetic sequence:

$$x_n = x_1 + d(n - 1)$$

where

n = the indicator of which term in the sequence is being referred to, such that x_n = nth term in the sequence;

x_1 = the first term in the sequence; and

d = difference between consecutive terms (ex: $x_2 - x_1$). Usually, we refer to consecutive terms by referring to x_n and $x_{(n+1)}$ (for example, if n = 5, then x_n becomes x_5 and $x_{(n+1)}$ becomes $x_{(5+1)}$ or x_6).

Typically, we're given the rule for the sequence by being told that x_n is defined by a rule that lets us calculate x_n, based on the previous term, $x_{(n-1)}$, but in this question, we're given the information in a different way: we're told about the relationship between x_n and the next term, x_{n+1}. Regardless, we're able to figure out the difference between consecutive terms, as $d = x_{n+1} - x_n$.

We start with:

$$x_{n+1} = x_n + 4$$

. . . which becomes:

$$x_{n+1} - x_n = 4$$

. . . which is our difference (d). Taking $d = 4$ and $x_1 = 1$ and substituting them into our formula $x_n = x_1 + d(n-1)$ gives us:

$$x_n = 1 + 4(n-1)$$
$$x_n = 1 + 4n - 4$$
$$x_n = 4n - 3$$

The correct answer is (C).

47. B

First, find the values for a and b.

$$a = 4(3-5) + 2$$
$$a = 4(-2) + 2$$
$$a = -8 + 2$$
$$a = -6$$
$$b = -4(5-3)$$
$$b = -4(2)$$
$$b = -8$$

So we have:

$$2|a| - |2b| =$$
$$2x|-6| - |2x(-8)| =$$
$$12 - |-16| =$$
$$12 - 16 = -4$$

(B) is the correct choice.

48. E

This algebra problem involves a tricky spatial element (the arrangement of the pickets and corresponding spaces) and a conversion step (the pickets and spaces have inch measurements, but the stem asks for an answer in terms of feet). Constructing an equation and solving for the length of the fence will most likely take longer than our backdoor option—Picking Numbers.

To make the Picking Numbers approach as straightforward as possible, we can work with just one pair of pickets ($x = 2$) to determine a target number. Since each picket is $\frac{1}{2}$ of an inch, and there are 6 inches of space between the pickets, the total length of a fence consisting of two pickets is $\frac{1}{2} + \frac{1}{2} + 6 = 7$ inches, or $\frac{7}{12}$ of a foot.

Now let's check our answer choices.

Note that this is a "which of the following" question, so there's a pretty good chance that the correct answer will be either (D) or (E). If we were short on time on Test Day, guessing one of these two choices would be a good bet. Since we're picking numbers on this question, we need to evaluate all choices. However, we can at least start with choice (E) to increase our chances of answering correctly in a time rush:

Choice (E):

$$\frac{13x - 12}{24} = \frac{13(2) - 12}{24} = \frac{26 - 12}{24} = \frac{14}{24} = \frac{7}{12}$$

Choice (D):

$$\frac{13x + 1}{24} = \frac{13(2) + 1}{24} = \frac{26 + 1}{24} = \frac{27}{24} \neq \frac{7}{12}$$

Choice (C):

$$\frac{13}{24}x = \frac{13 \times 2}{24} = \frac{26}{24} \neq \frac{7}{12}$$

Choice (B):

$$\frac{13}{2}x - 6 = \frac{13 \times 2}{2} - 6 = 13 - 6 = 7 \neq \frac{7}{12}$$

Choice (A):

$$\frac{13}{2}x = \frac{13 \times 2}{2} = 13 \neq \frac{7}{12}$$

As it turns out, only choice (E) matches our target number.

49. E

This question can be solved quickly by converting the "per second" rate provided in the stem to a "per minute" rate, and by using this converted rate to solve for the distance that the rocket travels.

Using the rate formula, we can find the rate for the rocket:

$$\text{Rate} = \frac{\text{Distance}}{\text{Time}} = \frac{\frac{x}{5}\,\text{miles}}{y\,\text{seconds}} = \frac{x\,\text{miles}}{5y\,\text{seconds}}$$

Since there are 60 seconds in a minute, we multiply by 60 to convert the rate from seconds to minutes:

$$\frac{x\,\text{miles}}{5y\,\text{seconds}} \times 60 = \frac{60x\,\text{miles}}{5y\,\text{minutes}} = \frac{12x\,\text{miles}}{y\,\text{minutes}}$$

Now use this rate to find how many miles the rocket can travel in z minutes:

$$\text{Rate} = \frac{\text{Distance}}{\text{Time}}$$

$$\frac{12x\,\text{miles}}{y\,\text{minutes}} = \frac{\text{distance}}{z\,\text{minutes}}$$

$$\text{distance} = \frac{12x\,\text{miles} \times z\,\text{minutes}}{y\,\text{minutes}}$$

$$\text{distance} = \frac{12xz}{y}$$

Choice (E) is correct.

Picking Numbers can also be used on this problem. Just make sure to pick numbers that are easy to calculate. If we make $x = 50$ and $y = 10$, then the rocket travels 10 miles every 10 seconds, or a mile a second. If we make $z = 2$, the rocket would travel 120 miles in 2 minutes, and 120 is our target number.

Applying these numbers to the answer choices, we find:

(A): $\frac{xy}{5z} = \frac{50 \times 10}{5 \times 2} = 50$

(B): $\frac{xz}{5y} = \frac{50 \times 2}{5 \times 10} = 2$

(C): $\frac{(50)(10)(2)}{6} = 166.67$

(D): $\frac{12xy}{z} = \frac{12 \times 50 \times 10}{2} = 3,000$

(E): $\frac{12xz}{y} = \frac{12 \times 50 \times 2}{10} = 120$

50. 2

Factor the quadratic and solve:

$$4x^2 - 16 = 0$$

$$4\left(x^2 - 4\right) = 0$$

$$4(x - 2)(x + 2) = 0$$

The possible values for x are 2 and –2. As $x > 0$, the correct answer is 2.

51. 5

We need to find the number of friends, x. They earn 20 × \$18 = \$360 selling the T-shirts. They spend 20(\$4 + \$1) = \$100 to buy the shirts and print the design. They spend another \$5 on promotion, for a total of \$105 in expenses. So, their profit is \$360 – \$105 = \$255. Each friend's share is \$51, so $51x = 255$. Solving for x, there are 5 friends in the group.

The correct answer is 5.

52. E

The unknown in this question is the total receipts that will result in equal earnings for both waiters. Since we have only one unknown (the total receipts must be the same for both waiters and will therefore have only one value) and two equal compensation figures, we can construct a single equation and solve for the total receipts.

Let's start with Waiter B's compensation since it seems to be a bit more straightforward. Using r to represent the total receipts for the week, we can write Waiter B's compensation as $0.25r$. Waiter A's compensation can be represented as \$500 + 0.15(r – \$600) since \$600 of the total receipts are not figured into her compensation.

Setting the two expressions equal to each other, we find:

$$0.25r = \$500 + 0.15(r - \$600)$$
$$0.25r = \$500 + 0.15r - 90$$
$$0.10r = \$410$$
$$r = \$4,100$$

When total receipts equal $4,100, Waiter A and B receive the same compensation. Choice (E) is correct.

53. A

The farmer's gross profit is the difference between the cost of producing the corn and the amount for which he sells it. In this question, however, we need to keep in mind that he does not sell all he produces since locusts destroy part of the crop. This must be factored into the solution. Let's begin by working out the cost to the farmer:

The farmer plants x acres of corn at a cost of p dollars per acre, so his total cost is xp.

Now for his profit:

The farmer sells part of the crop for q dollars per acre. The part he sells is less than the x acres he plants because y acres have been destroyed. Therefore, we can represent his profit as $(x - y)q$.

The gross profit is the difference between the two: $(x - y)q - xp$.

This question could also have been solved by Picking Numbers for each of the variables. This strategy helps makes an otherwise abstract word problem much more tangible. To begin, we must pick some numbers for each variable, being careful to follow the rules of the word problem.

Let's say that:

$$x = 10 \text{ acres}$$
$$p = \frac{\$2}{\text{acre}} \text{ (buying price)}$$
$$y = 3 \text{ acres destroyed by locusts}$$
$$q = \frac{\$5}{\text{acre}} \text{ (selling price)}$$

Notice that x must be greater than y, since y is the amount of the total x that is destroyed. Also, q must be greater than p, since the farmer sells the corn for a profit.

We can now calculate the costs and profits of the corn:

$$\text{Cost} = (10 \text{ acres})\left(\frac{\$2}{\text{acre}}\right) = \$20$$

$$\text{Profit} = (10 - 3 \text{ acres})\left(\frac{\$5}{\text{acre}}\right)$$
$$= (7)(5) = \$35$$

$$\text{Gross profit} = \$35 - \$20 = \$15$$

Next, we plug in our values for x, y, p, and q into each expression of the answer choices to find the correct answer:

(A): $(10 - 3)(5) - (10)(2) = (7)(5) - (10)(2) = 35 - 20 = 15$ Keep.

(B): $(10 - 3)(2) - (3)(5) = (7)(2) - (3)(5) = 14 - 15 = -1$ Eliminate.

(C): $(5 - 2)(3) - (10)(2) = (3)(3) - (10)(2) = 9 - 20 = -11$ Eliminate.

(D): $(10)(2) - (3)(5) = 20 - 15 = 5$ Eliminate.

(E): $(10 - 3)(5 - 2) = (7)(3) = 21$ Eliminate.

Only (A) matches the value calculated from the question stem, and is the correct answer.

54. 210

We can use the combination formula for this problem:

$$\text{Combination} = \frac{n!}{k!\,(n - k)!}$$

Here, $n = 12$ and $k = 3$.

$$\frac{12!}{(3!)(9!)}$$

This simplifies to:

$$\frac{(12 \times 11 \times 10)}{3!} = 220$$

However, this includes the teams that cannot work together. How many such teams are there? There are three available positions on the team. To find the number of prohibited teams, we must assume that two of those positions are held by the two employees who cannot work together. (If this condition were not true, the team would be valid.) That leaves only one position available on the team. There are 10 remaining employees to fill this remaining position, which leaves us with 10 teams that violate the conditions of this question. This means there are 10 teams that we should not have counted in our previous calculation. Our answer is thus 210.

55. 33

If we add up the given numbers, we get:

$$190 + 83 + 72 = 345$$

However, there are only 312 students in the class, which means that the difference between the two numbers, 33, must represent the students studying multiple languages. Since no students are taking either 0 or 3 language courses, we do not need to account for these possibilities. The answer is 33.

56. $\frac{9}{49}$

There are two ways to tackle this. One is the direct route: the probability that the first processor is defective is $\frac{5}{50}$, or $\frac{1}{10}$. If we pull a defective processor on our first try, the probability that the second is not defective is $\frac{45}{49}$.

The reason for this is that, after our first draw, there are only 49 processors remaining and, of those, 4 are defective (since we already

pulled one defective processor) and 45 are not. The joint probability of these two events occurring is the product of the two individual probabilities:

$$\left(\frac{1}{10}\right)\left(\frac{45}{49}\right) = \frac{45}{490} = \frac{9}{98}.$$

One more thing: we have found the probability of drawing a defective processor and then a working one. But it would also satisfy our problem if the first one worked and the second one were defective. Therefore, we need to *double* the probability we calculated:

$$2 \times \left(\frac{9}{98}\right) = \frac{18}{98} = \frac{9}{49}.$$

If you're worried about forgetting this last part (a common error), or want to check your result (but be careful with time), remember that there are three possibilities: either both processors work, one works and the other doesn't, or both are defective. Since these are the only three options, the sum of the three probabilities must equal one. So we can say the following:

1 – (probability that both work) – (probability that both are defective) = probability that one works

The probability that both work is:

$$\left(\frac{9}{10}\right)\left(\frac{44}{49}\right) = \frac{396}{490} = \frac{198}{245}$$

The probability that both are defective is:

$$\left(\frac{1}{10}\right)\left(\frac{4}{49}\right) = \frac{4}{490} = \frac{2}{245}$$

$$1 - \left(\frac{198}{245}\right) - \left(\frac{2}{245}\right) = \frac{45}{245} = \frac{9}{49}$$

57. B, C

One strategy we can use to solve this problem is to find either the greatest or lowest possible average for the entire class.

If we assume that there are exactly twice as many boys as there are girls in the class, we can set up an equation like this:

$$(2)(83) + (1)(92) = 166 + 92 = \frac{(258)}{3} = 86$$

In other words, if there were *exactly* twice as many boys as girls in the class, then the average for the entire class would be 86%.

However, we are told that there are *more* than twice as many boys as girls.

This means that the actual average will be less than 86%—the boys constitute a heavier weight toward the average because there are more of them, and because their average is lower they will drag the overall class average down.

This means we can eliminate answer choices (D), (E) and (F), all of which are too high.

On the other hand, the average cannot be less than 83, the boys' average. Because of this, we can eliminate (A).

This leaves us with only (B) and (C), which are indeed possible values for the whole class's average score on the test.

58. B, C, D

In order to solve this problem, let's first find out the minimum average speed of the entire trip.

We know that Haruna averaged exactly 30 mph, so that's fixed. Our variable is Rina's average speed, which is more than 60 mph. We don't know how much more.

To proceed, let's figure out the average speed if Rina had averaged *exactly* 60 mph. Keep in mind that this average will be the lower limit, and that the correct answers will need to be *more* than this.

How long or far they drove is not important. We can pick any value for the distance they drove and the averages will remain the same.

Let's use 60 miles and use the distance formula, $d = rt$:

For Rina:

$$60 = 60 \text{ mph } (t) = 60t$$
$$t = 1 \text{ hour}$$

For Haruna:

$$60 = 30 \text{ mph } (t) - 30t$$
$$t = 2 \text{ hours}$$

Now, for the entire trip:

120(60 each way)	=	(2 hours + 1 hour)(*r*)
120	=	(3 hours)*r*
r	=	40 mph

If Rina drove at an average rate of 60 mph, the total average would be 40 mph. Since we know she averaged *more* than 60 mph, however, the total average must be greater than 40. Therefore, (A) is incorrect, leaving the others as correct choices.

59. B, D

To find the average, we simply add two values together and divide by 2.

Since we want our average to equal 1, we need an initial sum that yields positive 2.

We can eliminate (A), the lowest negative number; when added to the largest positive number it will only yield 0, which is too low.

If we add –5 to 7, we get 2. This sum divided by 2 equals 1. No other combination of responses add together to produce the required sum of 2.

Thus, (B) and (D) are the correct responses.

60. A, C

This is a multiple choice question with one or more correct answers, so consider all the answer choices carefully.

We are asked which statements are sufficient to determine the chance of success of a randomly chosen child. The key thing to realize here is that, although we are given chances of success for girls and for boys separately, we don't know how the number of girls compares with the number of boys. If they were equal in number, then the chance of success would just be their average: $\frac{1}{2}$. In general, though, the probability of success of a mixed group for which we know the probabilities of success of the various subgroups is as follows:

probability of success for whole group = (fraction of the whole group represented by subgroup x × probability of success for subgroup x) + (fraction of the whole group represented by subgroup y × probability of success for subgroup y)

Here we know the probabilities of success, but not what fraction of the whole group is boys and what fraction is girls. Any answer choice that provides that information will be sufficient to answer the question.

(A) There are four times as many girls as boys.

If x is the number of boys, $4x$ is the number of girls, and $5x$ is the total size of the group. So boys are $\frac{1}{5}$ of the group, and girls are $\frac{4}{5}$. Now we have enough information to answer the question.

(You don't need to actually do the math once you realize that this information is sufficient, but just in case you're curious, here goes: $\left(\frac{4}{5}\right)\left(\frac{2}{3}\right) + \left(\frac{1}{5}\right)\left(\frac{1}{3}\right) = \frac{3}{5}$.

(B) Half of the group was under age 8, and they all found their way through the maze.

This tells us that at least half the total group found their way through the maze, which itself tells us that there are at least as many girls as boys (since the overall weighted average is at least $\frac{1}{2}$, and if there were an equal number of

boys and girls the overall chance of success would be exactly $\frac{1}{2}$). However, this doesn't give us any actual way of putting a precise number on the chance of success of the entire group. For that, we'd also need to know how the children over age 8 did, which we don't. This statement is not sufficient.

(C) 4 out of 10 children in the group did not find their way through the maze.

This answer choice gives the answer explicitly; you just have to realize it. The chance of an individual randomly selected child succeeding in the maze is equal to the overall chance of success of the entire group. If 4 out of 10 did not succeed, then 6 out of 10 did, and that's the likelihood that an individually selected child will make it through the maze.

Answer choices (A) and (C) are both correct.

61. C, D

$S \cap T$ means the intersection of sets S and T: those numbers which are elements of both S and of T.

$S = \{1, 2, 3, 4, 6, 8, 12, 24\}$. These are all the positive factors of 24.

Composite numbers are numbers that aren't prime. The number 1 is generally considered neither prime or composite, but this question doesn't require you to know that.

So $S \cap T$ contains the composite numbers that are also factors of 24.

In other words, $S \cap T = \{4, 6, 8, 12, 24\}$.

The correct answer choices are (C) and (D).

62. 33.60

In order to solve this problem, we need to first figure out how much Simon paid for both calls.

The first call was 8 minutes, so we can figure out the price according to the information we are given:

$$1.99 + 0.34\,(7) = 4.37$$

For the second call:

$$1.99 + 0.34\,(6) = 4.03$$

Now we add both together to get the total price:

$$4.37 + 4.03 = \$8.40$$

The next step is to find out the average price per hour. (A typical misstep at this stage in the problem is to find the average price *per call*, that is, the average of $4.37 and $4.03, which is $4.20.)

We can do this by setting up values in an equation that look like $\frac{\text{total price}}{\text{total time}}$:

$$\frac{\$8.40}{(8\,\text{min} + 7\,\text{min})} = \frac{\$8.40}{15\,\text{min}}$$

However, the question asks for the average per *hour*, meaning we need to convert 15 minutes to .25 hours.

$\frac{x = \$8.40}{0.25\,\text{hrs}} \Rightarrow$ multiply both the numerator and denominator by four:

$$x = \frac{\$33.60}{1\,\text{hr}}.$$

Our answer is 33.60.

63. 8

For this question, we need only refer to the principle that "when a number equal to an existing average is added, the new weighted average is equal to the old one."

In this case, we have 27 numbers with an average of 8. When 6 new numbers are added and the average doesn't change, that means the average of the new set of 6 numbers is 8 also.

64. A

The set of *J* will contain: {1, 2, 3, 4, 5, . . . 48, 49, 50}

The squares of the integers in set *J*, beginning with 1, are: {1, 4, 9, 16, 25, 36, 49 . . .}

Remember not to include any squares that are higher than fifty, as the questions asks for the "intersection" only, meaning the elements common to both sets.

Out of those squares, only 1, 9, 25, and 49 are also odd numbers and will therefore be in set *K*.

Since there are four of these elements, the answer is (A).

65. B

Here we are choosing 3 letters out of 5 total options. Since order is important here (because STR is different from SRT, for example) let's use the permutation formula to determine the total number of possible outcomes. Here $n = 5$ and $k = 3$.

$$Perm = \frac{n!}{(n-k)!}$$

$$Perm = \frac{5!}{(5-3)!}$$

$$Perm = \frac{5!}{2!}$$

$$Perm = 5 \times 4 \times 3$$

$$Perm = 60$$

So we know there are 60 ways possible to order five items three at a time. Logically, we have 5 choices for the first letter, 4 choices for the second letter, and 3 choices for the third and final letter.

$$5 \times 4 \times 3 = 60$$

The correct answer is (B).

66. D

Let's look at each round. The probability of getting heads is $\frac{1}{2}$ and the probability of rolling an even number is $\frac{3}{6} = \frac{1}{2}$. Therefore the probability of advancing to the second round is:

$$\frac{1}{2} \times \frac{1}{2} = \frac{1}{4}$$

For the second round, the probability will be the same even though the desired outcome is different (tails instead of heads and odds instead of evens), because there are only two sides to a coin, and the probability of rolling an odd number on a six-sided die is the same as rolling an even.

Therefore the probability of advance to the third round is also:

$$\frac{1}{2} \times \frac{1}{2} = \frac{1}{4}$$

To find the probability of advancing through the first round to the second and advancing from the second to the third, we multiply:

$$\frac{1}{4} \times \frac{1}{4} = \frac{1}{16}$$

The probability that an event will *not* occur is the probability that it *will* occur subtracted from 1:

$$1 - \frac{1}{16}$$

The probability that the event will not occur is $\frac{15}{16}$.

67. A

To solve this problem, we can use the average formula to solve for the sum of the "other three numbers." Once we find this sum, we can then find its average. First we need to set up the average formula for all five numbers:

$$\frac{\text{Sum of terms}}{\text{Number of terms}} = \text{Average}$$

$$\frac{2x + (\text{sum of 3 numbers})}{5} = 4x + 3$$

Solving for the sum of the three numbers, we find:

$$\frac{2x + (\text{sum of 3 numbers})}{5} = 4x + 3$$

$$\rightarrow 2x + (\text{sum of 3 numbers}) = 5(4x + 3)$$

$$\rightarrow 2x + (\text{sum of 3 numbers}) = 20x + 15$$

$$\rightarrow \text{sum of 3 numbers} = 18x + 15$$

Now that we know the sum of the three numbers, we can reapply the average formula for these particular values:

$$\frac{\text{Sum of terms}}{\text{Number of terms}} = \text{Average} \rightarrow \frac{18x + 15}{3} = 6x + 5$$

68. B

The correct answer is $\frac{5}{36}$. This is a weird setup, but let's think about the situation for a second. In this game, a player is "frozen" whenever another player lands on the spot where the first player already has her piece. Then the question asks for the probability that player B will be frozen by player A, who's 6 spaces behind player B. What does it depend on? It depends on whether player A gets a roll of exactly 6 on the dice. So what's the probability of getting 6 on the dice?

First, let's figure out the total possible outcomes for the roll. Since there are 6 numbers on each die, the total number of possible rolls will be 6 x 6, or 36. So there are 36 possible rolls. How many of them would allow player A to move exactly 6 spots? Well, any roll that adds up to 6.

So we could have 1/5, 2/4, and 3/3. But remember that since there are 2 dice, there are 2 ways to get 1/5 and 2/4, because either die could get the 1 or the 5, etc. So there's 1/5, 5/1, 2/4, 4/2, and 3/3. That's 5 rolls that add up to exactly 6. So 5 out of the 36 possible rolls would allow player A to freeze player B, which gives us a probability of $\frac{5}{36}$.

69.   A

The correct answer is (A), $\frac{14}{15}$. Here we've got 3 men and 7 women, and we're going to select 2 people at random.

The question asks for the probability that at least one woman is selected. This is a "multiple-scenario" question, since there are three ways to get at least one woman: woman first but not second; woman second but not first; woman first and second.

The direct way to answer this is to find the probabilities of each of these scenarios and add them. Or we could use the "subtraction" method, where we find the probability of what we don't want and subtract that from 1. In this case, there's only 1 way to get what we don't want and that's by getting *no* women.

So it's probably easier just to calculate that and subtract. The probability of getting a man for president is $\frac{3}{10}$ and the probability then of getting another man as vice-president is $\frac{2}{9}$ (since now there are only 9 people eligible and only 2 are men). So the probability of these two events occurring is $\frac{3}{10} \times \frac{2}{9} = \frac{6}{90} = \frac{1}{15}$. So if the probability of getting *no* women is $\frac{1}{15}$, then the probability of getting at least one woman must be $1 - \frac{1}{15}$, which is $\frac{14}{15}$.

70.   D

The correct answer is (D), 840. This problem will require us to use permutations. To find the number of permutations of a smaller group out of a larger group, we use the formula:

$$_nP_k = \frac{n!}{(n-k)!}$$

where n is the total number and k is the size of the group. So for our calculations, this means that $n = 7$ and $k = 4$. The formula gives us the total number of codes, that is, the number of possible groups of 4, multiplied by the number of ways each group can be arranged:

$$_7P_4 = \frac{7!}{(7-4)!} = \frac{7!}{3!}$$
$$= \frac{7 \times 6 \times 5 \times 4 \times 3 \times 2 \times 1}{3 \times 2 \times 1}$$
$$= 7 \times 6 \times 5 \times 4 = 840$$

Note that the formula ultimately reduces to $7 \times 6 \times 5 \times 4$, which we can also think of as having 7 choices for the first letter, 6 for the second (since the letter chosen for the first letter is now unavailable), 5 for the third, 4 for the fourth.

71.   B

The correct answer is (B), 14,400. This question will require us to use the permutation formula for ordered subgroups, $\frac{n!}{(n-k)!}$, where n is the total number of entities, and k is the number of entities in the subgroup. We know this is a permutation problem, and not a combination problem, because we have to figure out all the possible groups of 3 dogs that can win ribbons in each division where the order of the winners matters. First, let's figure out how many arrangements of 3 winners we can get out of a group of 6 dogs.

In this case, that means $n = 6$ and $k = 3$, so we get $\frac{6!}{(6-3)!}$, which is $\frac{6 \times 5 \times 4 \times 3 \times 2 \times 1}{3 \times 2 \times 1}$, or $6 \times 5 \times 4 = 120$ possible ways for 3 of the 6 dogs in a division to win ribbons. Because the numbers are the same in each division, if there are 120 possible ways to choose and arrange 3 of 6 dogs in one division, then there are 120 ways to do so in the other division as well. So for each of the 120 possible configurations of 3 in one division, there are also 120 for the 3 dogs in the other division. So altogether there are $120 \times 120 = 14,400$ ways for the 6 winning dogs to occupy the 6 winning positions.

72. E

The correct answer is (E), 37. The question asks us to figure out all the ways we can combine one singer with another singer who has a different vocal range. That means matching the sopranos with the mezzos, with the tenors, and with the baritones. Then we'd match the mezzos with the tenors and the baritones. Finally, we'd match the tenors with the baritones. So there are 3 sopranos and 3 mezzos, which makes 3 x 3 = 9 possible pairs of soprano/mezzo. 3 sopranos and 2 tenors = 6 pairs; 3 sopranos and 2 baritones = 6 pairs; 3 mezzos and 2 tenors = 6 pairs; 3 mezzos and 2 baritones = 6 pairs; 2 tenors and 2 baritones = 4 pairs. So that's 9 + 6 + 6 + 6 + 6 + 4 = 37.

A quicker way to solve this would be to use the combinations formula to find the total number of ways to choose 2 singers from a group of 10:

$$_{10}C_2 = \frac{10!}{(2!)(8!)} = \frac{(10 \times 9)}{(2 \times 1)} = \frac{90}{2} = 45$$

Then subtract the combinations included in that number that involve 2 singers from the same vocal range: there are 3 ways to combine 2 sopranos, 3 ways to combine 2 mezzos, 1 possible pair of baritones, and 1 possible pair of tenors. 45 – 3 – 3 – 1 – 1 = 37.

73. C

Average is determined by the following formula: Average = $\frac{\text{Sum of terms}}{\text{Number of terms}}$. We can use this formula in the rearranged form Sum of terms = Average × Number of terms. So if the average of 5 numbers is 35, then the sum of the 5 numbers is 35 × 5 = 175.

One number is removed, which means there are 4 numbers remaining. If the average of 4 numbers is 39, then the sum of the 4 numbers is 39 × 4 = 156.

Since we had a total of 175, and this has been reduced to 156, this means that the number

removed is the result of subtracting 156 from 175. The number removed is 175 – 156 = 19.

Therefore the correct choice is (C).

74. E

Let's begin by determining how many different ways there are to specify which 3 digits will each be one of the digits 5 or 7. Each of the other 3 digits will necessarily be one of the digits 1, 4, 6, or 8. The number of different ways to specify which 3 digits among the 6 digits will each be one of the digits 5 or 7 is the number of ways to select 3 different objects from 6 different objects.

In mathematics, $_nC_k$ is sometimes used to denote the number of different subgroups containing of k different objects that can be selected from a group of n different objects, where n is a positive integer, k is a non-negative integer, and $0 < k < n$. Then the combinations formula is $_nC_k = \frac{n!}{k!\,(n-k)!}$.

Using the formula with $n = 6$ and $k = 3$, we have

$$\begin{aligned}
_6C_3 &= \frac{6!}{3!\,(6-3)!} = \frac{6!}{3!\,(3!)} \\
&= \frac{6 \times 5 \times 4 \times 3 \times 2 \times 1}{3 \times 2 \times 1 \times 3 \times 2 \times 1} \\
&= \frac{6 \times 5 \times 4}{3 \times 2 \times 1} = 2 \times 5 \times 2 \\
&= 10 \times 2 = 20
\end{aligned}$$

There are 20 different ways to specify which 3 digits will each be one of the digits 5 or 7.

For each specification of which 3 digits will each be one of the digits 5 or 7, there are 2 possibilities for each of the 3 digits that are each one of the digits 5 or 7. Therefore the number of different ways to specify these 3 digits is 2 × 2 × 2 = 4 × 2 = 8.

For each specification of which 3 digits will each be one of the digits 5 or 7, and for each specification of which digit each of those 3 digits will be, there are 4 possibilities for each of the other 3 digits that are one of the digits 1, 4, 6, or 8. The number of ways to specify each of the 3 digits that are one of the digits 1, 4, 6, or 8 is 4 × 4 × 4 = 16 × 4 = 64.

Here is what we now know:

There are 20 different ways to specify which 3 digits will each be one of the digits 5 or 7.

For each specification of which 3 digits will each be one of the digits 5 or 7, there are 8 ways to specify each of these 3 digits.

For each specification of which 3 digits will each be one of the digits 5 or 7, and for each specification of what digit each of these 3 digits will be, there are 64 ways to specify which digit the other 3 digits will be, these other 3 digits being one of the digits 1, 4, 6, or 8.

Therefore the number of possible 6-digit integers that meet the all the requirements of the question stem is 20 × 8 × 64 = 10,240.

Choice (E) is correct.

75. $\frac{3}{26}$

The probability of an event occurring is defined by the formula:

$$P(E) = \frac{\text{Number of positive outcomes}}{\text{Numbers of possible outcomes}}.$$

In a deck of 52 cards, there are 2 red jacks, 2 red queens, and 2 red kings, for a total of 6 positive outcomes. The number of possible outcomes is 52 since there are 52 cards. The probability of selecting a red jack, queen, or king is $P(E) = \frac{6}{52} = \frac{3}{26}$. The correct answer is $\frac{3}{26}$.

Geometry

The geometry tested on the GRE is basic—but that doesn't mean it's easy. However, there are only a few fundamental definitions and formulas you need to know. The GRE emphasizes new ways of applying these elementary rules. Pay a lot of attention to diagrams. There can be a lot of information "hidden" in a diagram.

Geometry topics include lines and angles, triangles—including isosceles, equilateral, and special right triangles and the Pythagorean theorem—polygons, circles, multiple figures, three-dimensional figures (uniform solids), area, perimeter, and volume. You do not need to know how to do geometry proofs for the test.

Geometry Practice

Enter your answer in the answer box(es) below the question.

Equivalent forms of the correct answer, such as 2.5 and 2.50, are all correct. Fractions do not need to be reduced to lowest terms.

Enter the exact answer unless the question asks you to round your answer.

1. A circular pool is to be installed in a square plot. The pool is to be surrounded by a circular walkway 2 feet wide and is to be as large as possible. If the area of the plot is 144 ft², what is the ratio of the area of the pool (not including the walkway) to the area of the walkway?

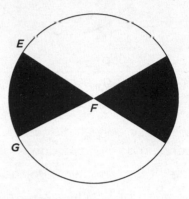

5. The circle shown has center *F* and radius 6. If the measure of angle *EFG* is 60˚, what is the combined area of the shaded regions, rounded to the nearest integer?

2. What is the area of a triangle with coordinates (3,5), (3,-2), (-1,3)?

3. A square is inscribed in a circle. If the area of the circle is 18π, what is the area of the square?

6. A cylindrical silo is 20 feet in diameter and 25 feet high. If the silo is 80% full of grain, and each 4π ft³ of grain weighs 10 pounds, what is the total weight of grain in the silo, in pounds?

 pounds

4. Line *l* has a slope of $\frac{1}{3}$. Line *r* is perpendicular to *l* and intersects *l* at (5,8). If the equation of line *r* is $y = mx + b$, what is the value of *b*?

7. Line *q* has a slope of 3 and passes through the point (4,6). Line *r* has a slope of –2 and an *x*-intercept of 12. What is the *y*-coordinate of the intersection point of lines *q* and *r*?

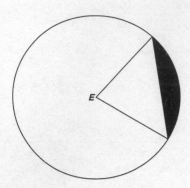

8. In the image shown, E is the center of the circle with radius 6. If angle E measures 60 degrees, what is the area of the shaded portion of the circle, rounded to the nearest integer?

☐

Select one or more answer choices according to the specific question directions.

If the question does not specify how many answer choices to select, select all that apply.

The correct answer may be just one of the choices or as many as all of the choices, depending on the question.

No credit is given unless you select all of the correct choices and no others.

If the question specifies how many answer choices to select, select exactly that number of choices.

9. What could possibly be the length of the third side of a triangle, if two sides both have a length of 12?

Indicate all possible lengths.

A 0.12

B 1

C 12

D 24

10. In cube s, each edge has a length of 7.5. Which of the following values is greater than or equal to the length of the diagonal of cube s?

Indicate all such numbers.

A 10

B $7.5\sqrt{2}$

C $7.5\sqrt{3}$

D 13

11. A right circular cylinder has a height of 10 cm and a diagonal 26 cm long. Which of the following values is larger than or equal to the volume of the cylinder?

Indicate all such amounts.

A 144π cm^3

B $1{,}440$ cm^3

C $1{,}440\pi$ cm^3

D $4{,}608$ cm^3

12. $x^2 + (y - 3)^2 = 9$

Which of the following points lie on the circle defined by the equation above?

Indicate all such points.

A $(0,-3)$

B $(0,6)$

C $(0,0)$

D $(6,0)$

E $(3,3)$

13. $(x + 4)^2 + (y - 2)^2 = 16$

    Which of the following points lie on the circle defined by the equation above?

    Indicate <u>all</u> such points.

    A (−4,6)

    B (−4,2)

    C (2,0)

    D (0,2)

14. If the length of two sides of a triangle are x and y, and $y \geq 2x$, then which of the following could be the length of the third side?

    Indicate <u>all</u> such lengths.

    A x

    B $2x$

    C $3x$

    D $100x$

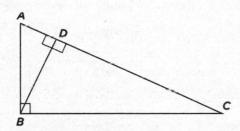

15. In the triangle shown, $BD = 8$ and $AD = 6$. Angles ABC, ADB, and CDB are all right angles. What is the perimeter of triangle ABC?

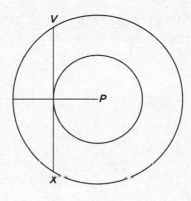

16. The two circles are concentric around point P. VX is tangent to the smaller circle and has a length of 12. The area of the larger circle is 100π. What is the radius of the smaller circle?

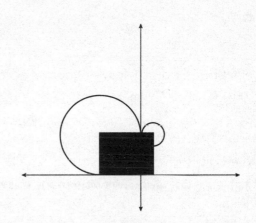

17. In the figure, the shaded rectangle lies on the x-axis as shown. Both circles are tangent to the y-axis at the same point. Both circles have centers at vertices of the rectangle. The larger circle is also tangent to the x-axis. If the distance between the centers of the circles is 9 and the area of the larger circle is 4 times greater than that of the smaller circle, find the area of the shaded rectangle.

18. What is the perimeter of an equilateral triangle inscribed in a circle with radius 12, rounded to the nearest integer?

☐

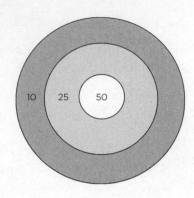

19. In the figure, the area of the 50-point bulls-eye (the inner circle) is 4π. The ratio of the radius of the bulls-eye to the width of the 25-point band to the width of the 10-point band is 1:1:1.5. What is the area of the 10-point band, rounded to the nearest integer?

☐

Select one or more answer choices according to the specific question directions.

If the question does not specify how many answer choices to select, select all that apply.

The correct answer may be just one of the choices or as many as all of the choices, depending on the question.

No credit is given unless you select all of the correct choices and no others.

If the question specifies how many answer choices to select, select exactly that number of choices.

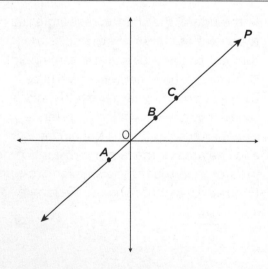

20. In the coordinate plane shown, line P has slope 1, and all four shown points—point A (a,a), the origin, point B (b,b), and point C (c,c)—lie on line P and are all equally spaced. Which of the following statements about a, b, and c must be true?

Indicate all such statements.

A $b - c = a$

B The distance from A to $C = 3b$

C $ba - ca > 0$

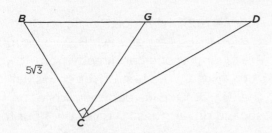

21. Which of the following statements <u>individually</u> provide(s) sufficient information to determine the area of triangle *BCD*?

Indicate <u>all</u> such statements.

- A $CG = GD = 5\sqrt{3}$
- B Triangle *BCG* is an equilateral triangle.
- C $CD = 15$
- D $CG = 5\sqrt{3}$
- E The length of the hypotenuse of triangle *BCD* equals $10\sqrt{3}$

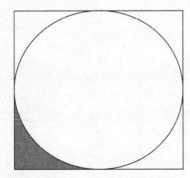

22. The circle in the figure above is inscribed in a square.

Which of the following statements <u>individually</u> provide(s) sufficient information to determine the area of the square?

Indicate <u>all</u> such statements.

- A The circumference of the circle = 4π.
- B The ratio of the area of the square to the area of the circle = $\frac{4}{\pi}$.
- C The area of the shaded section in the lower left, inside the square but outside the circle, is $4 - \pi$.

23. If the equation for line *L* is $y = 4x + 3$, which of the following statements *must* be true?

Indicate <u>all</u> such statements.

- A The line given by the equation $8x + 2y = \frac{2}{3}$ forms a right angle with line *L*.

- B The line given by the equation $3 + y = 4x$ is parallel to line *L*.

- C Line *L* passes through exactly two quadrants.

- D Line *M* is given by $y = 2x + b$, where *b* is positive; *L*'s *x*-intercept is greater than *M*'s *x*-intercept.

24. Rectangular solid *A* has a length 15% longer than the length of rectangular solid *B*, and a width that is 60% shorter. Both solids have the same height. What is the ratio of solid *A*'s volume to the volume of solid *B*?

25. Cube *m*'s side length is three times longer than the side length of cube *n*. What is the ratio of cube *m*'s surface area to the surface area of cube *n*?

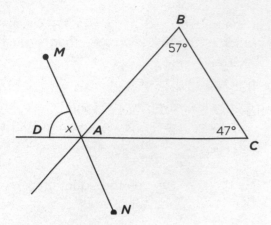

26. In the figure, if line segment *MN* bisects angle *DAB*, then what is the value of *x*?

27. Raj has cube-shaped crates of cornmeal with inside-edge lengths of $2\sqrt{2}$. What is the maximum number of full crates of cornmeal he can completely empty into a larger cube-shaped crate with inside-edge length $\sqrt{29}$?

    crates

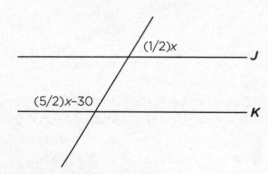

28. If line *j* and line *k* are parallel, what is the value of *x*, in degrees?

    degrees

29. Town A is 27 miles north of Town B. Town C is 46 miles east of Town B. Two people are driving in one car directly from Town A to Town C. The first driver drives half of the way at 10 miles per hour, while the second driver goes 20 miles per hour for the rest of the trip. Assuming time switching drivers is negligible, how many hours, rounded to the nearest hundredth, did it take them to drive from Town A to Town C?

    hours

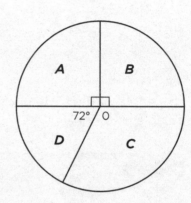

30. In the circle, line segments join at the center O to create the 4 regions. The area of region C is 9. What is the area of region A + B + D?

31. If a cube's diagonal has a length of $7\sqrt{3}$, what is the surface area of the cube?

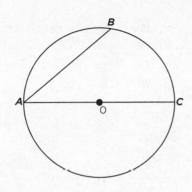

32. In the circle with center O, and radius of 3, what is the length of chord BC if $\angle BAC = 30^\circ$, rounded to the nearest tenths place?

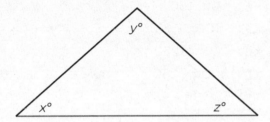

33. In the triangle above, what is the value of $\frac{(x+y+z)}{60}$?

Ⓐ 1

Ⓑ 2

Ⓒ 3

Ⓓ 4.5

Ⓔ 6

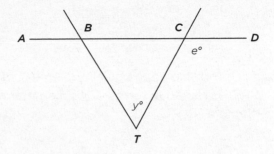

34. In the figure provided, $BT = CT$. If $e = 110$, then $y =$

Ⓐ 30

Ⓑ 40

Ⓒ 45

Ⓓ 70

Ⓔ 110

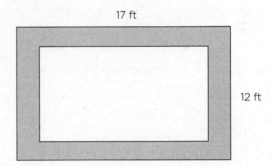

35. The rectangular pool in the figure above has a tile border 2 feet wide on all sides. What is the area, in square feet, of the pool that excludes the tile border?

Ⓐ 29

Ⓑ 104

Ⓒ 150

Ⓓ 196

Ⓔ 204

$$A = \frac{(\pi d^2)}{c}$$

36. If the formula above gives the area A of a circular region in terms of its diameter d, then $c =$

    (A) $\frac{1}{4}$

    (B) $\frac{1}{2}$

    (C) 1

    (D) 4

    (E) 8

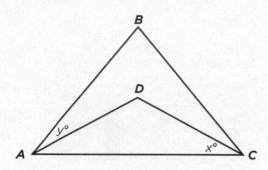

37. In the graphic above, ABC is an equilateral triangle and ADC is an isosceles triangle ($AD = CD$). If $x = 33$, what is the value of y?

    (A) 7

    (B) 17

    (C) 27

    (D) 57

    (E) Cannot be determined

38. If a circle has a radius of 10, what is its circumference?

    (A) 5π

    (B) 10π

    (C) 20π

    (D) 100π

    (E) 125π

39. If a brick which is 10 inches by 5 inches by 5 inches is placed inside a right circular cylinder with a radius of 5 and a height of 10, what is the volume (in cubic inches) of the portion of the cylinder that is not taken up by the brick?

    (A) 50π – 50

    (B) 1000π – 250

    (C) 250π – 250

    (D) 500π – 250

    (E) 1,000π – 250

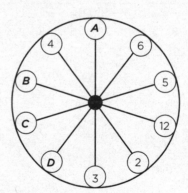

40. In the figure above, the product of any two numbers in adjacent circles is equal to the product of the two numbers that are opposite those circles So $B \times C = 12 \times 5$. What is the value of B?

    (A) 4

    (B) 6

    (C) 8

    (D) 12

    (E) 24

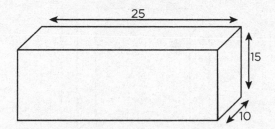

41. What is the maximum number of cubes, each 5 inches on each edge, that can be packed into a rectangular box with the inside dimensions as shown in the graphic above?

    Ⓐ 10

    Ⓑ 30

    Ⓒ 50

    Ⓓ 150

    Ⓔ 3,750

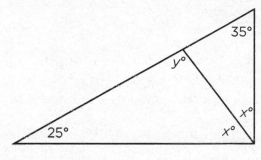

42. What is the value of *y* in the graphic above?

    Ⓐ 80

    Ⓑ 95

    Ⓒ 110

    Ⓓ 125

    Ⓔ 135

43. What is the perimeter, in feet, of a rectangular swimming pool 16 feet wide, that has the same area as a rectangular pool 32 feet long and 10 feet wide?

    Ⓐ 20

    Ⓑ 72

    Ⓒ 84

    Ⓓ 160

    Ⓔ 320

44. What is the length of a rectangle that has a width of 20 and a perimeter of 90?

    Ⓐ 20

    Ⓑ 25

    Ⓒ 30

    Ⓓ 35

    Ⓔ 50

45. If each curved section of the graphic above is a semicircle with a radius of 40 and the two parallel sides each have a length of 200, what is the area of the shaded region?

    Ⓐ 8,000

    Ⓑ 16,000

    Ⓒ 4,000 – 160π

    Ⓓ 8,000 – 320π

    Ⓔ 16,000 – 160π

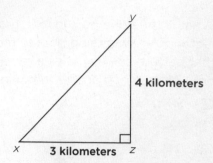

46. Based on the information in the figure above, how many kilometers shorter would the travel distance be if someone went from point X directly to point Y, rather than going from point X to point Z and then from point Z to point Y?

   Ⓐ 0

   Ⓑ 1

   Ⓒ 2

   Ⓓ 5

   Ⓔ 7

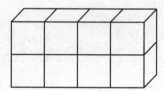

47. The rectangular solid above is made up of eight cubes of the same size, each of which has exactly one face painted green. What is the greatest fraction of the total surface area of the solid that could be green?

   Ⓐ $\dfrac{1}{3}$

   Ⓑ $\dfrac{1}{6}$

   Ⓒ $\dfrac{9}{28}$

   Ⓓ $\dfrac{2}{7}$

   Ⓔ $\dfrac{3}{14}$

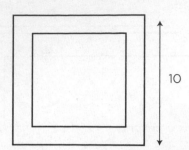

48. In the figure shown, the larger square has a side length of 10. The area of the smaller square is $\dfrac{1}{2}$ the area of the larger square. How many units longer is the diagonal of the larger square than the diagonal of the smaller square?

   Ⓐ $10(\sqrt{2} - 1)$

   Ⓑ $\sqrt{200}$

   Ⓒ 20

   Ⓓ 5

   Ⓔ $\sqrt{2}$

49. A circle with radius 4 is intersected by a line at points x and y. The maximum possible distance between x and y is

   Ⓐ 2

   Ⓑ π

   Ⓒ 4

   Ⓓ 8

   Ⓔ 8π

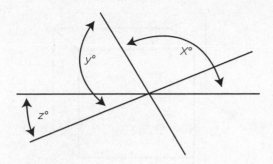

50. In the figure above, if $x - 100$ and $y = 110$, then $z =$

Ⓐ 80

Ⓑ 70

Ⓒ 40

Ⓓ 30

Ⓔ 10

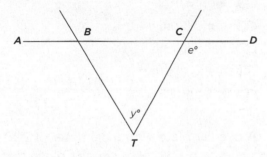

51. In the figure provided, $BT = CT$. If $y = 54.6$, then $e =$

Ⓐ 54.6

Ⓑ 62.7

Ⓒ 117.3

Ⓓ 109.2

Ⓔ 180

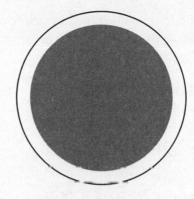

52. The circular pool in the figure above has a tile border 3 feet wide (the white area surrounding the pool) and the area, in square feet, of the pool and tile included is 225π. What is the area, in square feet, of the pool that excludes the tile border?

Ⓐ 12π

Ⓑ 24π

Ⓒ 81π

Ⓓ 144π

Ⓔ 156π

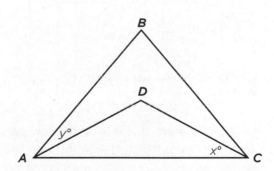

53. In the graphic above, ABC is an equilateral triangle and ADC is an isosceles triangle ($AD = CD$). If $y = 25$, what is the value of x?

Ⓐ 15

Ⓑ 25

Ⓒ 30

Ⓓ 35

Ⓔ 60

54. If a circle has a radius of approximately π, what is its approximate circumference?

    Ⓐ 2π

    Ⓑ π²

    Ⓒ π³

    Ⓓ 2π³

    Ⓔ 2π²

55. If a brick which is .2 inches by .05 inches by .05 inches is placed inside a right circular cylinder with a radius of .05 and a height of .2, what portion of the cylinder is not taken up by the brick?

    Ⓐ .005π – .005

    Ⓑ .0005π – .0005

    Ⓒ .05π – .05

    Ⓓ .0005π

    Ⓔ 0

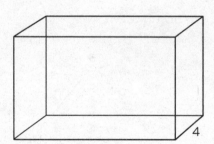

56. Each dimension of the rectangular solid (volume = 24) pictured is an integer less than 6. Which of the following is the total surface area of the solid?

    Ⓐ 24

    Ⓑ 52

    Ⓒ 60

    Ⓓ 68

    Ⓔ 78

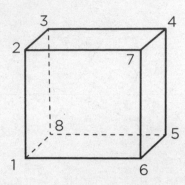

57. Which of the following statements about the cube must be true?

    I. Line 1-3 is parallel to Line 4-6
    II. Triangle 3-4-7 has the same area as Triangle 1-6-8
    III. Line 3-6 = Line 1-4

    Ⓐ II only

    Ⓑ I and II only

    Ⓒ I and III only

    Ⓓ II and III only

    Ⓔ I, II, and III

58. A circular plate with a diameter of 20 inches is placed on a circular place mat with a diameter of 24 inches. What fraction of the place mat's surface area is not covered?

    Ⓐ $\frac{11}{144}$

    Ⓑ $\frac{11}{36}$

    Ⓒ $\frac{25}{36}$

    Ⓓ $\frac{20}{24}$

    Ⓔ $\frac{41}{44}$

59. What is the radius of the largest sphere that could fit inside a cube with a volume of 125?

    (A) $\frac{1}{4}$

    (B) $\frac{3}{2}$

    (C) $\frac{5}{2}$

    (D) π

    (E) 5

60. Set A consists of all points (x, y) such that $x^2 + y^2 = 4$, and $x \neq 0 \neq y$. If a point (m, n) is selected from set A at random, what is the probability that $n > m + 2$?

    (A) $\frac{3}{4}$

    (B) $\frac{1}{2}$

    (C) $\frac{1}{4}$

    (D) $\frac{1}{8}$

    (E) The probability cannot be determined.

Enter your answer in the answer box(es) below the question.

Equivalent forms of the correct answer, such as 2.5 and 2.50, are all correct. Fractions do not need to be reduced to lowest terms.

Enter the exact answer unless the question asks you to round your answer.

---

61. What is the area of a rectangle with a side of 5 and a diagonal of 13?

62. If a square parking lot has an area of z, what is the longest distance on a straight line that a car could drive on the lot?

    (A) $\sqrt{z}$

    (B) $\sqrt{2z}$

    (C) $2\sqrt{z}$

    (D) $z\sqrt{2}$

    (E) $2z$

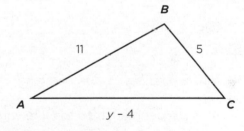

63. Which of the following describes the possible range of values of y?

    (A) $9 < y < 11$

    (B) $5 < y < 11$

    (C) $9 < y < 15$

    (D) $5 < y < 15$

    (E) $10 < y < 20$

64. Jonna and Russell meet at a diner that is directly south of Jonna's house and directly west of Russell's house. If the diner is exactly 10 miles from Jonna's house and Russell's house is 2 miles closer to the diner than to Jonna's house, how far apart is Russell's house from the diner?

    (A) 8

    (B) 14

    (C) 16

    (D) 24

    (E) 26

65. If the number of square units in the surface area of a cylinder with a radius of 6 is $\frac{1}{2}$ of the number of cubic units in the cylinder, what is the number of square units in the surface area?

    (A) 128π

    (B) 192π

    (C) 216π

    (D) 324π

    (E) 432π

66. Line A is perpendicular to the line with the equation $y = -\frac{1}{5}x$, and the point (3,−10) is on line A. Which of the following is the equation of line A?

    (A) $y = -\frac{1}{5}x - \frac{47}{5}$

    (B) $y = \frac{1}{5}x - \frac{53}{5}$

    (C) $y = 5x$

    (D) $y = 5x - 5$

    (E) $y = 5x - 25$

67. Starting from point A on a flat savanna, a cheetah walks 10 miles due north, then 8 miles due east, and then 4 miles due south, arriving at point B. What is the shortest distance, in miles, that the cheetah can walk to return to point A?

    (A) 18

    (B) 16

    (C) 14

    (D) 12

    (E) 10

68. If a rectangular piece of cloth measuring 20 inches by 10 inches is cut into exactly two squares, each of which are then cut into exactly two triangles, what is the area of one of the triangles, in square inches?

    (A) 20

    (B) 40

    (C) 50

    (D) 60

    (E) It cannot be determined from the information given.

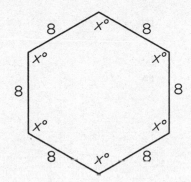

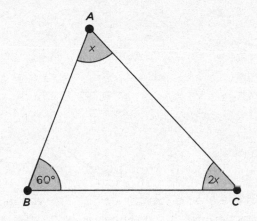

69. What is the area of the figure shown?

Ⓐ $96\sqrt{3}$

Ⓑ 256

Ⓒ $256\sqrt{3}$

Ⓓ 512

Ⓔ It cannot be determined by the information given.

70. The base of an isosceles triangle has its endpoints at coordinates (5,2) and (1,2). Which of the following coordinate pairs could be the third vertex of the triangle?

Indicate *all* possible choices.

Ⓐ (4,7)

Ⓑ (4,-7)

Ⓒ (3,6)

Ⓓ (5,-6)

Ⓔ (3,-6)

71. What is the degree measure of angle *ACB*?

72. One side of a triangle measures 10 inches. Which of the following could be the lengths of the other two sides?

Indicate *all* possible correct answers.

Ⓐ 2 and 7

Ⓑ 4 and 7

Ⓒ 6 and 5

Ⓓ 8 and 2

Ⓔ 10 and 10

Ⓕ 12 and 22

Ⓖ 14 and 23

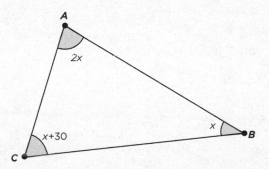

73. What is the measure of angle *C*? Enter your answer in degrees.

[   ] degrees

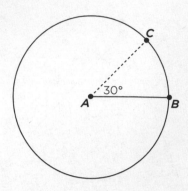

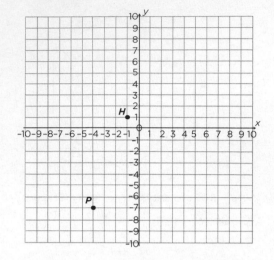

74. If the area of sector *ABC* is 3π, what is the length of the diameter of the circle?

75. If *M* is the midpoint of a line segment $\overline{PQ}$ (point *Q* not shown), what is the *y*-coordinate of *Q*?

Answers and explanations begin on the next page.

Answer Key

GEOMETRY PRACTICE

1. $\frac{4}{5}$
2. 14
3. 36
4. 23
5. 38
6. 5,000
7. 12
8. 3
9. A, B, C
10. C, D
11. C, D
12. B, C, E
13. A, D
14. B, C, D
15. 40
16. 8
17. 54
18. 62
19. 104
20. A, C
21. A, B, C, E
22. A, C
23. B
24. $\frac{23}{50}$
25. $\frac{9}{1}$

26. 52
27. 6
28. 70
29. 4
30. 21
31. 294
32. 3
33. C
34. B
35. B
36. D
37. C
38. C
39. C
40. B
41. B
42. B
43. B
44. B
45. B
46. C
47. D
48. A
49. D
50. D
51. C

52. D
53. D
54. E
55. B
56. B
57. E
58. B
59. C
60. C
61. 60
62. B
63. E
64. D
65. C
66. E
67. E
68. C
69. A
70. C, E
71. 80
72. B, C, E, G
73. 67.5
74. 12
75. 9

Answers and Explanations

GEOMETRY PRACTICE

1. $\dfrac{4}{5}$

Since the plot is a square, we can take the square root of the area to find the length of its sides. This works out to 12 ft. From there we can find the diameter of the pool. The diagram is below.

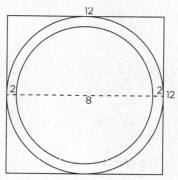

The diameter of the pool is 8, meaning the radius is 4. Therefore the area of the pool is:

$$4^2\pi = 16\pi$$

The area of the walkway equals the area of the entire circular region minus the area of the pool. This is given by:

$$6^2\pi - 4^2\pi = 36\pi - 16\pi = 20\pi$$

So the ratio of pool area to walkway area is $\dfrac{16\pi}{20\pi} = \dfrac{4}{5}$.

2. 14

The area of a triangle is $0.5 \times$ base $\times$ height.

The easiest base to use is the vertical line between (3,5) and (3,–2), since we can find its length easily.

Since these points lie along a vertical line, the distance is the difference between their y-coordinates:

$$5 - (-2) = 7$$

The height is the distance from the third vertex to the vertical line, for which we need only to deal with the x-coordinates:

$$3 - (-1) = 4$$

The area is therefore $0.5 \times 4 \times 7 = 14$.

3. 36

The area of the circle is πr^2, which means that:

$$A = \pi r^2 = 18\pi$$
$$18 = r^2$$
$$\sqrt{18} = r$$
$$3\sqrt{2} = r$$

This means the diameter of the circle is $6\sqrt{2}$. The diameter of a circle is also the diagonal of the inscribed square. If the diagonal of the square is $6\sqrt{2}$, we can use the ratio of a 45-45-90 triangle to find that the side length of the square is 6. The area of the square is therefore 6^2, or 36.

4. 23

Perpendicular lines have slopes that are negative reciprocals of one another. If the slope of l is $\frac{1}{3}$, then the slope of the perpendicular line is –3. Thus, the equation of the line is $y = -3x + b$.

Since we know that this line passes through (5,8), we can substitute these values in for x and y:

$$8 = -3(5) + b$$
$$8 = -15 + b$$
$$b = 23$$

5. 38

In the diagram, point *F* does not appear to be at the center of the circle, but the question stem tells you that it is. Remember that, on the GRE, you cannot always rely on the diagram to identify things like right angles or relative lengths of sides of figures, but you *can* always rely on information given in the question stem. Consequently, ignore the fact that point *F* may not *look like* it's at the center.

The shaded area of the circle is composed of two sectors formed by two lines that intersect at *F*, the center of the circle. When two lines intersect, they form two pairs of congruent, vertical angles; in this case, one pair of the angles so formed are central angles that intercept the shaded sectors of the circle. This means that the central angles in question are congruent, and therefore that the sectors themselves will have equal areas. In order to answer the question, we can thus find the area of one sector and then double that result.

The area of the circle is πr^2, which in this case is 36π. In any circle, the ratio of the area of a sector to the area of the circle will be equal to the ratio of the central angle (in degrees) to 360. Sector *EFG* is bounded by angle *EFG*, which measures 60 degrees, so the area of sector *EFG* can be found using the following proportion:

$$\frac{60}{360} = \frac{x}{36\pi}$$
$$360x = 2{,}160\pi$$
$$x = 6\pi$$

Extending this to both shaded sectors gives us the area of the entire region. The area of both sectors is thus 12π, or 37.699. Round up to 38.

6. 5,000

We first want to find the volume of the silo. The volume of a cylinder is $\pi r^2 h$. The diameter of the silo is 20 ft, so the radius is 10 ft. The volume of the silo is thus:

$$(10)^2\pi 25 = 2{,}500\pi \text{ ft}^3$$

Since the silo is 80% full, the volume of grain in the silo is:

$$.8(2{,}500\pi \text{ ft}^3) = 2{,}000\pi \text{ ft}^3$$

Now we can use a proportion to find the weight of the grain:

$$\frac{10\text{lbs}}{4\pi} = \frac{x}{2{,}000\pi}$$
$$x = \frac{20{,}000\pi \text{ lbs}}{4\pi}$$

The grain weighs 5,000 lbs.

7. 12

First we should find the equations of lines *q* and *r*.

The equation of line *q* is:

$$y = 3x + b$$

Plugging in the values (4,6), we can find the value of the *y*-intercept of the line:

$$6 = 3(4) + b$$
$$6 = 12 + b$$
$$b = -6$$

The equation of line *q* is:

$$y = 3x - 6$$

Line *r* has a slope of –2 and it passes through the point (12,0). The equation is:

$$0 = -2(12) + b$$
$$0 = -24 + b$$
$$b = 24$$

The equation of line *r* is:

$$y = -2x + 24$$

Setting the lines equal, we have:

$$3x - 6 = -2x + 24$$
$$5x = 30$$
$$x = 6$$

Plugging 6 back into one of our linear equations gives us:

$y = -2(6) + 24$

$y = -12 + 24$

$y = 12$

8. 3

Angle E marks off a sector of the circle. If we find the area of the sector and subtract the area of the triangle with vertex at E, we will have our answer.

The area of a sector can be solved using a proportion: the ratio of angle E to the entire degree measure of the circle is proportional to the ratio of the area of the sector to the area of the circle. The area of the circle is given by πr^2, which means we can set up the following:

$$\frac{60}{360} = \frac{x}{36\pi}$$
$$\frac{1}{6} = \frac{x}{36\pi}$$
$$x = 6\pi$$

This is approximately 18.84.

To find the area of the triangle, it helps to note that this is an equilateral triangle. We know that it is at least isosceles, since all radii of a circle are congruent, and since angle E measures 60° and the other angles are equal to one another (because their corresponding sides, both radii, are equal.) So, all angles must be 60°. (If the other two angles are defined as x, then $2x + 60 = 180$, and $x = 60$.)

This establishes that this triangle is equilateral, which means we can divide it as follows:

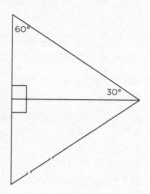

The radius 6 corresponds to the hypotenuse of the right triangle. The side length ratio of a 30-60-90 triangle is $x : x\sqrt{3} : 2x$, which in this case means $3 : 3\sqrt{3} : 6$.

The area of a triangle is .5 × base × height. The base is 6 and the height is $3\sqrt{3}$, which makes the area of the triangle $9\sqrt{3}$, or approximately 15.6.

Subtracting the area of the triangle from the area of the sector gives us:

$$18.84 - 15.6 = 3.24$$

This rounds down to 3.

9. A, B, C

In order to solve this problem, it's important to know the properties of triangles.

The length of the third side of any triangle must be greater than the difference of the two remaining sides and less than the sum of the two remaining sides.

In other words, with the two sides 12 and 12, the length of the third side MUST be greater than 12 − 12 = 0 and less than 12 + 12 = 24.

Although it is not an integer, choice (A), 0.12, is still correct because it is greater than 0. The question does not specify that the length must be an integer.

On the other hand, choice (D) is incorrect: the third side must be less than 24.

This means that any value between 0 and 24 is correct, which includes (A), (B), and (C).

10. C, D

In order to solve this problem, we must know how to find the diagonal of a cube.

There is an equation to memorize for the diagonal of a cube (this works ONLY for cubes).

$d = s\sqrt{3}$ where d = diagonal and s = length of the side.

Since we know that the side = 7.5, the diagonal is $7.5\sqrt{3}$, so anything greater than or equal to this will be our correct answer.

However, if we don't know this formula, we can figure the answer out via the Pythagorean theorem.

If we draw a diagram of a cube, we can see that the diagonal is actually the hypotenuse of a right triangle whose legs are (1) the diagonal of an entire face of the cube and (2) the side of the cube.

First, we must find the diagonal of one face of the cube. Let c = diagonal of a face of the cube.

$$7.5^2 + 7.5^2 = c^2$$
$$56.25 + 56.25 = c^2$$
$$112.5 = c^2$$

So $c = \sqrt{112.5}$

Now that we have the diagonal of the face, we can figure out the diagonal of the entire cube.

The sides of the right triangle are c and s; the hypotenuse is the diagonal of the cube.

So let d = diagonal of the cube.

$$c^2 + s^2 = d^2$$
$$(\sqrt{112.5})^2 + (7.5)^2 = d^2$$
$$112.5 + 56.25 = 168.75 = d^2$$

We can either reduce this, or just figure out the numerical value of the square root of 168.75.

It ends up being $7.5\sqrt{3}$, or almost 13.

11. C, D

The formula for the volume of a cylinder is:

$$V = \pi r^2 h$$

We know that h = 10 cm, but we need to find the length of the radius.

Since the diagonal is 26 cm, we can figure out the diameter using the Pythagorean theorem. The diagonal is the hypotenuse, and the height and diameter are the other two sides.

Let d = length of the diameter:

$$26^2 = 10^2 + d^2$$
$$676 = 100 + d^2$$
$$576 = d^2$$
$$d = 24$$

So if the diameter is 24, then the radius will be half of that.

$$r = 12$$

Now that we know r = 12 cm, we can fill in the equation and figure out the volume.

$$V = \pi(12 \text{ cm})^2 (10 \text{ cm}) = 1{,}440\pi \text{ cm}^3$$

So any answer choice greater than or equal to $1{,}440\pi$ cm^3 is correct. $1{,}440\pi$ is approximately 4,524.

This means (A) and (B) are incorrect. (C) is correct because it is exactly the volume of the cylinder, and (D) is correct because 4,608 = 1,440 × 3.2, and 3.2 is greater than π.

12. B, C, E

To solve this problem, we can plug in the answer choices to see if they make a valid statement. If they do, the point lies on the circle.

(A) (0,−3): $0^2 + (-3 - 3)^2 = 36 \neq 9$

(B) (0,6): $0^2 + (6 - 3)^2 = 9$

(C) (0,0): $0^2 + (0 - 3)^2 = 9$

(D) (6,0): $6^2 + (0 - 3)^2 = 45 \neq 9$

(E) (3,3): $3^2 + (3 - 3)^2 = 9$

Thus, (B), (C), and (E) are the correct answers.

13. A, D

To solve this problem, we can simply plug in the answer choices to see if they make a valid statement. If they do, the point lies on the circle.

(A) (−4,6); $(−4 + 4)^2 + (6 − 2)^2 = 16$

(B) (−4,2): $(−4 + 4)^2 + (2 − 2)^2 = 0 \neq 16$

(C) (2,0): $(2 + 4)^2 + (0 − 2)^2 = 40 \neq 16$

(D) (0,2): $(0 + 4)^2 + (2 − 2)^2 = 16$

Thus, (A) and (D) are the correct answers.

14. B, C, D

In order to solve this problem, we can refer to the properties of triangles. Recall that the third side of a triangle must be less than the sum of the two known sides, and greater than the difference.

We know that the smallest y can be is $2x$.

If we set $y = 2x$, and we know that the third side must be greater than the difference between the two known sides, then we know that the third side must be greater than $y − x$; through substitution, this becomes:

third side $> 2x − x$

third side $> x$

So we know that the third side must be greater than x. However, because we know that $y \geq 2x$, the sum of the two sides can be anything greater than $3x$, and so there is no upper limit: y could equal $5x$, or $200x$, or $1,000x$, etc.

For example, if we set $y = 1,000x$, then the third side would have to be less than the sum of the other two sides:

third side $< 1,000x + x$

third side $< 1,001x$

We see that the upper limit can always get higher, but the third side can never be less than x.

So (B), (C), and (D) are the correct answers.

15. 40

An altitude drawn from the right angle of a right triangle divides the triangle into smaller, proportional triangles. First, we can use the Pythagorean theorem to find AB: triangle ADB is a Pythagorean triple in the ratio of 3-4-5. In this case, the legs are 6 and 8, so the hypotenuse will be 10.

Since the triangles are proportional, their perimeters are proportional as well. The perimeter of triangle ADB is 24 (6 + 8 + 10), so we can set up the following equation, comparing the smallest sides of both triangles we're considering:

$$\frac{6}{10} = \frac{24}{\text{Perimeter of } ABC}$$

$$6(\text{Perimeter of } ABC) = 240$$

$$\text{Perimeter of } ABC = 40$$

16. 8

The area of a circle is given by πr^2, where r is the radius of the circle. If the area of the larger circle is 100π, this makes $r^2 = 100$, which makes the radius of the large circle 10.

There are a few things to remember about chords like VX. Any radius that passes through a chord serves as a perpendicular bisector of the chord, meaning that we can form a right triangle out of any radius of the large circle, the radius of a small circle, and half of the length of VX.

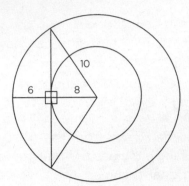

Setting r as the radius of the small circle and using the Pythagorean theorem, we have:

$$r^2 + 6^2 = 100$$
$$r^2 + 36 = 100$$
$$r^2 = 64$$
$$r = 8$$

The radius of the small circle is 8.

17. 54

Since we know the circles are tangent to the y-axis at the same point, we know that the top edge of the rectangle is as long as both radii of the two circles added together. This means that this edge has a length of 9. The other side is equal to the radius of the larger circle. Let's set a = longer radius and b = shorter radius. The ratios of the areas of the circles would be:

$$\frac{\pi a^2}{\pi b^2} = \frac{a^2}{b^2} = \left(\frac{a}{b}\right)^2$$

Since that ratio is 4, we can further state:

$$\left(\frac{a}{b}\right)^2 = 4$$

$$\frac{a}{b} = 2$$

This means $a = 2b$. Since the distance between the centers is equal to the combined radii of the two circles, we can set up another equation, $a + b = 9$. Through substitution, this gives us:

$$2b + b = 9$$
$$3b = 9$$
$$b = 3$$
$$a = 6$$

With length = 9 and a = width = 6, length × width = 9 × 6 = 54.

Therefore, the area of the rectangle is 54.

18. 62

Let's sketch out the diagram. Furthermore, it is helpful to draw two radii from the center of the circle to two vertices of the triangle, and one additional radius perpendicular to the side of the triangle. It will look like this:

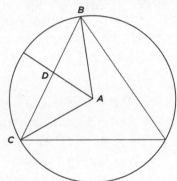

Angle BAC is 120°; we know this because it encompasses exactly one-third of the circle. We know that AD must bisect angle BAC. Since triangle BAC is isosceles, an altitude drawn to the base must bisect the angle, which means that BAD is a 30-60-90 triangle. The sides are thus in an x- $x\sqrt{3}$-$2x$ ratio. The $2x$ side is 12, so BD must be $6\sqrt{3}$. That means that BC is $12\sqrt{3}$, and the perimeter of the triangle is $36\sqrt{3}$. This rounds off to 62.

19. 104

The area of a circle is given by πr^2. If the area of the inner circle is 4π, then $r^2 = 4$ and $r = 2$. This means, in keeping with the ratio we are given, that the width of the second ring is 2 as well, and that the width of the outer ring is 3. To find the area of the shaded region, we subtract the area of the white area from the area of the entire figure. The radius of the entire figure is:

$$2 + 2 + 3 = 7$$

The radius of the white concentric circles is:

$$2 + 2 = 4$$

Therefore the area of the shaded area is

$$(7)^2\pi - (4)^2\pi = 49\pi - 16\pi = 33\pi$$

This works out to approximately 104.

20. **A, C**

Given that the points are equally spaced, we know that $b = -a$, and $c = 2b$.

Since we need to select all true statements, let's examine each of them one by one.

(1) $b - c = a$

We can see graphically that this must be true. Since b is one unit away from the origin and c is two units away, subtracting c from b yields a result one unit away from the origin: a.

To confirm by doing the math, $b - c = b - 2b = -b = a$. True.

(2) The distance from A to $C = 3b$

Don't be tricked: just because the points on the line are equally spaced, and B is one unit away from the origin, doesn't mean the distance between each of them is b! The distance from the origin to B, which is also the distance from the origin to A or from B to C, is not b but rather $b\sqrt{2}$ —remember the Pythagorean theorem. Therefore the distance from A to C is actually $3b\sqrt{2}$, not $3b$. False.

(3) $ba - ca > 0$

ba is negative, as is ca, but which has the greater absolute value? Graphically, clearly $|ca| > |ba|$, so subtracting the larger negative number will yield a result that is positive.

Mathematically, $ba - ca = a(b - c)$, where $b - c$ is negative and so is a, so the product will be positive. True.

You could also evaluate each of these statements by substituting acceptable values for the coordinates of each point—for example, A could be (-1,-1), B could be (1,1), and C could be (2,2)—and then calculate the results for each statement.

21. **A, B, C, E**

The area of a triangle is $\frac{1}{2}$ × base × height. In our case, the diagram shows that $\angle BCD$ is a right angle, and we are given the length of BC. Therefore, if we can determine the length of CD, we can determine the area of triangle BCD.

This is a multiple-choice question with one or more correct answers. Let's consider each statement in turn, remembering that for the answer to be correct it must be sufficient by itself—without any of the other statements—to enable us to determine the area of BCD.

Also remember that you do not need to make each of these calculations when answering the question. The question asks about what information is sufficient to solve for the area of BCD.

(A) $CG = GD = 5\sqrt{3}$

If $CG = GD$, then triangle CGD is isosceles, and so $\angle GCD = \angle GDC$—let's call that angle x. This means that $\angle CGD = 180 - 2x$.

We also then know that $\angle CGB = 2x$.

And we know that $\angle CBG = 2x$, since $CG = BC = 5\sqrt{3}$, making triangle BCG isosceles.

Thus, if $\angle CDG = x$ and $\angle CBG = 2x$, then $x + 2x = 90$, since $\angle BCD$ is 90 and those three angles must sum to 180.

Since $x + 2x = 90$, then $x = 30$, $2x = 60$, and triangle BCD is a 30:60:90 triangle.

Thus, in keeping with the proportions of sides of 30:60:90 triangles, $CD = 5\sqrt{3} \times \sqrt{3} = 15$. Now we know the base and height of the triangle, so we know the area too.

(B) Triangle BCG is an equilateral triangle.

If BCG is an equilateral triangle, then $\angle CBG = 60$, which means that BCD is a 30:60:90 triangle with sides $5\sqrt{3}$ and 15. These double as our base and height, so we can calculate the area.

(C) $CD = 15$

Since BCD is a right triangle, its area is just $\frac{1}{2} \times BC \times CD$. Since we already have BC and this statement tells us the value of CD, we have enough information to calculate the area.

(D) $CG = 5\sqrt{3}$

This by itself does not tell us enough. This statement plus the given tells us that triangle BCG is isosceles, but this information isn't sufficient for determining CD or the area of the triangle.

(E) The length of the hypotenuse of triangle $BCD = 10\sqrt{3}$

Since BCD is a right triangle, and we began with the value of one of the sides, then the length of the hypotenuse gives us enough information to apply the Pythagorean theorem to determine the value of the other side, CD. Then we'll have the values of both the base and the height, with which we can determine the area of the triangle.

Answer choices (A), (B), (C), and (E) are all correct.

22. A, C

This is a multiple-choice question with one or more possible correct answers, so let's examine each statement in turn to select the correct answers.

(A) The circumference of the circle = 4π

Since the circumference = diameter × π, this means that the diameter of the circle is 4. That diameter is also the length of a side of the circumscribed square, whose area would then be 16.

(B) The ratio of the area of the square to the area of the circle = $\frac{4}{\pi}$.

Let r be the radius of the circle. In this case, the area of the square will be $4r^2$ and the area of the circle πr^2.

The ratio of the area of the square to the area of the circle will be $\frac{4r^2}{\pi r^2} = \frac{4}{\pi}$. This statement will always be true for any circle inscribed in a square, so it doesn't tell us any useful information about this particular square.

(C) The area of the shaded section in the lower left, inside the square but outside the circle, is $4 - \pi$.

This looks promising. The area of the shaded area is $\frac{1}{4}$ the area of the square minus $\frac{1}{4}$ the area of the circle.

If r is the radius of the circle, then $\frac{1}{4}$ the area of the square is just r^2, and $\frac{1}{4}$ the area of the circle is $\frac{\pi r^2}{4}$.

We can set up our equation using this new statement:

$$r^2 - \frac{\pi r^2}{4} = 4 - \pi.$$

Multiply each side by 4 to get:

$$4r^2 - \pi r^2 = 4(4 - \pi)$$

Factor the left side $\Rightarrow r^2(4 - \pi) = 4(4 - \pi)$

Divide out the $4 - \pi$ from both sides $\Rightarrow r^2 = 4$

Square root both sides $\Rightarrow r = 2$.

The length of a side of the square = $2r = 4$, and the area of the square is 16.

Answer choices (A) and (C) are each individually sufficient to answer the question.

23. B

This is a multiple-choice question with one or more correct answers. In this case we must evaluate each of the statements in the answer choices to select the ones that are definitely true.

(A) The line given by the equation $8x + 2y = \frac{2}{3}$ forms a right angle with line L.

If two lines form a right angle with one another, they will be perpendicular, and the slopes of the two lines are negative inverses of each other, meaning their product is –1. For line L, the slope is 4.

What's the slope of the line given in this statement? Let's rewrite the equation in slope-intercept form.

$$8x + 2y = \frac{2}{3}$$

$$2y = -8x + \frac{2}{3}$$

$$y = -4x + \frac{1}{3}$$

So the slope is –4, which is the negative of L's slope but not the negative *inverse* (which would be $-\frac{1}{4}$). Thus, this line is not perpendicular to L. Not true.

(B) The line given by the equation $3 + y = 4x$ is parallel to line L.

Two lines that are parallel share the same slope but have different y-intercepts. Let's rewrite the equation for the line given in this statement and put it into slope-intercept form.

$$3 + y = 4x$$

$$y = 4x - 3$$

The slope is 4 (same as L), but the y-intercept is –3 (not 3, as for line L). Thus, the two lines are parallel, and this statement is true.

(C) Line L passes through exactly two quadrants.

The coordinate plane is divided into four quadrants. Because lines continue infinitely, almost all lines pass through exactly three quadrants. However, lines that are vertical or horizontal pass through only two quadrants. Since line L is neither vertical nor horizontal, and does not pass through the origin, it will pass through three quadrants. This statement is not true.

(D) Line M is given by $y = 2x + b$, where b is positive; L's y-intercept is greater than M's x-intercept.

Given that L and M both have a positive slope and a positive y-intercept, we know that they both have a negative x-intercept (draw it to see why this is the case).

What is L's x-intercept? Calculate it by letting $y = 0$.

$$0 = 4x + 3, \; x = -\frac{3}{4}$$

For example, if $b = \frac{1}{4}$, then line M is $y = 2x + \frac{1}{4}$. If $y = 0$, then $x = -\frac{1}{8}$, which is greater than $-\frac{3}{4}$.

Thus, although this statement is true for most positive values of b, it's not true for all of them. For any $b < \frac{3}{4}$ it will be false, so we can't say this statement must be true.

Only answer choice (B) is correct.

24. $\frac{23}{50}$

In order to solve this problem, we do not need to know the exact values of solid A's dimensions. Because we're just looking for a ratio, we need to know only how the two solids' dimensions differ.

Solid B's dimensions are l, w, and h.

Solid A's dimensions: its length is 15% longer, or 1.15l;

its width is 60% shorter, or 100% – 60% = 40% of B's width: 0.4w;

and its height is the same.

So Solid A's dimensions are 1.15l, 0.4w, and h.

To figure out the volumes, we just multiply all three dimensions together.

Solid B volume = v = lwh

Solid A volume = v = (1.15)(0.4)(lwh) = (0.46)lwh

Now we can figure out the ratio of volumes between A and B.

$$(0.46)lwh : lwh = \frac{0.46}{1} = 0.46$$

$$\frac{46}{100} = \frac{23}{50}.$$

25. $\frac{9}{1}$

To solve this problem, we can use any value for the side length of cube m. We can use a variable or an actual numerical value; for this example, let's use the number 3.

The side length of cube n = 3

This means the side length of cube m = 9, because it is three times larger.

Now we can find the surface area of each cube.

$$SA = 6s^2$$

SA for cube n:

$$SA = 6(3^2) = 54$$

SA for cube m:

$$SA = 6(9^2) = 486$$

So the ratio will be

$$486 : 54 = 9$$

The answer is 9. We will reach this answer regardless of what we set as the side length of cube n, whether we use a variable or integer.

26. **52**

In order to solve this problem, we need to find the value of angle DAB.

We see that angle DAB plus the missing angle of triangle ABC is a straight line, meaning that these angles will add up to 180 degrees.

We also know that there are 180 degrees inside a triangle, which means that the sum of the two known angles, 57 and 47 degrees, is the same as angle DAB.

57 + 47 = 104 degrees total.

Finally, we know that line segment MN bisects angle DAB, or cuts it in half, which means that the value of x will be half of that value.

angle DAB = 104

$$x = \frac{104}{2}$$
$$x = 52$$

27. **6**

To solve this problem, we must find the volume of both cubes. Volume of a cube is expressed by the length of a side cubed:

$$\left(2, \sqrt{2}^3\right) = \text{(approx) } 22.627$$

$$\sqrt{29}^3 = \text{(approx) } 156.169$$

With these volumes, we can divide the smaller cube into the larger one.

$$\frac{156.169}{22.627} = 6.901$$

The answer is 6, because we can fit a maximum of 6 cubes—not quite 7.

28. 70

To solve this problem, we must know the properties of angles when a line intersects two parallel lines.

Since opposite angles will sum to 180, we can add the two angles with x values in them and set them equal to 180.

$$\left(\frac{5}{2}\right)x - 30 + \left(\frac{1}{2}\right)x = 180$$

$$\left(\frac{6}{2}\right)x = 210$$

$$3x = 210$$

$$x = 70$$

29. 4

To solve this problem, we can draw a diagram of where the towns are in relation to each other.

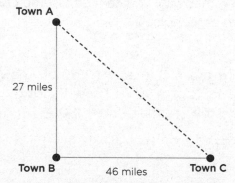

If we connect a line from Town A to Town C, it makes a right triangle.

We can use the Pythagorean theorem to find the distance between Town A and Town C:

$$27^2 + 46^2 = c^2$$

$$729 + 2{,}116 = c^2$$

$$2{,}845 = c^2$$

$$c \approx 53.338$$

Then we can use the distance formula to find the answer to the question.

$$d = rt$$

Since we're dealing with two different times for the two different halves of the journey, let's make t_1 represent the time it took for the first driver and t_2 the time it took for the second; at the end of the problem, we'll add these two times together to get the total time.

We know that the first driver drove half the distance, or $\frac{53.338}{2} \approx 26.669$ miles.

$$26.669 \text{ miles} = 10\text{mph} \times t_1$$

$$t_1 \approx 2.669 \text{ hours.}$$

For the second driver:

$$26.669 \text{ miles} = 20\text{mph} \times t_2$$

$$t_2 \approx 1.333 \text{ hours}$$

Then we can add these two values together.

$$1.333 \text{ hours} + 2.669 \text{ hours} = 4.002 \text{ hours}$$

Rounding to the nearest hundredth, we get 4 hours.

30. 21

To solve this problem, we can set up a ratio to find the total area of the circle.

Since the angle given for area D is 72 degrees, the central angle of region C must be 108 degrees.

Thus we can set up this ratio, where x represents the total area of the circle:

$$\frac{108 \text{ degrees}}{360 \text{ degrees}} = \frac{9}{x}$$

Cross-multiply:

$$108x = 3{,}240 \rightarrow x = 30$$

If the entire circle's area is 30, we need to subtract the area of region C to find the area of the other regions added together.

$$30 - 9 = 21.$$

31. 294

There are two ways to solve this problem. The first way is simpler.

The diagonal of a cube is $s\sqrt{3}$, where s = the length of the side of the cube. Since this is the case, the length of the side is 7.

If you don't know this formula, use the Pythagorean theorem.

The diagonal of a cube is the hypotenuse of a right triangle, within a cube, whose other two side lengths are the side length of the cube and the diagonal of one of the faces of the cube.

$$a^2 + b^2 = c^2$$

a = side length of the cube

b = diagonal of the face of one of the sides

We can find the value of the diagonal of the face in terms of the side lengths by using the Pythagorean theorem for just that face:

$$a^2 + a^2 = b^2$$
$$2a^2 = b^2$$

We can plug this into the original equation:

$$a^2 + 2a^2 = c^2$$
$$3a^2 = (7\sqrt{3})^2$$
$$3a^2 = (49) \times (3)$$
$$a^2 = 49$$
$$a = 7$$

Now, since we know the length of one side of the cube, we can find the surface area, which is six times the area of a single side.

$$SA = 6s^2$$
$$SA = 6(7^2)$$
$$SA = 6(49)$$
$$SA = 294$$

32. 3

When we connect a point on a circle to the ends of a diameter, the resulting angle is always a right angle.

This means that because point B is connected to points A and C, which are the ends of the diameter, angle ABC is 90°.

If this is the case, then chord BC makes up a leg of a right triangle, where the diameter is the hypotenuse.

AC = 6 (twice the radius)

BC = 3 (this is a 30-60-90 triangle, and the side opposite the 30° angle is always half the hypotenuse)

BC has a length of 3.

Note: Do not be deceived by the diagram, which is not drawn to scale. It may be tempting to draw OB and BC and make a right triangle that way. You cannot assume OB and OC are perpendicular.

33. C

Despite the fact that we do not know any values for x, y, or z, we know that if they are inside a triangle their sum is 180.

Since $\frac{180}{60} = 3$ we can quickly find the solution here.

The correct answer is (C).

34. B

First, we must remember that a straight line has 180 degrees in it, so the angle opposite angle e is 180 – 110 = 70. Also, we are given that $BT = CT$, so both of the interior angles opposite of y must equal to one another, as shown in the diagram below. Given this information, the measure of y is 180 – 70 – 70 = 40.

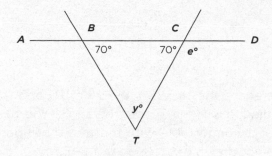

$$\frac{16\pi}{c} = 4\pi$$

$$\frac{16}{c} = 4$$

$$16 = 4c$$

$$4 = c$$

The correct answer is (B).

35. B

We are given the length and width of the pool with the tile included, as well as the size of the tile border. So without the tile border, the length of the pool is 17 – (2)(2) = 13 feet. The width of the pool is 12 – (2)(2) = 8 feet. Taking this together, the area of the pool only is 13 × 8 = 104 square feet.

The correct answer is (B).

36. D

The area of a circular region is normally given as $A = \pi r^2$, where r is the length of the radius. Since $r = \frac{d}{2}$, the formula, in terms of d, is

$$A = \pi\left(\frac{d}{2}\right)^2 = \pi\frac{d^2}{4} = \pi\frac{d^2}{4}.$$

The correct answer is (D).

We can also pick a number for the diameter and see what c would need to be to get the area.

Let's say $d = 4$, so the radius is 2.

According to the equation given, $A = \frac{\left(\pi 4^2\right)}{c} = 16\frac{\pi}{c}$ would need to equal $A = (\pi 2^2) = A = 4\pi$. Therefore:

37. C

Since ABC is an equilateral triangle, each side is equal and each angle is 60°.

If ADC is placed inside of it and is an isosceles (where angle D is the one larger angle), we know that two of the angles are equal.

If the angles are equal, then x is also the compliment to angle y, which means that $x + y = 60$.

If $x = 33$ then $33 + y = 60$

$y = 60 – 33$

$y = 27$.

The correct answer is (C).

38. C

First you must remember the formulas for finding the circumference of a circle. The circumference of a circle can be figured out from its diameter: $C = \pi \times d$ or by using its radius and calculating $C = 2 \times r \times \pi$.

Since we're given the radius in this question, we'll want to find the circumference by using the radius. If we replace the r with a 10 we get $2 \times 10 \times \pi = 20\pi$.

The correct answer is (C).

39. C

We know that the volume of the cylinder can be found by $r^2\pi h$ and the volume of the brick can be found by $b \times h \times w$. Since we have all of these figures we can easily solve.

Cylinder = $5^2 \times \pi \times 10 = 250\pi$

Brick = $10 \times 5 \times 5 = 250$

So the answer is 250π – 250

The correct answer is (C).

40. B

This is simply algebra once we set up the right equation. If the numbers in the opposite circles have the same product, then we can set up the equation as follows:

$$4B = 12 \times 2$$
$$4B = 24$$
$$B = \frac{24}{4}$$
$$B = 6$$

The correct answer is (B).

41. B

To calculate the answer we need to determine how many cubes fit in each dimension of the solid (heightwise, lengthwise, and widthwise). Luckily for us, the cube length of 5 divides evenly into each measurement of the rectangle.

So:

Height: $15 \to \frac{15}{5} = 3$ cubes high

Width: $10 \to \frac{10}{5} = 2$ cubes wide

Length: $25 \to \frac{25}{5} = 5$ cubes long

So we can fit 2 cubes along the bottom, 3 cubes high, and 5 cubes long or $2 \times 3 \times 5 = 30$ cubes.

The correct answer is (B).

42. B

To solve this, we need to realize that these two triangles actually make up a larger triangle. Secondly, every triangle has three angles, which sum to 180.

So $25 + 2x + 35 = 180$

$$2x = 180 - 25 - 35$$
$$2x = 120$$
$$x = 60$$

Disregard that $x = 60$ and $2x = 120$ and that angle looks like a 90 degree angle. You need to get comfortable with the fact that figures are not drawn to scale on the GRE.

Now that we know x, we can solve for the larger of the two triangles:

$$25 + y + x = 25 + y + 60 = 180$$
$$y = 180 - 25 - 60$$
$$y = 95$$

The correct answer is (B).

43. B

This equation depends on knowing the equation for the area of a rectangle $l \times w$. To solve this, we should set up an equation and solve for the missing variable l.

So

$$l \times 16 = 32 \times 10$$
$$l \times 16 = 320$$
$$l = \frac{320}{16}$$
$$l = 20$$

Now that we know that $l = 20$, we know the perimeter of the pool is $2l + 2w$ or $2 \times 16 + 2 \times 20$

$32 + 40 = 72$. The correct answer is (B).

44. B

The perimeter of a rectangle is equal to $2(l + w)$.

Here, we know the perimeter and the width, so we can solve for the length.

$$2(l + 20) = 90$$
$$\Rightarrow 2l + 40 = 90$$
$$\Rightarrow 2l = 50$$

l = 25. As a check, we can see that 25 + 25 + 20 + 20 = 90. The correct answer is (B).

45. B

This looks much more difficult than it is. In fact you do not even need to know how to find the area of a circle to solve this. We know that each side of the rectangle has a length of 200, and that the figure has a height equal to twice the radius of the semicircle, or 2 × 40 = 80. The semicircle that extends to the left is equal to the semicircle that is missing from the right, so we can replace one with the other and we are left with a basic rectangle with dimensions of 200 × 80.

Therefore, the area is 80 × 200 = 16,000.

The correct answer is (B).

46. C

A regularly occurring set of values for right triangles is 3, 4, and 5. This should be something you memorize for the GRE, but we can also calculate the distance from X to Y using the Pythagorean theorem:

$a^2 + b^2 = c^2$ where c represents the hypotenuse (or XY in this case).

$3^2 + 4^2 = c^2 \Rightarrow 9 + 16 = c^2 \Rightarrow 25 = c^2 \Rightarrow \sqrt{25} = c \Rightarrow 5 = c$

Now that we know XY = 5 kilometers, we can do the math.

$XZ + ZY \Rightarrow 3 + 4 = 7$

So one would travel 7 kilometers by traveling through point Z versus 5 if traveling via the direct route of XY. The difference between these two distances is 2.

The correct answer is (C).

47. D

First we need to determine how many exposed faces there are:

Front and back: 8 × 2 = 16

Both sides: 2 × 2 = 4

Top and bottom: 4 × 2 = 8

Total: 28

Now that we know that there are 28 exposed faces and we know that the best case is that each cube has its one painted face exposed, we know that, at best, $\frac{8}{28}$ are exposed.

We can simplify $\frac{8}{28} \Rightarrow$ rewrite as $\frac{(2 \times 4)}{(7 \times 4)} \Rightarrow$ cancel out the 4s and we have $\frac{2}{7}$.

The correct answer is (D).

48. A

We need to first calculate the area of the larger square, using the formula for the area of a square, $A = s^2$, where s is the length of any side. In this case, $A = 10^2 = 100$.

$\frac{1}{2}$ of 100 = 50, so the area of the smaller square is 50.

To get the length of one of the sides we need to take the square root of the smaller square to get the length of one side of the smaller square.

$\sqrt{50}$ = length of side of smaller square.

(The GRE will not ask you to take the root of a value like this, so leave it in this form because either the answer will include a root, or you will be squaring this value later in the question.)

Now that we know the sides, we can calculate the diagonals using $a^2 + b^2 = c^2$.

Small:

$$(\sqrt{50})^2 + (\sqrt{50})^2 = c^2$$
$$\Rightarrow 50 + 50 = c^2$$
$$\Rightarrow 100 = c^2$$
$$\Rightarrow 10 = c$$

Larger:

$$10^2 + 10^2 = C^2$$
$$\Rightarrow 100 + 100 = C^2$$
$$\Rightarrow 200 = C^2$$
$$\Rightarrow \sqrt{200} = C$$

We can simplify $\sqrt{200}$:

$$C = \sqrt{200} = \sqrt{(100 \times 2)} = (\sqrt{100}) \times (\sqrt{2}) = 10\sqrt{2}$$

So the difference between the two is is $C - c$ or $10\sqrt{2} - 10$; $10\sqrt{2} - 10$ can be written as $10(\sqrt{2} - 1)$.

The correct answer is (A).

49. D

The greatest distance between any two points on a circle will be at the circle's widest: its diameter. A line drawn between two points on a circle forms a chord, and the longest possible chord in any circle is, by definition, the diameter.

A circle's diameter is equal to $2 \times r$.

Thus, since we are given that the circle has a radius of 4, the diameter of the circle is $4 \times 2 = 8$.

The correct answer is (D).

50. D

The best way to solve this is to first look at what we are given and put them into equation form.

We know that there are 180 degrees in a straight line. Also, we know that with intersecting lines, opposite angles are equal. This tells us that the angle opposite of z (the smaller angle that is part of angle x) is equal to z.

Thus:

$$x + y - z = 180$$

Substituting in, we get:

$$100 + 110 - z = 180$$
$$z = 30$$

The correct answer is (D).

51. C

First, we must remember that a straight line has 180 degrees in it, so the angle opposite angle e is $180 - e$. Also, we are given that $BT = CT$, so both of the interior angles opposite of y must be equal to one another. Once we find these angles, we can subtract from 180 to find e.

Given this information, the measure of the angle opposite of e must be $\frac{(180 - 54.6)}{2} = 62.7$.

As a check, we want to make sure that the interior angles measure to 180. $2 \times 62.7 + 54.6$ must equal 180, and as a check, it does.

The final step is to subtract 62.7 from 180 to find e.

$$180 - 62.7 = 117.3$$

The correct answer is (C).

52. D

We are given the area of the pool with the tile included, as well as the size of the tile border.

So with the tile border, the area of the pool is 225π, meaning that the length of the radius is 15 (because the area of a circle is πr^2, we take the square root of 225 to find the radius). $\sqrt{225} = 15$.

If the radius of the pool and tile is 15, and the tile border is 3 feet wide, then the radius of the pool alone is $15 - 3 = 12$.

With this info, we can find the area of the pool alone using the formula for the area of a circle.

$$\text{Area of circle} = \pi r^2$$

$$\pi 12^2 = 144\pi = \text{area of the pool}$$

The correct answer is (D).

53. D

If *ABC* is an equilateral triangle, that means each side is equal and each angle is 60.

If *ADC* is placed inside of it and is an isosceles triangle (where angle *D* is the one larger angle) we know that two of the angles are equal.

If the angles are equal, then $x + y = 60$.

If $y = 25$ then $25 + x = 60$

$$
\begin{aligned}
y &= 60 - 25 \\
x &= 35.
\end{aligned}
$$

The correct answer is (D).

54. E

First you must remember the formulas for finding the circumference of a circle. The circumference of a circle can be figured out from its radius by calculating $C = 2 \times r \times \pi$.

If we replace the *r* with π, we get $2 \times \pi \times \pi = 2\pi^2$.

The correct answer is (E).

55. B

In this question we need to first figure out what we're being asked. The question is just asking us to find the volume of the cylinder and then subtract the volume of the brick. "Portion" may sound like "proportion," which makes it sound like we're looking for a ratio, but portion just means a quantity, not a ratio. If wording in a question stem like this puts you in doubt, don't be afraid to look at the answer choices for clues: we can see from the answer choices that we're not asked for a ratio.

We know that the volume of the cylinder can be found by $r^2\pi h$ and the volume of the brick can be found by $b \times h \times w$. Since we have all of these figures, we can easily solve, as long as we keep track of our decimal places.

Cylinder $= .05^2 \times \pi \times .2 = .0005\pi$

Brick $= .2 \times .05 \times .05 = .0005$

So the answer is .0005π − .0005.

The correct answer is (B).

56. B

The formula for the volume (*V*) of a rectangular solid is the length × width × height or, $V = l \times w \times h$.

The question tells us that $w = 4$ and $V = 24$.

$$
\begin{aligned}
24 &= 4 \times l \times h \\
6 &= l \times h
\end{aligned}
$$

We know that the dimensions of the solid are all integers, and that the factors of 6 are 1, 2, 3, and 6.

The question tells us that 6 *cannot* be one of the dimensions, so the remaining dimensions must be 2 and 3.

For a rectangular solid, the surface area is the sum of the areas of all 6 sides, with three different sizes of side.

If the dimensions of the solid are 2 × 3 × 4, we can solve for the surface area, starting with the first type of side:

$$
\begin{aligned}
2 \times 3 &= 6 \\
6 \times 2 &= 12
\end{aligned}
$$

Now the second type of side:

$$
\begin{aligned}
2 \times 4 &= 8 \\
8 \times 2 &= 16
\end{aligned}
$$

Finally, the third type of side:

$$
\begin{aligned}
3 \times 4 &= 12 \\
12 \times 2 &= 24
\end{aligned}
$$

Now we add up all of the sides to find the total surface area:

$$12 + 16 + 24 = 52$$

The correct answer is (B).

57. E

When you encounter Roman numeral questions, evaluate each statement individually.

For I, notice that Line 1-3 and Line 4-6 lie within opposite faces of the cube, and opposite faces of a cube are parallel. Lines 1-8 and 6-5 are parallel edges of the cube, and lines 3-8 and 4-5 are also parallel edges of the cube; since 1-3 and 4-6 are hypotenuses joining 1-8 and 6-5 to 8-3 and 5-4, the two lines are parallel hypotenuses of opposite faces. This statement is true.

For II, triangle 3-4-7 is half of one face of the cube. Triangle 1-6-8 is also half of one face of the cube. Since all the faces of a cube are equal, the two triangles must have the same area. This statement is true.

For III, Line 3-6 and Line 1-4 are two diagonals of the cube. If you did not already know they must be equal, you could draw two right triangles using the height of the cube and the diagonal of the base. Since the two triangles would have corresponding legs, their hypotenuses would also have to be of the same length. This statement is true. (E) is the correct answer.

58. B

The area of a circle is given by the formula: $A = \pi \times r^2$ and the radius of a circle is half of the diameter.

To find the area of the place mat:

$$A = \pi \times r^2$$
$$A = \pi \times (12)^2$$
$$A = 144\pi$$

To find the area of the plate:

$$A = \pi \times r^2$$
$$A = \pi \times (10)^2$$
$$A = 100\pi$$

The part of the place mat that is not covered is $144\pi - 100\pi = 44\pi$.

$$\frac{44\pi}{144\pi} = \frac{11}{36}$$

The correct answer is (B).

59. C

It might be helpful to draw a diagram of this to visualize. The sphere will touch the cube at six points, each point being the center of one of the cube's faces.

The diameter of the sphere will have the same length as the edge of the cube. Let's use what we know about the volume of a cube to find the side length.

$$Vol = s^3$$
$$125 = s^3$$
$$5 = s$$

The diameter of the sphere is 5, so the radius of the sphere is $\frac{5}{2}$.

The correct answer is (C).

60. C

We know that the standard equation of a circle is:

$$(x - h)^2 + (y - k)^2 = r^2.$$

where (h,k) is the center of the circle and r is the radius.

For the given equation, the center of the circle is the origin and we can quickly solve for the radius:

$$r^2 = 4$$
$$r = 2$$

For a moment let's imagine that $n > m + 2$ is a line in the standard slope-intercept format of $y = mx + b$.

The line would be $y = x + 2$. Graph both the circle and the line:

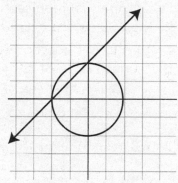

The points where $n > m + 2$ will be true for all points above the line $y = x + 2$. If you are unsure of this, choose a coordinate above the line, such as (–3,2).

$$2 > -3 + 2$$
$$2 > -1$$

True!

$\frac{1}{4}$ of the points on the circumference of the circle (the points that are true for $x^2 + y^2 = 4$) will make $n > m + 2$ true. (C) is the correct answer.

61. 60

The diagonal of a triangle is the hypotenuse of a right triangle with the legs equal to the sides of the rectangle. A triangle with one leg equal to 5 and hypotenuse equal to 13 should jump out at you as being two sides of a Pythagorean triple, 5:12:13. So the length and width of the triangle are 12 and 5. The area of the rectangle is length × width:

$$5 × 12 = 60.$$

62. B

The area of a square is a side squared, or s^2. In this case:

$s^2 = z \Rightarrow$ Take the square root of each side of the equation:

$$s = \sqrt{z}.$$

Within a square, the longest distance on a straight line is the diagonal. The diagonal of a square divides the square into two 45°/45°/90° triangles, for which the diagonal will be the hypotenuse of each. The ratio of the lengths of the sides of 45°/45°/90° triangles is $x : x : x\sqrt{2}$. Therefore, to find the diagonal we must multiply the length of a side, $\sqrt{z}$, by $\sqrt{2}$, which gives us $\sqrt{2z}$.

63. E

The question asks us to put limits on the possible values of y. Since this isn't any type of special triangle, we are left with the triangle inequality theorem: one side is greater than the positive difference of the other two sides, and it's less than the sum of the other two sides. Applied to AC this means that:

$$11 - 5 < y - 4 < 11 + 5$$
$$6 < y - 4 < 16$$
$$6 + 4 < y - 4 + 4 < 16 + 4$$
$$10 < y < 20.$$

64. D

Let's begin by sketching out the scenario described in the question stem:

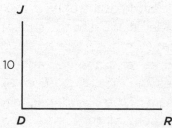

We are given an actual value for the distance between the diner and Jonna's house, but we will need to use variables to represent the remaining distances. We are told that Russell is two miles closer to the diner than he is to Jonna's house, so we can use x to represent his distance from Jonna and $x - 2$ to represent his distance from the diner:

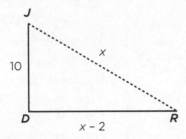

Since the placement of the houses and the diner forms a right triangle, we can use the Pythagorean theorem to find the value of x, which in turn will give us the value of $x - 2$, the distance from Russell's house to the diner:

$$10^2 + (x - 2)^2 = x^2$$
$$\rightarrow 100 + (x^2 - 4x + 4) = x^2$$
$$\rightarrow 100 - 4x + 4 = 0$$
$$\rightarrow -4x = -104$$
$$\rightarrow x = 26$$

If $x = 26$, then $x - 2$ (the distance between Russell's house and the diner) is $26 - 2 = 24$.

65. C

First let's figure out a way to represent the square units and the cubic units of the cylinder.

The number of square units in the surface area of a cylinder is equal to the sum of the circular areas that compose the top and bottom of the cylinder and the rectangular area that composes the curved portion. Since the top and bottom of the cylinder are circles of equal area, the sum of their areas may be represented by $\pi r^2 + \pi r^2 = 2\pi r^2$.

The lateral surface of the cylinder is actually rectangular, with the circumference of the circular top (or bottom) as one side, and the height of the cylinder as the other side (picture an "unrolled" cylinder). This area is therefore equal to $2\pi rh$. Together, these elements form the surface area of the cylinder: $2\pi r^2 + 2\pi rh$. The number of cubic units in a cylinder is represented by the formula for the volume of a cylinder: $\pi r^2 h$.

Now let's return to the question stem. It tells us that the surface area of a cylinder with radius of 6 is equal to $\frac{1}{2}$ of the volume. Now we can construct the following equation:

$$2\pi(6)^2 + 2\pi(6)h = \frac{1}{2}\left[\pi\left(6^2\right)h\right].$$

Solve this for the height h:

$$2\pi(6)^2 + 2\pi(6)h = \frac{1}{2}\left[\pi(6)^2 h\right]$$
$$2\pi(36) + 12\pi h = \frac{1}{2}(36\pi h)$$
$$72\pi + 12\pi h = 18\pi h$$
$$6\pi h = 72\pi$$
$$h = \frac{72\pi}{6\pi} = 12$$

If the height is 12, then the surface area of the cylinder is: $2\pi(6^2) + 2\pi(6)(12) = 72\pi + 144\pi = 216\pi$. (C) is the correct answer.

66. E

If a line has a nonzero slope of m, any line perpendicular to the line has a slope which is the negative reciprocal of m—that is, any line perpendicular to this line has a slope of $-\frac{1}{m}$. Since the slope of the line with the equation $y = -\frac{1}{5}x$ has a slope of $-\frac{1}{5}$, the slope of any line perpendicular to this line has a slope of $-\frac{1}{\left(-\frac{1}{5}\right)} = -(-5) = 5$. Therefore, line A has a slope of 5. So line A has an equation of the form $y = 5x + b$.

We also know that line A passes through the point $(3, -10)$. If we substitute $x = 3$ and $y = -10$ into $y = 5x + b$ and then solve for b, we can find the correct equation for line A:

$$
\begin{aligned}
y &= 5x + b \\
\rightarrow \quad 10 &= 5(3) + b \\
\rightarrow \quad -10 &= 15 + b \\
\rightarrow \quad -25 &= b
\end{aligned}
$$

The equation of line A is $y = 5x - 25$. (E) is the correct answer.

67. E

To solve this problem, we must first diagram it out like so:

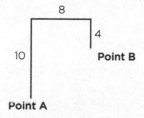

According to our diagram, the cheetah will get to Point A most directly by walking in a southwest direction, indicated below by the dotted line. To find this distance, we can draw a right triangle, making the dotted line the hypotenuse:

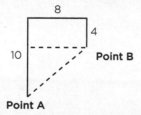

To find the length of the hypotenuse, we must find the lengths of the sides of the triangle. One side is represented above by the dashed line; this side forms a rectangle with the three pathways, and it is opposite the pathway with length 8. Therefore, it must also measure 8.

The other side of the triangle is formed by a portion of the pathway with length 10. Since this side begins where the pathway with length 4 ends, it must measure $10 - 4 = 6$.

Now we have a right triangle with sides of 6 and 8. The hypotenuse must equal 10 since 6:8:10 is a variant of the 3:4:5 Pythagorean triplet. If we did not know this, we could work out the length of the hypotenuse by using the Pythagorean theorem:

$$
\begin{aligned}
6^2 + 8^2 &= \text{side}^2 \\
36 + 64 &= \text{side}^2 \\
100 &= \text{side}^2 \\
\sqrt{100} &= \sqrt{\text{side}^2} \\
\text{side} &= 10
\end{aligned}
$$

The shortest distance from Point A to Point B is 10. Choice (E) is correct.

68. C

Let's begin by sketching the rectangle described in the question stem:

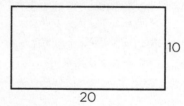

Now, if the rectangle is to be cut into exactly two squares, we have only one possible scenario—we can divide the *length* of the rectangle into two segments of 10, each of which forms a side of one square. The *width* remains undivided with a length of 10; this dimension also serves as a side of each square. We are left with two squares with dimensions of 10 × 10.

Note that we *cannot* divide the width of the rectangle into two segments to form the two squares. Each segment would be less than

10—too short to form a square with the length of the rectangle.

Now we must divide each square into two triangles. The only way to accomplish this is to divide the square along its diagonal to form two equal 45:45:90 triangles. Any other division would result in other shapes, as shown below:

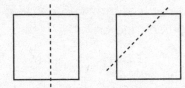

Since each square is composed of two triangles of equal size, the area of one triangle must equal half the area of the square. The area of the square is $10 \times 10 = 100$, so the area of the triangle must be 50. (C) is the correct answer.

69. A

A regular hexagon is a polygon with six equal sides and six equal angles. For any polygon, the sum of the degree measures of the interior angles is given by the formula $180(n - 2)$, where n is the number of sides.

In this case, $n = 6$. Hence, the interior angles sum to $180(6 - 2) = 720$ degrees. So we have that $6x = 120$.

Consider that this hexagon can be divided into a rectangle (middle section) and two triangles (upper and lower sections). If we add the areas of these figures, then we get the area of the entire hexagon.

The upper triangular area consists of two identical 30°-60°-90° triangles, as does the lower triangular area. The leg length to leg length to hypotenuse length ratio in a 30°-60°-90° triangle is 1 to $\sqrt{3}$ to 2. Since the hypotenuse of each 30°-60°-90° triangle is 8, the length of the leg opposite the 30° angle

is $\frac{8}{2} = 4$ and the length of the leg opposite the 60° angle is $4 \times \sqrt{3} = 4\sqrt{3}$.

The area of any triangle is given by the formula Area $= \frac{1}{2} \times$ base $\times$ height. In a right triangle, one leg can be considered to be the base and the other leg can be considered to be the height. Therefore the area of a right triangle can be found by using the formula Area $= \frac{1}{2} \times$ leg$_1 \times$ leg$_2$. The area of each 30°-60°-90° triangle in this question is $\frac{1}{2} \times 4\sqrt{3} \times 4 = 8\sqrt{3}$. So the sum of the areas of all four 30 -60 -90 triangles is $4(8\sqrt{3}) = 32\sqrt{3}$.

For the rectangular section, the length of the horizontal dimension is $4\sqrt{3} + 4\sqrt{3} = 8\sqrt{3}$. The vertical dimension of the rectangular section is 8. The area of a rectangle is length $\times$ width. The area of the rectangular section is:

$$(4\sqrt{3} + 4\sqrt{3})(8) = (8\sqrt{3})(8) = 64\sqrt{3}.$$

Therefore the area of the hexagon is $32\sqrt{3} + 64\sqrt{3} = 96\sqrt{3}$.

Choice (A) is correct.

70. C, E

The base of the triangle is a horizontal segment. Because this is an isosceles triangle, we know the other two sides, the legs, are equal. They may be above or below the base, but they'll meet at the x-coordinate that is exactly in the middle of the base's two endpoints. You can calculate this x-coordinate as follows: $\frac{5+1}{2} = 3$. Answer choices (A), (B), and (D) are eliminated because in each case, the x-coordinate is not 3. The correct choices are (C) and (E).

71. 80

In a triangle, the measures of the interior angles have a sum of 180 degrees. Thus, we can write an equation to find the degree measure of angle *ACB* by adding all the angles. Then, we need to solve for *x*:

$$60 + x + 2x = 180$$
$$3x + 60 = 180$$
$$3x = 120$$
$$x = 40$$

Angle *ACB* has a measure of 2*x*, or 2 × 40° = 80°.

The correct answer is 80.

72. B, C, E, G

Any side of a triangle must be less than the sum *and* greater than the difference of the remaining two sides. This means that 10 must be less than the sum *and* greater than the difference. To test the choices, simply add and subtract each pair of numbers:

(A) 2 + 7 = 9. 10 is greater than the sum. Eliminate.

(B) 4 + 7 = 11 and 7 – 4 = 3. 10 is less than the sum (11) and greater than the difference (3). This works.

(C) 6 + 5 = 11 and 6 – 5 = 1. This works.

(D) 8 + 2 = 10. Eliminate. 10 is not less than itself!

(E) 10 + 10 = 20 and 10 – 10 = 0. This works.

(F) 12 + 22 = 34 but 22 – 12 = 10. Eliminate.

(G) 14 + 23 = 37 and 23 – 14 = 9. This works.

Answer choices (B), (C), (E), and (G) are the correct answers.

73. 67.5

The angles of a triangle must sum to 180°, so set up an equation to solve for *x*:

$$2x + x + x + 30 = 180$$
$$4x = 150$$
$$x = 37.5$$

Angle *C* is represented by the expression *x* + 30, so it must measure 37.5° + 30° = 67.5°.

The correct answer is 67.5.

74. 12

We can find the diameter of the circle if we know the circle's area. We can find the area of the circle from the sector area given. Recall that the ratio of the sector area to the area of the entire circle is equal to the ratio of the measure of the central angle of the sector, ∠*BAC*, to 360°. We represent this mathematically as:

$$\frac{\text{Area of } ABC}{\text{Area of Circle}} = \frac{m\angle BAC}{360°}$$
$$\frac{3\pi}{\text{Area of Circle}} = \frac{30°}{360°}$$
$$\frac{3\pi}{\text{Area of Circle}} = \frac{1}{12}$$
$$\text{Area of Circle} = 36\pi$$

The area of a circle is π*r*², so the radius of this circle is 6. That makes the diameter 6 × 2 = 12.

The correct answer is 12.

75. 9

We need to find the coordinates of one endpoint of a line segment given the other endpoint and the segment's midpoint.

The *y*-coordinate of point *P* is 8 less than the *y*-coordinate of point *M*. Adding 8 to point *M*'s *y*-coordinate should give you point *Q*'s *y*-coordinate: (1) + 8 = 9.

The correct answer is 9.

Alternately, note that we can use the midpoint formula to find the coordinates of the unknown endpoint *Q*.

The coordinates of the midpoint are $\left(\frac{x_1+x_2}{2}, \frac{y_1+y_2}{2}\right)$, given the endpoints (x_1, y_1) (x_2, y_2). Using this formula with the points *P* and *M* given, we have:

$$\left(\frac{x_P + x_Q}{2}, \frac{y_P + y_Q}{2}\right) = (-1, 1)$$

$$\left(\frac{-4 + x_Q}{2}, \frac{-7 + y_Q}{2}\right) = (-1, 1)$$

This yields two equations we need to solve: one to find the x-coordinate of Q and one to find the y-coordinate of Q:

$$\frac{-7 + y_Q}{2} = 1$$

$$-7 + y_Q = 2$$

$$y_Q = 9$$

The y-coordinate of Q is 9.

It is not necessary to find the x-coordinate of Q, and so you would be wasting time in finding it, but this is how you would do it:

$$\frac{-4 + x_Q}{2} = -1$$

$$-4 + x_Q = -2$$

$$x_Q = 2$$

Introduction to Data Interpretation Questions

Data Interpretation questions are based on information located in tables or graphs and are often statistics oriented. The data may be located in one table or graph, but you might also need to extract data from two or more tables or graphs. There will be a set of questions for you to answer based on each data presentation.

You may be asked to choose one or more answers from a set of answer choices or to enter your answer in a Numeric Entry field.

The directions for Data Interpretation questions will look like this:

Questions 1–5 are based on the following table.

	May	June	July
The Home Touch	45%	25%	48%
Curtains Unlimited	30%	23%	23%
Max's Curtain Supply	9%	23%	17%
Valances by Val	13%	20%	8%
Wendy's Windows	3%	9%	4%

PERCENTAGE OF SALES PER CLIENT FOR CURTAIN FABRIC OVER THREE MONTHS

A Data Interpretation question that requires you to choose exactly one correct answer will look like this:

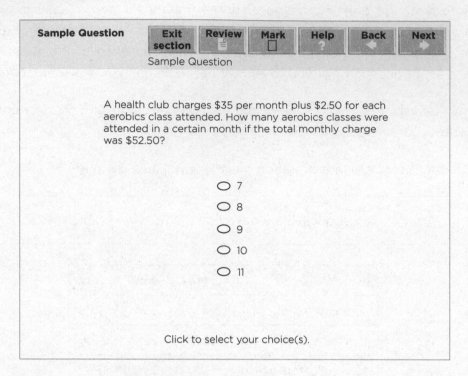

A Data Interpretation question that requires you to select all the answer choices that apply will look like this:

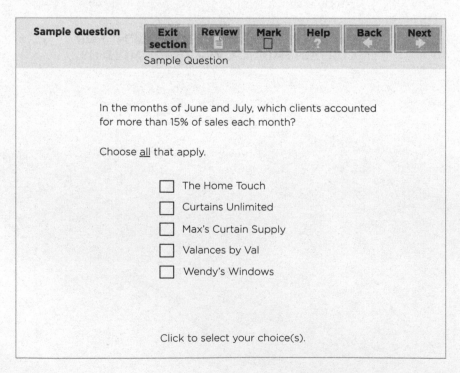

A Data Interpretation question that requires you to enter your numeric answer in a box will look like this:

| Sample Question | Exit section | Review | Mark | Help ? | Back | Next |

Sample Question

In May, the two clients representing the greatest percentages of sales accounted for $81,000 in sales. What were the total sales for the month of May?

$ [   ]

Click in the box and type your numeric answer. Backspace to erase.

Data Interpretation Practice

Select one or more answer choices according to the specific question directions.

If the question does not specify how many answer choices to select, select all that apply.

The correct answer may be just one of the choices or as many as all of the choices, depending on the question.

No credit is given unless you select all of the correct choices and no others.

If the question specifies how many answer choices to select, select exactly that number of choices.

Liberal Studies	19%
English	20%
History	21%
Art	15%
Anthropology	12%
Sociology	13%

1. The table shown lists the distribution of a certain number of humanities students by major. If there are a total of 1,500 students, which of the following majors have fewer than 225 students?

   Indicate all such majors.

   A Liberal Studies

   B English

   C Art

   D Anthropology

   E Sociology

2. The table shown lists the distribution of a certain number of humanities students by major. Which of the following could be the total number of students if at least 190 students are History majors?

   Indicate all such numbers.

   A 900

   B 904

   C 905

   D 950

   E 1000

3. The table shown lists the distribution of a certain number of humanities students by major. If there are a total of 3,600 students, which of the following majors have more than 700 students?

   Indicate all such majors.

   A Liberal Studies

   B English

   C History

   D Anthropology

   E Sociology

Pop	x%
Rock	y%
Jazz	12%
Dance	10%
Hip Hop	25%
Country	11%

4. The chart above shows the percentage of all the different genres of music CDs sold in a record store. If $x = 2y$, and there is a total of 1,200 CDs, which genres could have at least 180 CDs?

Indicate <u>all</u> such genres.

A Pop

B Rock

C Jazz

D Dance

E Hip Hop

F Country

5. The chart above shows the percentage of all the different genres of music sold in a record store. If $x = 2y$ and there is a total of 1,200 CDs, which genres have fewer than 160 CDs?

Indicate <u>all</u> such genres.

A Pop

B Rock

C Jazz

D Dance

E Hip Hop

F Country

6. The chart above shows the percentage of all the different genres of music CDs sold in a record store. If $x = y$ and there is a total of 1,200 CDs, which genres would have more than 240 CDs?

Indicate <u>all</u> such genres.

A Pop

B Rock

C Jazz

D Dance

E Hip Hop

F Country

7. The chart above shows the percentage of all the different genres of music CDs sold in a record store. If $x = y$ and there is a total of 5,000 CDs, which genres have at least 500 CDs?

Indicate <u>all</u> such genres.

A Pop

B Rock

C Jazz

D Dance

E Hip Hop

F Country

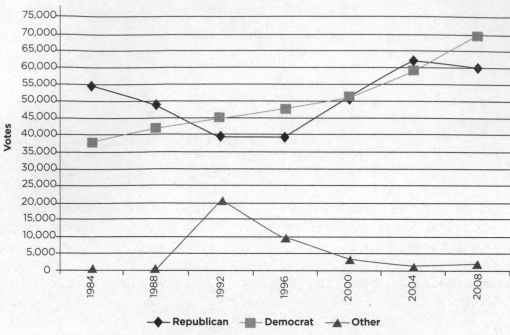

Presidential Vote by Party (Votes are in thousands.)

8. For how many of the years shown did the Republican candidate receive more votes than the Democratic candidate?

   (A) 1
   (B) 2
   (C) 3
   (D) 4
   (E) 5

9. The difference between the vote the Republican candidate received and the Democratic candidate received was greatest in what year?

   (A) 1984
   (B) 1988
   (C) 1996
   (D) 2004
   (E) 2008

10. In the year that the Other candidate received the most votes, approximately what percentage of the total vote did his vote make up?

    (A) 10%
    (B) 20%
    (C) 25%
    (D) 30%
    (E) 35%

11. Of the seven elections shown, for which year(s) could the losing major party candidate have won if he had received all of the Other candidate's votes?

    A   1984
    B   1988
    C   1992
    D   1996
    E   2000
    F   2004
    G   2008

Comedy	19%
Drama	18%
Action	16%
TV	27%
Horror	15%
Documentary	5%

12. The chart above represents the inventory of a video store, by genre. When restocking the store, the owner receives a shipment of new DVDs that includes x Documentary DVDs, which he adds to the 75 already in stock. If the percentages in the chart shift after the new shipment arrives, such that Documentaries are now less than or equal to 5% of the total stock, which of the following could be the new total number of DVDs in the store?

Indicate all such amounts.

A 1,400

B 1,480

C 1,500

D 1,520

13. The chart above shows the percentage of different kinds of movies sold at a store. Which genres have more than 513 units if there is a total of 2,700 movies?

Indicate all such genres.

A Comedy

B Drama

C Action

D TV

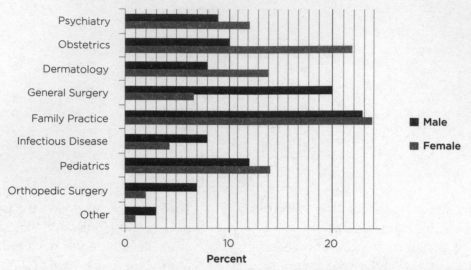

Percentage of Male Doctors and Percentage of Female Doctors at Hospital Y, by Specialty (*Total male doctors: 200; Total female doctors: 75*)

14. There are 16 medical students currently doing clinical rotations in the hospital's Family Practice unit. Approximately what is the ratio of the number of medical students learning family practice to the number of doctors in their department?

    Ⓐ 1 to 1

    Ⓑ 1 to 3

    Ⓒ 1 to 4

    Ⓓ 1 to 6

    Ⓔ 1 to 17

15. For which specialty (or specialties) is the number of male doctors more than twice the number of female doctors?

    Ⓐ Psychiatry

    Ⓑ Dermatology

    Ⓒ Family Practice

    Ⓓ Infectious Disease

    Ⓔ Pediatrics

16. In Pediatrics and Orthopedic Surgery, $\frac{1}{3}$ of the female doctors and $\frac{1}{2}$ of the male doctors have staff positions, and the rest are fellows or contract doctors. What fraction of all the doctors in those two specialties combined have staff positions? Express your answer as a decimal.

    ☐

17. The odds that a randomly selected male doctor at hospital Y is a surgeon is what percentage larger than the odds he is an obstetrician?

    Ⓐ 34

    Ⓑ 60

    Ⓒ 63

    Ⓓ 100

    Ⓔ 170

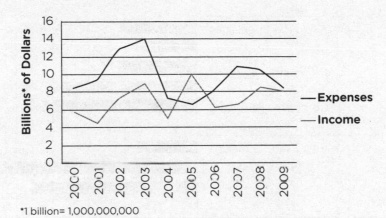

*1 billion= 1,000,000,000

Total Expenses and Income for Federal Government of Country P, 2000–2009 (in United States dollars)

18. For which of the 10 years from 2000 to 2009 did country P run a deficit (expenses minus income) of more than $3 billion?

Indicate all such years.

Ⓐ 2000

Ⓑ 2001

Ⓒ 2002

Ⓓ 2003

Ⓔ 2004

Ⓕ 2005

Ⓖ 2006

Ⓗ 2007

Ⓘ 2008

Ⓙ 2009

19. What is the best approximation of the average (arithmetic mean) of the changes in federal expenses between each consecutive year from 2000 to 2009?

Ⓐ $0 million

Ⓑ $200 million

Ⓒ $850 million

Ⓓ $2 billion

Ⓔ $9.7 billion

20. In 2003, the federal government's expenses were approximately what percentage greater than the federal government's income?

Ⓐ 5%

Ⓑ 36%

Ⓒ 56%

Ⓓ 73%

Ⓔ 180%

21. If it were discovered that, due to corruption and embezzlement, the actual income for 2008 was $2.5 billion less than reported, by how many million dollars would the average income for the period 2006–2009 change?

$ ☐ million

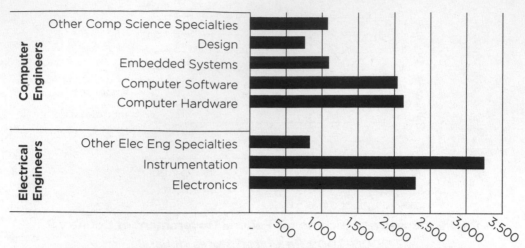

Number of Engineers at SoboCon within Computer Science and Electrical Engineering

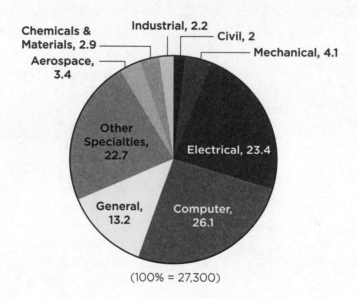

(100% = 27,300)

Percentage of Engineers by Category at SoboCon

22. Approximately what is the ratio of electrical engineers to industrial engineers at SoboCon?

   Ⓐ 12 to 1

   Ⓑ 11 to 1

   Ⓒ 8 to 1

   Ⓓ 1 to 10

   Ⓔ 1 to 11

23. How many more mechanical engineers are there than civil engineers?

   [   ] mechanical engineers

24. Approximately how many computer engineers were not in computer hardware?

Ⓐ 1,100

Ⓑ 2,125

Ⓒ 5,000

Ⓓ 7,125

Ⓔ 11,200

25. There are twice as many embedded systems engineers who have been at SoboCon for 5+ years as there are aerospace engineers who had been at SoboCon for 5+ years. If 14% of aerospace engineers have been at SoboCon for 5+ years, then approximately what percentage of embedded systems engineers have been at SoboCon for 5+ years?

Ⓐ 13%

Ⓑ 24%

Ⓒ 35%

Ⓓ 71%

Ⓔ 85%

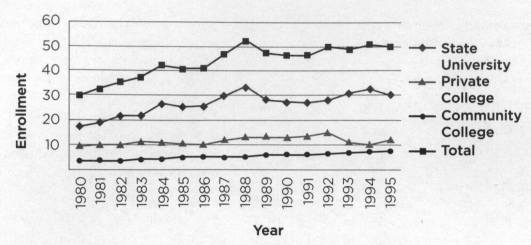

University Enrollment by Type of Institution *(in millions of students)*

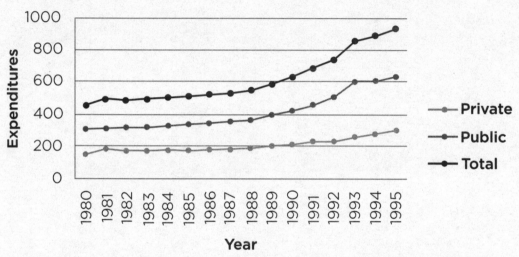

Public and Private University Expenditures 1980–1995 *(in billions of dollars)*

26. Of the following years, which showed the least difference between public and private university expenditures?

    Ⓐ 1980

    Ⓑ 1981

    Ⓒ 1988

    Ⓓ 1990

    Ⓔ 1995

27. In 1990, approximately how many billions of dollars were spent on public community colleges?

    Ⓐ 7

    Ⓑ 27

    Ⓒ 210

    Ⓓ 420

    Ⓔ It cannot be determined from the given information.

28. Which of the following period(s) showed a continual increase in the total university enrollment?

    Ⓐ 1983–1985

    Ⓑ 1984–1986

    Ⓒ 1986–1988

    Ⓓ 1987–1989

    Ⓔ 1992–1994

29. In 1989, public university expenditures were approximately what percentage of the total university expenditures?

    Ⓐ 33%

    Ⓑ 50%

    Ⓒ 67%

    Ⓓ 80%

    Ⓔ 85%

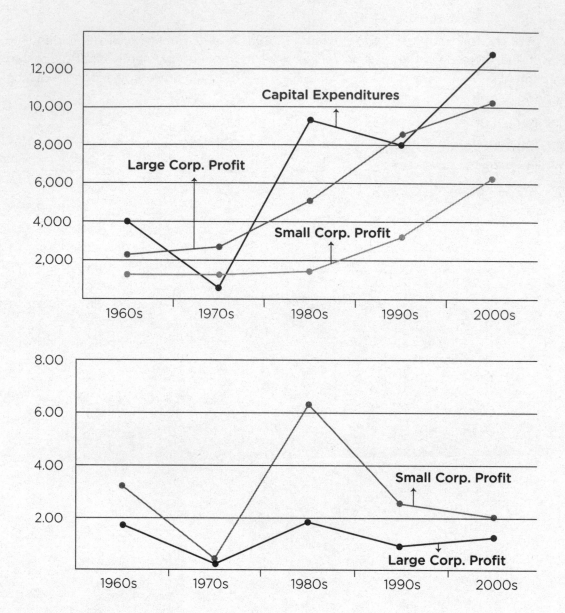

The graphs above detail the average corporate profits (small and large corporations), in thousands, for all corporations for each decade, and the average capital expenditures, in thousands, as well. The lower graph illustrates the ratio between the average capital expenditures and the small and large corporate profits.

30. Approximately what was the average capital expenditure, in thousands, for a corporation in the 1970s?

    Ⓐ 600
    Ⓑ 3,000
    Ⓒ 4,000
    Ⓓ 9,000
    Ⓔ 13,000

31. In the 1990s, what was the approximate difference between the average small corporate profits and large corporate profits?

    Ⓐ 1,000
    Ⓑ 3,000
    Ⓒ 3,500
    Ⓓ 6,000
    Ⓔ 8,000

32. For which decade(s) was the ratio of capital expenditures to small corporate profits less than 1 or greater than 4?

    Ⓐ 1960s
    Ⓑ 1970s
    Ⓒ 1980s
    Ⓓ 1990s
    Ⓔ 2000s

33. In order to make the ratio of capital expenditures to small corporation profits in the 1980s equal to the ratio of capital expenditures to large corporation profits in the same decade, without changing the capital expenditures, what would the small corporate profits have to be changed to?

    Ⓐ 4,000
    Ⓑ 5,000
    Ⓒ 6,000
    Ⓓ 8,000
    Ⓔ 9,000

INCOME AND EXPENDITURES OF A LOCAL GOVERNMENT AGENCY—May 1988

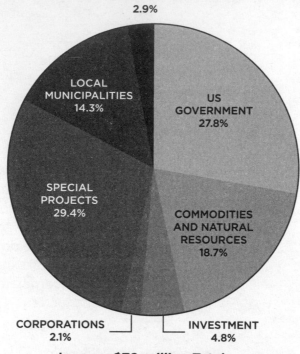

Income $70 million Total

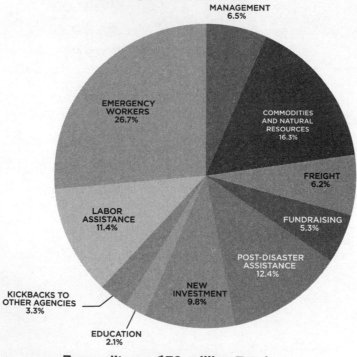

Expenditures $70 million Total

34. Rounded to the nearest million dollars, how much of the agency's income was provided by the US Government?

$ [_____] million

35. Income from which of the following source(s) exceeded $20 million?
   - Ⓐ Local Municipalities
   - Ⓑ Taxes/Tolls
   - Ⓒ Special Projects
   - Ⓓ Corporations
   - Ⓔ Investment
   - Ⓕ Commodities and Natural Resources
   - Ⓖ US Government

36. In May 1988, $\frac{1}{2}$ of the agency's emergency workers expenditures, $\frac{1}{4}$ of its freight expenses, and $\frac{2}{3}$ of its post-disaster assistance were directly related to one natural disaster. The total of these expenditures was approximately how many millions of dollars?
   - Ⓐ $9 million
   - Ⓑ $13 million
   - Ⓒ $16 million
   - Ⓓ $20 million
   - Ⓔ Cannot be determined from the given information.

37. Of the following, which is the closest approximation to the percentage of fundraising expenditures in excess of income from corporations?
   - Ⓐ 35%
   - Ⓑ 50%
   - Ⓒ 60%
   - Ⓓ 67%
   - Ⓔ 75%

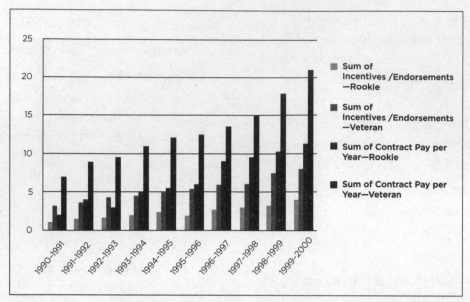

Average Annual Total Pay* for Rookie and Veteran Professional Athletes, 1990–2000, in millions of dollars (*The total compensation consists of contracts as well as incentives and endorsements)

38. In what year shown was the total annual pay for veterans closest to $15 million?

    (A) 1991–1992

    (B) 1992–1993

    (C) 1993–1994

    (D) 1995–1996

    (E) 1997–1998

39. Which of the following forms of annual pay increased the least from the first to the last of the ten years represented on the graph?

    (A) Sum of Contract pay per year for rookies

    (B) Sum of Contract pay per year for veterans

    (C) Sum of Incentives/Endorsement pay for veterans

    (D) Sum of Incentives/Endorsement pay for rookies

    (E) Total annual pay for veterans

40. For the year in which annual contract pay for rookies was closest to $10 million, what was the approximate Incentives/Endorsements pay for veterans?

    (A) $3.0 million

    (B) $5.5 million

    (C) $7.5 million

    (D) $15 million

    (E) $20 million

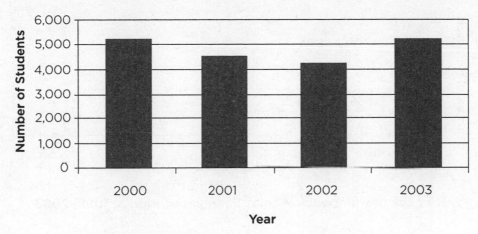

Year

Students Living on Campus at University X

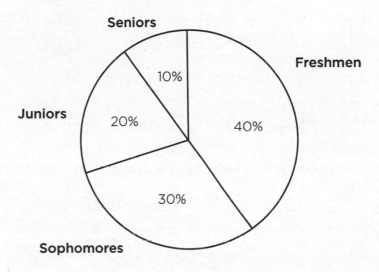

Students Living on Campus at University X in 2002

41. How many more students were living on campus at University X in 2003 than in 2001?

 (A) 1000

 (B) 700

 (C) 500

 (D) 300

 (E) 200

42. In 2002, how many of the students living on campus were sophomores?

 (A) 420

 (B) 1,260

 (C) 1,350

 (D) 1,680

 (E) 1,800

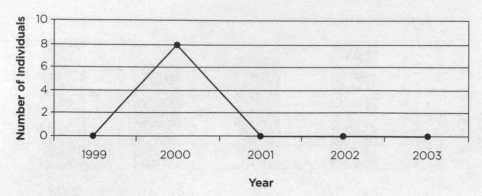

Number of Humpback Whales Seen in Location X, 1999–2003

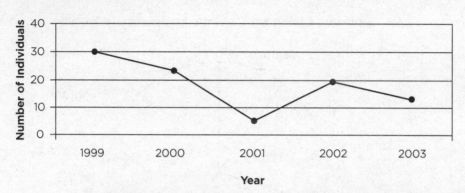

Number of Porpoises Seen in Location X, 1999–2003

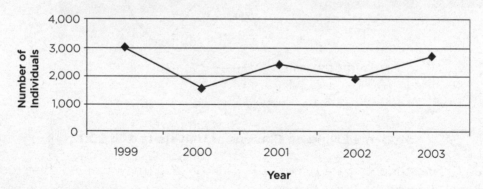

Number of Dolphins Seen in Location X, 1999–2003

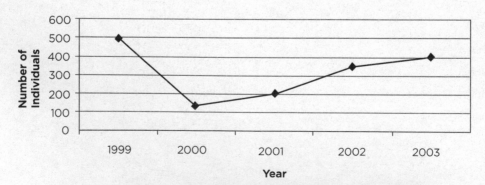

Number of Blue Whales Seen in Location X, 1999–2003

43. What was the average (arithmetic mean) number of humpback whales seen each year from 1999 through 2003?

    Round your answer to the nearest tenth.

    ☐ humpback whales

44. By what percentage did the number of blue whales spotted at location X decrease between 1999 and 2003?

    Ⓐ 20%

    Ⓑ 30%

    Ⓒ 40%

    Ⓓ 70%

    Ⓔ 80%

45. From the graphs provided, which animal is most likely to be spotted in Location X from 1999–2003?

    Ⓐ Humpback Whales

    Ⓑ Porpoises

    Ⓒ Dolphins

    Ⓓ Blue Whales

    Ⓔ It cannot be determined from the information provided.

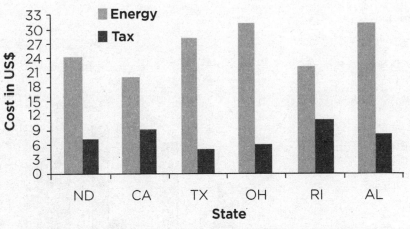

Electricity Prices (Average Monthly Household Bill)

46. Approximately what percentage of the total electricity bill in AL does tax account for?

    Ⓐ 19%

    Ⓑ 21%

    Ⓒ 26%

    Ⓓ 31%

    Ⓔ 39%

47. In which of the states is the ratio of tax to energy cost the smallest?

    Ⓐ CA

    Ⓑ RI

    Ⓒ TX

    Ⓓ OH

    Ⓔ AL

48. In states where the tax is above 6 dollars, what is the standard deviation of the cost of energy?

    Ⓐ 1.8

    Ⓑ 4.2

    Ⓒ 5.9

    Ⓓ 7

    Ⓔ 17.5

49. What is the approximate positive difference, in dollars, between the range of tax and the range of energy cost across all states?

    Ⓐ 2

    Ⓑ 5

    Ⓒ 9

    Ⓓ 11

    Ⓔ 12

50. If the tax in CA increases by 20% each year for the next 4 years, and the energy cost in CA remains the same each year for the next 4 years, what will be the positive difference, in dollars, between the CA tax and the CA energy cost in 4 years?

    Ⓐ 0

    Ⓑ 1.34

    Ⓒ 2.59

    Ⓓ 3.12

    Ⓔ It cannot be determined from the information given.

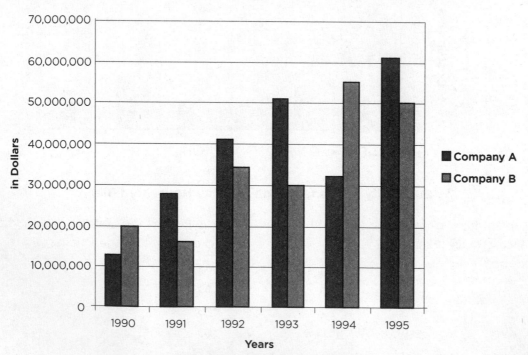

Profits of Companies A and B

51. By approximately what percentage did the profits of Company B increase from 1990 to 1995 ?

    Ⓐ 75%

    Ⓑ 150%

    Ⓒ 250%

    Ⓓ 300%

    Ⓔ 450%

52. What was the approximate average (arithmetic mean) yearly profit of Company A for those years when the profits of Company A were greater than the profits of Company B?

    Ⓐ $31,000,000

    Ⓑ $37,000,000

    Ⓒ $39,000,000

    Ⓓ $45,000,000

    Ⓔ $53,000,000

Total sales = $24,000,000

Sales of Department Store X in the Year 2003

53. The sales from clothing were less than the sales from sporting goods by how many percent?

    Ⓐ 4%

    Ⓑ 5%

    Ⓒ 8%

    Ⓓ 12%

    Ⓔ 16%

54. Approximately how many million dollars in sales did department store X have from home improvement tools in 2003?

    Ⓐ 4.1

    Ⓑ 4.3

    Ⓒ 5.0

    Ⓓ 5.8

    Ⓔ 6.0

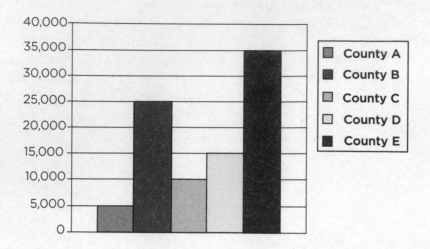

Numbers of People Who Were Surveyed about a Car in Different Counties

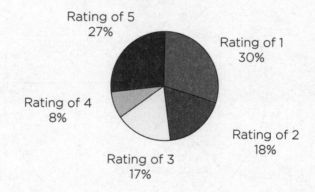

Distribution of the Durability Ratings Given to the Car by the People Surveyed in County E

The bar graph provided shows the numbers of people who were surveyed about a car in 5 counties. The pie chart above shows the distribution of how the people in County E rated the car for durability, where each person rated the car for durability with one of the integers 1, 2, 3, 4, and 5, where 1 is the worst and 5 is the best.

55. Approximately what percentage of the total number of people surveyed in all 5 counties was the number of people surveyed in County E who gave the car a durability rating of 4?

Ⓐ 0.3%

Ⓑ 3.1%

Ⓒ 7.0%

Ⓓ 8.0%

Ⓔ 11.7%

56. What was the average (arithmetic mean) rating of the durability of the car in County E?

Ⓐ 1.25

Ⓑ 1.42

Ⓒ 2.53

Ⓓ 2.84

Ⓔ 3.00

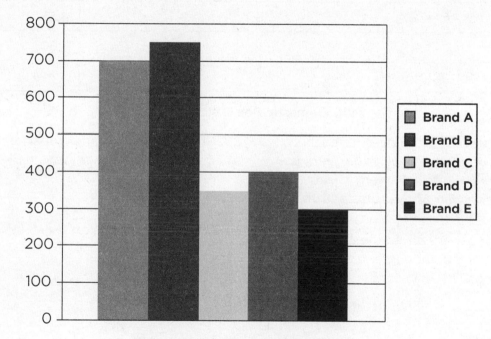

Sales of Clothing Store T, by Brand, in Thousands of Dollars, in the Year 2000

57. Approximately what percentage less than the sales of brand B clothing by store T in the year 2000 were the sales of brand E clothing by store T in the year 2000?

Ⓐ 30%

Ⓑ 40%

Ⓒ 50%

Ⓓ 60%

Ⓔ 75%

Movie Title	Gross Sales (Millions of Dollars)	Number of Theaters
Toy Story 3	415	4,028
Alice in Wonderland (2010)	334.2	3,739
Iron Man 2	312.4	4,390
The Twilight Saga: Eclipse	300.5	4,468
Harry Potter and the Deathly Hallows Part I	294.6	4,125
Inception	292.6	3,792
Despicable Me	251.5	3,602
Shrek Forever After	238.7	4,386
Tangled	195.8	3,603
The Karate Kid (2010)	176.6	3,740

2010 Domestic Box Office Grosses

58. If it is true that gross sales for each movie completely depend on average sales per theater, how many theaters would *Iron Man 2* have to be shown in to gross $385.4 million?

    (Round your answer to the nearest whole number, and do not enter a comma for thousands.)

    ☐☐☐☐ theaters

59. Of the movies listed below, which movie had the highest gross per theater?

    Ⓐ Alice In Wonderland

    Ⓑ Harry Potter and the Deathly Hallows Part I

    Ⓒ Inception

    Ⓓ Iron Man 2

    Ⓔ The Twilight Saga: Eclipse

60. What is the median number of theaters in which the movies in the table were shown?

    Ⓐ 3,792.0

    Ⓑ 3,910.0

    Ⓒ 3,958.5

    Ⓓ 3,987.3

    Ⓔ 4,028.0

| Type of Student | Percentage of Prime Time Program Viewing | | | | | | | | Average Weekly Prime Time Viewing (in hours) |
| | Sitcoms | Documentaries | News | Television Movies | | | Sports | Other | |
				Fact-Based	Action	Comedy			
Preschool	87	0	0	0	0	3	10	0	7
Grade School	40	2	0	2	17	13	25	1	11.5
High School	22	13	6	5	8	12	25	9	12
Vocational School	24	10	4	3	11	13	32	3	12.8
College	10	22	11	6	7	8	30	6	15.4

Average Weekly Viewing of Prime Time Television

61. What is the percentage increase in the average number of hours spent watching prime time sports programs between high school and college?

(A) 2%

(B) 5%

(C) 34%

(D) 40%

(E) 54%

The graph below represents a professional football league's total scouting makeup for all teams. The top graph shows the total number of scouts working for the league in the categories of Offensive and Defensive players. The second graph illustrates their total compensation in thousands of dollars.

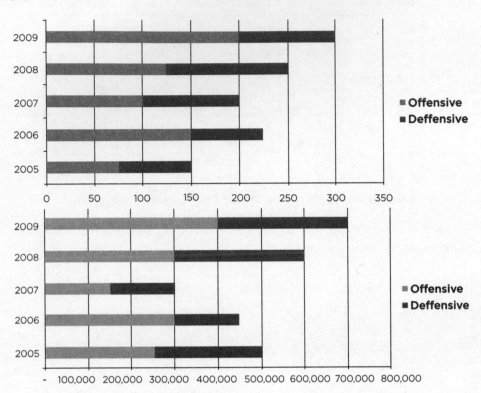

62. By what percentage did the total number of defensive scouts increase from 2006 to 2007?

Ⓐ 0%

Ⓑ 25%

Ⓒ 33.33%

Ⓓ 66.66%

Ⓔ 100%

63. What was the increase in offensive scouts from 2008 to 2009?

Ⓐ 25

Ⓑ 60

Ⓒ 65

Ⓓ 75

Ⓔ 100

64. If 50% of the 2008 offensive scout salaries were switched to defensive scouts salaries, how much, in thousands of dollars, would the new total defensive scout salaries be?

$ ☐ thousand

65. What was the total spent on defensive scouts in the years 2005, 2006, and 2007 combined?

Ⓐ 150,000

Ⓑ 450,000

Ⓒ 550,000

Ⓓ 600,000

Ⓔ 750,000

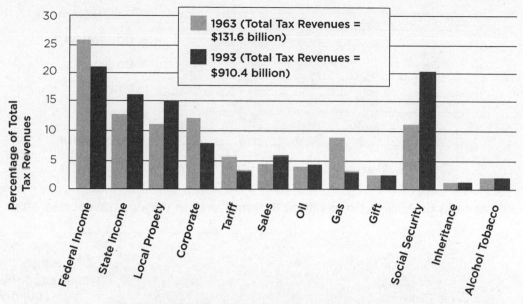

Tax Revenues in Country F, 1963 and 1993

66. Which of the following statements can be inferred from the graph?

Indicate <u>all</u> such statements.

Ⓐ The number of corporations paying taxes decreased from 1963 to 1993.

Ⓑ The amount of gas tax revenue was greater in 1993 than in 1963.

Ⓒ In 1993, the amount of local property tax revenue was more than twice as much as the revenue from tariffs.

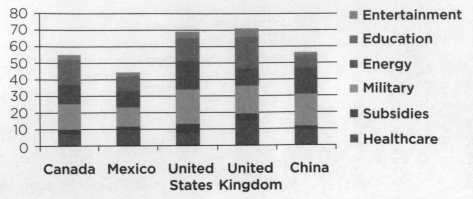

Percentage of Annual Government Expenditures in Various Categories, 1994

Country	Oil	Natural Gas/ Coal	Solar	Wind	Hydro	Nuclear	Other	Average monthly energy expenditures (billions of dollars)
Canada	65	20	3	2	2	3	5	**10.6**
Mexico	76	10	2	2	1	1	8	**8.4**
United States	72	8	4	2	3	3	8	**32.9**
United Kingdom	74	12	2	2	1	7	2	**21.3**
China	59	15	3	2	3	5	13	**30.2**

Percentage of Total Energy Expenditures, 1994

67. In millions of dollars, what average amount per month did the Canadian government spend on nuclear, hydro, and wind power combined?

    $ ⬚ million

68. Approximately what percentage of the average monthly energy expenditures of China were spent on coal?

    (A) 30%

    (B) 16%

    (C) 15%

    (D) 4%

    (E) It cannot be determined from the information given.

69. Approximately what percentage of the United Kingdom's total annual government expenditures are spent on oil?

Ⓐ 74%

Ⓑ 21%

Ⓒ 11%

Ⓓ 8%

Ⓔ It cannot be determined from the information given.

70. Which of the following statements can be inferred from the information given?

I. Of the countries shown, the United Kingdom had the greatest annual government expenditures.

II. For all the countries shown, the average amount spent per month on wind energy was the same.

III Of the countries shown, the average amount spent on natural gas/coal energy per month was greatest for China.

Ⓐ I

Ⓑ II

Ⓒ III

Ⓓ None of the above

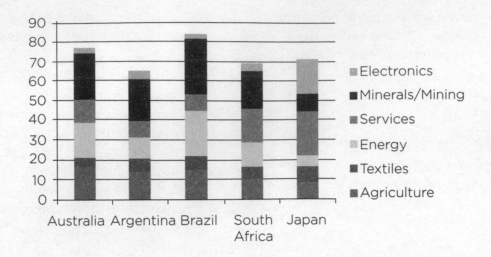

Percentage of Annual GDP from Various Sources, 2001

Country	Gold	Silver and Other Precious Metals	Iron Ore	Copper	Precious Stones	Bauxite	Other	Average Quarterly GDP from Minerals/ Mining (billions of dollars)
Australia	64%	20%	8%	2%	2%	1%	3%	**194**
Argentina	49%	18%	11%	8%	1%	1%	12%	**173**
Brazil	19%	8%	30%	23%	9%	3%	8%	**219**
South Africa	70%	11%	2%	2%	8%	5%	2%	**207**
Japan	1%	2%	1%	2%	3%	73%	18%	**11**

71. Approximately how much of Argentina's average quarterly GDP from Minerals/ Mining come from iron ore, copper, precious stones, and bauxite combined?

    Ⓐ $865 billion

    Ⓑ $173 billion

    Ⓒ $36 billion

    Ⓓ $21 billion

    Ⓔ $4 billion

72. Approximately what percentage of the average quarterly GDP of Japan was derived from silver?

    Ⓐ 8%

    Ⓑ 4%

    Ⓒ 2%

    Ⓓ 1%

    Ⓔ It cannot be determined from the information given.

73. Approximately what percentage of South Africa's total GDP is derived from gold?

Ⓐ 70%

Ⓑ 20%

Ⓒ 14%

Ⓓ 4%

Ⓔ It cannot be determined from the information given.

74. Which of the following statements can be inferred from the information given?

Ⓐ Of the categories shown, Brazil had the greatest GDP in 2001.

Ⓑ Japan produces more bauxite than South Africa.

Ⓒ The Japanese derived the most GDP (absolute dollar amount) from electronics in 2001 as compared to the other countries.

Ⓓ None of the above

Answer Key

DATA INTERPRETATION PRACTICE

1.	D, E	**25.**	B	**50.**	B
2.	C, D, E	**26.**	B	**51.**	B
3.	B, C	**27.**	E	**52.**	D
4.	A, E	**28.**	C	**53.**	E
5.	C, D, F	**29.**	C	**54.**	A
6.	A, B, E	**30.**	A	**55.**	B
7.	A, B, C, D, E, F	**31.**	D	**56.**	D
		32.	B, C	**57.**	D
8.	C	**33.**	B	**58.**	5416
9.	A	**34.**	19	**59.**	A
10.	B	**35.**	C	**60.**	B
11.	C, D, E	**36.**	C	**61.**	E
12.	D	**37.**	C	**62.**	C
13.	D	**38.**	C	**63.**	D
14.	C	**39.**	D	**64.**	450
15.	C, D, E	**40.**	C	**65.**	C
16.	0.46	**41.**	B	**66.**	B, C
17.	E	**42.**	B	**67.**	742
18.	B, C, D, H	**43.**	1.6	**68.**	E
19.	A	**44.**	A	**69.**	D
20.	C	**45.**	C	**70.**	C
21.	625	**46.**	B	**71.**	C
22.	B	**47.**	C	**72.**	E
23.	573	**48.**	B	**73.**	C
24.	C	**49.**	B	**74.**	D

Answers and Explanations

DATA INTERPRETATION PRACTICE

1. D, E

In order to solve this problem, it is best to figure out what percentage 225 is of 1,500.

We can figure this out by setting up the following equation:

$$\frac{225 \text{ students}}{1,500 \text{ students}} = 0.15 = 15\%$$

However, we want *fewer than* 225 students, or less than 15%. Thus, Art is not valid because it has exactly 225 students, not fewer. Only Anthropology and Sociology have fewer than 225 students.

This means (D) and (E) are our correct answers.

2. C, D, E

In order to solve this problem, we can set up an equation.

First, we know that History majors account for 21% of the total number of students.

We also know that we want 21% to equal *at least* 190 students.

This equation will yield the smallest possible number of students needed for 190 to equal 21%:

$$\frac{21}{100} = \frac{190}{x}$$
$$21x = 19,000$$
$$x = 904.76$$

Since we cannot have .76 of a person, we round up to 905: this is the lowest possible total number of students for 21% to equal at least 190 students. Thus, any total equal to or greater than 905 works.

This means that (C), (D), and (E) are our answers.

3. B, C

In order to solve this problem, it is best to figure out what percentage 700 is of 3,600.

We can figure this out by setting up the following equation:

$$\frac{700 \text{ students}}{3600 \text{ students total}} = 0.1944 = 19.4\%$$

We want a value that is greater than 19.4%, because we want *more than* 700 students.

This means that any major with more than a 19.4% share of the student body will work: English and History.

Thus, (B) and (C) are our correct answers.

4. A, E

In order to solve this, first we must find what percentage 180 is of 1,200:

$$\frac{180}{1,200} = 0.15$$

So we know that we need at least 15% to be a correct answer.

Out of the known percentages, we see that only (E) is a correct answer so far.

Next, we must find x and y.

When we add all known values, we get 58%, meaning that $x + y = 42\%$.

We also know that $x = 2y$, so we can plug in:

$$2y + y = 42$$
$$3y = 42$$
$$y = 14$$
$$\text{so, } x = 28.$$

This means that (A) is greater than 15%, so it is also correct.

The correct answers are (A) and (E).

5. C, D, F

In order to solve this problem, we must first figure out what percentage 160 is of 1200:

$$\frac{160}{1200} = 0.1333$$

So we want a percentage that is less than 13.3%.

Out of our known values, we see that (C), (D), and (F) fit that description, so they are all correct.

To check the other two, we must figure out the values of x and y.

When we add all known values, we get 58%, which means that $x + y = 42\%$.

We also know that $x = 2y$, so we can plug in $2y + y = 42$:

$$
\begin{aligned}
3y &= 42 \\
y &= 14 \\
\text{so, } x &= 28.
\end{aligned}
$$

This means that both x and y are greater than 13.3%, so neither is correct.

6. A, B, E

In order to solve, first we must figure out what percentage 240 is of 1,200:

$$\frac{240}{1200} = 0.2$$

So we know that we want a value greater than 20%.

Out of our known values, we see that only (E) qualifies.

To check the other two, we must figure out the values of x and y.

When we add all known values, we get 58%, which means that $x + y = 42\%$.

We also know that $x = y$, so we can plug in $y + y = 42$:

$$
\begin{aligned}
2y &= 42 \\
y &= 21 \\
\text{so, } x &= 21.
\end{aligned}
$$

This means that both x and y are greater than 20%, so both are correct.

Answers (A), (B), and (E) are correct.

7. A, B, C, D, E, F

This question includes a lot of potential equations and possible calculations. Make sure you do only what is necessary.

We first find that 500 is 10% of 5,000.

The question asks for "at least 500," or at least 10%, so 10% is correct also.

Every known percentage is at least 10%, so they are all correct.

To check the two unknown percentages, we must figure out the values of x and y.

When we add all known values, we get 58%, which means that $x + y = 42\%$.

We also know that $x = y$, so we can plug in $y + y = 42$:

$$
\begin{aligned}
2y &= 42 \\
y &= 21 \\
\text{so, } x &= 21.
\end{aligned}
$$

This means both are greater than 10%, so both are correct.

Thus all answers are correct.

8. C

The Republican candidate received more votes in the years 1984, 1988, and 2004, so, three years.

The correct answer is (C).

9. A

We have to look at the graph to find the year in which the gap between the Republican candidate (diamond) and the Democratic candidate (squares) is greatest.

1984: Rep 55 vs Dem 37 = 18

2008: Rep 60 vs Dem 69 = 9

1984 is the largest, so the correct answer is (A).

10. B

The year that the Other candidate received the most votes is clearly 1992, so we just have to figure out the values for the three components.

Rep:	39,000
Dem:	45,000
Other:	20,000
Total:	104,000

So $\frac{20,000}{104,000}$ = 19.3%, which is roughly 20%.

The correct answer is (B).

11. C, D, E

The best way to approach this is to eyeball the obvious answers and then calculate the close ones. To ask this question another way, in what years was the Other candidate's vote share larger than the difference between the Republican and the Democrat?

Based on a quick look, we know that in 1984 and 1988 the Other candidate received negligible votes and the winning candidate had a large majority, which is also the case with 2008. Secondly, in 1992 and 2000 we can see that the Other candidate took enough of the vote to keep the winning candidate from receiving a majority. This leaves us with 1996 and 2004 to calculate.

1996:

Rep: ~ 39

Dem: ~ 47

A difference of 8

Other: Max of 9

This is enough.

2004:

Rep: ~ 62

Dem: ~ 59

A difference of 3

Other: Max of 2

This is not enough.

Not Enough: 1984, 1988, 2004, and 2008

Enough: 1992, 1996, and 2000

The correct answers are (C), (D), and (E).

12. D

Because we do not have all the information we need, we can plug in values that we know must be true.

We know that we already have 75 Documentary DVDs in stock, plus x to be added. So we have a total of $75 + x$ Documentary DVDs.

Next, we know that this value is less than or equal to 5% of the total. Now we can set up an equation to better visualize this:

(Total DVDs) (5%) $\geq 75 + x$

Then change 5% into 0.05

(Total DVDs) (0.05) $\geq 75 + x$

Now we can plug in the answer choices, which are potential total DVD numbers, into our equation.

(A) (1,400) (0.05) = 70

$$70 \geq 75 + x$$
$$x \leq -5$$

This is incorrect; we can't have a negative shipment of DVDs. The value has to be at least 1.

(B) (1,480) (0.05) = 74

$$74 \geq 75 + x$$
$$x \leq -1$$

This is incorrect for the same reason as (A).

(C) (1,500) (0.05) = 75

$$75 \geq 75 + x$$
$$x \leq 0$$

This is incorrect: we know the store received at least 1 new DVD.

(D) (1,520) (0.05) = 76

$$76 \geq 75 + x$$
$$x \leq 1$$

This is correct; the store could possibly have received a shipment of 1 Documentary DVD.

Thus, (D) is our correct answer.

13. D

In order to solve, we must find the percentage of 513 out of 2,700:

$$\frac{513}{2,700} = 0.19$$

However, we want *more* than 513, or *more* than 19%.

Answer choice (D) is more than 19%. Comedy, which is exactly 19%, is not eligible.

The correct answer is (D).

14. C

Be careful in interpreting the data in these questions: make sure you understand exactly what the graph is and isn't showing. Here we are told the total number of doctors in the hospital (200 men, 75 women), and the graph shows the percentage of male and female doctors in each department. The graph is comparing percentages, not total numbers.

From the chart, we see that about 23% of all the male doctors and about 24% of all the female doctors in the hospital work in Family Practice. Thus, there are about 200×.23 = 46 male doctors, and about 75×.24 = 18 female

doctors, in Family Practice, for a total of 64 doctors.

Thus the ratio of medical students to doctors in Family Practice is 16 to 64, or 1 to 4, making (C) the correct answer.

15. C, D, E

It isn't enough to compare the percentages of male and female doctors in each specialty. You must calculate or at least estimate the actual number of male and female doctors for each specialty.

Psychiatry:

9% male out of 200 = .09 × 200 =18

12% female out of 75 = .12 × 75 = 9

$\frac{18}{9}$ = 2 So, the number of male doctors is *not* more than twice the number of female doctors.

Dermatology:

8% male out of 200 = .08 × 200 = 16

14% female out of 75 = .14 × 75 = 10.5

$\frac{16}{10.5}$ < 2 So, the number of male doctors is *not* more than twice the number of female doctors.

Family Practice:

23% male out of 200 = .23 × 200 = 46

24% female out of 75 = .24 × 75 = 18

$\frac{46}{18}$ > 2 So, the number of male doctors *is* more than twice the number of female doctors.

Infectious Disease:

8% male out of 200 = .08 × 200 = 16

4% female out of 75 = .04 × 75 = 3

$\frac{16}{3}$ > 2 So, the number of male doctors *is* more than twice the number of female doctors.

Pediatrics:

12% male out of 200 = .12 × 200 = 24

14% female out of 75 = .14 × 75 = 10.5

$\frac{24}{10.5} > 2$ So, the number of male doctors *is* more than twice the number of female doctors.

So the correct answer choices are (C), (D), and (E).

16.   0.46
This is the credited response.

Here we just have to read the chart precisely. 12% of the male doctors are in Pediatrics, and 7% of the male doctors are in Orthopedic Surgery, so combined we have 19% of the male doctors in these two specialties, or 200 × .19 = 38 doctors. Of these, $\frac{1}{2}$ × 38 = 19 have staff positions.

14% of the female doctors are in Pediatrics, and 2% are in Orthopedic Surgery, so combined we have 16% of the female doctors in these two specialties, or 75 × .16 = 12 doctors. Of these $\frac{1}{3}$ × 12 = 4 have staff positions.

All told, in these two specialties, there are 38 + 12 = 50 doctors, and of them 19 + 4 = 23 have staff positions. The correct answer is $\frac{23}{50}$ or 0.46.

17.   E
Begin by collecting the data. There are two kinds of surgery specialties (General Surgery and Orthopedic Surgery), but the question does not specify one or the other, so we need to add them together.

The odds are 20% that a male doctor is a general surgeon, and 7% that he is an orthopedic surgeon. All told, the odds are 27% that he is a surgeon.

From the chart again, the odds are 10% that he is in Obstetrics.

To calculate the percentage larger one number is over another, take the difference of the two numbers and divide by the smaller number, then convert to a percentage. In our case, take 27 − 10 = 17. Then divide by the smaller number, 10, to yield 1.7. Convert to a percentage by multiplying by 100: the odds are 170% greater that the random doctor will be a surgeon. (E) is the correct answer.

18.   B, C, D, H
This just requires looking at the chart for each year to see where the difference between the top line (expenses) and the lower line (income) is more than $3 billion. For some years it's obvious at a glance; some years require taking a closer look.

2000: Look closely. Expenses are just over 8 and income just under 6. That's a difference of under $3 billion.

2001: Expenses 9.5, income 4.4: clearly over 3. Correct.

2002: Easily over 3 (over 13 vs. under 8). Correct.

2003: Clearly over 3. Correct.

2004: Needs a closer look, but the answer is no: expenses around 7.5, income around 5.

2005: Obviously not. Income is higher than expenses.

2006: Expenses are just $2 billion more than income.

2007: Expenses around 11, income under 7. Correct.

2008: Expenses are a bit over 10 and income a bit over 8, which is not a difference of $3 billion.

2009: Obviously not; the values are almost equal.

So the correct answer choices to select are (B), (C), (D), and (H) (2001, 2002, 2003, and 2007).

19. A

The average of all the changes is the same as the total change divided by the 9 years of measured changes. Since the expenses in 2009 are about the same as the expenses in 2000, the total change is 0, so the average change is also 0, making (A) the correct answer.

Just to spell it out more, if necessary: The average of the changes is equal to the sum of the 9 changes, divided by 9:

For the expenses within each year:

$$\frac{(2001 - 2000) + (2002 - 2001) + \ldots + (2009 - 2008)}{9}$$

Looking more closely at the numerator, all but two terms will cancel out, and we're left with:

$$\frac{2009 - 2000}{9} = \frac{8.5 - 8.5}{9} = 0$$

Logically speaking, the average of all the differences, some of which show growing expenses and some of which show declining expenses, is obtained by looking at the overall change and dividing it up among the 9 parts.

20. C

According to the chart, the 2003 expenses were about $14 billion, and the income was about $9 billion. To find out how much *greater* one value is than another value, calculate their difference and divide by the second term:

$\frac{14 - 9}{9} = .5$, or about 56%. (C) is the correct answer.

21. 625

The average income for a period is just the sum of each year's income divided by the number of years. So if the income goes down by $2.5 billion in one single year, the total income for this four-year period also goes down by $2.5 billion. But since the average is the total divided by the number of years, even

though the *total* goes down by $2.5 billion, the *average* will go down only by $\frac{\$2.5 \text{ billion}}{4} = \$625$ million.

22. B

To do this one, we must look at the chart that shows the percentages of different categories of engineers. We can simply compare the percentage of electrical engineers to the percentage of industrial engineers, which is a ratio of $\frac{23.4}{2.2} = 10.63$, so 11 to 1 is the closest answer.

The correct answer is (B).

23. 573

To answer this question, we must first multiply 4.1% by 27,300 (the total number of engineers at SoboCon, provided in the second chart) to get 1,119 mechanical engineers.

To get civil engineers, we multiply 2.0% by 27,300 = 546 civil engineers. Now subtract: 1,119 - 546 = 573 more mechanical engineers.

24. C

First, we must get the total number of computer engineers by multiplying 27,300 by 26.1% to get 7,125. Next, we need to subtract the number of computer engineers who are in computer hardware (which we can estimate from the first graph), so the answer is 7,125 - 2,125 = 5,000.

The correct answer is (C).

25. B

To calculate this, we must first calculate how many aerospace engineers have been at SoboCon for 5+ years. To get this, we multiply the total number of engineers by the percentage of aerospace engineers and the percentage of aerospace engineers who have been at SoboCon for 5+ years. This is calculated as 27,300(.034)(.14) to arrive at approximately 130. We know that there were twice as many embedded systems engineers who have been at SoboCon for 5+ years, so 2 × 130 = 260. Now, to find the percentage of embedded systems engineers who have been at SoboCon for 5+ years, we take $\frac{260}{1,100}$ to arrive at approximately 24%.

The correct answer is (B).

26. B

Here we need to refer to the graph that shows expenditures and see what year has the smallest difference between public and private expenditures. It is easy to see that 1981 has the smallest difference, so the answer is (B).

27. E

The graphs give us information on public and private universities and on enrollment figures for state universities, private colleges, and community colleges, but nowhere in the graphs can we see how much was spent on public community colleges (since there could be private community colleges), so the answer is (E).

28. C

Here we must refer to the University Enrollment graph and observe the trends. We want to find a period where the total enrollment is continuously increasing for the given period. Here, we can see that the period 1986–1988 shows an increase without any decrease. The other periods given as answer choices show declines, so the answer is (C).

29. C

Here we need to look at the total public university expenditures and compare it to the total university expenditures for 1989. We see that the total expenditures in 1989 were approximately $600 billion and the public

university expenditures were approximately $400 billion, so the percentage is $\frac{400}{600}$ = 67%. The correct answer is (C).

30. A

We can use the top graphic to figure this out. In the 1970s, the second decade given on the x-axis, the corresponding capital expenditures, represented by the line, were less than 1,000, and only one answer, 600, is below 1,000.

The correct answer is (A).

31. D

We can see that the 1990s show small corporate profits at roughly 3,000 and large corporate profits at just under 9,000. Since we are only asked for an approximate difference, we can go with 9,000 – 3,000 = 6,000.

Answer (D) is correct.

32. B, C

For this we need to go to the lower graph and look at the small corporate profit line. The only decade in which the ratio is less than 1 is the 1970s, and the only decade in which the ratio is greater than 4 is the 1980s.

The correct answers are (B) and (C).

33. B

Since these ratios are based on the same numerator, capital expenditures, and we are asked to set them equal, all we have to do is make the small corporate profits equal the large corporate profits for that same year. That would make them roughly 5,000.

The correct answer is (B).

34. 19

For this question, we simply multiply $70 million (the total income for the agency) by

27.8% and we arrive at 19.46. Rounded to the nearest million, this is 19.

35. C

This question can be translated to $70x = 20$ (ignoring the millions), or what percentage of 70 million is 20 million?

When solving for x, we get $\frac{20}{70} = \frac{2}{7}$ or approximately .286, or 28.6% The only category for which income exceeds 28.6% is Special Projects.

The correct answer is (C).

36. C

To solve this question, we must first figure out how much was spent in each category, then apply the fractions to each. We can also approximate, as the question is not looking for an exact number.

Emergency workers = .267 × 70 = $18.7 million

Freight = .062 × 70 = $4.34 million

Post-disaster Assistance = .124 × $70 million = $8.7 million.

Now we apply the fractions:

Emergency workers = $18.7 million × $\frac{1}{2}$ = $9.35 million

Freight = $4.34 million × $\frac{1}{4}$ = $1.1 million

Post-disaster Assistance = $8.7 million × $\frac{2}{3}$ = $5.8 million

Adding them up we get $9.35 + $1.1 + $5.8 = $16.25 million, and we can round down to $16 million. The correct answer is (C).

37. C

This is just a simple calculation. We first need to see how much corporations donated, then compare that to the total of the fundraising expenditures.

Corporations = .021 × 70 = $1.47 million

Fundraising expenditures: .053 × 70 = $3.71 million

Thus the percentage of income not covered by corporations is:

($3.7 − $1.5)$3.7 = $\frac{\$2.2}{\$3.7}$ = approximately 60%.

The correct answer is (C).

38. C

We must total both the contract pay and incentives/endorsements to arrive at annual pay for veterans and find the years in which the total is closest to $15 million.

In this case, we must sum the 2nd and 4th bars in each group (veterans) to see which sum is closest to $15 million, and it is in year 1993–1994, where the two columns are very close to $11 million and $4 million, for a total of $15 million.

The correct answer is (C).

39. D

Here we must find the column that has the smallest increase from 1990 to 2000.

Do not get fooled into thinking that this is a percentage problem; we need to consider the change in actual amounts.

Looking at the graph, we see that the 1st column, the sum of incentives/endorsements for rookies, increases the least, with an increase of about $3 million.

The correct answer is (D).

40. C

We see that the year when contract pay for rookies (3rd bar) was closest to $10 million was 1998–1999.

Therefore, we want to see what the approximate Incentives/Endorsements pay was for veterans (2nd bar), and we can see that in the same year the figure is approximately $7.5 million.

The correct answer is (C).

41. B

There were 5,200 students living on campus in 2003, and 4,500 students living on campus in 2001. Thus, there were 5,200 − 4,500 = 700 more students living on campus in 2003 than in 2001.

Choice (B) is correct.

42. B

In 2002, there were 4,200 students living on campus. Of those, 30% were sophomores. Thus, 0.3 × 4,200 = 1,260 of the students living on campus in 2002 were sophomores. (B) is the correct answer.

43. 1.6

During four out of the five years, no humpback whales were spotted. During 2000, however, 8 were spotted. Thus, the average for the five years is:

$$\frac{0+8+0+0+0}{5} = \frac{8}{5} = 1.6.$$

44. A

In 1999, 500 blue whales were spotted. In 2003, 400 blue whales were spotted. Percent change is calculated as $\frac{\text{New value} - \text{Orig. value}}{\text{Orig. value}}$ × 100%. Therefore, we have that the percent decrease in blue whales spotted from the year 1999 to the year 2003 is:

$$\frac{500 - 400}{500} \times 100\% =$$

$$\frac{100}{500} \times 100\% =$$

$$\frac{1}{5} \times 100\% = 20\%$$

Thus, there was a 20% decrease in the number of blue whales spotted.

Therefore, the answer is (A).

45. C

This question tests your ability to examine the information from all four graphs at the same time. Notice that there were no more than 8 humpback whales spotted in any given year, no more than 30 porpoises spotted in any given year, and no more than 500 blue whales spotted in any given year. However, there were always more than 1,000 dolphins spotted each year. Thus, the animal most likely to be spotted is a dolphin, making (C) the correct answer.

46. B

The tax in AL is approximately 8 dollars, and the energy cost is approximately 31 dollars. The total bill is 8 + 31 = 39. The percentage that the 8 dollar tax is of the total 39 dollar bill is $\frac{8}{39} \times 100\% = \frac{800}{39}\%$, which to the nearest percent is 21%. (B) is the correct answer.

47. C

In both CA and RI, the tax is a relatively large fraction of the energy cost. Answer choices (A) and (B) can be eliminated first. Then, the approximate ratios of the remaining three states can be determined:

$$\text{TX}: \frac{5}{28}$$

$$\text{OH}: \frac{6}{31}$$

$$\text{AL}: \frac{8}{31}$$

Since the ratio in OH is smaller than in AL (they have the same denominator, so the numerators can be compared), (E) can be eliminated.

Then, by comparing TX and OH by cross-multiplication, 5 × 31 = 155 and 6 × 28 = 168, the ratio in OH is larger than in TX. Thus, the ratio of tax to energy cost in TX is the smallest of all states. Choice (C) is correct.

48. B

Only in ND, CA, RI, and AL is the tax above 6 dollars, so TX and OH can be ignored. The first step in calculating the standard deviation is to calculate the mean. The mean energy cost for the four states of interest is approximately $\frac{(23 + 20 + 22 + 31)}{4} = \frac{96}{4} = 24$.

The next step is to take the absolute value of the difference between each value and the mean. For ND, CA, RI, and AL this yields 24 − 23 = 1, 24 − 20 = 4, 24 − 22 = 2, and 31 − 24 = 7, respectively. Then, squaring the differences and adding them together, we have $1^2 + 4^2 + 2^2 + 7^2 = 1 + 16 + 4 + 49 = 70$.

Finally, to obtain the standard deviation, we divide the sum by the number of values, $\frac{70}{4} = 17.5$ and take the positive square root of the result. The standard deviation is the positive square root of 17.5. The positive square root of 17.5 can be approximated as slightly greater than the positive square root of 16, which is 4. Only choice (B), 4.2, is slightly greater than 4. Choice (B) is correct.

49. B

The range of a list of numbers is the greatest number minus the smallest number. For tax, the state with the greatest tax is RI, with a tax that is approximately 11 dollars, and the state with the smallest tax is TX, with a tax that is approximately 5 dollars. So the range of the tax, in dollars, is approximately 11 − 5 = 6. For energy cost, the states with the greatest energy cost are AL and OH, with an energy cost of approximately 31 dollars each, and the state with the smallest energy cost is CA, with an energy cost of approximately 20 dollars.

So the range of the energy cost, in dollars, is approximately 31 − 20 = 11. So the positive difference, in dollars, between the range of tax and the range of energy cost across all

states, is approximately 11 − 6 = 5. Choice (B) is correct.

50. B

To begin, we must calculate the tax in 4 years. In 1 year, the tax is 20% higher, so in dollars, the tax will be 9 × 1.2 = 10.80. In 2 years, the tax is 20% higher than in year 1, so in dollars, the tax will be 10.8 × 1.2 = 12.96. In 3 years, the tax, in dollars, will be 12.96 × 1.2, which to the nearest hundredth is 15.55, and in 4 years, the tax, in dollars, will be 15.55 × 1.2 = 18.66. The energy cost, in dollars, is 20, so the positive difference, in dollars, between the energy cost and the tax will be 20 − 18.66 = 1.34, so (B) is correct.

51. B

The formula for percent increase is

$$\frac{\text{New value} - \text{Original value}}{\text{Original value}} \times 100\%.$$

The correct answer is (B). In 1990, the profits of company B were approximately 20 million dollars. In 1995, the profits of company B were approximately 50 million dollars. The percent increase in profits of Company B from 1990 to 1995 was approximately:

$$\frac{50,000,000 - 20,000,000}{20,000,000} \times 100\%$$
$$= \frac{30,000,000}{20,000,000} \times 100\%$$
$$= \frac{3}{2} \times 100\%$$
$$= 3 \times 50\%$$
$$= 150\%$$

52. D

The average formula is Average = $\frac{\text{Sum of the terms}}{\text{Number of terms}}$. The years in which the profits of Company A were greater than the profits of Company B were 1991, 1992, 1993, and 1995.

In 1991, the profits of Company A were approximately 28,000,000 dollars.

In 1992, the profits of Company A were approximately 41,000,000 dollars.

In 1993, the profits of Company A were approximately 51,000,000 dollars.

In 1995, the profits of Company A were approximately 61,000,000 dollars.

The average of the profits of Company per year in the years 1991, 1992, 1993, and 1995 was approximately: $\frac{(28M + 41M + 51M + 61M)}{4} = \frac{181M}{4} =$ $45.25M.

This is closest to choice (D).

53. E

We do not even have to use the total of $24,000,000 in our calculations.

Answer choice (E) is correct. We can say that $24,000,000 is t. Then the sales from clothing were 25% of t, which is $0.25t$. The sales from sporting goods were 21% of t, which is $0.21t$. The percentage that the sales from sporting goods is less than the sales from clothing is $\frac{0.25t - 0.21t}{0.25t} \times 100\%$

We were actually finding the percent that 21% is less than 25%. However, we included the total sales t in our calculation for clarity. We can see that the t's will cancel:

$$\frac{0.25t - 0.21t}{0.25t} \times 100\% =$$

$$\frac{0.04t}{0.25t} \times 100\% =$$

$$\frac{4}{25} \times 100\% =$$

$$4 \times 4\% = 16\%$$

54. A

The total sales were $24 million and 17% of the sales were for home improvement. So the

sales for home improvement were 0.17 × 24,000,000 = 0.17 × 24 = $4.08 million ≈ $4.1 million. (A) is correct.

55. B

To answer this question, let's find the total number of people in the 5 counties who were surveyed, and the number of people surveyed in County E who gave the car a durability rating of 4.

From the first graph, which is a bar graph, the total number of people surveyed in the 5 counties was 5,000 + 25,000 + 10,000 + 15,000 + 35,000 = 90,000.

From the first graph, the number of people surveyed in County E was 35,000. From the second graph, which is a pie chart, 8% of the people in County E gave the car a rating of 4. So the number of people in County E who gave the car a rating of 4 was 8% of 35,000. The decimal equivalent if 8% is 0.08. So the number of people surveyed in County E who gave the car a rating of 4 was 0.08(35,000) = 2,800.

Therefore, there were a total of 90,000 people surveyed, and 2,800 people in County E gave the car a durability rating of 4. So the percentage of all the people surveyed in the 5 counties who were people from County E who gave the car a durability rating of 4 was $\frac{2,800}{90,000}$, which is approximately 3.1%. (B) is the correct answer.

56. D

There is no need to use the first graph to obtain the actual numbers of people surveyed in County E who gave the car the durability ratings of 1, 2, 3, 4, and 5. We can find the average by just finding the weighted average by using the pie chart. So the average rating of the car by the people surveyed in County E was:

$0.30(1) + 0.18(2) + 0.17(3) + 0.08(4) + 0.27(5) =$

$0.3 + 0.36 + 0.51 + 0.32 + 1.35 =$

2.84

The correct answer is (D).

57. D

The formula for the decrease in percent is:

$$\frac{\text{Original value - New value}}{\text{Original value}} \times 100\%.$$

From the first graph, which is a bar graph, the sales of brand B clothing were approximately $750,000, and the sales of brand E clothing were approximately $300,000. So the percent decrease is approximately:

$$\frac{\$750,000 - \$300,000}{\$750,000} \times 100\% =$$

$$\frac{\$450,000}{\$750,000} \times 100\% =$$

$$\frac{45}{75} \times 100\% =$$

$$\frac{3}{5} \times 100\% =$$

$$3 \times 20\% = 60\%$$

The correct answer is (D).

58. 5416

We can solve this problem by using a proportion. We know from the table that the movie grossed $312.4 million when it played in 4,390 theaters. We can use this ratio to write a proportion to solve the problem:

$$\frac{312.4}{4,390} = \frac{385.4}{x}$$

$$312.4x = 4,390 \times 385.4$$

$$312.4x = 1,691,906$$

$$x = 5,415.8$$

Rounding to the nearest whole number, the number of theaters needed to gross $385.4 million is 5,416.

59. A

The best strategy for this problem is to use straight math.

To determine the gross per theater, we need to divide the gross sales for each movie by the number of theaters the movie played in:

(A) $\frac{334.2}{3,739} = 0.08938$

(B) $\frac{294.6}{4,125} = 0.07142$

(C) $\frac{292.6}{3,792} = 0.07716$

(D) $\frac{312.4}{4,390} = 0.07116$

(E) $\frac{300.5}{4,468} = 0.06726$

The correct answer is (A).

60. B

The median of a set is the middle value in the set when the terms in that set are arranged from least to greatest. If there is an even number of terms in the set—and, therefore, two middle values—the average of the two middle terms is the median of the set.

To solve this question, let's first list the values in order from least to greatest: 3,602, 3,603, 3,739, 3,740, 3,792, 4,028, 4,125, 4,386, 4,390, 4,468. Since this list contains 10 numbers, we must find the average of the two middle values, 3,792 and 4,028.

The average of 3,792 and 4,028 is 3,910, so that's our median. The correct answer is (B).

61. E

Examine the title first. "Average Weekly Viewing of Prime Time Television" tells us that the chart deals with prime time only, and the chart breaks this viewing down further into a number of smaller categories which are listed along the top of this chart. Notice that these numbers are also in percentages with the exception of the column of numbers on the far right, which shows the average weekly prime time viewing in hours. That means that in order to find the number of hours spent watching a prime time program type, we need to use the percentage values and the number of hours value over in the far right column.

High school students spent 25% of their 12 hours watching sports. 25% is one quarter, so they spent a quarter of 12 or 3 hours per week watching sports. College students spent 30% of their 15.4 hours of prime time viewing sports. 30% of 15.4 = (0.3)(15.4) = 4.62. So the increase in viewing was 4.62 – 3 = 1.62 hours.

The percent increase was:

$\frac{1.62}{3}$ × 100% = 0.54 × 100% = 54%. (E) is the correct answer.

62. C

In this case we need to determine two values: the defensive scouts in 2006 and 2007. Go to the top chart and down the y axis find 2006.

We can see that in 2006 there were 75 defensive scouts and in 2007 there were 100.

So we need to calculate the increase of 75 to 100:

100 – 75 = 25 (increase) so $\frac{25}{75}$ = 33.33%

The correct answer is (C).

63. D

We need to find two values to solve this: the offensive scouts in 2008 and in 2009. This is not a percentage question, so we only need to solve for the actual number.

Looking at the top chart, we can go down the y-axis to the year 2008 and find that there were 125 offensive scouts in 2008 and 200 in 2009:

200 – 125 = 75.

Answer (D) is the correct choice.

64. 450

We need two values to solve this question, the offensive and defensive scout salaries in 2008.

Using the lower chart, we can see in 2008 that the offense and defense scout total salaries were each 300,000. If we take 50% of the offensive scout salaries (150,000) and add that to the 300,000 of the defensive salaries, we get a new total defensive scout salaries of 300,000 + 150,000 = 450,000. Therefore, in thousands of dollars, the answer is 450.

65. C

We need to determine three values here: the defensive scout salaries in 2005, 2006, and 2007.

To do this we can use the lower chart and determine the following:

2005: 250,000

2006: 150,000

2007: 150,000

Combining these we get:

250,000 + 150,000 + 150,000 = 550,000.

Answer (C) is correct.

66. B, C

The graph uses two differently shaded bars, so be careful not to get them confused when evaluating the choices. To find the actual dollar values of a type of tax revenue in a given year, we need to know what percent of the total tax revenue was raised by that tax and the total tax revenues that year, which is given in the legend. Let's evaluate the choices:

(A) We don't have any information about the number of corporations, only the revenue raised, so this statement cannot be inferred.

(B) Gas tax revenues in 1963 were about 9% of $131.6 billion, and gas tax revenues in 1993 were about 3% of $910.4 billion. We know that

9% of $131.6 billion is the same as 3% of three times $131.6 billion, or 3% of $394.8 billion, so we can infer that the gas tax revenues were greater in 1993 than in 1963.

(C) Tariffs accounted for about 3% of the total tax revenue in 1993, and local property tax accounted for about 15% of the total tax revenue that year. Since 15% is more than twice 3%, even before factoring in the overall increased revenue in 1993, this statement is true.

The correct answers are (B) and (C).

67. 742

This question is about monthly expenditures on energy, which can be found in the chart. For Canada, we are given that the monthly average expenditures on energy is $10.6 billion. We now must find what percentage of that was spent on nuclear, hydro, and wind power. We see that the total percentage spent on these three sources was 3%, 2%, and 2%, respectively, for a total of 7%. Now multiply $10.6 billion by 7% and the answer is $.742 billion, which is equal to $742 million.

68. E

Here, we need to look at the chart to see what percentage of China's average monthly expenditures are spent on coal. However, there is not a category only for coal; the category for coal is combined with natural gas (which is 15% for China). Therefore, the answer cannot be determined, as we don't know the exact percentage for coal alone.

The correct answer is (E).

69. D

We must use both the chart and graph to answer this question. From the graph, we can see that the United Kingdom spends approximately 11% of its annual expenditures on energy. From the chart, we know that 74%

of its totally energy expenditures is spent on oil. Therefore, 11% × 74% = approximately 8% spent on oil each year.

The correct answer is (D).

70. C

You are to determine which of the three given statements can be inferred from the data. Statement I cannot properly be inferred since the graph shows percentages of annual government expenditures. (Although the bar for the United Kingdom is tallest, this does not mean that their annual expenditures was greatest; rather it means that they spend a greater percent of their annual expenditures in these categories than the other countries listed). Statement II cannot be inferred either—although each country spends the same percent of their annual expenditures on wind energy, the expenditures differed. For example, 2% of $10.6 billion is less than 2% of $32.9 billion. Thus III is the only possible correct inference.

The correct answer is (C).

71. C

This question is about quarterly GDP from minerals and mining, which can be found in the chart. For Argentina, we are given that the quarterly average GDP from minerals and mining is $173 billion. We now must find what percentage of that was derived from iron ore, copper, precious stones, and bauxite, and we see that the total percentage on these four sources was 11%, 8%, 1%, and 1%, respectively, for a total of 21%. Now multiply $173 billion by 21%, and the answer is approximately $36 billion.

The correct answer is (C).

72. E

Here, we need to look at the chart to see what percentage of Japan's average quarterly GDP was derived from silver. However, there is not a category only for silver; the category for silver is combined with other precious metals (which is 2% for Japan). Therefore, the answer cannot be determined, as we don't know the exact percentage for silver alone.

The correct answer is (E).

73. C

We must use both the chart and graph to answer this question. From the graph, we can see that South Africa derives approximately 20% of its total GDP from minerals and mining. From the chart, we know that 70% of its total minerals and mining GDP is derived from gold. Therefore, 20% × 70% = approximately 14%.

The correct answer is (C).

74. D

You are to determine which of the three given statements can be inferred from the data.

Statement I cannot properly be inferred, since the graph shows percentages of GDP totals. (Although the bar for Brazil is tallest, this does not mean that its GDP was greatest; rather it means that they derived a greater percent of their 2001 GDP in these categories than the other countries listed).

Statement II is actually false—although Japan derives 73% of its quarterly GDP from minerals and mining on bauxite, South Africa actually has a higher absolute amount on bauxite. (5% of $207 billion is greater than 73% of $11 billion).

Statement III also cannot be inferred. Similar to statement I, we are given only percentages of GDP, not absolute values. Even though Japan derived the highest percentage of GDP from electronics as compared to the other countries, it does not imply that they had the highest absolute dollar amount. We would need the total GDP for each country in 2001 to verify this.

The correct answer is (D).

Introduction to Quantitative Comparison

In each Quantitative Comparison question, you'll see two mathematical expressions. One is Quantity A, the other is Quantity B. You will be asked to compare them. Some questions include additional centered information. This centered information applies to both quantities and is essential to making the comparison. Since this type of question is about the relationship between the two quantities, you often won't need to calculate a specific value for either quantity. Therefore, you do not want to rely on the onscreen calculator to answer these questions. The art of quantitative comparison problems is getting away with the bare minimum to save time. Many quantitative comparisons are designed to look time consuming, which is a good indicator that there is a much faster way to solve the problem.

The directions for a Quantitative Comparison question will look like this:

Directions: Select the correct answer.

A Quantitative Comparison question will look like this:

Sample Question

| Exit section | Review | Mark | Help | Back | Next |

Sample Question

$$h > 1$$

Quantity A	Quantity B
The number of minutes in h hours	$\dfrac{60}{h}$

- ◯ Quantity A is greater.
- ◯ Quantity B is greater.
- ◯ The two quantities are equal.
- ◯ The relationship cannot be determined from the information given.

Click to select your choice.

Quantitative Comparison Practice

Compare the quantities in Column A and Column B and select the appropriate answer. If there is an image or text between the columns, assume that it represents the same thing for both columns.

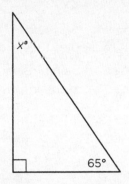

1.　　Column A　　　　Column B

　　　　25　　　　　　　x

    Ⓐ　The quantity in Column A is greater.

    Ⓑ　The quantity in Column B is greater.

    Ⓒ　The two quantities are equal.

    Ⓓ　The relationship cannot be determined from the information given.

2.　For each home in Dutch County, the amount of property tax is p percent of the value of the home. The property tax on a home whose value is $55,000 is $5,500.

　　　　Column A　　　　Column B

The property tax on a home in Dutch County whose value is $65,000.	$6,600

    Ⓐ　The quantity in Column A is greater.

    Ⓑ　The quantity in Column B is greater.

    Ⓒ　The two quantities are equal.

    Ⓓ　The relationship cannot be determined from the information given.

3.　Triangle regions Q_1 and Q_2 have equal areas and have heights h_1 and h_2, respectively.

　　　　Column A　　　　Column B

　　　　　h_1　　　　　　h_2

    Ⓐ　The quantity in Column A is greater.

    Ⓑ　The quantity in Column B is greater.

    Ⓒ　The two quantities are equal.

    Ⓓ　The relationship cannot be determined from the information given.

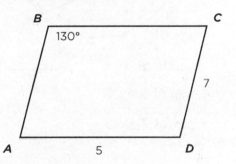

4.　　Column A　　　　Column B

　　The area of region $ABCD$　　35

    Ⓐ　The quantity in Column A is greater.

    Ⓑ　The quantity in Column B is greater.

    Ⓒ　The two quantities are equal.

    Ⓓ　The relationship cannot be determined from the information given.

5.
$$k + n = 14$$
$$n + 4 = 9$$

Column A	Column B
k	n

Ⓐ The quantity in Column A is greater.

Ⓑ The quantity in Column B is greater.

Ⓒ The two quantities are equal.

Ⓓ The relationship cannot be deter-mined from the information given.

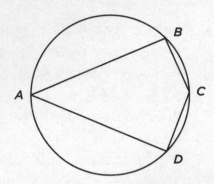

6.

Column A	Column B
The area of the region enclosed by quadrilateral *ABCD*	80

Ⓐ The quantity in Column A is greater.

Ⓑ The quantity in Column B is greater.

Ⓒ The two quantities are equal.

Ⓓ The relationship cannot be deter-mined from the information given.

7. $x, y,$ and z are positive integers.

Column A	Column B
The product of x, y, and z	The sum of $x, y,$ and z

Ⓐ The quantity in Column A is greater.

Ⓑ The quantity in Column B is greater.

Ⓒ The two quantities are equal.

Ⓓ The relationship cannot be deter-mined from the information given.

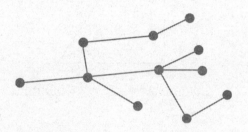

8.

Column A	Column B
The total number of joints	The total number of connectors

Ⓐ The quantity in Column A is greater.

Ⓑ The quantity in Column B is greater.

Ⓒ The two quantities are equal.

Ⓓ The relationship cannot be deter-mined from the information given.

9.

Column A	Column B
The greatest prime factor of 15	The greatest prime factor of 14

Ⓐ The quantity in Column A is greater.

Ⓑ The quantity in Column B is greater.

Ⓒ The two quantities are equal.

Ⓓ The relationship cannot be deter-mined from the information given.

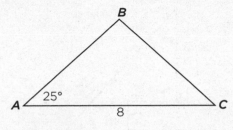

10.

Column A	Column B
AB	*BC*

- Ⓐ The quantity in Column A is greater.
- Ⓑ The quantity in Column B is greater.
- Ⓒ The two quantities are equal.
- Ⓓ The relationship cannot be determined from the information given.

11. Mr. Tharp figured out that to find his golf ball company's net profits in terms of the number of golf balls sold, represented by x, he would use the formula $2x^2 + 3x - 200$.

Column A	Column B
The number of golf balls sold to break even	12

- Ⓐ The quantity in Column A is greater.
- Ⓑ The quantity in Column B is greater.
- Ⓒ The two quantities are equal.
- Ⓓ The relationship cannot be determined from the information given.

12.

$$x^3 = 27$$
$$y^2 = 9$$

Column A	Column B
x	y

- Ⓐ The quantity in Column A is greater.
- Ⓑ The quantity in Column B is greater.
- Ⓒ The two quantities are equal.
- Ⓓ The relationship cannot be determined from the information given.

13.

$$h - r = 4$$
$$r - (-1) = 6$$

Column A	Column B
h	11

- Ⓐ The quantity in Column A is greater.
- Ⓑ The quantity in Column B is greater.
- Ⓒ The two quantities are equal.
- Ⓓ The relationship cannot be determined from the information given.

14. Chase's salary, which is greater than $20,000, is 80 percent of Katy's salary. Timan's salary is 80% of Chase's salary.

Column A	Column B
Katy's salary	Timan's salary

- Ⓐ The quantity in Column A is greater.
- Ⓑ The quantity in Column B is greater.
- Ⓒ The two quantities are equal.
- Ⓓ The relationship cannot be determined from the information given.

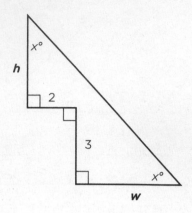

15.

Column A	Column B
The number that is halfway between points x and y.	$\frac{3}{4}$

Ⓐ The quantity in Column A is greater.

Ⓑ The quantity in Column B is greater.

Ⓒ The two quantities are equal.

Ⓓ The relationship cannot be determined from the information given.

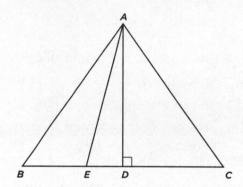

16.

Column A	Column B
The length of segment AE	The length of segment AC

Ⓐ The quantity in Column A is greater.

Ⓑ The quantity in Column B is greater.

Ⓒ The two quantities are equal.

Ⓓ The relationship cannot be determined from the information given.

17.

Column A	Column B
h	w

Ⓐ The quantity in Column A is greater.

Ⓑ The quantity in Column B is greater.

Ⓒ The two quantities are equal.

Ⓓ The relationship cannot be determined from the information given.

18. For all numbers x, $x^{\#} = 24 - x$.

Column A	Column B
$(x^{\#})^{\#}$	x

Ⓐ The quantity in Column A is greater.

Ⓑ The quantity in Column B is greater.

Ⓒ The two quantities are equal.

Ⓓ The relationship cannot be determined from the information given.

19. a and b are each greater than 1.

Column A	Column B
$3ab$	$(3a)(3b)$

Ⓐ The quantity in Column A is greater.

Ⓑ The quantity in Column B is greater.

Ⓒ The two quantities are equal.

Ⓓ The relationship cannot be determined from the information given.

20.　　　　　　　$500 < x < 1{,}000$

Column A	Column B
$1{,}000 - x$	$x - 500$

Ⓐ The quantity in Column A is greater.

Ⓑ The quantity in Column B is greater.

Ⓒ The two quantities are equal.

Ⓓ The relationship cannot be determined from the information given.

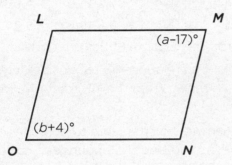

21.

Column A	Column B
a	b

Ⓐ The quantity in Column A is greater.

Ⓑ The quantity in Column B is greater.

Ⓒ The two quantities are equal.

Ⓓ The relationship cannot be determined from the information given.

22. Team V scored 5 runs in the first inning in the first game of the World Series, but then team P scored 10 more runs in the second inning than team V.

Column A	Column B
First inning runs scored by team V	Second inning runs scored by team P

Ⓐ The quantity in Column A is greater.

Ⓑ The quantity in Column B is greater.

Ⓒ The two quantities are equal.

Ⓓ The relationship cannot be determined from the information given.

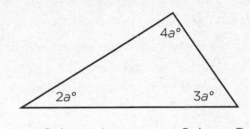

23.

Column A	Column B
a	25

Ⓐ The quantity in Column A is greater.

Ⓑ The quantity in Column B is greater.

Ⓒ The two quantities are equal.

Ⓓ The relationship cannot be determined from the information given.

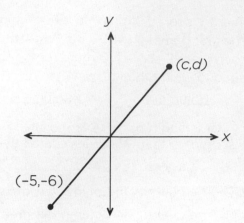

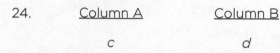

Average score for the boys	92
Average score for the girls	83
Average score for the class	86

24.   Column A   Column B

         c d

  Ⓐ The quantity in Column A is greater.

  Ⓑ The quantity in Column B is greater.

  Ⓒ The two quantities are equal.

  Ⓓ The relationship cannot be determined from the information given.

25. $(a + 6)(a - 6) = 0$

         $(b + 6)(b - 6) = 0$

     Column A   Column B

     $a + 6$ $b + 6$

  Ⓐ The quantity in Column A is greater.

  Ⓑ The quantity in Column B is greater.

  Ⓒ The two quantities are equal.

  Ⓓ The relationship cannot be determined from the information given.

26.   Column A   Column B

    The number of   The number of
    boys in the class   girls in the class
    who took the test   who took the test

  Ⓐ The quantity in Column A is greater.

  Ⓑ The quantity in Column B is greater.

  Ⓒ The two quantities are equal.

  Ⓓ The relationship cannot be determined from the information given.

27.   Ellen went to the store to buy coffee beans and bought 5 pounds of coffee A for $9.85 and 7 pounds of coffee B for $8.33.

     Column A   Column B

    The price Ellen   The price Ellen
    paid per pound   paid per pound
    for coffee A   for coffee B

  Ⓐ The quantity in Column A is greater.

  Ⓑ The quantity in Column B is greater.

  Ⓒ The two quantities are equal.

  Ⓓ The relationship cannot be determined from the information given.

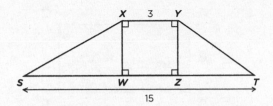

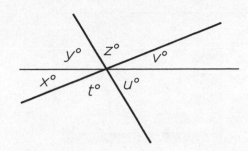

28.

Column A	Column B
The area of the rectangle *WXYZ*	The area of the triangle *WXS*

Ⓐ The quantity in Column A is greater.

Ⓑ The quantity in Column B is greater.

Ⓒ The two quantities are equal.

Ⓓ The relationship cannot be determined from the information given.

29.

$$2x + 5y = 14$$
$$x + 3y = 20$$

Column A	Column B
$x + y$	-32

Ⓐ The quantity in Column A is greater.

Ⓑ The quantity in Column B is greater.

Ⓒ The two quantities are equal.

Ⓓ The relationship cannot be determined from the information given.

30.

$$a + b = 10$$
$$a - b = 4$$

Column A	Column B
a	b

Ⓐ The quantity in Column A is greater.

Ⓑ The quantity in Column B is greater.

Ⓒ The two quantities are equal.

Ⓓ The relationship cannot be determined from the information given.

31.

Column A	Column B
$x + z + u$	$y + v + t$

Ⓐ The quantity in Column A is greater.

Ⓑ The quantity in Column B is greater.

Ⓒ The two quantities are equal.

Ⓓ The relationship cannot be determined from the information given.

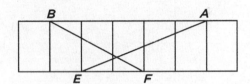

32.

Column A	Column B
The length of *BF*	The length of *EA*

Ⓐ The quantity in Column A is greater.

Ⓑ The quantity in Column B is greater.

Ⓒ The two quantities are equal.

Ⓓ The relationship cannot be determined from the information given.

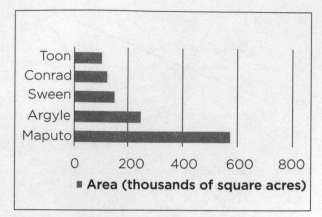

Area of the five largest lakes in Oak County

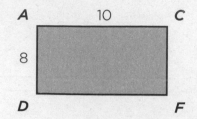

33.

Column A	Column B
Sum of the areas of the four smallest lakes	Area of the largest lake

Ⓐ The quantity in Column A is greater.

Ⓑ The quantity in Column B is greater.

Ⓒ The two quantities are equal.

Ⓓ The relationship cannot be determined from the information given.

35.

Column A	Column B
The area of a square region with a perimeter equal to the perimeter of rectangular region *ADFC*	81

Ⓐ The quantity in Column A is greater.

Ⓑ The quantity in Column B is greater.

Ⓒ The two quantities are equal.

Ⓓ The relationship cannot be determined from the information given.

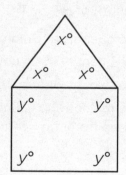

34.

Column A	Column B
$2x + 2y$	270

Ⓐ The quantity in Column A is greater.

Ⓑ The quantity in Column B is greater.

Ⓒ The two quantities are equal.

Ⓓ The relationship cannot be determined from the information given.

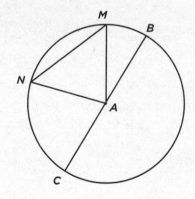

36.

Column A	Column B
$\dfrac{CB}{NM}$	2

Ⓐ The quantity in Column A is greater.

Ⓑ The quantity in Column B is greater.

Ⓒ The two quantities are equal.

Ⓓ The relationship cannot be determined from the information given.

37. Ms. Moss bought a surfboard on the installment plan. The cash price of the surfboard was $650. The amount she paid at the time of purchase was $170 and then she paid 24 monthly payments of $23 each.

Column A	Column B
The amount in dollars she paid for the surfboard in excess of the cash price.	71

Ⓐ The quantity in Column A is greater.

Ⓑ The quantity in Column B is greater.

Ⓒ The two quantities are equal.

Ⓓ The relationship cannot be determined from the information given.

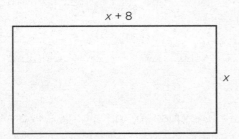

38.

Column A	Column B
The length of a side of A	$x + 4$

Ⓐ The quantity in Column A is greater.

Ⓑ The quantity in Column B is greater.

Ⓒ The two quantities are equal.

Ⓓ The relationship cannot be determined from the information given.

39.
$$O < x < y < z$$

Column A	Column B
$\dfrac{y}{x}$	$\dfrac{z}{y}$

Ⓐ The quantity in Column A is greater.

Ⓑ The quantity in Column B is greater.

Ⓒ The two quantities are equal.

Ⓓ The relationship cannot be determined from the information given.

40.

Column A	Column B
2^x	3^x

Ⓐ The quantity in Column A is greater.

Ⓑ The quantity in Column B is greater.

Ⓒ The two quantities are equal.

Ⓓ The relationship cannot be determined from the information given.

41.

Column A	Column B
The sum of all the integers from 19 to 49, inclusive	The sum of all the integers from 22 to 49, inclusive

Ⓐ The quantity in Column A is greater.

Ⓑ The quantity in Column B is greater.

Ⓒ The two quantities are equal.

Ⓓ The relationship cannot be determined from the information given.

42.

$$y > x > 0$$

Column A	Column B
$\dfrac{y}{x}$	$\dfrac{x}{y}$

Ⓐ The quantity in Column A is greater.

Ⓑ The quantity in Column B is greater.

Ⓒ The two quantities are equal.

Ⓓ The relationship cannot be determined from the information given.

43. The average (arithmetic mean) of x, y, and 12 is 8.

Column A	Column B
$\dfrac{(x+y)}{2}$	8

Ⓐ The quantity in Column A is greater.

Ⓑ The quantity in Column B is greater.

Ⓒ The two quantities are equal.

Ⓓ The relationship cannot be determined from the information given.

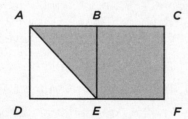

44.

Column A	Column B
The area of the shaded region	36 + 16

Ⓐ The quantity in Column A is greater.

Ⓑ The quantity in Column B is greater.

Ⓒ The two quantities are equal.

Ⓓ The relationship cannot be determined from the information given.

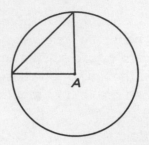

45.

Column A	Column B
The perimeter of the triangle	Half the perimeter of the circle

Ⓐ The quantity in Column A is greater.

Ⓑ The quantity in Column B is greater.

Ⓒ The two quantities are equal.

Ⓓ The relationship cannot be determined from the information given.

46.

$$h - r = 6$$
$$r - (-3) = 6$$

Column A	Column B
h	8.5

Ⓐ The quantity in Column A is greater.

Ⓑ The quantity in Column B is greater.

Ⓒ The two quantities are equal.

Ⓓ The relationship cannot be determined from the information given.

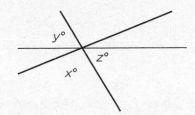

47.

Column A	Column B
$180 - z$	$180 - y$

Ⓐ The quantity in Column A is greater.

Ⓑ The quantity in Column B is greater.

Ⓒ The two quantities are equal.

Ⓓ The relationship cannot be determined from the information given.

48.

Column A	Column B
$\lvert(x + y + z)\rvert$	$\lvert x\rvert + \lvert y\rvert + \lvert z\rvert$

Ⓐ The quantity in Column A is greater.

Ⓑ The quantity in Column B is greater.

Ⓒ The two quantities are equal.

Ⓓ The relationship cannot be determined from the information given.

49. For every integer x from 1 to 10, inclusive, the xth term of a certain sequence is given by:

$$(-1)^{x+1} \times \frac{1}{2^x}$$

S is the sum of the first 10 terms in the sequence.

Column A	Column B
S	$\frac{1}{4}$

Ⓐ The quantity in Column A is greater.

Ⓑ The quantity in Column B is greater.

Ⓒ The two quantities are equal.

Ⓓ The relationship cannot be determined from the information given.

50. A cube of cheese is completely covered in a rind and has an edge of 2 inches.

Column A	Column B
The percent of the total surface area that is not covered by rind when the cheese is cut down the middle into 2 equal pieces	50%

Ⓐ The quantity in Column A is greater.

Ⓑ The quantity in Column B is greater.

Ⓒ The two quantities are equal.

Ⓓ The relationship cannot be determined from the information given.

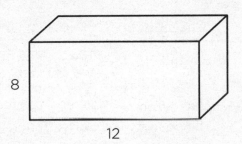

51.

Column A	Column B
The volume of the rectangular solid	96

Ⓐ The quantity in Column A is greater.

Ⓑ The quantity in Column B is greater.

Ⓒ If the two quantities are equal.

Ⓓ The relationship cannot be determined from the information given.

52. Cylinder A has twice the radius but half the height of Cylinder B.

Column A	Column B
The volume of Cylinder A	The volume of Cylinder B

Ⓐ The quantity in Column A is greater.

Ⓑ The quantity in Column B is greater.

Ⓒ The two quantities are equal.

Ⓓ The relationship cannot be determined from the information given.

53. The longest distance between any two points in a right cylinder is 13. The height and the diameter are positive integers such that the height exceeds the diameter.

Column A	Column B
75π	The volume of the cylinder

Ⓐ The quantity in Column A is greater.

Ⓑ The quantity in Column B is greater.

Ⓒ The two quantities are equal.

Ⓓ The relationship cannot be determined from the information given.

54. There are 8 emeralds and 6 rubies in a bag, from which a boy selects two gems without replacement.

Column A	Column B
The probability of choosing two rubies	The probability of choosing an emerald, and then a ruby

Ⓐ The quantity in Column A is greater.

Ⓑ The quantity in Column B is greater.

Ⓒ The two quantities are equal.

Ⓓ The relationship cannot be determined from the information given.

55.
$$x < 0 < y$$

Quantity A	Quantity B
x^2	$x - y$

Ⓐ The quantity in Column A is greater.

Ⓑ The quantity in Column B is greater.

Ⓒ The two quantities are equal.

Ⓓ The relationship cannot be determined from the information given.

56. Drawing a diagonal between opposite vertices of a quadrilateral creates two isosceles right triangles out of the original quadrilateral.

Quantity A	Quantity B
The number of square units of the area of the quadrilateral	The number of units of the perimeter of the quadrilateral

Ⓐ The quantity in Column A is greater.

Ⓑ The quantity in Column B is greater.

Ⓒ The two quantities are equal.

Ⓓ The relationship cannot be determined from the information given.

57. Used continuously at maximum speed, Pipe X can fill a silo with grain in 5 hours.

    Used continuously at maximum speed, Pipe Y can fill the same silo with grain in 2 hours.

Quantity A	Quantity B
The minimum number of minutes it will take both pipes to fill 35% of the silo	30

    Ⓐ The quantity in Column A is greater.
    Ⓑ The quantity in Column B is greater.
    Ⓒ The two quantities are equal.
    Ⓓ The relationship cannot be determined from the information given.

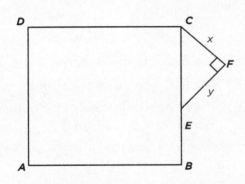

58.

Quantity A	Quantity B
$x^2 + y^2$	$\dfrac{p^2}{32}$

    Ⓐ The quantity in Column A is greater.
    Ⓑ The quantity in Column B is greater.
    Ⓒ The two quantities are equal.
    Ⓓ The relationship cannot be determined from the information given.

59. The first term of an infinite sequence of numbers is positive, and each term of the sequence other than the first term is $\frac{5}{12}$ of the previous term.

Quantity A	Quantity B
The ratio of the tenth term to the third term	$\dfrac{5^8}{12^8}$

    Ⓐ The quantity in Column A is greater.
    Ⓑ The quantity in Column B is greater.
    Ⓒ The two quantities are equal.
    Ⓓ The relationship cannot be determined from the information given.

60. When the positive integer t is divided by 36, the remainder is 30.

Quantity A	Quantity B
The remainder when $\frac{t}{3}$ is divided by 6	4

    Ⓐ The quantity in Column A is greater.
    Ⓑ The quantity in Column B is greater.
    Ⓒ The two quantities are equal.
    Ⓓ The relationship cannot be determined from the information given.

61.
    $$y > 0$$
    $$\sqrt{25x^4 + 40x^2y + 16y^2} = 5x^2 + y^2 - 8y + 35$$

Quantity A	Quantity B
y	3

    Ⓐ The quantity in Column A is greater.
    Ⓑ The quantity in Column B is greater.
    Ⓒ The two quantities are equal.
    Ⓓ The relationship cannot be determined from the information given.

62. The original price of a radio was $48.00. When the original price of the radio was decreased by x percent, the new price of the radio was $42.00.

Quantity A	Quantity B
x	14

    Ⓐ The quantity in Column A is greater.
    Ⓑ The quantity in Column B is greater.
    Ⓒ The two quantities are equal.
    Ⓓ The relationship cannot be determined from the information given.

63. $x \triangle y = x^2 + xy$

Quantity A	Quantity B
$5 \triangle 3$	$4 \triangle 5$

    Ⓐ The quantity in Column A is greater.
    Ⓑ The quantity in Column B is greater.
    Ⓒ The two quantities are equal.
    Ⓓ The relationship cannot be determined from the information given.

64. For all real numbers y, $\#y\# = \frac{y^2 + y}{2}$.

Quantity A	Quantity B
$\#(\#3\#)\#$	24

    Ⓐ The quantity in Column A is greater.
    Ⓑ The quantity in Column B is greater.
    Ⓒ The two quantities are equal.
    Ⓓ The relationship cannot be determined from the information given.

65. $\frac{27^x}{3^y} = 81$

Quantity A	Quantity B
$3x$	$y + 4$

    Ⓐ The quantity in Column A is greater.
    Ⓑ The quantity in Column B is greater.
    Ⓒ The two quantities are equal.
    Ⓓ The relationship cannot be determined from the information given.

66. The 360 seniors in a school are 30% of the total number of students in the school.

Quantity A	Quantity B
The total number of students in the school	1,080

    Ⓐ The quantity in Column A is greater.
    Ⓑ The quantity in Column B is greater.
    Ⓒ The two quantities are equal.
    Ⓓ The relationship cannot be determined from the information given.

67. $y = 6$

Quantity A	Quantity B
$2y^2 + y + 1$	80

    Ⓐ The quantity in Column A is greater.
    Ⓑ The quantity in Column B is greater.
    Ⓒ The two quantities are equal.
    Ⓓ The relationship cannot be determined from the information given.

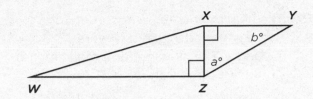

68.

Quantity A	Quantity B
The perimeter of a quadrilateral *WXYZ*	78

Ⓐ The quantity in Column A is greater.

Ⓑ The quantity in Column B is greater.

Ⓒ The two quantities are equal.

Ⓓ The relationship cannot be determined from the information given.

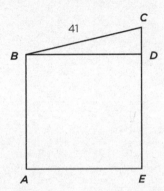

69.

Quantity A	Quantity B
The length of *CD*	10

Ⓐ The quantity in Column A is greater.

Ⓑ The quantity in Column B is greater.

Ⓒ The two quantities are equal.

Ⓓ The relationship cannot be determined from the information given.

70. The average (arithmetic mean) of a, b, c, d, and e is 61. The average (arithmetic mean) of c, d, and e is 43.

Quantity A	Quantity B
The average (arithmetic mean) of a and b	81

Ⓐ The quantity in Column A is greater.

Ⓑ The quantity in Column B is greater.

Ⓒ The two quantities are equal.

Ⓓ The relationship cannot be determined from the information given.

71.
$$5p + 6q = 74$$
$$q = 8$$

Quantity A	Quantity B
p	5

Ⓐ The quantity in Column A is greater.

Ⓑ The quantity in Column B is greater.

Ⓒ The two quantities are equal.

Ⓓ The relationship cannot be determined from the information given.

72.
$$7c + 5d = 81$$
$$5c + 2d = 50$$

Quantity A	Quantity B
$2c + 3d$	30

Ⓐ The quantity in Column A is greater.

Ⓑ The quantity in Column B is greater.

Ⓒ The two quantities are equal.

Ⓓ The relationship cannot be determined from the information given.

73.
$$a^2 + b^2 = 25$$
$$a^3 = -27$$

Quantity A	Quantity B
a	b

(A) The quantity in Column A is greater.
(B) The quantity in Column B is greater.
(C) The two quantities are equal.
(D) The relationship cannot be determined from the information given.

74.
$$x^2 - 8 = 17, \ x > 0$$

Quantity A	Quantity B
$-x$	-5

(A) The quantity in Column A is greater.
(B) The quantity in Column B is greater.
(C) The two quantities are equal.
(D) The relationship cannot be determined from the information given.

75. The high temperatures recorded for a five-day period in January were 35, 30, x, 32, and x. The average (arithmetic mean) of the five temperatures is 31.

Quantity A	Quantity B
The mode of the list of temperatures	29

(A) The quantity in Column A is greater.
(B) The quantity in Column B is greater.
(C) The two quantities are equal.
(D) The relationship cannot be determined from the information given.

Answers and explanations begin on the next page.

Answer Key

QUANTITATIVE COMPARISON PRACTICE

1.	C	26.	B	51.	D		
2.	B	27.	A	52.	A		
3.	D	28.	D	53.	C		
4.	B	29.	C	54.	B		
5.	A	30.	A	55.	A		
6.	D	31.	C	56.	D		
7.	D	32.	B	57.	C		
8.	A	33.	A	58.	B		
9.	B	34.	A	59.	A		
10.	D	35.	C	60.	C		
11.	B	36.	B	61.	A		
12.	D	37.	A	62.	B		
13.	B	38.	C	63.	A		
14.	A	39.	D	64.	B		
15.	B	40.	D	65.	C		
16.	B	41.	A	66.	A		
17.	B	42.	A	67.	B		
18.	C	43.	B	68.	B		
19.	B	44.	A	69.	B		
20.	D	45.	D	70.	A		
21.	A	46.	A	71.	A		
22.	B	47.	C	72.	A		
23.	B	48.	D	73.	D		
24.	B	49.	A	74.	C		
25.	D	50.	B	75.	C		

Answers and Explanations

QUANTITATIVE COMPARISON PRACTICE

1. C

Adding up all the angles in any triangle will result in 180°. The diagram shows that one of the angles is a right angle or 90°, which leaves 180 – 90 = 90 for the remaining two angles. The diagram also provides the value for the second angle, 65°, which leaves 90 – 65 = 25 for the final angle designated by x. If $x = 25$ then it is equal to (B), which is also 25. The correct answer is (C).

2. B

The most accurate way to solve this equation is to do the calculations and determine the property tax rate, or p. $p = \frac{5,500}{55,000}$ or 10%. With the value of p determined, (A) can be solved to be 65,000 × 10% = 6,500, which is less than 6,600, making the correct answer (B).

3. D

The equation for the area of a triangle is $\frac{1}{2}$ × base × height.

If h_1 and base$_1$ are the height and base, respectively, of triangle Q_1, and h_2 and base$_2$ are the height and base, respectively, of triangle Q_2, then since the areas of Q_1 and Q_2 are equal, we can say:

$$\frac{1}{2} \times h_1 \times \text{base}_1 = Q_1 = Q_2 = \frac{1}{2} \times h_2 \times \text{base}_2$$

$$h_1 \times \text{base}_1 = h_2 \times \text{base}_2$$

This is as far as we can go.

Many different values could work to satisfy the equation at this point, and you can simply plug in some values. If you put $h_1 = 2$ and $h_2 = 4$ then base$_1$ = 4 and base$_2$ = 2 or vice versa. It is true that, if you set $h_1 = h_2$, then base$_1$ = base$_2$, but we don't know whether or not $h_1 = h_2$. Thus, the correct answer is (D), the relationship cannot be determined from the information given.

4. B

It is necessary to know the formula for the area of a parallelogram, which is base × height. Note that while the base is one side of the parallelogram, the height is NOT the length of the other side. Do not be confused and use the product of the length of the two sides by mistake. In this question the maximum area of this parallelogram, which would be the case if it were a rectangle, would be 5 × 7 = 35. However, since we are given that angle ABC is greater than 90°, we know that this is not a rectangle, so the height *must* be less than 7, and thus the area will be less than 35. The correct answer is (B).

5. A

We are given two equations and need to find the values of both k and n. From the second equation, we know that $n = 9 – 4 = 5$. By plugging this value of n into the first equation, we are left with $k + 5 = 14$ and $k = 14 – 5 = 9$. The correct answer is (A), as $k = 9$ is greater than $n = 5$.

6. D

We are given the diameter of the circle as 20, however we are not given any information about the location of points A, B, C, and D. It might look like line segment AC is the diameter and that BC and CD are equal, but we cannot assume this. We also cannot assume that there are two right triangles.

One possibility would have B, C, and D being very close to each other on the circumference of the circle, such that the quadrilateral would have a tiny area, close to zero. This would make Column B bigger. All that remains is to determine if there is any way that Column A could be bigger: is there any way that the area of the quadrilateral could have an area greater than 80?

If *ABCD* were a square (again, we don't have to assume this is impossible just because of the way the diagram looks), it would have a diagonal equal to the diameter of the circle, which is 20.

A square with side *x* has a diagonal of $x\sqrt{2}$, so a diagonal of 20 means:

$$x\sqrt{2} = 20$$

$x = \dfrac{20}{(\sqrt{2})}$ = the side length of a square *ABCD*.

Since the area of the square is just (side length)², the area of a square *ABCD* would be:

$$\left[\frac{20}{\sqrt{2}}\right]^2 = \frac{400}{2} = 200$$

This tells us that the area could definitely be greater than 80, and Column A could be greater than Column B. Because more than one relationship between these quantities is possible, the correct answer is (D).

7. D

We can find the answer by plugging in values for the variables. Note that the question never specifies that *x*, *y* and *z* can't all be the same positive integer. It doesn't affect the answer to this question, but be careful about making assumptions the question doesn't allow you to make.

If the three positive integers happen to be 1, 2, and 3 for example, then (1)(2)(3) = 6 and 1 + 2 + 3 = 6, and the two columns would be equal to each other.

If the integers are 2, 3, and 4, however, then (2)(3)(4) = 24 and 2 + 3 + 4 = 9 so we'd

get a different result, with A being the greater quantity.

These examples show that the relative values of the sum and product can vary according to the numbers chosen. The correct answer is (D), not enough information.

8. A

If we count the joints and connectors in this figure, we come up with 11 joints and 10 connectors, making (A) the correct answer. There is no need to complicate this with a permutation or combination formula, as we must count them anyway.

9. B

The way to approach this is to list the factors of the numbers in columns A and B:

To *factor* a number means to break it up into numbers that can be multiplied together to get the original number (e.g. 6: 6, 3, 2, 1).

So for this question we have 15 and 14.

Factors are:

15 = 15, 5, 3, 1

14 = 14, 7, 2, 1

Since 7 is the greatest prime factor of 14, and it is greater than 5, which is 15's greatest prime factor, (B) is the correct answer.

10. D

Here we are given one angle of a triangle and one side length, leaving us with two unknown angles. Even though the angles and sides look similar, we cannot assume that they are equal, and therefore we cannot be sure what type of triangle it is. If we were given either of the other two angles we could get closer to an answer, but we cannot determine whether the side *AB* is the same as *BC*. The correct answer is (D), the relationship cannot be determined from the information given.

11. B

Because "break even" means that the net profit is equal to zero we can find the quantity in Column A by using the equation $2x^2 + 3x - 200 = 0$. If we find an x that produces a value greater than 0, we know that value for x is greater than the break-even x.

The easiest way to solve this is to plug 12 in to the formula and test the result, because you know that if 12 produces a value greater than 0, then the number of golf balls you need to break even is fewer than 12.

So $2 \times 12 \times 12 + 3 \times 12 - 200 = 124$. From this, we can deduce that the number of golf balls needed to break even, or make this equation equal to 0, is less than 12.

The correct answer is (B).

12. D

To find the answer we need to solve for x and y.

In column A we can solve for x by finding the cube root of 27, which is 3 (because $3 \times 3 \times 3 = 9 \times 3 = 27$). We know x has to be 3, but y could be 3 or –3, since you can square either of these and end up with positive 9. If y is 3, the two quantities are equal, but if y is –3, column A is greater.

The correct answer is (D).

13. B

In order to compare the columns, we must solve for h.

From the second statement, we know that $r + 1 = 6$, so r must equal 5.

Next, by plugging this into the equation above it, we get $h - 5 = 4$, so h must equal 9 by adding 5 to both sides. Because 9 is less than 11, the correct answer is (B).

14. A

We don't know Chase's exact salary, other than that it is greater than $20,000. We know that Chase's salary is 80% of Katy's salary, so it must be less than her salary.

Timan's salary is 80% of Chase's salary, which is less than Katy's salary, so Timan's salary must be less than Katy's salary.

The correct answer is (A).

15. B

The number line diagram is more of a distraction than anything else. The best way to approach finding a halfway point is simply to take the average.

To find the average, we need to sum the two values and divide by 2. To simplify the addition, we should find a common denominator.

$-\frac{1}{2}$ and $\frac{7}{4}$ have 4 as a common denominator, so they can be written as $-\frac{2}{4}$ and $\frac{7}{4}$. Next, add them to get $\frac{5}{4}$. The average is half of $\frac{5}{4}$, and $\frac{5}{4} \times \frac{1}{2} = \frac{5}{8}$.

Quantity B is $\frac{3}{4}$, which can be written as $\frac{6}{8}$, which is clearly greater than our Quantity A $\left(\frac{5}{8}\right)$. The correct answer is (B).

16. B

Although this is not drawn to scale, we are given some hints as to the relationships of each point. As D is the midpoint and BDA and CDA both have 90° angles, we know that there are two equal right angle triangles here which make up one isosceles (two equal sides) triangle. Given that BDA and CDA are mirror images of each other, $AC = AB$, and we can compare Column A and Column B by comparing AE to AB.

Using the Pythagorean theorem ($a^2 + b^2 = c^2$) we know:

$$AD^2 + BD^2 = AB^2$$
$$AD^2 + ED^2 = AE^2$$

AD^2 is common to both equations, so we can rearrange them to make them equal to each other:

$$AD^2 = AB^2 - BD^2$$
$$AD^2 = AE^2 - ED^2$$

So $AB^2 - BD^2 = AE^2 - ED^2$.

Since we know that $BD > ED$ (and that they are both positive values), we know that $BD^2 > ED^2$. In order for the above equality to hold, it follows that $AB^2 > AE^2$, and therefore that $AB > AE$. The correct answer is (B).

17. B

There are three right angles, and the two other angles are equal to one another.

If this odd-looking shape were to be made into one big triangle by "pushing back" the segment that is 3 long to line up with the h segment, this would make a right triangle with two sides of $h + 3$ and $w + 2$. Since the two non-right angles of the figure are equal to each other (measuring x degrees), our new triangle would also be an isosceles triangle, as any triangle with two equal angles is an isosceles triangle. This would mean that the two side lengths would have to be equal to each other as well, so we can set up this equation:

$h + 3 = w + 2 \Rightarrow$ subtract 3 from both sides:

$h + 3 - 3 = w + 2 - 3 \Rightarrow$

$h = w - 1$

From this, we can conclude that w is 1 greater than h; thus (B) is greater and the correct answer.

18. C

The simplest way to solve this might be to plug in an easy value to work with. Let's set $x = 10$. We can do this because it says "for all

numbers x." When we choose this number as x, we must substitute it for x anywhere in the equation and also put $24 - x$ wherever we see $x^{\#}$:

Column A: $24 - (24 - 10)$

Column B: 10

For A, we can simply do the math. Inside the parentheses is $24 - 10 = 14$, which gives us $24 - 14$ remaining. $24 - 14$ is 10, which is equal to B.

To do it algebraically we can just set it up the same way.

Column A: $24 - (24 - x)$

Column B: x

$24 - (24 - x)$ can be changed to $24 - 24 + x$ using the property $[a - (b - c)] = a - b + c$

So $24 - 24 + x \Rightarrow x$. So A $= x$ and B $= x$.

Either way you do it, the columns are equal and the correct answer is (C).

19. B

Column A reads "3 times the product of a and b" while column B reads "3 times a times 3 times b", so if it is not apparent that column B is a magnitude 3 times bigger than column A, we can plug values in for a and b and see the result.

Let's say $a = 2$ and $b = 3$, column A $= 3(2 \times 3) = 18$ and column B $= (3 \times 2)(3 \times 3) = 54$. Let's say $a = 5$ and $b = 1$: column A $= 3(5 \times 1) = 15$ and column B $= (3 \times 5)(3 \times 1) = 45$. Column B is consistently greater, so the correct answer is (B). This will be true for all values of a and b greater than 1.

20. D

We are given that x must be between 500 and 1,000.

The best way to solve for this one is to use two extreme variables for x, such as $x = 501$ and $x = 999$. It is always best to use extreme values when you are given a range, to test the limits of the range.

When $x = 501$, column A is equal to $1{,}000 - 501 = 499$ and column B equals $501 - 500 = 1$. so column A is bigger for this value.

When we use $x = 999$, we get $1{,}000 - 999 = 1$ for column A and $999 - 500 = 499$ for column B, so column B is greater in this case. We see that the relationship cannot be determined from the given information and the correct answer is (D).

21. A

Here we know that $LMNO$ is a parallelogram, with lines LO and MN being parallel and LM and ON being parallel.

Therefore, all the angles opposite one another in the parallelogram are equal (angle OLM is equal to MNO). With this information, we know that angle LMN is equal to LON.

Even though we don't know the exact value of these angles, we know that

$a - 17 = b + 4$

$a = b + 4 + 17$

$a = b + 21$, so angle a is greater than b and (A) is the correct answer choice.

22. B

Although we do not know the actual number of runs scored by team P in the second inning (let's label that amount P_2), we know that it is 10 more than team V scored in the second inning (V_2).

$V_1 = 5$

$P_2 = V_2 + 10$.

Let's say team V scored 0 runs in the second inning. V_2 would then be equal to 0, which makes the equation $P_2 = 0 + 10$ or $P = 10$.

That would make column B greater. The least amount team P could have scored in the

second inning is 10 (since team V can't score less than 0), which is more than 5.

The correct answer is (B).

23. B

The sum of the interior angles of a triangle are equal to 180 degrees. To solve for a, we must add all the like terms (they all have a), so $2a + 3a + 4a = 9a$.

Next, $9a = 180$, so $a = 20$.

Column B is bigger and the correct answer is (B).

24. B

Here, we are given $(-5,-6)$ in the third quadrant and the origin $(0,0)$ as points on this line. This is enough to give us the slope, which we can calculate easily using the formula $\dfrac{(y_2 - y_1)}{(x_2 - x_1)}$, where (x_1, y_1) and (x_2, y_2) are points on the line:

$$\frac{(0 - (-6))}{(0 - (-5))}$$

$$\Rightarrow \frac{(0 + 6)}{(0 + 5)}$$

$$\Rightarrow \frac{6}{5}$$

Since we know the y-intercept is at the origin, we can use slope-intercept form ($y = mx + b$) to generate the equation for our line as $y = \left(\frac{6}{5}\right)x + 0$, which just simplifies to $y = \left(\frac{6}{5}\right)x$.

Once we have this equation, we can see that, when x is positive, y is always greater. Since (c,d) is in the first quadrant, where x is positive, d will have to be greater than c, and Column B must be greater.

Choice (B) is the correct answer.

25. D

In order to get a product equal to zero, one of the amounts inside the parentheses must be equal to zero. In each of the equations, each of –6 and 6 can take the place of a and b to satisfy the equation to make it zero.

However, what we do not know is whether $a = 6$ or –6 and whether b equals –6 or 6. There is not enough information to establish a consistent relationship between Column A and Column B.

As an example, one possibility would have $a = 6$ and $b = -6$, which would be consistent with both equations. With these values, Column A would be 12 and Column B would be 0.

Another possibility would have $a = -6$ and $b = 6$, which leads to 0 for Column A and 12 for Column B.

These two different possibilities produce different relationships between Column A and Column B.

Therefore, the correct answer is (D).

26. B

We are given the average test scores for a certain class, but we are not given any information on how many boys and girls are in the class. However, we can use the information in the graph to make an equation to solve for the number of boys (or girls).

Use logic to find the answer: since the class average of 86 is closer to the 83 average of the girls than to the 92 average of the boys, there must be more girls, because the class average is more heavily influenced (weighted) by the girls' scores.

You can also solve mathematically:

Let's assume that there are 10 students in the class, so then the total score for the class is 86 × 10 or 860. Let x be the number of boys, and 10 – x be the number of girls.

$$
\begin{aligned}
x(92) + (10 - x)83 &= 860 \\
92x - 83x + 830 &= 860 \\
9x &= 30 \\
x &= 3.33 \\
\text{and } 10 - x &= 6.67
\end{aligned}
$$

This proves that there are more girls in the class. The correct answer is (B).

27. A

Since Ellen paid more for 5 pounds of coffee A than she did for 7 pounds of coffee B, the price per pound of coffee A must be greater.

You can also solve this with division. Set up the equations and figure out the per pound price.

A: $\dfrac{9.85}{5} = \dfrac{1.97}{\text{pound}}$

B: $\dfrac{8.33}{7} = \dfrac{1.19}{\text{pound}}$

The correct answer is (A).

28. D

To determine which column is greater, we would need to know the length of segment SW, and then determine if it is more than 2 × 3, since the area of the rectangle is $b \times h$ (3 × h), and the area of the triangle is $\frac{1}{2}b \times h$, and they share the same value for h.

Since we don't have enough information to determine the length of segment SW, we cannot determine the relationship, so the correct answer is (D).

29. C

We must solve for x and y in these simultaneous equations. To solve for y, the easiest way to solve is to multiply the bottom equation by –2 (because the top equation is $2x$) to get –$2x$ –$6y$ = –40. Now, we must add the two equations to get:

$$2x + 5y = 14$$
$$+ -2x - 6y = -40$$
$$\overline{0x - 1y = -26}$$

This is equal to $-y = -26$, so if you multiply both sides by -1 then $y = 26$. Now, to solve for x, we can plug y into any equation.

$$2x + 5(26) = 14$$
$$2x = -116$$
$$\text{so } x = -58.$$

Finally, add x and y to get $26+(-58) = -32$. The amounts are the same, so the correct answer is (C).

30. A

This is a system of equations problem that is solved by adding or subtracting the two equations to single out one variable.

$$a + b = 10$$
$$+a - b = 4$$
$$\overline{2a = 14} \Rightarrow \text{divide each side by 2}$$
$$a = \frac{14}{2} = 7$$

Now that we have a, we can plug 7 into either equation and solve for b:

$$7 + b = 10 \Rightarrow \text{substract 7 from both sides}$$
$$b = 10 - 7 = 3$$
$$a = 7$$
$$b = 3$$
$$a > b$$

The correct answer is (A).

31. C

Here we are shown an image with 6 different angles and then are given two equations to compare. To answer this question, we must know that all the angles opposite each other are equal. This is true for any opposite angles as a result of intersecting lines. Therefore in the diagram, angle x = angle v, angle y = angle u and angle z = angle t.

We also know that a straight line has 180 degrees in it; therefore, angles x, y, and z total to 180 degrees, just as angles t, u, and v do.

With this info, we know that $x + z + u = 180$ because angle u is equal to angle y. Also, $y + v + t = 180$ because y is equal to u. Therefore, both columns are the same; they both equal 180 degrees.

The correct answer is (C).

32. B

We are given a rectangle whose width is split into equal segments. Because the segments have equal widths, and each line starts and ends at the same height as the other, we know the line that spans more segments will be the longer one.

By looking at the diagram, we see that segment *BF* spans 3 of the segments while segment *EA* spans 4 of the segments. There is no further math needed; *EA* must be longer than *BF*.

The correct answer is (B).

33. A

The chart we are given shows the areas of five different lakes, and we are asked to see if the sum of the size of four smaller lakes is greater than the size of the largest one.

In order to answer this question, we simply need to look at the graph and see what the total area of the four smaller lakes is. By looking at the graph, we see that the sums of the four lakes are approximately $100 + 120 + 150 + 250 = 620$.

This is larger than the approximately 575 for the largest lake, so (A) is the answer.

34. A

For this, we are given a triangle and a quadrilateral and are asked to compare angle measurements.

Since we know that the angles in a triangle add up to 180 degrees, we can say $3x = 180$, so $x = 60$.

We also know that the angles of a quadrilateral sum to 360 degrees, so $4y = 360$, and $y = 90$.

We can now plug in the these values for x and y to arrive at a comparison.

Column A: $2(60) + 2(90) = 120 + 180 = 300$

Because 300 is greater than 270, the answer is (A).

35. C

We must first determine the total perimeter of the rectangle, then divide this amount by 4 (because a square has four equal sides) to find the sides of the square.

The perimeter of a rectangle is $2(l + w) = 2(10 + 8) = 36$.

Therefore, each side of the square is $\frac{36}{4} = 9$.

Now that we have the sides of the square, we can find the area by squaring the length of one side.

Area of square = $9^2 = 81$.

The quantities are equal; the answer is (C).

36. B

We are given that line *CAB* is the diameter of the circle, as *A* is the center. Also, we know that angle *NAM* is a right angle (even though it does not look like a 90-degree angle in the diagram), and, since sides *AM* and *AN* are both radii of the circle and therefore the same length, triangle *MAN* is a 45-45-90 triangle.

Let's use x for the radius of this circle.

Now let's find the ratio of *CB* to *NM*. Even though we are not given exact lengths, we can solve for this. We know that because the triangle is a 45-45-90 triangle, NM must be equal to $x\sqrt{2}$ (because it is opposite the 90-degree angle) and both *NA* and *MA* are of size x in length.

We also know that *CB* (the diameter) is equal to $2x$ (because a diameter is equal to 2 times the radius and *NA* and *MA* are radii). Therefore, the ratio is equal to $\frac{2x}{x\sqrt{2}}$.

We can cancel out the x's to get $\frac{2}{\sqrt{2}}$, which equals $\sqrt{2}$.

Since the root of any integer greater than 1 must be less than that integer, $\sqrt{2}$ must be less than 2. Thus, the correct answer is (B).

37. A

To calculate this, we must sum all of the cash she paid for the surfboard on the installment plan and then subtract the cash price.

Down payment: $170

24 payments of $23: $552

Total: $722

Difference: $722 – $650 = $72

72 > 71, so A > B; the answer is (A).

38. C

We need to set up the equation to calculate the perimeter of the rectangle and then compare it to $x + 4$.

Perimeter of rectangle: $2(x + 8 + x) \Rightarrow 2(2x + 8) \Rightarrow 4x + 16$

Since the square has the same perimeter as the rectangle, we know that the perimeter divided by 4 is the length of any side of the square. So the length of a side of square A:

$$\frac{(4x + 16)}{4} = x + 4$$

Thus, Column A equals Column B, so the correct answer is (C).

39. D

Since this should work with any values that fit the $0 < x < y < z$ inequality, let's start by plugging in some values:

$0 < 1 < 2 < 3$

A: $\frac{2}{1} = 2$

B: $\frac{3}{2} = 1.5$

So, in this case A is larger, but let's try changing z to 10, which still fits the inequality:

A: $\frac{2}{1} = 2$

B: $\frac{10}{2} = 5$

Now B is larger, which means that we cannot be sure, thus (D) is the correct answer.

40. D

Here we are given two numbers raised to the exponent x; however, we don't know if x is positive or negative. This should be a red flag for you immediately.

If x is a positive number greater than 1, then column B will be larger.

We can test this. Say $x = 2$

Column A = $2^2 = 4$ and Column B = $3^2 = 9$

But say x is –2.

Column A = $\left(\frac{1}{2^2}\right) = \frac{1}{4}$ and B = $\left(\frac{1}{3^2}\right) = \frac{1}{9}$. In this case, A is bigger.

Thus, we cannot determine with the information given and the answer is (D).

41. A

There is a much quicker way to solve this than to manually add up all the numbers. Use logic to determine that the set of numbers described in Column A is the same as the set

in Column B, except that Column B is missing 19, 20, and 21. Therefore, Column A's set must sum to a greater number.

The answer is (A).

42. A

The equation makes it clear that both x and y are positive numbers (greater than zero) and y is the greater of the two. Because both of the numbers are positive and y is greater than x, $\frac{x}{y}$ has to be less than 1 and $\frac{y}{x}$ has to be greater than 1, making Column A greater.

For example if $x = 1$ and $y = 2$, then $\frac{1}{2} < \frac{2}{1}$.

The correct answer is (A).

43. B

To solve this question, you must isolate $x + y$. The easiest way to do this is to set up an equation that is given to us:

$\frac{(x + y + 12)}{3} = 8 \Rightarrow x + y + 12 = 24 \Rightarrow x + y = 12$

$\frac{12}{2} = 6$, which is less than 8.

The correct answer is (B).

44. A

We know that both squares have sides of length 6, so the area of each square is $6^2 = 36$.

The area of the triangle is half of one of the squares, so the area of the triangle must be $\frac{(6 \times 6)}{2} = 18$. Then, to find the area of the shaded region, we take 18 plus the area of the shaded square to get $18 + 36 = 54$.

Column A is larger, since $36 + 18$ is greater than $36 + 16$.

The correct answer is (A).

45. D

We cannot calculate the perimeter of the triangle. All we know is that the triangle has 2 sides of 5 (2 radii), but we don't know the value of the third side. We cannot calculate it because we don't know if it's a right triangle.

We do know that the circumference (the perimeter) of the circle is equal to $2 \times \pi \times$ radius $= 2 \times 5 \times \pi = 10\pi$, so half the perimeter is 5π. However, we cannot assume that the third side of the triangle is more or less than 5 (even though it looks similar), so we don't have enough information to determine which column is larger.

If you're unsure here, pick some values for the third (non-radius) side of the triangle (let's call it s):

if s is 1, then our perimeter is $1 + 5 + 5 = 7$

if s is 9, then our perimeter is $9 + 5 + 5 = 19$

Half the perimeter of the circle is 5π, or about 5×3.14, which is between 15 and 16. Thus, depending on the length of s, either column might be larger.

The correct answer is (D).

46. A

In order to compare the columns, we must solve for h.

From the second statement, we know that $r + 3 = 6$, so r must equal 3.

Next, by plugging this into the equation above it, we get $h - 3 = 6$, so h must equal 9.

Because 9 is greater than 8.5, the correct answer is (A).

47. C

Here we have 3 straight lines that intersect.

A straight line has a measurement of 180 degrees. Angle y and the angle opposite it, z, are called vertically opposite angles, and such angles are always equal. Thus, $180 - z$ and $180 - y$ must be the same amount if y and z are equal.

Angle x here is merely a distraction; it is not relevant to our solution.

The correct answer is (C).

48. D

Let's pick numbers for this one. Remember, if we can choose two sets of numbers that give us different outcomes, then the answer will be (D).

If $x = 1$, $y = 1$, and $z = 1$, then the two columns are equal.

However we can also choose a value to make one column greater.

If $x = -3$, $y = 1$, and $z = 1$, then we can solve for Column A:

$|(x + y + z)|$

$|(-3) + (1) + (1)| =$

$|-1| = 1$

and Column B:

$|x| + |y| + |z|$

$|-3| + |1| + |1| =$

$3 + 1 + 1 = 5$

In this case, Column B would be larger.

The correct answer is (D).

49. A

To solve this question, let's use the formula for the sum of a geometric series:

$$\text{Sum} = \frac{a\left(1 - r^n\right)}{1 - r}$$

a = first term

r = ratio between terms (second term divided by the first term)

n = number of terms

Now let's look at the given equation for a moment. We are told that x = # of terms in the sequence. If we plug in $x = 1$, we find that the first term is $\frac{1}{2}$. If we plug in $x = 2$, we find that the second term in the sequence is $\frac{-1}{4}$.

The ratio is the second term divided by the first term:

$$\frac{\frac{-1}{4}}{\frac{1}{2}}$$

$r = \frac{-1}{2}$

So, for this question $a = \frac{1}{2}$, $r = \frac{-1}{2}$, and $n = 10$.

$$S = \frac{1}{2} \times \frac{\left(1 - \frac{-1}{2}^{10}\right)}{\left(1 - \frac{-1}{2}\right)}$$

$$S = \frac{1}{2} \times \frac{\left(1 - \frac{1}{1,024}\right)}{\frac{3}{2}}$$

$$S = \frac{\left(\frac{1,023}{1,024}\right)}{3}$$

From here we can estimate. $\frac{1,023}{1,024} =$ approximately 1, so $S \approx \frac{1}{3}$.

Since $\frac{1}{3}$ is larger than $\frac{1}{4}$, the answer is (A).

50. B

Here it might help to draw a picture to visualize. The surface area of a square cube is the area of one of the sides multiplied by six. Here we know the cube of cheese has a side length of 2 inches.

The surface area is $2 \times 2 \times 6 = 24$.

When the cube is cut into 2 equal pieces, it makes two rectangular blocks. Four of the sides of each block will have the dimensions 1 × 2, and two of the sides will have the dimension 2 × 2.

The new total surface area will be 32, since cutting the block in half creates two new surfaces, each with the dimension 2 × 2.

Only the two new surfaces will have no rind on them, and to find their total we merely add the areas of those sides: 4 + 4 = 8.

$$\frac{8}{32} = \frac{1}{4} = 25\%$$

Column B is larger, therefore the correct answer is (B).

51. D

To find the volume of a rectangular solid, we use the formula:

$$Vol = l \times w \times h$$

Without knowing the width of the rectangular box, it is impossible to determine a numerical value for Column A. It may have occurred to you that that the width must have a positive numerical value. Remember that you multiply the width by 96 to get the volume. Depending on whether the width is greater than or less than 1, the volume will be greater than or less than 96.

Therefore the answer is (D).

52. A

The equation for the volume of a right cylinder is: area of base × height = $\pi r^2 \times h$

If Cylinder B has radius r and height h, then Cylinder A has radius $2r$ and height $\frac{1}{2}h$.

The volume of Cylinder B: $V_B = \pi r^2 \times h$

The volume of Cylinder A:

$$V_A = \pi(2r)^2 \times \left(\frac{1}{2}\right)h = \pi\left(4r^2\right)\left(\frac{1}{2}h\right) = 2\pi r^2 \times h$$

Cylinder B's volume is $\pi r^2 h$, and Cylinder A's volume is $2\pi r^2 h$. Cylinder A has twice the volume of Cylinder B and is therefore greater.

The correct answer is (A).

53. C

Here it is helpful to draw a picture to visualize the cylinder:

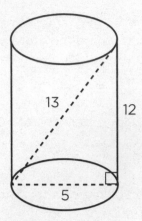

The longest distance between any two points in a right circular cylinder must be the distance from one point of the circumference to the farthest point on the other base's circumference. This becomes the hypotenuse of a right triangle.

Since we are told that the height and diameter are positive integers, and the height is greater than the diameter, we can recognize that this must be the common 5: 12: 13 right triangle ratio (Pythagorean triplet), making the height 12 and the diameter 5. The radius is half of the diameter, $\frac{5}{2}$.

Now we can find the volume using the formula:

$$Vol = \pi \times r^2 \times h$$

$$Vol = \pi \times \left(\frac{5}{2}\right)^2 \times (12)$$

$$Vol = \pi \times \frac{25}{4} \times (12)$$

$$Vol = 75\pi$$

The columns are equal.

The correct answer is (C).

54. B

Examine each column individually.

For Column A, we are choosing a ruby out of 14 possible gemstones. It can be any of the 6 rubies, so the probability is $\frac{6}{14} = \frac{3}{7}$. Then we are choosing a second ruby, but this time we only have 5 rubies to choose out of 13 total gemstones remaining, so $\frac{5}{13}$. Since we want both events to occur, we must multiply them together to find the probability:

$$\frac{3}{7} \times \frac{5}{13} = \frac{15}{91}$$

For Column B, we want our first stone to be an emerald, and 8 out of the 14 stones are emeralds, so the probability is $\frac{8}{14} = \frac{4}{7}$. For the second stone, we want a ruby. We have 6 rubies to choose from out of 13 possible stones, so the probability is $\frac{6}{13}$. Now we multiply them together to get the probability of both events occurring:

$$\frac{4}{7} \times \frac{6}{13} = \frac{24}{91}$$

You could bypass all of these calculations merely by noticing that there are more emeralds than rubies, which means the probability of picking an emerald and a ruby must be greater than the probability of picking two rubies.

Column B is greater, so the answer is (B).

55. A

The value of x^2 is greater than 0 for all values of x, so Quantity A is positive. The value in column B is negative, so (A) is the correct choice.

56. D

The relationship between the quantities cannot be determined. If a diagonal divides a quadrilateral into two isosceles right triangles, then the quadrilateral must be a square.

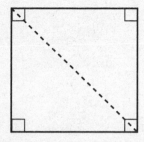

This is an important step because it tells us which area formula to use when simplifying Quantity A. Area = side × side. Also, because all four sides of a square are congruent, perimeter = 4 × side.

Which is greater, the number of square units of the area or the number of units of the perimeter, depends on what numbers we pick for each side of the square. We're not given any information about the length of the diagonal (which is also the hypotenuse of each isosceles triangle), so we can pick any positive number for the side length of the square.

If $s = 10$, the area of the square is 100 and the perimeter is 40. But if $s = 1$, the area of the square is 1, and the perimeter is 4. Therefore, it is impossible to compare these two quantities. Choice (D) is correct.

57. C

Rate = $\frac{\text{Work}}{\text{Time}}$, and we know the work (1 silo to fill) and the time required for each pipe to fill the silo, so we can plug in the numbers and find the relevant maximum rates:

$$\text{max rate of pipe X} = \frac{1\,\text{silo}}{5\,\text{hours}}$$

$$= \frac{1}{5}\ \text{of a silo per hour}$$

$$\text{max rate of pipe Y} = \frac{1\,\text{silo}}{2\,\text{hours}}$$

$$= \frac{1}{2}\ \text{of a silo per hour}$$

Since the minimum number of minutes will occur when both pipes are working at their maximum rates, we must add these two rates to find the total maximum rate:

$$\frac{1}{5}(\text{rate of Pipe X}) + \frac{1}{2}(\text{rate of Pipe Y})$$

$$= \frac{1}{2} + \frac{1}{5}$$

$$= \frac{5}{10} + \frac{2}{10}$$

$$= \frac{7}{10}\ \text{of a silo per hour}$$

If both pipes working together at their maximum rates would fill 70% of the silo in an hour, they would fill 35% of a silo in 30 minutes. Therefore, the quantities are equal and the correct answer is (C).

58. B

In looking at the columns, we can see that Column A is really one part of the Pythagorean formula, and because of this, it is equal to the square of the length of the hypotenuse of a right triangle where x and y form the remaining sides.

The diagram shows that x and y are both legs of right ΔFCE, with the remaining side being the hypotenuse CE. The Pythagorean formula can be used with this triangle so that Column A is equal to CE^2, the square of the hypotenuse of ΔFCE. Because E is the midpoint of one side, we know that CE will be equal to half the length of one side of the square.

Since the perimeter of square $ABCD$ is p, one side of the square must be $\frac{p}{4}$. $CE = \frac{1}{2}CB$, so $CE = \frac{1}{2}\left(\frac{p}{4}\right) = \frac{p}{8}$. Column A is CE^2, which is $\left(\frac{p}{8}\right)^2$, which is $\frac{p^2}{64}$. This is less than $\frac{p^2}{32}$. Column B is greater, and the correct answer is (B).

59. A

Let's say that the first term of the sequence is a_1, the second term of the sequence is a_2, the third term of the sequence is a_3 ... and the 10th term of the sequence is a_{10}.

The centered information says: $a_2 = \frac{5}{12}a_1$, $a_3 = \frac{5}{12}a_2$, $a_4 = \frac{5}{12}a_3$ ... and $a_{10} = \frac{5}{12}a_9$.

If we work with the equations $a_2 = \frac{5}{12}a_1$ and $a_3 = \frac{5}{12}a_2$, we can substitute $\frac{5}{12}a_1$ for a_2 in the equation $a_3 = \frac{5}{12}a_2$. We then have:

$$a_3 = \frac{5}{12}\left(\frac{5}{12}a_1\right) = \left(\frac{5}{12}\right)^2 a_1.$$

If we think about how each term after the first term is related to the first term, we see that to go from the first term, which is a_1, to the nth term, where n is a positive integer greater than 1, we must multiply a_1 by $n-1$ factors of $\frac{5}{12}$. Thus, if n is an integer: $a_n = a_1\left(\frac{5}{12}\right)^{n-1}$.

For the tenth term, which is a_{10}, we have:

$$a_{10} = a_1\left(\frac{5}{12}\right)^{10-1} = a_1\left(\frac{5}{12}\right)^9$$

The ratio of the 10th term to the third term:

$$\frac{a_{10}}{a_3} = \frac{a_1\left(\frac{5}{12}\right)^9}{a_1\left(\frac{5}{12}\right)^2} = \frac{\left(\frac{5}{12}\right)^9}{\left(\frac{5}{12}\right)^2}$$

We will now rewrite $\dfrac{\left(\frac{5}{12}\right)^9}{\left(\frac{5}{12}\right)^2}$ by using the law of exponents that says that, to divide powers with the same base, we subtract the exponent of the denominator from the exponent of the numerator and keep the same base (that is, $\frac{b^x}{b^y} = b^{x-y}$).

$$\frac{a_{10}}{a_3} = \frac{\left(\frac{5}{12}\right)^9}{\left(\frac{5}{12}\right)^2} = \left(\frac{5}{12}\right)^{9-2} = \left(\frac{5}{12}\right)^7.$$

So Quantity A is $\left(\frac{5}{12}\right)^7$.

Another law of exponents tells us that $\left(\frac{a}{b}\right)^n = \frac{a^n}{b^n}$, so Quantity B = $\frac{5^8}{12^8} = \left(\frac{5}{12}\right)^8$.

Now that we see Quantity A is $\left(\frac{5}{12}\right)^7$ and Quantity B is $\left(\frac{5}{12}\right)^8$. Since $\frac{5}{12}$ is a positive fraction less than 1, $\left(\frac{5}{12}\right)^7$ is greater than $\left(\frac{5}{12}\right)^8$ and Quantity A is greater. Choice (A) is correct.

60. C

Since the remainder when t is divided by 36 is 30, we can say that $t = 36n + 30$, where n is a non-negative integer. Since $t = 36n + 30$:

$$\Rightarrow \frac{t}{3} = \frac{36n + 30}{3}$$

$$\Rightarrow \frac{t}{3} = 12n + 10$$

$$\Rightarrow \frac{t}{3} = 12n + 10.$$

Let's find the remainder when $12n + 10$ is divided by 6. Now 12 is a multiple of 6 ($12 = 2 \times 6$) and n is an integer. Therefore $12n$ is a multiple of 6. Since $12n$ is a multiple of 6. the remainder when $12n$ is divided by 6 is 0. When 10 is divided by 6, the quotient is 1 and the remainder is 4.

Thus, the remainder when $12n$ is divided by 6 is 0 and the remainder when 10 is divided by 6 is 4. So the remainder when $12n + 10$ is divided by 6 is $0 + 4 = 4$. The quantities in both columns are equal and choice (C) is correct.

61. A

We have the algebraic identity $(a + b)^2 = a^2 + 2ab + b^2$.

Let's take apart the expression on the left side of the equation of the centered information. Underneath the radical sign, we have:

$25x^4 + 40x^2y + 16y^2$

$\Rightarrow (5x^2)^2 + 40x^2y + (4y)^2$.

If we think of $5x^2 = a$ and $4y = b$, we can rewrite this expression in the form $(a + b)^2$:

$\Rightarrow (5x^2)^2 + 40x^2y + (4y)^2$

$\Rightarrow (5x^2)^2 + 2(20x^2y) + (4y)^2$

$\Rightarrow (5x^2)^2 + 2(5x^2)(4y) + (4y)^2$

$\Rightarrow (5x^2 + 4y)^2$.

Thus, $25x^4 + 40x^2y + 16y^2 = (5x^2 + 4y)^2$. So we can replace $25x^4 + 40x^2y + 16y^2$ with $(5x^2 + 4y)^2$ in this equation:

$\sqrt{25x^4 + 40x^2y + 16y^2} = 5x^2 + y^2 - 8y + 35$

of the centered information.

This equation becomes

$\sqrt{\left(5x^2 + 4y\right)^2} = 5x^2 + y^2 - 8y + 35.$

Now let's recall the radical convention. If $z > 0$, then $\sqrt{z}$ means the positive square root of z. Since x^2 is always nonnegative, $5x^2$ is nonnegative. The question stem says that $y > 0$. So $4y > 0$. Since $5x^2$ is nonnegative and $4y$ is positive, $5x^2 + 4y$ is positive.

Because of this, we can replace $\sqrt{\left(5x^2 + 4y\right)^2}$ with $(5x^2 + 4y)$:

$\sqrt{\left(5x^2 + 4y\right)^2} = 5x^2 + y^2 - 8y + 35 \Rightarrow$

$5x^2 + 4y = 5x^2 + y^2 - 8y + 35 \Rightarrow$ Subtract $5x^2$ from both sides:

$4y = y^2 - 8y + 35 \Rightarrow$ Subtract $4y$ from both sides:

$0 = y^2 - 12y + 35 \Rightarrow$ Factor using reverse FOIL:

$0 = y^2 - 12y + 35 = (y - 5)(y - 7)$

If $(y - 5)(y - 7) = 0$, then $y - 5 = 0$ or $y - 7 = 0$, so the possible values of y are 5 and 7. If $y = 5$, then the quantity in Quantity A is greater than the quantity 3 in Quantity B. If $y = 7$, then the quantity in Quantity A is again greater than the quantity 3 in Quantity B. Thus, the quantity in Quantity A is always greater. Choice (A) is correct.

62. B

The formula for percent decrease is:

$$\frac{\text{Original value} - \text{New value}}{\text{Original value}} \times 100\%.$$

When the price is decreased from \$48.00 to \$42.00, the percent decrease is:

$$\frac{\$48.00 - \$42.00}{\$48.00} \times 100\% = \frac{6}{48} \times 100\%$$

$$= \frac{1}{8} \times 100\%$$

$$= \frac{100}{8}\%$$

$$= 12\frac{1}{2}\%$$

Therefore, Quantity A = $x = 12\frac{1}{2}$ and Quantity B is 14. Quantity B is greater, so choice (B) is correct.

63. A

Let's find the value of Quantity A. Using the defining equation $x \triangle y = x^2 + xy$, let's replace x with 5 and let's replace y with 3. Then $5 \triangle 3 = 5^2 + (5)(3) = 25 + 15 = 40$. Quantity A is 40.

Let's find the value of Quantity B. Using the defining equation $x \triangle y = x^2 + xy$, let's replace x with 4 and let's replace y with 5. Then $4 \triangle 5 = 4^2 + (4)(5) = 16 + 20 = 36$. Quantity B is 36.

Quantity A is 40 and Quantity B is 36. Quantity A is greater and choice (A) is correct.

64. B

Let's begin by finding #3#, which is inside the parentheses. Let's use the defining equation #y# = $\frac{y^2+y}{2}$. Replacing y with 3, we have #3# = $\frac{3^2+3}{2}$ = $\frac{9+3}{2}$ = $\frac{12}{2}$ = 6. Thus, #(#3#)# = #6#.

Let's use the defining equation #y# = $\frac{y^2+y}{2}$ again. Replacing y with 6, we have #6# = $\frac{6^2+6}{2}$ = $\frac{36+6}{2}$ = $\frac{42}{2}$ = 21. Thus, #(#3#)# = 21. Quantity A is 21 and Quantity B is 24. Quantity B is greater and choice (B) is correct.

65. C

Let's try to rewrite the equation of the centered information so that all the powers have the same base.

We have that:

$27 = 3 \times 9 = 3 \times 3 \times 3 = 3^3$

$81 = 3 \times 27 = 3 \times 3 \times 9 = 3 \times 3 \times 3 \times 3 = 3^4$

Now let's replace 27 with 3^3 and 81 with 3^4 in $\frac{27^x}{3^y}$ = 81. We then have $\frac{\left(3^3\right)^x}{3^y}$ = 3^4.

When we raise a power to an exponent, we multiply the exponents and keep the same base. Algebraically, $(b_a)c = b_{ac}$. Therefore $(3^3)x = 3^{3x}$. Then the equation $\frac{\left(3^3\right)^x}{3^y}$ = 3^4 can be rewritten as $\frac{3^{3x}}{3^y}$ = 3^4.

When we divide powers with the same base, we subtract from the exponent of the numerator the exponent of the denominator and keep the same base. Algebraically, $\frac{b^a}{b^c} = b^{a-c}$.

Therefore, $\frac{3^{3x}}{3^y}$ = 3^{3x-y}. The equation $\frac{3^{3x}}{3^y}$ = 3^4 can be rewritten 3^{3x-y} = 3^4.

When equal powers have the same base, where that same base is a number other than 1, 0, or –1, the exponents must be equal. The equal powers 3^{3x-y} and 3^4 have the same base 3, so the exponents $3x - y$ and 4 must be equal. Thus, $3x - y = 4$. If we add y to both sides of the equation $3x - y = 4$, we have $3x = y + 4$. The quantities $3x$ in Quantity A and $y + 4$ in Quantity B are equal. Choice (C) is correct.

66. A

Let's say that the total number of students in the school is t. Then the number of seniors in the school, 360, is 30% of t. The decimal equivalent of 30% is 0.3. Therefore, $0.3t = 360$. So:

$$t = \frac{360}{0.3} = \frac{360 \times 10}{0.3 \times 10} = \frac{3,600}{3} = 1,200.$$

The quantity in Quantity A is 1,200 and the quantity in Quantity B is 1,080. Quantity A is greater, so choice (A) is correct.

67. B

Let's substitute 6 for y in the expression $2y^2 + y + 1$:

$2(6^2) + 6 + 1$

$2(36) + 6 + 1$

$72 + 6 + 1$

$78 + 1 = 79$.

Quantity A is 79 and Quantity B is 80. Quantity B is greater, so choice (B) is correct.

68. B

The perimeter of quadrilateral $WXYZ$ is $WX + XY + YZ + WZ$. We must find the lengths of YZ and WZ.

The sum of the degree measures of the angles in any triangle is 180 degrees. In triangle XYZ, we have:

$a + b + 90 = 180$

⇒ $a + b = 90$.

Since $a = 2b$, let's substitute $2b$ for a in the equation $a + b = 90$:

⇒ $2b + b + 90$

⇒ $3b = 90$

⇒ $b = \frac{90}{3} = 30$.

Since $a = 2b$, $a = 2(30) = 60$. So triangle XYZ is a 30 60 90 right triangle. In a 30-60-90 right triangle, the ratio of the side lengths to each other is $1 : \sqrt{3} : 2$. Side XY, whose length is $7\sqrt{3}$ is opposite the angle whose measure is $a = 60$ degrees. So side XZ, which is opposite the angle whose measure is $b = 30$ degrees, must have a length of $\frac{7\sqrt{3}}{\sqrt{3}} = 7$. Then side YZ, which is the hypotenuse of right triangle XYZ, must have a length of $2(7) = 14$.

Now let's look at triangle WXZ in order to try to find the length of WZ. We are given that the hypotenuse WX of this right triangle is 25 and we have found when working with triangle XYZ that the length of leg XZ is 7. We can use the Pythagorean theorem in right triangle WXZ to find the one missing side of our quadrilateral, WZ. We have:

$$
\begin{aligned}
(WX)^2 &= (XZ)^2 + (WZ)^2 \\
25^2 &= 7^2 + (WZ)^2 \\
625 &= 49 + (WZ)^2 \\
576 &= (WZ)^2
\end{aligned}
$$

Since lengths are never negative, $WZ = \sqrt{576} = 24$.

So we know that $WX = 25$, $XY = 7\sqrt{3}$, $YZ = 14$, and $WZ = 24$. So the perimeter of the quadrilateral is:

$25 + 7\sqrt{3} + 14 + 24 = 63 + 7\sqrt{3}$ = approximately 75.1 = Quantity A.

Quantity B is 78, so Quantity B is greater. Choice (B) is correct.

69. B

The area of a square is its side squared. Since the area of the square in this question is 1,600, the length of a side of this square is $\sqrt{1,600} = 40$. In particular, the length of side BD of the square, which is a leg of right triangle BCD, is 40. Now we can use the Pythagorean theorem in right triangle BCD to find the length of CD. We have:

$$
\begin{aligned}
(BC)^2 &= (BD)^2 + (CD)^2 \\
41^2 &= 40^2 + (CD)^2 \\
1,681 &= 1,600 + (CD)^2 \\
81 &= (CD)^2
\end{aligned}
$$

Since lengths are never negative, $CD = \sqrt{81} = 9$. Quantity A is 9 and Quantity B is 10. Quantity B is greater, so choice (B) is correct.

70. A

The average formula is Average $= \frac{\text{Sum of the terms}}{\text{Number of terms}}$. In solving this question, we will use this formula in the rearranged form Sum of the terms = Average × Number of terms. Since the average of a, b, c, d, and e is 61, the sum of a, b, c, d, and e, which is $a + b + c + d + e$, is $61 × 5 = 305$. Since the average of c, d, and e is 43, the sum of c, d, and e, which is $c + d + e$, is $43 × 3 = 129$. So the sum of a and b, which is $a + b$ is equal to $(a + b + c + d + e) - (c + d + e) = 305 - 129 = 176$. So the average of a and b is $\frac{a+b}{2} = \frac{176}{2} = 88$. Quantity A is 88 and Quantity B is 81. Quantity A is greater, so choice (A) is correct.

71. A

Let's try to find the value of p. Let's substitute 8 for q in the equation $5p + 6q = 74$. Then $5p + 6(8) = 74$, $5p + 48 = 74$, $5p = 26$, and $p = \frac{26}{5} = 5\frac{1}{5}$. So Quantity A is $5\frac{1}{5}$ and Quantity B is 5. Quantity A is greater, so choice (A) is correct.

72. A

We could solve the two equations for the values of c and d and then substitute these values into the expression $2c + 3d$ of Quantity A; however, there is a faster way to solve this question. We can subtract the corresponding sides of the equation $5c + 2d = 50$ from the corresponding sides of the equation $7c + 5d = 81$:

$$\begin{array}{rcl} 7c + 5d & = & 81 \\ - (5c + 2d & = & 50) \\ \hline 2c + 3d & = & 31 \end{array}$$

The number on the right side of the equation is the value of Quantity A, since it is equal to $2c + 3d$.

Thus, Quantity A, which is $2c + 3d$, is 31, and Quantity B is 30. Quantity A is greater, so choice (A) is correct.

73. D

Because a cube always has the same sign as its cube root, we can tell from the second equation that a is negative. Since the cube root of 27 is 3, $a = -3$. Plugging this into the first equation, we find:

$$\begin{array}{rcl} -3^2 + b^2 & = & 25 \\ 9 + b^2 & = & 25 \\ b^2 & = & 16 \\ b & = & 4 \text{ or } -4 \end{array}$$

Since one of the possible values is greater than a, and one is less than a, we can't tell for sure which is greater, a or b.

The correct answer is (D).

74. C

Because $x^2 = 25$, $x = 5$ or $x = -5$. Because $x > 0$, $x = 5$. Quantity A is $-x = -5$. The quantities are equal, so the correct answer is (C).

75. C

Remember the definition of mode: the value that occurs most often in a group of terms. In this case then, the mode is x, as it occurs at least twice (and possibly three times, if it turns out to be one of 30, 32, or 35). So the quantity in Quantity A is x, and you are comparing x with 29 in Quantity B.

You are given the average and a group of terms. Find the value of the unknown terms by using the average formula:
$\frac{35 + 30 + x + 32 + x}{5} = 31$, or $\frac{97 + 2x}{5} = 31$.

Multiplying both sides by 5 gives you $97 + 2x = 155$. Subtracting 97 from both sides gives $2x = 58$; dividing both sides by 2 gives you $x = 29$. The quantities are equal, so the answer is (C).

Chapter 4

Analytical Writing Assessment

GRE Analytical Writing Section Overview

The Analytical Writing section assesses not only how well you write, but also the thought processes you employ to formulate and articulate a position. Your analytical and critical thinking skills will be tested by questions that ask you to evaluate complex arguments and form an argument of your own. The goal of the Analytical Writing section is to make the test an accurate indicator of your ability to understand and formulate an argument, and to assess your reasoning skills. These skills are exactly those you will need to perform well as a student at the graduate level.

The Analytical Writing section consists of two separately timed tasks:

- **A 30-Minute Issue Essay**

  The Issue task will provide a brief quotation on an issue of general interest and instructions on how to respond. You must evaluate the issue and develop your own argument with support for your side of the issue.

- **A 30-Minute Argument Essay**

  The Argument task will contain a short argument that may or may not be complete, and specific instructions on how to respond. It requires you to analyze and critique an argument. You must evaluate the logical soundness of the argument presented in the prompt rather than take a side.

You can (and should) outline your essays on scratch paper, but your final answer must be typed into the computer before the end of the timed segment in order to receive a grade for your work.

The essay scoring for the Analytical Writing sections is holistic, which means that the graders base your score on their overall impression of your essay, rather than deducting specific point values for errors. The scoring scale is from 0 to 6, with 6 being the highest score. Two graders will read and score each essay. If their scores differ by more than one point, a third reader will also score the essay. Although the Analytical Writing section comprises two separate essays, you will receive a single score that represents the average of your scores for the two essays, rounded up to the nearest half-point.

Argument Essays

Note: Grockit does not provide feedback on these essays. This prompt is for your independent practice. We recommend taking 30 minutes to respond to this prompt in a word-processing program. Then use the sample and feedback provided to assess your own writing.

1. In 1992, many farmers in Jalikistan began using a hormone designed to produce larger cows that would produce more milk. Since then, childhood obesity in Jalikistan has grown by 200 percent. The amount of milk and dairy consumed by children in this area has not increased or decreased. Children in the same area who are lactose intolerant, and who drink almond milk or soy milk, have not had the same increase in childhood obesity. The only clear explanation is that the introduction of the hormone is responsible for the increase in childhood obesity in that area.

   Write a response in which you discuss one or more viable alternatives to the proposed explanation. Justify, with support, why the alternatives could rival the proposed explanation and explain how those explanation(s) can plausibly account for the facts presented in the argument.

2. Several charitable organizations in Pleasantville provide opportunities for teenagers to engage in community service. These organizations have a great need for volunteers, but in recent years, the number of teenage volunteers has significantly declined.

   The Pleasantville School Board should take measures to increase the number of volunteers. Teachers, parents, and other community members agree that it is important for young people to learn the value of community service. Requiring high-school students to engage in community service would provide much-needed assistance to worthy local charities and would also help young people understand the importance of giving back to their community. For this reason, the Pleasantville School Board should institute a program requiring students of Pleasantville High School to complete 40 hours of community service prior to graduation.

   Write a response in which you examine the stated and/or unstated assumptions of the argument. Be sure to explain how the argument depends on these assumptions and what the implications are for the argument if the assumptions prove unwarranted.

3. A recent survey of 250 adults between the ages of 30 and 45 showed an association between the number of hours adults spend online each day and self-reporting of symptoms commonly associated with depression. The survey found that adults who spend 30 hours or more online each week were twice as likely as others to report that they "frequently" had trouble concentrating. Of adults who reported spending more than 30 hours per week online, 20 percent also reported that they had felt "sad, down, or blue" at least three times within the past month.

   These results suggest that spending too much time online is linked to depression and people who want to improve their well-being should strictly limit the time they spend online.

   Write a response in which you discuss what questions would need to be answered in order to decide whether the recommendation and the argument on which it is based are reasonable. Be sure to explain how the answers to these questions would help to evaluate the recommendation.

4. One increasingly popular policy for promoting renewable energy is a feed-in tariff. Under such a policy, investors on any scale, from large corporations to individual homeowners, produce their own energy from solar panels installed on their property. Electricity companies are then required to purchase the energy through a long-term contract at an increased rate that allows the investors to more than offset the cost over time. There is no denying that the initial cost of solar installation is a burden on the investor. In strenuous economic times, both businesses and homeowners might be reluctant to make the investment due to concern that the payout could be less than sufficient or the plan might prove unfeasible. However, research has shown that a feed-in tariff plan is not only stable but also exceptionally effective and it ought to be more actively pursued.

   Write a response in which you examine the stated and/or unstated assumptions of the argument. Be sure to explain how the argument depends on these assumptions and what the implications are for the argument if the assumptions prove unwarranted.

5. In fall 2010, the Transportation Security Administration (TSA) stepped up its security efforts in U.S. airports by incorporating random full-body searches as part of its counterterrorism efforts. These full-body searches were a response to the refusal of some people to accept the use of full-body scanners, which were judged by some to be excessively revealing. The chief of the TSA and the secretary of state both stated that, while they acknowledge every citizen's desire for privacy, this desire must be considered in balance with safety measures. However, whatever safety full-body searches provide is not a reasonable trade-off for the invasion of privacy that citizens must now suffer, so the TSA must abandon such measures.

    Write a response in which you discuss what questions would need to be answered in order to decide whether the advice and the argument on which it is based are reasonable. Be sure to explain how the answers to these questions would help to evaluate the advice.

Answers and explanations begin on the next page.

Answers and Explanations

ARGUMENT ESSAYS

Sample Response 1 (as written, including original errors)

While the hormone may well contribute to an increase in childhood obesity, it does not have to be the only problem. A 200 percent rise in obesity over a given period of time begs the question of whether other factors are at work. Obesity in all ages can be linked to many different factors: physical activity, increased consumption of solid food, or the type of food being ingested. A milk hormone—while being a potential source—is not the "only clear explanation." Other factors, from diet to physical activity, could be at work.

The argument concludes that the hormone is causing obesity in children. This an assumption that is not necessarily true. This scenario says nothing about the activity level of the children; this is a large gap in the reasoning that could help the reader further understand the role that the hormone played in the children's obesity. If the hormone usage in 1992 converged with a decline in physical activity, then either factor, or both, could have caused the uptick in obesity rates. The fact that the use of the hormone coincided with the start of a period in which, due to the availability of automotive transportation, people are more sedentary, is worth investigating. During the time in question, television and video games may become more prevalent, furthering a sedentary lifestyle. Nothing is mentioned about the levels of physical activity among these two groups of children.

The argument states that the children's dairy consumption hasn't change, but says nothing else about their dietary habits. It's possible that the children who eat dairy products also have, since 1992, taken to eating richer foods, fewer vegetables, or more carbohydrates. Such a change in diet could account for the obesity rates within the population. It is also possible that, during the time in question, lactose-tolerant children have been eating more fattening food products that, while not dairy products themselves, employ milk, cheese, or butter in the preparation. This could cause the increase in obesity rates and the lactose intolerant children would be unaffected.

Given that we do not know the answers to these questions, the argument goes beyond the available data in asserting that it must be true that the hormone is to blame for the obesity rates among children who are lactose tolerant.

Sample Feedback

The author of this essay easily recognizes that the argument depends on two unqualified assumptions and that simply stopping the use of the hormone may or may not have the desired effect. The author argues throughout the essay that the only difference between the two groups of children that we are made aware of is the type of milk they drink or do not drink. We do not know:

1. The effect of diet (aside from dairy products)
2. Level of physical ability

Because we don't know the facts pertinent to the environmental or behavioral factors affecting the two groups of children, both diet and exercise can be considered as potential alternative explanations. The argument in the prompt simply assumes that both groups are otherwise identical, and that assumption stretches beyond the known information.

Throughout the essay the author uses well-organized paragraphs—each starts with a broad statement followed by supporting statements—and his ideas logically flow from one sentence to the next. He uses succinct, economical diction and rotates complex and simple sentences. Though containing a few grammar errors, the essay remains focused and clear throughout, earning a score of 6.0.

Sample Response 2 (as written, including original errors)

Instituting a community-service requirement might benefit local teenagers and their community. The author argues that doing so would assist local charity organizations while also instilling important values. However, this argument depends on a number of unproven assumptions, and as such, it is not strong enough to justify instituting the requirement.

First, the author believes the new requirement would help worthy local charitable organizations accomplish important work. The truth of this assertion depends on several other unstated assumptions. The author assumes that local charities which are not described in detail are accomplishing work that is of significant value to the community. However, perhaps some of the organizations labeled as charities or nonprofits are not substantially benefiting the community. A charitable organization may have a narrow mission that only benefits a few; it may be inept or even corrupt. Without knowing more about the charities that would be affected by this measure, it is impossible to gauge the potential benefit to the community.

Even if we could assume that the affected organizations work is valuable, it doesnt necessarily follow that the new program would help them to accomplish this valuable work. The author does not provide data about how much the charities depend on volunteers, how volunteering has declined, how many charities would take part in the program, or how they would be selected. We also dont know how many students would be involved or how the high school would work with local charities to implement the program. Would the 40-hour requirement suffice to meet the organizations needs? Do teenagers have skills that match well with the tasks that need to be done? Do the high school and the local charities have sufficient resources to implement this program successfully? Are the charities even interested in having short-term high school volunteers involved with their work? The author seems to assume so, but these assumptions are groundless.

Even if schools should teach the value of community service, we cannot assume the new graduation requirement would instill this value. Forty hours might not have a significant impact on students thinking, or students might have a bad or indifferent experience working with a particular organization, or they might resent the extra demand on their time, especially if they do not get to choose where they volunteer. The goal may be laudable, but we cannot assume this is the best way to achieve it.

Volunteer work may benefit the Pleasantville community and the teenagers who live there, and instituting a community-service graduation requirement may help accomplish both of those ends. For this reason, the

School Board may choose to implement the new requirement. However, the authors argument is not, in and of itself, strong enough to persuade the School Board to take this action.

Sample Feedback

In addressing the specific task directions, a 6.0 response presents a cogent, well-articulated examination of the argument and conveys meaning skillfully. Here the test taker identifies and analyzes the main contention of this argument that local charities are in need of volunteers and that instituting a community service requirement at the high school will help in meeting that need. She identifies weaknesses in the argument, noting that the author of the argument does not define the scope of the needs of local charities and whether those needs are compatible with what high-school students could provide. This test taker uses rhetorical questions, but only sparingly, to focus on key elements; develops ideas cogently and organizes them well; and provides solid support for them. She examines ways to both weaken and strengthen the argument, accepting that the proposal could be a good one even though this author has not supported it adequately. She is fluent, uses precise vocabulary and sentence variety, and shows facility with the conventions of standard English. There are a few grammatical errors, as would occur under normal test conditions, but they will not detract from the score. Essays with some small errors or imperfections can still earn a score of 6.0. The essay is focused and clear throughout, earning it a score of 6.0.

Sample Response 3 (as written, including original errors)

The survey may have uncovered a link between time spent online and two symptoms commonly associated with depression–difficulty concentrating and subjective feelings of sadness. However, the evidence provided does not make this case strongly enough to justify taking the recommended action. Several questions would need to be answered to determine whether the author's recommendation is reasonable and would lead to improved well-being.

One obvious question is "What else is known about the adults surveyed who reported spending 30 or more hours online per week?" The survey found that these adults often reported symptoms of depression, but correlation alone does not guarantee that time spent online caused these symptoms. It is quite possible that they were caused by some other factor. For instance, these adults may have had plenty of time to spend online because they were unemployed; if so, this life circumstance could be the underlying cause of their symptoms. Alternatively, perhaps adults who are predisposed to have trouble concentrating and experience feelings of sadness are also likely to spend time more online. In other words, it might be the depressive symptoms causing the behavior, rather than the behavior causing the depressive symptoms.

Another important question is "What did other adults surveyed report about their ability to concentrate and their subjective feelings of depression?" The author provides information about only those adults who reported spending 30 or more hours per week online. We cannot make a meaningful comparison between groups without raw data about all of the survey participants. For instance, the author states that "adults who spend 30 hours or more online each week were twice as likely as others to report that they 'frequently' had trouble concentrating." Does this mean that 50 percent of adults in this group frequently had trouble concentrating, but only 25 percent of adults in other groups did? Or is the ratio 2 percent compared to 1 percent? The author also states that 20 percent of adults in this group reported feeling "sad, down, or blue" at least three times in the past month. This may be significant, but if 18 percent of adults in other groups experienced these feelings with similar frequency, it probably isn't.

A final crucial question is "How did the researchers assess the accuracy of subjects' self-reporting?" Survey data is often rife with inaccuracies, and this problem is compounded when subjects answer questions about subjective mental states. Were any other, more objective measures employed in addition to subjects' self-reported data? Answering these questions would help us evaluate the data the researchers collected.

Spending a great deal of time online may be correlated with experiencing symptoms of depression, and for this reason, some people may choose to limit the time they spend online. However, without access to more complete data and assurances that the study was rigorous, there is no justification for recommending that everyone do so.

Sample Feedback

In addressing the specific task directions, a 6.0 response presents a cogent, well-articulated examination of the argument and conveys meaning skillfully. Here the test taker identifies and analyzes the main contention of this argument—that spending significant time online is correlated with symptoms of depression in adults. He identifies questions that need to be answered in order to decide whether the recommendation that adults curtail time spent online and the argument on which it is based are reasonable.

This test taker focuses on key elements of the argument, particularly on the potential drawbacks to using data from surveys; develops ideas cogently; and organizes them well. He examines ways to both weaken and strengthen the argument, accepting that the recommendation could be a good one even though this author has not supported it adequately. He is fluent, uses precise vocabulary and sentence variety, and shows facility with the conventions of standard English. There are a few grammatical errors, as would occur under normal test conditions, but they will not detract from the score. Essays with some small errors or imperfections can still earn a score of 6.0. The essay is focused and clear throughout, earning it a score of 6.0.

Sample Response 4 (as written, including original errors)

The argument that feed-in tariffs, as an efficient means to reduce energy bills and promote renewable energy, should be more aggressively promoted seems reasonable, but relies on several assumptions that it fails to establish. Perhaps of greatest concern is the "guarantee" that the solar panels will "more than offset the cost over time." Like any investment, it inevitably has its risks, which are compounded by the fact that the owners are forced to sign a long-term contract with their electricity company.

The author fails to properly consider the implications, particularly concerning homeowners. While reducing energy bills in the long term might seem desirable, no consideration is given to the potential effects on the value of the house and how these types of contracts adapt to change in ownership of the house. Additionally, solar panels are machines, and like all machines, may break or be faulty to begin with. The money saved by the tariff might cover the initial cost of installation, but this assumes that no maintenance will be necessary.

The author is writing with a fixed state of the establishment in mind bearing the solar panels–assuming the same owners, a lack of required maintenance, and so on. Should the solar panels break or the building be purchased, the contract would most likely continue, thus forcing the owners to either pay for the maintenance (which could negate the profit) or remain in the contract without gaining the benefits of the tariff.

This is particularly concerning because the electricity companies would likely increase rates to compensate for the cost of purchasing energy–which the author also fails to take into account. Simply by reason, it can be discerned that the money to cover the electricity companies' purchasing of energy must come from somewhere. Whether by federal funding or increased rates, the burden will eventually return to the same people whose bills the feed-in tariff is supposed to lessen. It almost forces the members of the community to participate, because it increases everyone's rates, but only those who join the tariff plan accrue any benefits.

Additionally, the author relies heavily upon the "effectiveness" that the unnamed research has proved. This seems vague and unconvincing, assuming that the research was performed on a wide variety of communities to ensure that the benefits it espouses would be comparable in the reader's community. Furthermore, no mention of the effects is made–the passage seems to focus entirely on the financial side of the feed-in tariff policy, rather than the environmental effects. The author does not seem to consider whether the "effectiveness" demonstrated by the research was financial, environmental, or both. It is difficult to tell for what sort of audience the author is writing. A major aspect of the feed-in tariff's policy seems to be expanding renewable energy sources, but the author assumes that this would be of little consequence to the reader. Although there is a degree of validity to the author's argument, it relies on too many crucial assumptions to present a convincing stance on feed-in tariffs.

Sample Feedback

In addressing the specific task directions, a 6.0 response presents a cogent, well-articulated examination of the argument and correctly identifies the unproven assumptions that the argument relies upon. This author successfully identifies and analyzes the argument's main contention: that feed-in tariffs should be increased as a means of promoting renewable energy sources.

In the opening paragraph, the essay restates the argument and then cites its unsupported assumptions. In the following paragraphs, the author insightfully identifies flaws in the assumptions, such as the contention that solar panels will offset the cost over time. She effectively addresses the assignment's requirement that she discuss the implications for the argument if the assumptions prove unwarranted.

Throughout the essay, the author uses well-organized paragraphs—each starts with a broad statement followed by supporting statements—and her ideas flow logically from one sentence to the next. She uses succinct, economical diction and rotates complex and simple sentences.

The essay concludes strongly by summarizing the major flaws in the argument (i.e., the fact that the author ignores the effects of the policy). The essay remains focused and clear throughout, earning it a score of 6.0.

Sample Response 5 (as written, including original errors)

It is well known that the threat to the safety of airline passengers is real and that the authorities must take measures to protect that safety. The above argument hinges on the perceived lack of balance between safety and privacy in enforcing airport security. In order to establish that objections to the process are defensible–and that the new safety measures need to be repealed–opponents to the measures have to demonstrate that the rights of citizens are being violated to excess with no proportional gain in security.

The question of the violation of privacy is very much a matter of extent. For example, airline passengers now almost universally accept X-rays of luggage; no controversies are currently raging in order to prevent TSA from screening checked or carry-on luggage. On the other hand it may be that it is the physical searches and scans of the actual people that cross the line. This is a potentially more cogent argument than simply stating that things as they are not acceptable.

This raises a second question: what would be a suitable replacement for the searches? If there is, indeed, a necessity for increased security, particularly regarding what people may be carrying on their persons, is there currently a viable alternative to the searches or body scans? If there is not, then we have to ask whether it is instead in the best interests of citizens to simply not increase security measures at all. By answering these initial questions, the author of the argument could strengthen his or her position by demonstrating what, precisely, is objectionable about the searches and what the alternatives to them are.

Yet another question the author of the argument would need to face is how effective these searches are. If they are demonstrably ineffective, then the claim that citizens' rights are being forfeited for the sake of no significant gain would greatly improve the author's position. However, if the evidence showed that the searches have been critical in preventing numerous threats that would have gone otherwise undetected, the author would be forced to adopt a new approach to the argument.

A final concern is the absence of detail connected with use of the new terminology. Although "full-body search" is relatively self-explanatory, the author makes no mention of the conditions under which these searches occur. The author does not indicate whether the TSA selects passengers at random, a certain amount from among any given number of passengers, or if the TSA performs the full search on every passenger who refuses the scanner. The author also does not discuss whether or not children are subject to these searches or if they are an exception. If children are, indeed, an exception, then the claim that the TSA makes random searches–because it is impossible to know who precisely could be carrying illegal items–becomes much weaker.

The author uses emotional, negative phrases such as "full-body search" and "invasion of privacy" to strengthen his or her position, because it seems that the basic argument falls down on other grounds. Therefore it is important to resolve the resulting critical questions before one can give serious consideration to a proposal such as the abandonment of the new security measures.

Sample Feedback

In addressing the specific task directions, a 6.0 response presents a cogent, well-articulated examination of the argument and conveys meaning skillfully. The test taker identifies and analyzes the main contention of this argument—that the

Transportation Security Administration is overstepping its bounds in enforcing new and more extreme security measures when screening airline passengers. She identifies weaknesses in the argument—notably that it relies on general assertions, gives too few details about the procedures at issue, and uses emotional terms that invite negative reactions.

This test taker uses rhetorical questions, but only sparingly, to focus on key elements; develops ideas cogently and organizes them well; and provides good support for them. She is fluent, uses precise vocabulary and sentence variety, and shows facility with the conventions of standard English. There are a few grammatical errors, as would occur under normal test conditions, but they will not detract from the score. Essays with some small errors or imperfections can still earn a score of 6.0. The essay is focused and clear throughout, earning it a score of 6.0.

Issue Essays

> Note: Grockit does not provide feedback on these essays. This prompt is for your independent practice. We recommend taking 30 minutes to respond to this prompt in a word-processing program. Then use the sample and feedback provided to assess your own writing.

1. The emergence of the online "blogosphere" and social media has significantly weakened the quality of political discourse in the United States.

    Reason: When anyone can publish political opinions easily, standards for covering news and political topics will inevitably decline.

    Write a response in which you examine your own position on the statement. Explore the extent to which you either agree or disagree with it, and support your reasoning with evidence and/or examples. Be sure to reflect on ways in which the statement might or might not be true, and how this informs your thinking on the subject.

2. Some people believe it is imperative for individuals living in developed nations to reduce their energy consumption and lead a more sustainable lifestyle, given the evidence for global climate change. Others believe that such drastic lifestyle changes are unwarranted, based on the existing evidence for global climate change.

    Write a response in which you discuss which view more closely aligns with your own position and explain your reasoning for the position you take. In developing and supporting your position, you should address both of the views presented.

3. So long as they are aware of the dangers involved, adults should not be legally bound to use seat belts.

    Write a response in which you discuss the extent to which you agree or disagree with the statement and explain your reasoning for the position you take. In developing and supporting your position, you should consider ways in which the statement might or might not hold true and explain how these considerations shape your position.

4. Children should not be forced by law to be educated by either public schools or homeschooling if their parents do not wish them to be.

    Write a response in which you discuss your views on the policy and explain your reasoning for the position you take. In developing and supporting your position, you should consider the possible consequences of implementing the policy and explain how these consequences shape your position.

5. Parents should be able to monitor and restrict which books, digital media, or other information their children access at or check out of the public library.

   Write a response in which you discuss the extent to which you agree or disagree with the statement and explain your reasoning for the position you take. In developing and supporting your position, you should consider ways in which the statement might or might not hold true and explain how these considerations shape your position.

Answers and Explanations

ISSUE ESSAYS

Sample Response 1 (as written, including original errors)

The claim posits that technological advances in communications media have negatively affected the quality of discourse within those media. Certainly the Internet has revolutionized both personal and public communication, and the rise of the "blogosphere" and other social media has blurred the line between public and private discourse. People use private blogs and social media to post personal details about their own lives and to link to news articles, informational websites, and the like. The online format also makes it easier than ever to respond publicly to others' ideas—and in turn, to respond to comments from readers. Thus, techno-logical advances have also blurred the lines between formal and informal writing and between media creators and consumers.

The claim focuses solely on how these changes have weakened public political discourse. The reasoning is that when anyone can publish ideas easily, "quality control" disappears, because the rigorous standards of traditional print journalism no longer apply. Although this is one possible outcome, the claim does not present a complete picture.

First, if public discourse is actually declining, it is not a new phenomenon caused by the rise of the blogosphere. Granted, blogs and social media may not always undergo a rigorous editorial and fact-checking process before publication. However, this standard has declined in mainstream journalism as well. The "New York Times" once published several falsified articles by reporter Jayson Blair. It was the attention of online petitions and social media that prevented the implementation of a change in grant policy at a breast cancer charity. This example demonstrates that non-professionals who don't need to worry about losing access to high-profile political figures may be in a better position to discuss sensitive topics. They are accountable only to their readers.

Furthermore, citizen writers are less subject to financial constraints than are mainstream news publications and programs. U.S. media outlets are largely owned by just a handful of major conglomerates. Their dependence on advertising revenue means that advertising or corporate interests can influence news and political coverage, especially as each outlet competes with many others for people's attention. Bloggers, meanwhile, may depend somewhat on mainstream media for information (and in some cases are closely affiliated with mainstream outlets). However, most blogs are not directly tied to major corporations or as heavily dependent on advertising revenue, and few people writing on social media receive any financial compensation for their work.

Finally, the emergence of the blogosphere encourages people to actively participate in discussions of news events and politics, rather than passively consuming mass media. True, many people will squander this opportunity by posting uninformed opinions or vitriolic comments. However, others may use the opportunity to research important issues, think through their positions, and respond thoughtfully—and, when necessary, critically—to others' published ideas. It is simply not valid to make a blanket claim that this new medium has weakened public discourse.

Sample Feedback

A 6.0 response presents a cogent, well-articulated analysis of the issue and conveys meaning skillfully. Here the test taker establishes her position on the issue of whether the participation of nonprofessionals in political discourse weakens that discourse. She accepts that there are some disadvantages to opening up such discussions but comes to the conclusion that there are many pluses. She develops this position with logical and appropriate reasons, especially the ability to influence public policy quickly and without regard to financial constraints. She connects ideas logically and generally with fluency and a facility with varied, clear, and interesting writing. Her use of transition keywords is particularly useful, helping the reader follow her argument. There are a few grammatical errors, as would occur under normal test conditions, but they will not detract from the score. Essays with some small errors or imperfections can still earn a score of 6.0. For these reasons, this essay receives a score of 6.0.

Sample Response 2 (as written, including original errors)

Climate change—and what should be done about it—has received a great deal of media attention, especially within the last decade. Environmental activists believe changing weather patterns provide irrefutable evidence for climate change (or global warming), with potentially dire consequences for the planet and for humanity. Some argue that individuals living in developed nations must make major changes to their way of living before it is too late; indeed, some claim that we have already delayed such changes so long that crisis is inevitable. Others claim that the evidence for climate change has been greatly exaggerated, or that climate change is occurring but is unrelated to (and therefore cannot be mitigated by) human activity. Thus, the latter groups do not think drastic lifestyle changes are warranted.

The first view aligns most closely with my position. The evidence for climate change is substantial. NASA has documented various phenomena attributed to increasing carbon dioxide levels in our atmosphere, including rising sea levels, increased land surface temperatures and ocean temperatures, and decreasing ice near the Earth's poles. If unchecked, this geologically rapid shift in temperatures could drastically reduce the global supply of potable water and the amount of land usable for agriculture, thus leading to mass starvation, along with an increase in the frequency of extreme, destructive weather events such as 2005s Hurricane Katrina.

Scientific experts and government authorities have addressed this grave issue repeatedly. Making individual lifestyle changes–such as biking to work instead of driving a car, or turning on the air-conditioning in one's home only when absolutely necessary–is an important step in reducing our collective "carbon footprint." These changes not only reduce overall energy consumption, but also set an example for others to follow.

However, individual lifestyle changes will not be enough to solve this global problem. Large-scale social changes, such as reducing factory pollution, are also necessary. Furthermore, infrastructure development and policy changes at the municipal, state, and national level would help make it possible to individuals to adjust to a "greener" lifestyle.

It is important to address claims from the other side of the debate—specifically, that climate change is being exaggerated or cannot be affected by human actions. It is true that, like any other major social movement, this one is sometimes associated with factual errors or distortions. For instance, a recent report from a United Nations panel apparently exaggerated the possibility that glaciers in the Himalayas would soon disappear; quickly rising temperatures in the 1990s led some activists to speculate (incorrectly) that the rate of temperature increase was accelerating. These distortions are unfortunate, but they are the exception and not the rule, and as such they should not be taken as grounds for dismissing the problem entirely.

Internationally, the vast majority of our scientists and world leaders agree that climate change is a pressing problem that requires us to take action, individually and collectively.

Sample Feedback

A 6.0 response presents a cogent, well-articulated analysis of the issue and conveys meaning skillfully. Here the test taker establishes his position on the issue of whether individual lifestyle changes are necessary to abate the spread of global climate change. He accepts that there is some controversy surrounding this view but concludes that scientific and social opinion is on his side. He develops this position using good reasoning and evidence.

The writer connects ideas logically and generally writes with fluency and facility using varied, clear, and interesting language. His use of transition keywords is particularly useful, helping the reader follow his argument. His concluding paragraph is thin, but an otherwise well-developed essay that lacks a well-developed conclusion will not be penalized. Essays with some small errors or imperfections can still earn a score of 6.0. For these reasons, this essay receives a score of 6.0.

Sample Response 3 (as written, including original errors)

In a country that prides itself in its personal liberties, it is tempting to constantly advocate for increased individual freedom, with the belief that people should be allowed to do whatever they want with their lives and bodies, so long as they are only hurting themselves. This argument holds that it is not fair for us to dictate such control over each other's lives. The flaw in this philosophy is that there is no way to limit the extent of damaging actions, and what may have been intended to harm only one person will also affect other people. This cannot be tolerated. When we use safety devices, we are also safeguarding our ability to contribute to our society.

Intentionally foregoing simple safety measures, such as using seat belts, significantly increases the risk of serious bodily injury or death in the occurrence of an accident. By the nature of their profession, doctors and other hospital staff cannot refuse to treat and heal anyone, regardless of the origin of their injury; however, if these preventable injuries were avoided, the very same time, resources, and energy could be used to tend to others. Furthermore, by living in a civilized society, using the machines, roads, and other services provided by other members of the community, you become responsible for contributing substantially to the community whose resources you use. As an active member of the community, it is your duty to protect yourself and ensure that you are able to continue to add to the community in recompense for what you take away.

Another point to recognize is the non-intrusiveness of the requirement. While ensuring that all citizens eat properly and exercise frequently would certainly be a strong limitation of their personal freedom, a seat belt does not restrict one's ability to drive or otherwise interfere with one's life. It is a simple and nonrestrictive measure that allows the community to protect its members and assets. Intentionally endangering yourself, without any benefits, is as much a threat to your community as it is to yourself. Harm done to yourself is harm done to your community. This is not a limitation on activities, a ban on potentially dangerous hobbies, or any unreasonable restriction imposed by the government. It is a matter of protection against potential unnecessary damage. Because you live in a community, your life is not entirely your own. As a contributor to the community, either professionally or personally, you must accept a certain responsibility to protect yourself–to protect a community's worker, a child's parent, a friend. The community that protects and ensures our personal freedom requires, almost paradoxically, that we provide certain contributions to enable the community to flourish.

Sample Feedback

A 6.0 response presents an insightful, in-depth analysis of complex ideas, developing and supporting main points with logically compelling reasons and/or highly persuasive examples. It addresses the specific directions that are given in the task in a well-focused and organized way.

This particular essay is well constructed; the author begins by acknowledging arguments against compulsory seat belt laws, then states her opinion ("The flaw in this philosophy is that there is no way to limit the extent of damaging actions, and what may have been intended to harm only one person will also affect other people"). She proceeds to support her position with compelling evidence, citing the effect of safety regulations upon society at large and the relatively nonintrusive nature of seat belts. The writing is clear, direct, and error-free and reveals skillful use of diction. There is no clear concluding paragraph, but an otherwise well-developed essay that lacks a conclusion will not be penalized. For all these reasons, this essay receives a score of 6.0.

Sample Response 4 (as written, including original errors)

The basis of this issue lies in the question of whether or not parents have the right to raise their children as they see fit. Although in theory, it might seem reasonable, and even desirable, to allow parents to do what they believe to be best for their child, parents do not have unlimited control over every aspect of their child's life.

Parents do not, for instance, have a right to starve or imprison their children. The state has some responsibility toward children in general, ensuring protection for them against abuse and negligence in their rearing. Further, because children are obviously not born with all the necessary information and skills to function as independent adults, the state also insists that all children must undertake a certain number of years of education so they may acquire those skills, and the state provides free schooling for that purpose.

Compulsory education does not force parents to relinquish control of their children's education (as the possibility of homeschooling shows), but it does ensure that children are given an equal opportunity to learn the fundamentals of reading, mathematics, and other subjects that allow them later to effectively follow a walk of life of their own choosing.

The argument that compulsory education is tantamount to the government dictating what a child does and does not learn is fundamentally flawed, in that it does not account for parental freedom in choosing to home-school their child or to educate their child in a system other than the public one. In addition, in school associations and in electing their local representatives, parents have a degree of influence in the education the system gives their child. On the other hand, while parents may also choose to have their child instructed according to whatever doctrine or ideas they believe to be right, they must not prevent the child from learning certain fundamentals. For example, while the parents may have a right to refuse to teach a child about a philosophy they object to, they should not have the right to deny the child the opportunity to learn to read–a potential consequence of permitting parents to decide not to educate their children at all.

Part of encouraging individual freedom is educating children in how to use their knowledge and skills to enjoy that freedom. Ideally, parents should not deny their child the opportunity to pursue a path of his or her own choosing by restricting the child's education. Compulsory education is a policy that, although seeming to limit the possibilities of how parents raise their children, in fact extends the possibilities of what the children choose to do with their lives as adults. This is a key freedom that requires protection–the right of every person to have an equal opportunity to do with his life as he pleases. This is what a basic education allows, and this is why the enforcement of compulsory education is necessary–to provide in education as in most things the proper balance between compulsion and unrestricted freedom.

Sample Feedback

A 6.0 response presents a cogent, eloquent analysis of the issue and conveys meaning skillfully. This essay establishes a clear, thoughtful position on the issue, basing the argument on the rights of parents to raise their children as they see fit while acknowledging limitations on those rights. The writer develops the position using sound examples (extremes of parental neglect, instances of the rights of the state, possible careers a child might wish to pursue) and connects ideas logically throughout, particularly when examining the tensions between the rights of parents and of the state. The writing is fluent and clear, showing good use of vocabulary and sentence structure with few errors. For these reasons, this essay receives a score of 6.0.

Sample Response 5 (as written, including original errors)

Although it is reasonable for parents to be interested in, or even concerned about, what their children are checking out from the library, to allow parents to monitor that activity or prevent their children accessing information would be a great ethical wrong. To clarify, this view does not concern lascivious or pornographic content–such things would be restricted by library policy in any case–but there are many issues that children might not feel comfortable discussing with their parents or would be reluctant to talk about should their parents find out.

A classic example of this is teenage pregnancy. Regardless of personal stances on abortion, it is important for information resources to be readily available through confidential channels. The same is true of matters such as sexually transmitted diseases, depression, suicide, or other particularly sensitive subjects. To make resources available to assist youths with difficult problems or concerns would be self-defeating if young people had to announce their interest or concern, even to their parents.

Particularly since the advent of the Internet, youths have no difficulty finding information on personal–or even taboo–subjects. Unfortunately, the Internet has also opened up a vast body of unreliable or incorrect information, which, when related to crucial topics such as those mentioned above, should not form the basis of a young person's knowledge. It is far better for children to use the library, which can evaluate the materials it receives, to search for reliable and accurate information than for them to seek it from unmonitored sources.

Finally, it is also not the role of the library or librarian to act as censor or monitor over what children show interest in. It is the place of the library to make accurate information readily accessible to all patrons. Given the broad range of ages, maturity, and levels of parental restrictiveness, it is simply impractical and unfeasible to mandate policies restricting what information patrons can and cannot access. Many libraries do have graphic material, and it would be a reasonable compromise to restrict the borrowing of such materials, which clearly exist only for adult entertainment rather than for significant educational value. However, this is a decision which rests with library policy, not in the hands of a particular set of patrons wishing to exercise control over the usage of another set, even their own offspring. It is reasonable for the library to restrict access by children to erotica, but not to information of educational value, no matter how controversial it may be.

Sample Feedback

A 6.0 response presents a cogent, well-articulated analysis of the issue and conveys meaning skillfully. Here the test taker establishes his position on the issue of parental monitoring and restriction of what children take from the library. He accepts that parents have legitimate concerns about what their children access but shows that libraries exercise their own controls. He develops this position using good reasons, especially the reluctance of youths to discuss deeply personal anxieties with their parents. He connects ideas logically and generally with fluency and facility, using varied, clear, and interesting writing. There are a few grammatical errors, as would occur under normal test conditions, but they will not detract from the score. Essays with some small errors or imperfections can still earn a score of 6.0. For these reasons, this essay receives a score of 6.0.

Chapter 5

Getting Ready for Test Day

s it starting to feel as if your whole life is a buildup to the GRE? You've known about it for years, worried about it for months, and now spent at least a few weeks in solid preparation for it. As the test gets closer, you may find that your anxiety is on the rise. To help calm any pre-test jitters that you may have, however, let's go over a few strategies for the couple of days before the test.

Tips for the Days Just Before the Exam

• The best test takers do less as the test approaches. Taper off your study schedule and take it easy on yourself. Give yourself time off, especially the evening before the exam. By that time, if you've studied well, everything you need to know is firmly stored in your memory bank.

• It's in your best interest to marshal your physical and psychological resources for the last 24 hours or so before the test. Keep the test out of your consciousness; go to a movie, take a pleasant walk, or just relax. Eat healthy meals and try to steer clear of sugar and caffeine. And, of course, get plenty of rest that night, and also two nights before. It's hard to fall asleep earlier than you're used to, and you don't want to lie there worrying about the test.

• Make sure you know where the test will be held and the quickest, easiest way to get there. You'll have great peace of mind by knowing that all the little details are set before Test Day.

• Visit the test site a few days in advance, particularly if you are especially anxious.

Preparing for Test Day

The night before Test Day, gather the following things together:

• ID
• admission ticket
• a watch
• a bottle of water
• aspirin or other painkiller, in case you get a headache
• a snack, such as nuts or an energy bar, to keep your energy up for the later sections of the test
• names of schools you'd like to receive your scores

Test Day should start with a moderate, high-energy breakfast. Avoid anything with a lot of sugar. Also, unless you are utterly catatonic without it, it's a good idea to stay away from coffee. Yes, perhaps you drink two cups every morning and don't even notice it, but it's different during the test. Coffee won't make you alert (your adrenaline will do that much more effectively); it will just give you the jitters.

When you get to the test center, you will need to present your ID and must also complete an additional ID verification, including fingerprinting, photographing, videotaping, or another form of electronic ID confirmation. The test administrator will assign you a seat at a computer station. You will receive a supply of scratch paper before you begin the test, and you can replenish this supply by asking the test administrator. You may not bring your own scratch paper to the test. Some administrative questions will be asked before the test begins, and once you're done with those, you're set to go. While you're taking the test, a small clock will count down the time you have left in each section. The computer will tell you when you're done with each section and when you've completed the test.

Test Day and Beyond

Here are some last-minute reminders to help guide your work on the test:

- Take a few minutes before the test to look back over your preparation and give yourself credit for all the work you put into it. Confidence is far more useful than distress.
- Don't bother trying to figure out which section is the experimental section. It can't help you, and you might make a tragic mistake if you guess wrong. Instead, just do your best on every section.
- Dress in layers for maximum comfort. This way, you can adjust to the room's temperature accordingly.
- During the exam, try not to fixate on what your score is or how you're doing so far. It's counterproductive to continue to think about questions you've already answered or ones you haven't gotten to yet. If you worry about the next section, or the one you've just completed, you'll just feel overwhelmed. Instead, focus on the question-by-question task of picking the correct answer choice. Try to take things one step at a time.
- Keep moving forward instead of getting bogged down in a difficult question. You don't have to get everything right to achieve a solid score. So don't linger out of desperation on a question that is going nowhere even after you've spent considerable time on it.

- Breathe! Weak test takers tend to share one major trait: they don't breathe properly as the test proceeds. They might hold their breath without realizing it or breathe irregularly. Improper breathing hurts confidence and accuracy. Just as importantly, it interferes with clear thinking.

Once you've completed the GRE, here are some next steps to focus on:

- Congratulate yourself for all the hard work you've put in. Make sure you celebrate afterward—and start thinking about your exciting path to the graduate school of your choice!
- Plan your approach to graduate school applications, including references and essays.
- Expect to wait approximately 10–15 days for your official scores (which include your Analytical Writing score) to be posted online.